T0208673

SCHOOL ENVIRONMENT AND SUSTAINABLE DEVELOPMENT GOALS BEYOND 2030

Fourth Edition

Princewill I. Egwuasi Ph.D
Jake M. Laguador Ph.D
Emad K. Hussein Ph.D
Ohene B. Apea Ph.D
Joan I. Egwuasi CNA
George N. Shava

authorHOUSE®

AuthorHouse™
1663 Liberty Drive
Bloomington, IN 47403
www.authorhouse.com
Phone: 1 (800) 839-8640

Published by AuthorHouse 06/05/2020

ISBN: 978-1-7283-6332-5 (sc)
ISBN: 978-1-7283-6331-8 (e)

Library of Congress Control Number: 2020910153

Print information available on the last page.

ABOUT THE EDITORS

Princewill I. Egwuasi Ph.D NCE, BA Ed. (English), M.Ed, Ph.D (Educational Management and Planning), is of the University of Uyo, Uyo, Nigeria. He is currently the Business Editor of three reputable journals, an international reviewer to several global online and print journals. His areas of specialization are English Education and Educational Management and Planning. A recipient of the Nigerian Merit Gold Award for Productivity 2011 and Nigerian Hall of Fame Awards 2013, Dr. Egwuasi has over 45 publications in both national and international journals. He is the initiator of the book on School Environment in Nigeria and the Philippines, published in 2015, the 2nd edition, School Environment in Nigeria, Ghana and the Philippines published in 2017, and School Environment in Africa and Asia Pacific published in 2018. Dr. Egwuasi belongs to several academic professional bodies and is currently serving as the Vice Chairman, World Educators Forum.

Jake M. Laguador Ph.D is currently of the Lyceum of the Philippines University, Batangas City, Philippines and *Research Journal Editor,* Lyceum Engineering Research Journal, Lyceum of the Philippines University. He is also the Associate Editor of Asia Pacific Journal of Education, Arts and Science. He has published several papers in reputable international journals. He has served as an editor in all the previous editions of this book.

Emad K. HUSSEIN Ph.D is a professor in the Pumps Engineering Department, Al-Mussaib Technical College, TCM, Al-Furat Al-Awsat Technical University ATU, Al-Mussaib Babil, Iraq.

Ohene B. Apea Ph.D is currently the Vice Dean, Students Affairs and lecturer in Applied Chemistry and Biochemistry Department, University for Development Studies, Navrongo, Ghana. He is a research and development consultant wit articular emphasis on Programme Planning and Execution, Product Design and Development. Dr. Apea is a consultant to ON GHANA LIMITED and Managing Editor of Novel Publications.

Joan I. Egwuasi CNA is of the Basic Programme, Obong University, Obong Ntak, Nigeria. She is a professional Accountant and teaches Accounting courses with stronghold in Oil

& Gas and Environmental Accounting. She is a research assistant to several international and locally referred journals with several publications to her credit.

George N. Shava is of the Department of Education Leadership and Policy Studies, Faculty of Education, University of Pretoria, Pretoria South Africa. He is a widely travelled scholar and an editor to several international referred journals.

PREFACE

This publication on *School Environment and SDGs Beyond 2030 is* a continuation of our maiden, second and third publications of *School Environment in Nigeria and the Philippines*, published in February, 2015; *School Environment in Nigeria, Ghana and the Philippines* published in March, 2017 and *School Environment in Africa and Asia Pacific published in 2018*. The philosophy being that since there is a shift from globalization to internationalization and to cross-border education, there is the urgent need to revisit some topical issues in our school environment towards the realization of an internationalized, qualitative and cross-border teaching and learning, using all the parameters of the Sustainable Development Goals. The focus on Sustainable Development Goals in this edition is a conviction of the strategic positions of the global drive for a sustained developed economy all over the world, using the United Nations' laid down benchmark. In this edition, all the articles are theoretically, conceptually and/or empirically assembled to address diverse but all-important facets of the SDGs, with a view of proffering solutions, suggestions and recommendations to several questions that may have arisen over time, not to ignore the contributions to existing knowledge and literature of the academia. The articles were also subjected to international peer review and went through insightful scrutiny for standardization. It is the utmost belief of the editors, that this book would become a springboard to all scholars and nations of the world that sincerely require the best in their educational system, hence, the editors welcome more collaborations globally.

Editors

ACKNOWLEDGMENT

The production of this academic project would not have been possible without the benevolence of the Almighty God, through whose grace, wisdom was bestowed on the initiator of the project, Dr. Princewill I. Egwuasi, of the Department of Curriculum Studies, Educational Management and Planning, University of Uyo, Nigeria, to visualize this work. From the maiden edition to the present, several individuals shall be continually acknowledged for their roles in making the book a reality. The Lyceum of the Philippines University, Batangas-City, Philippines, South Asia, is worthy of recognition. Through its Dean, Postgraduate School, Dr. Jake M. Laguador, the university has continued to support this vision. We are also indebted to Emad K. HUSSEIN Ph.D, professor in the Pumps Engineering Department, Al- Mussaib Technical College, TCM, Al-Furat Al-Awsat Technical University ATU, Al-Mussaib Babil, Iraq; Ohene B. Apea Ph.D, the Vice Dean, Students Affairs and lecturer in Applied Chemistry and Biochemistry Department, University for Development Studies, Navrongo, Ghana and Joan I. Egwuasi CNA of the Basic Programme, Obong University, Obong Ntak, Nigeria. Finally, the Book Coordinator is appreciative of all the efforts of the chapter contributors to this publication and wishes to thank them immensely for believing in our commitment and genuine dedication to this course. At this point, we state categorically that the views and findings as expressed in this book are strictly those of the authors.

Princewill I. Egwuasi ***Ph.D***
Book Coordinator

LIST OF CONTRIBUTORS

WORDU Chiduhiegem C. R.
Department of Technical Education
Ignatius Ajuru University of Education Port Harcourt
Nigeria

SAUE Baritule P.
Department of Technical Education,
Ignatius Ajuru University of Education Port Harcourt
Nigeria

ANIAH Solomon A.
Department of Educational Management
Faculty of Education
University of Calabar, Calabar
Nigeria

EDEM Felix B.
National Teachers' Institute
WAPI Study Centre, Calabar
Nigeria

UDOM Cosmas A.
Department of Sociology
Obong University, Obong Ntak
Nigeria

USORO Nsidibe *Ph.D*
Department of Sociology and Anthropology
University of Uyo, Uyo
Nigeria

PETER Peter E.
Department of Sociology and Anthropology
University of Uyo, Uyo
Nigeria

IKEANYIONWU, Chioma L. *Ph.D*
Federal College of Education (Technical) Umunze
Nigeria

ENWERE Judith O.
Federal College of Education (Technial) Umunze
Nigeria

OKAFOR Chinagolum V.
Federal College of Education (Technical) Umunze
Nigeria

GEORGE Sogbege T. *Ph.D*
Department of Physical and Health Education,
University of Uyo, Nigeria

Udokop Christopher A. *Ph.D*
Department of Physical and Health Education
University of Uyo, Nigeria

UZOH Uche V. *Ph.D*
St. John of God Secondary School, Awka
Nigeria

AJOKU Lawrence I. *Ph.D*
Department of Curriculum Studies and Instructional Technology
Ignatius Ajuru University of Education
Rumuolumeni, Port Harcourt
Nigeria

CHINDAH Worokwu *Ph.D*
Department of Chemistry
Ignatius Ajuru University of Education
Rumuolumeni, Port Harcourt
Nigeria

ALLISON B. R.
Department of Sociology,
Faculty of Humanities,
Federal University Wukari
Nigeria

PAUL A. H.
Department of Agricultural Economic and Extension
Faculty of Agriculture and Life Science
Federal University Wukari,
Nigeria

DUNU Benson T. *Ph.D*
Department of Educational Management
Faculty of Arts and Education
University of Africa/UAT Toru-Orua
Nigeria

NWOSU Nancy *Ph.D*
Department of Educational Management
Faculty of Arts and Education
University Of Africa/UAT Toru-Orua
Nigeria

THOMPSON John D.
Senior Assistant Registrar,
Office of the Dean of Students' Affairs,
University for Development Studies,
Tamale Campus, Ghana

ANSOGLENANG Gilbert
Senior Assistant Registrar and Campus Officer
Navrongo Campus
University for Development Studies
Tamale, Ghana

EGHAGHA Patricia N.
Department of Integrated Science
College of Education, Warri
Nigeria

ADEDAYO Temitayo G.
Academics Board Unit, Academic Affairs Office
Tai Solarin of College of Education
Nigeria

SENNUGA Mabayoje A.
Department of Economics
Tai Solarin of College of Education
Nigeria

DANIA Clement M.
Department of Physics
Federal College of Education, Kontagora,
Nigeria

OTI Elizabeth C.
Department of Biology
Federal College of Education, Kontagora
Nigeria

OLUBELA Afolabi *Ph.D*
Department of Arts and Social Sciences Education (ASSED)
Faculty of Education
Olabisi Onabanjo University
Ago-Iwoye
Nigeria

OGUNSANYA Adeola *Ph.D*
Department of Arts and Social Sciences Education (ASSED)
Faculty of Education
Olabisi Onabanjo University
Ago-Iwoye
Nigeria

HUSSEIN Emad K.
Pumps Engineering Department, Al- Mussaib Technical College
TCM, Al-Furat Al-Awsat Technical University ATU
Al-Mussaib Babil, Iraq

SUBHI Kussay A.
Department of Machine Elements and Tribology
The Polytechnic University of Bucharest, Romania

TUDOR Andrei
Department of Machine Elements and Tribology
The Polytechnic University of Bucharest, Romania

KANU Chikaodili L.
Department of Library and Information Science
Federal College of Education (Technical), Umunze
Nigeria

AGU Bartholomew O. (Rev. Fr. CSSp)
Department of Library and Information Science
University of Nigeria, Nsukka
Nigeria

LAWAL M. O.
Tai Solarin College of Education
Omu-Ijebu
Nigeria

ADEDAYO T. G.
Tai Solarin College of Education
Omu-Ijebu
Nigeria

OBAKOYA T. T.
Tai Solarin College of Education
Omu-Ijebu,
Nigeria

LAGUADOR Jake M. *Ph.D*
Lyceum of the Philippines University,
Batangas City, Philippines

MENEZ Norma L. *Ph.D*
Lyceum of the Philippines University
Center for Research and Innovation Development
Batangas City, Philippines

BADILLO Elmer
Lyceum of the Philippines University
Center for Research and Innovation Development
Batangas City, Philippines

OSARO Christiana A. *Ph.D*
Ignatius Ajuru University of Education
Port Harcourt
Nigeria

OBINDAH Fortune *Ph.D*
Ignatius Ajuru University of Education
Port Harcourt
Nigeria

AGI Ugochukwu K. *Ph.D*
Department of Educational Management,
Faculty of Education,
Ignatius Ajuru University of Education,
Port Harcourt, Nigeria.

ORDUA Victor N. *Ph.D*
Department of Educational Psychology,
Guidance and Counselling
School of Education,
Federal College of Education (Technical) Omoku
Nigeria

UDECHUKWU Joachim A. *Ph.D*
Department of Educational Psychology
Federal College of Education (Technical), Umunze
Nigeria

ANAZODO C. E. *Ph.D*
Department of Early Childhood & Primary Education
Federal College of Education (Technical), Umunze
Nigeria

YARO, Joseph Bawa
Department of Arts and Social Science Education (ASSE)
Faculty of Education
Nasarawa State University, Keffi
Nigeria

George N. Shava
Department of Education Leadership and Policy Studies,
Faculty of Education,
University of Pretoria,
Pretoria South Africa

Lwazi Sibanda
Faculty of Science and Technology Education,
National University of Science and Technology,
Zimbabwe

GUIDELINES FOR AUTHORS

The Project Co-ordinator and Board of Editors welcome scholarly articles on *Contemporary Issues in School System across the globe* for publication in its 5th edition of a book titled, **"SCHOOL ENVIRONMENT: DRUG POLICIES, MANAGEMENT AND USE"**. It is an international book with editors from the academia, which aims at showcasing their educational systems. Interested contributors are to abide by the following instructions;

- Submit an online copy of manuscript(s), including abstract and references, in MS Word format to dr.princewilluniuyoedu@gmail.com
- The title page of the article should carry the authors' names, status/rank and address, place of work and affiliations.
- Abstract of not more than 250 words.
- Manuscripts are received on the understanding that they are original and unpublished works of the author(s) not considered for publication elsewhere.
- Current APA style of referencing should be maintained.
- Author(s) e-mail addresses and phone numbers should accompany the paper.
- Figures, tables, charts and drawings should be clearly drawn and the position marked in the text.
- All manuscripts should reach the Project Co-ordinator on or before 31st March, 2021.

Dr. Princewill I. Egwuasi
Department of Curriculum Studies
Educational Management and Planning
University of Uyo, Uyo
Akwa Ibom State
Nigeria
princewilliegwuasi@uniuyo.edu.ng
+2348038955075, +2348094454419

CONTENTS

1

Exploring Customer Relationship Management Strategies in a Higher Educational Institution in the Philippines

LAGUADOR Jake M.

Abstract

HEIs create physical environment with the purpose of nurturing the learning and working experiences of stakeholders. Customizing the services for each client is considered a challenging strategy for the organization. This study aims to determine the customer relationship management practice of an academic institution focusing on key customers like students, employees and alumni using the Plan, Do, Check/Study Act approach of Deming. Quantitative Descriptive type of research was utilized in the study with 355 randomly selected respondents. Results showed that there is a high level of planning through assessing the needs of the customers but observed low in customizing the services while still considered high in terms of on-going dialogue and customer responsiveness. Employees have significantly higher level of assessment on Customer Relationship Management practices than students and alumni. Maintaining a positive atmosphere of customer relationship entails a productive system involving everyone in the academic community. As a developing country like the Philippines, giving priority to the customers is an ultimate goal to build long term connections and giving add on value to the services is sometimes being neglected due to lack of resources.

Key Words: *Knowledge Management, Knowledge-based Culture, Innovation, Quality Management, Intellectual Capital*

Introduction

One of the challenging roles and responsibilities faced by most higher education institutions is on how to maintain the quality of their educational services in making excellent customer experiences most especially the students, employees and alumni. Finding, attracting, recruiting and winning new clients and nurturing and retaining them (Zamil, 2011) as active members of the organization are the goals of the customer relationship management. Identifying their essential needs and requirements to fulfil their goals and expectations is an obligation of the company in order to sustain the operation especially of the private academic institutions. Allameh, Shahin and Tabanifar (2012) emphasized that customer knowledge has been known as a main source that can be used to support research and development, improvement and innovation, facilitate better understanding of market opportunities and support long-term relation with customers.

Managing effectively the data and information of the stakeholders leads to certain level of knowledge where its relevance and ultimate purpose could be utilized to strengthen customer relationship and maximize available resources to create more opportunities and possibilities. Most academic institutions are formulating strategies on how they can create value to their services in order to make their customers satisfied especially the students and the parents as primary stakeholders. In modern competitive environments, graduates are expected to contribute to the sustainable development of various sectors and industries where they can apply what they have learned from formal schooling. Therefore, to elevate the educational system, the country must adhere to the global standard of accreditation and qualification frameworks.

Quality assurance mechanisms facilitate business results that emphasize customers. Customer relationship management builds important data and information that are being analyzed for utilization as input in formulating business strategies and implementing programs relevant to the preferences of the customers. Its main process is to collect information about customers in order to find and record customers' important features to implement marketing activities based on customers' demand and quality (Allameh *et al.*, 2012). Chalmeta (2006) also cited that "CRM is a customer-focused business strategy that dynamically integrates sales, marketing and customer care service in order to create and add value for the company and its customers".

This study is anchored in the Deming Cycle of Plan-Do-Check/Study-Act, PDCA or PDSA which is very common approach for continuous improvement in most organization to address issues and concerns as well as how to deliver quality outcomes. The creation of environment based on ÇRM as component of knowledge management activities is concerned with adopting appropriate organizational norms and values relating to knowledge (Rowley, 2000). This is where the community builds the security and credibility of the teachers and researchers which are dependent upon their knowledge base. Experts are identified in various areas and disciplines as part of developing the database and process of recognizing the capacity of people to contribute and share their knowledge and expertise to the needs of the institution and answer the demands of the society. Abburu and Babu (2013) investigated a framework for ontology based knowledge management which provides a better support for integration of related knowledge sources and searching. Knowledge representation is important for effective and efficient knowledge management of a domain where Ontology is considered good technology for this purpose.

Through the use of CRM, the unified views and voice of the customers can be systematically collected, analyzed, processed, interpreted and utilized for the interest of the organization to take to the new level of value creation. Putting the school environment into a wider perspective would include the multichannel communication (Payne & Frow, 2004; Chan, 2005; Jayachandran et al., 2005) using social media and other networks for customer engagement which raises interesting challenges for traditional CRM approaches (Baird & Parasnis, 2011) and value chain (Chan, 2005). Organizations recognize the need to develop cordial relationships with customers and serve them in their preferred ways (Chua & Banerjee, 2013). Taking advantage of the usefulness of social media can be a good channel of communication among millennials to secure information and connect with them in answering their concerns and other demands. Reaching them out creates value to what they really need from the institution.

Knowing the preferences of the students through diagnostics examination, addressing their cognitive ability could be able to understand by the teachers the appropriate approach or teaching methodology that would be suitable for unique and diverse types of students. Several information about students' personality, attitude, and behavior are already available in the records section of the academic institution which can be analyzed and interpreted in order for the teachers to be informed about the nature of students they have in specific classes or group of students in one course. HEIs can create an atmosphere to encourage active student service learning experiences and opportunities to explore deeply their respective fields of specialization (Kuh, Schuh & Whitt, 1991 ; Ackerman & Schibrowsky, 2008) based on what they really value and considered worthwhile. It should be consistently delivered the educational services that explicitly promises a quality level and intends to provide for the learners (Berry et al., 2006).

Soliciting opinions from the students regarding their insights on how they wanted the activities to be carried out would basically capture the customer views and requirements (Baird & Parasnis, 2011) through the implementation of the customer-centric management system (Jayachandran et al., 2005; Chua & Banerjee, 2013). Joseph, Yakhou and Stone (2005) noted that administrators should recognize that each student and each group of students is different from his/her predecessors. The participation of the students in the decision making creates ownership and responsibility on the outcomes of their collective ideas. The customer-driven strategies as inputs to the realization of goals and objectives of the institution build a strong foundation and advocacy to the brand affinity being sought.

With many academic institutions in the Philippines competing with highly qualified students to enter universities, those highly performing HEIs always win the most of the best students. Universities must be true to what they advertised. Some of them failed to deliver appropriate services resulting to the decision of students with the consent of the parents to transfer to another academic institution or shift to another degree program. Knowing what really the customer needs, wants and demands creates an atmosphere of commitment in delivering quality services to satisfy the expectations and build a strong foundation towards a long term relationship with the community and society.

Methods

The descriptive type of research was utilized in the study. Descriptive survey method is appropriate for data derived from simple observational situations, whether these are actually physically observed or observed through the use of a questionnaire or poll techniques (Zulueta, & Costales Jr., 2001). This study has 355 randomly selected respondents from the group of employees (n=97, 27.3%); students (n=148, 41.7%) and alumni (n=110, 31%) from one private university in the Philippines.

A survey questionnaire adapted from the study of Ejaz, Ahmed and Ahmad (2013) was utilized for the study to determine the CRM practices of the respondents. Some statements were modified to make it more suitable for the setting and kind of respondents. The instrument underwent face-to-face content validation from the three experts in marketing management, educational psychology, and measurement and evaluation. It was also pilot-tested to 35 respondents who are not part of the study and obtained a Cronbach's alpha values of 0.832 which implies that the instrument used for the study has a good internal consistency.

The questionnaires were personally administered by the researchers to the employees and students while online survey forms were sent to the alumni. They were informed regarding the purpose of the survey and ensured that the data and information gathered from the study will solely be used for the continuous improvement of the delivery of educational services in the university under study. Only those respondents who were willing to participate in the survey were given the questionnaires. Strict confidentiality of their identity as one of the respondents in the study was observed. They were also informed about their rights to withdraw their participation anytime they feel uncomfortable or inconvenience answering the statements in the questionnaire.

Weighted mean and ranking were the statistical tools used to describe the result of the survey. Since the gathered data were normally distributed, Analysis of Variance was used to test the significant difference on the CRM strategies when the respondents are grouped according to category. The given scale was used to determine the extent of observation of the respondents: 3.50 - 4.00: Very High (VH); 2.50-3.49: High (H); 1.50 - 2.49: Low (L); 1.00-1.49: Very Low (VL).

Results and Discussion

Table 1: Customer Relationship Management Strategies in terms of Needs Assessment

Plan: Needs Assessment The University has provided...	Employee	Students	Alumni	WM	f-value	p-value
1. Efforts to know customer needs and requirements	2.56 (H)	2.51 (H)	2.81 (H)	2.62 (H)	4.672	.010
2. System of prioritizing key customers' needs	2.76 (H)	2.55 (H)	2.55 (H)	2.61 (H)	2.994	.051
3. Continuous customer satisfaction assessments	3.62 (VH)	3.64 (VH)	3.29 (H)	3.53 (VH)	13.094	.000
Composite Mean	2.98 (H)	2.90 (H)	2.88 (H)	2.92 (H)	1.643	.195

**Significant at p-value < 0.05*

Table 1 presents the Customer Relationship Management Strategies in terms of Needs Assessment. There is a very high observation on the continuous customer satisfaction assessments (3.53) as part of the CRM strategies wherein students and employees have significantly higher observation compared to alumni as denoted by the computed p-value of less than 0.01 alpha level. Part of the Quality Management System is the semestral evaluation of the institutional services and faculty performance before the end of the semester. Students are being given enough time to visit the evaluation room to simultaneously answer the computer-based instrument for evaluation while teaching and non-teaching personnel have also their facilities on their respective offices to evaluate the quality of the delivery of the services of the university to its stakeholders and how they see the processes, the attitude and behaviour of the employees could still be improved. The Customer Measurement Survey is being conducted as part of the feedback mechanism of the institution in order to identify areas for improvement which is considered a good CRM practice.

Meanwhile, alumni have significantly higher observation on the efforts of the university in knowing the customer needs and requirements compared to employees and students as denoted by the computed p-value of 0.01 which is less than 0.05 alpha level. It is good to note that alumni recognized the efforts of the institution to determine their needs through college alumni council. The needs of the teaching personnel in different perspective are determined based on the learning needs assessment survey being conducted every end of the semester while members of the non-teaching personnel are also accomplishing the same annually. They considered this mechanism as useful to identify their professional needs but their personal needs are not being addressed directly. Likewise, the needs of the students are also being addressed by their respective colleges but there is no established system on how each student could able to share their needs and requirements which resulted to providing system of prioritizing key customers' needs obtained the least score of 2.61. Though it is still high, but the score falls within the lower range and the responses have no significant difference.

When computed the composite mean scores, the observation of the three groups in the planning stage of the University in conducting needs assessment is highly observed and the responses do not vary significantly as denoted by the computed p-value of 0.195. There is a good practice for the university in identifying the quality of the delivery of educational services and instruction but these are based on the pre-defined set of criteria. The adequacy of data gathered is limited only in the perspective of the management but not really grounded in the direct needs of the stakeholders. The importance of collecting data and information from the grassroots of the issues and challenges in the educational system and practices of Higher Learning would provide insights on how to establish the necessary processes and manage the situation through making sound decisions based from the scientific method of analyzing the problem and sharing the knowledge to the members of the organization through an aid of technology.

The planning approach to make the collection of data systematically is the initial step towards maintaining a complete database of the needs and requirements of the customers and other stakeholders. Knowing their demands and the approach on how they need to be treated and served is one way of expressing the sincerity of the services.

Table 2: Customer Relationship Management Strategies in terms of Customized Services

Do: Customized Services	**Employee**	**Students**	**Alumni**	**WM**	**f-value**	**p-value**
1. Customized educational services to key customers.	2.61 (H)	2.32 (L)	2.10 (L)	2.33 (L)	12.696**	.000

2. Modification of services based on customer requirements.	2.53 (H)	2.92 (H)	2.46 (L)	2.67 (H)	13.656**	.000
3. Personalized services to key customers	2.33 (L)	2.46 (L)	2.61 (H)	2.47 (L)	3.823*	.023
Composite Mean	2.49 (L)	2.57 (H)	2.39 (L)	2.49 (L)	5.075**	.007

**Significant at p-value < 0.05; **Significant at p-value < 0.01*

Table 2 presents the Customer Relationship Management Strategies in terms of Customized Services. Modification of services based on customer requirements is highly observed according to employees (2.53) and students (2.92) but significantly low among the alumni (2.46) as denoted by the computed p-value of less than 0.01 alpha level. Institutions of higher learning provide curricular offerings based on the regulatory requirements of the Commission on Higher Education in the Philippines and other quality assurance mechanisms. Organizations modify and improve their services based on the results of external audits and customer satisfaction measurement. It is rarely being practiced in academic institutions that students are being asked on how they wanted the school programs and projects to be implemented and carried out. The same situation with the employees that traditional way of training and development is being provided throughout all ages without considering the needs of the millennial, baby boomers and generation X and Y. Alumni sought to consider their needs as they move forward their careers. The university is not focusing their resources to build strong relationship with the alumni through having constant communication and projects.

Meanwhile, personalized services to key customers as strategy is significantly highly observed among alumni (2.61) but significantly low for employees as denoted by the computed p-value of 0.023. There are certain colleges with sustainable projects where alumni can possibly participate and enjoy the camaraderie of each member of the alumni association. But there are some colleges with established college alumni council but no implemented sustainable projects due to inactive participation of both officers and members. Designing personalized services to each customer is a tedious and complicated approach to management. They are thinking the practicality and applicability of the idea based on the resources that the organization may provide for delivering such kind of services.

Furthermore, customized educational services to key customers is highly observed among employees (2.61) but significantly low among students (2.32) and alumni (2.10). There are educational services to regular employees as part of their privilege in professional growth. They can choose whatever degree program aligned or not aligned to their completed bachelor's degree to enroll in the graduate program. They can also choose whether to pursue the graduate degree in the university under study or to other universities within the region or outside the region. It gives them better option to improve their educational background. However, educational services for students are dictated by the curriculum and mandated by the CHED Memorandum Orders. The curriculum is designed based on the needs of the degree program and student outcomes. Different colleges have their own way of providing co-curricular activities where the students can enjoy the learning and teaching process within and outside the university.

The university has also career placement office that caters to the needs of the graduating students and alumni. This is considered a basic requirement for HEIs to have strong connections with the partner industries in order to absorb their graduates. Bejou (2005) added that the school should make an excellent career placement office as one of its top priorities that will support the graduate employment. It is not only the responsibility of the HEIs to hone the skills of the students but also to find good employers from the partner-industries. It demonstrates the capability of the academic institution on how strong its networks and linkages in assisting the graduates to find suitable work place for the graduates. This is also adding extra value to the existing educational services. Petruzzellis et al. (2006) emphasized that Universities become relational services, in which demand and supply cooperate to improve and design satisfying outputs.

The computed composite mean score in terms of customized services is observed significantly higher among students (2.57) than alumni (2.39) as denoted by the computed p-value of 0.007 which is less than 0.01 alpha level with low overall observation when taken as a whole. Part of the doing stage in PDCA cycle is the execution based on the strategic and annual operational plan. Knowledge sharing is an important process in management to support the decision and strengthen the views and ideas of people in providing suitable strategies to meet the demands of the customers. Ramachandran et al. (2009) believed that it can lead to the establishment of a higher standard of education. Meanwhile, Rowley (2000) emphasized that the main asset which determines the employability of the individuals is their knowledge together with the appropriate skills and values. Giving leadership training to the students with potential to become part of the student government body is very beneficial but how about those students without capability as of the moment to become leaders due to lack of self-esteem and other characteristics of an active student. Making them also as future leaders is a great achievement for the institution and a gift for the parents where the University tried its best to shape their character and build their spirit to become successful alumni and citizens of the country.

Table 3: Customer Relationship Management Strategies in terms of On-going Dialogue

Study: Ongoing Dialogue	**Employee**	**Students**	**Alumni**	**WM**	**f-value**	**p-value**
1. regular contacts with the customers while assessing the implementation of the services	3.26 (H)	2.74 (H)	2.46 (L)	2.79 (H)	27.098**	.000
2. Means of getting feedback from customers through social media about the educational services	2.47 (L)	2.42 (L)	2.57 (H)	2.48 (L)	1.183	.307
3. Means of communication through sending email and newsletter to the customers to inform of their services and school activities	3.16 (H)	2.66 (H)	2.41 (L)	2.72 (H)	28.302**	.000
Composite Mean	2.97 (H)	2.60 (H)	2.48 (L)	2.66 (H)	29.109**	.000

***Significant at p-value < 0.01*

Table 3 presents the Customer Relationship Management Strategies in terms of On-going Dialogue, where alumni (2.48) have significantly lower observation compared to employees (3.26) when they were asked regarding if the university has provided regular contacts with the customers while assessing the implementation of the services (2.79). Employees being the customers of the organization at the same time have regular contacts with the management. The top and middle management through regular meetings provide some updates regarding the challenges and concerns of the work units in everyday activities and the status of operational plans. However, alumni have very limited access and contact with the university. Dedicated social media for the alumni is not being given emphasis and regular update to the information provided is also limited. Zamil (2011) noted that if the implementation of CRM is effective, the people, processes, and technology work in synergy to increase profitability, and reduce operational costs.

Likewise, the university has provided means of communication through sending email and newsletter to the customers to inform of their services and school activities is observed significantly higher among employees (3.16) but significantly lower among alumni (2.41) as denoted by the computed p-value of less than 0.01 alpha level. Studying on how information is being disseminated to customers is also part of PDCA cycle where effective communication is being evaluated. One form of communication could be effective to one group of people but may not be as effective to other groups. Therefore, ongoing dialogue with them in different forms and personalizing services are better ways to continuously improve the strategies on how to win and retain customers.

However, the university has provided means of getting feedback from customers through social media about the educational services (2.48) is considered low among the respondents but there is no significant difference among their responses. Social Media users make more significant contributions to the creation of knowledge as content publishers of their ideas, thoughts, feelings and emotions where these can be useful source of information for the organizations. Chua and Banerjee (2013) analyzed the extent to which the use of social media can support customer knowledge management (CKM) in organizations relying on a traditional bricks-and-mortar business model. They emphasized the three CKM strategies that organizations use to manage customer knowledge: management of knowledge (1) for customers, (2) from customers, and (3) about customers. Social Media encourages people to do knowledge sharing as part of the customer-centric approach in order to determine their expectations, behavior, sentiments and preferences.

CRM strategies in terms of on-going dialogue is observed significantly higher among employees (2.97) than alumni (2.48) as denoted by the computed p-value of less than 0.01 alpha level with high overall observation when taken as a whole. Program accreditations have included in their process of validating some documents through dialogues with the students, employees and alumni where the result of this is included in the report submitted by the accrediting body. The information taken from this process served as important input on how the university can still provide enhancement of its curriculum design, facilities, delivery of quality instruction and educational services. Allameh, Shahin and Tabanifar (2012) emphasized that company can make sense of the information exchange with customers exploiting appropriate facilities and the latest technology and using group interviews and surveys periodically in order to overcome shortcomings in their products and services and enhance customer loyalty rates may apply.

Table 4: Customer Relationship Management Strategies in terms of Customer Responsiveness

Act: Customer Responsiveness	**Employee**	**Students**	**Alumni**	**WM**	**f-value**	**p-value**
1. Mechanism on addressing conflicts through listening from customer complaints	3.01 (H)	3.14 (H)	2.77 (H)	2.98 (H)	7.100**	.001
2. Positive response on the results of customer satisfaction	3.05 (H)	2.94 (H)	3.02 (H)	2.99 (H)	.705	.495
3. Immediate actions on the needs and inquiries of the customers	2.88 (H)	2.63 (H)	2.46 (L)	2.65 (H)	6.218**	.002
Composite Mean	2.98 (H)	2.90 (H)	2.75 (H)	2.88 (H)	7.673	.001

***Significant at p-value < 0.01*

Table 4 presents the Customer Relationship Management Strategies in terms of customer responsiveness. Having positive response on the results of customer satisfaction is highly being observed by the respondents with no significant difference on their responses as denoted by the computed p-value of 0.495 which is greater than 0.05 alpha level. The university under study provides its best action plan to maintain the harmonious relationship with the students, alumni and employees. One of the ultimate goals of business organizations is to obtain high customer satisfaction and getting the result of this measure defines how the management delivers the services to different types of customers. Not all customers are the same. There is a diversity of cultural background and behaviour where appropriate service needs to be identified to different kinds of clients. The result of customer satisfaction is being used to address some important issues in the organization that needs major attention. The responsiveness of the management in closing the gaps between expectations and experiences is one way of creating long term relationships with the customers.

Meanwhile, the mechanism in addressing conflicts through listening from customers is highly observed significantly among students (3.15) compared to the responses of alumni (2.77) while employees (2.88) have significantly higher observation in terms of providing immediate actions on the needs and inquiries of the customers than alumni (2.46) with low observation. The university provides appropriate channel on how students can bring their complaints through written views and concerns using drop boxes located in visible corners of the buildings. They can also be invited by the guidance counsellors through one-on-one interview to hear their problems either related to studies, family and peers. They also have teachers who can also listen to their grievances and conflicts. Addressing all these challenges through listening is an essential part of the action plan of the management in maintaining the balance of school and family life of the students. On the other hand, alumni have lesser chance of experiencing how to manage their conflicts because they have already different environment. But it is good to note if the university can also provide means on how alumni can still acquire counselling services. Furthermore, employees are service-oriented regarding how actions on the inquiries must always be instantaneous and the problems of the clients must be given enough attention. Allameh, Shahin and Tabanifar (2012) used interaction management and channel management as mediating tools for knowledge exchange and interaction between companies and customers which proper use of these tools lead to achieving of customer knowledge management goals.

Overall, employees (2.98) have significantly higher level of observation in terms of customer responsiveness than alumni (2.75) as denoted by the computed p-value of 0.001 which is less than 0.01 alpha level. Employees are the ones providing information and answers to the needs and inquiries of the students and alumni. The teachers have direct contact with the students, and they are acknowledgeable about the problems of the student.

Department secretaries as well are also involved in the management of behaviour of the students. They are aware of the concerns of the students and they really provide assistance on how students could face and surpass their challenges. They are always ready to listen to the stories of the students.

Conclusion and Recommendations

HEIs create physical environment with the purpose of nurturing the students' learning experiences. The respondents believed that the University has high level of CRM strategies in terms of planning for having needs assessment through customer satisfaction assessment. Another high level rating in terms of having an on-going dialogue through regular contacts with the customers; high level rating on customer responsiveness. However, the university has low level in customizing educational services. Significant difference exists on customized services where students have significantly higher assessment than alumni and employees. In terms of on-dialogue and customer responsiveness, employees have significantly higher level of assessment of strategies than alumni.

All organizations need to maintain its presence and making it possible is through building a special relationship with its customers in order to fulfil the short-term and long-term goals. Ensuring the proper management of customer relations is one of the challenges of most HEIs where majority of them have no dedicated office or center that caters to the specific functions of knowledge management. Although they manage customer relations in different ways according to the nature and demand of their respective clients but integrating knowledge management to the system would somehow address the gap on the implementation of programs for students and low level of collaboration between partner institutions and other stakeholders. Exploring all the possibilities to strengthen the involvement of people to various opportunities is one of the objectives of customer relationship and knowledge management system approach. It gives better position for the organization to become dynamic and competitive.

Integrating the process as part of the institutional programs makes CRM as part of the culture in the organization. Establishing a knowledge management office with CRM component can bring another perspective for the administrators on how they should go towards a better direction. From the study of Allameh, Shahin and Tabanifar (2012), they emphasized the Knowledge management (KM) and customer relationship management (CRM) for the allocation of resources to business supportive activities in order to gain competitive advantages. This will also serve as part of the institutional innovation and solution to sustain various quality assurance mechanisms and strategic directions. This is an approach of dynamically leveraging the expertise of people for value creation and enhancement of organizational performance.

Including retention strategies in the plans of the universities for the key industry-partners of large multinational corporations would provide specific direction for a long term goal which is designed to build relationships. Strategic choice theorists emphasize the ability of managers to redesign internal organizational networks to fit changing tasks and environments (Campbell, 2011). Identifying the specific skills requirement of the industry-partners from the graduates also gives substantial insights to the enhancement and revision of the program curriculum.

A well-informed academic community could possibly think of alternative solutions from the given problem or situation. Human resources, processes and technological infrastructures are the key components of the knowledge management that facilitate the complete operation of the CRM system suitable for the needs and requirements of certain HEI.

Further may consider the Customer Knowledge Management (CKM) that creates new knowledge sharing platforms and processes between companies and their customers. Gibbert, Leibold & Probst (2002) emphasized the five styles of CKM which can be prosumerism, group learning, mutual innovation, communities of creativity, and joint intellectual capital.

The needs and requirements of the industry-partners must also be considered as part of future investigation in establishing mechanism on how they will be served by the HEIs in sustaining partnership towards the attainment of higher employment rating of the graduates. Industry as important partner of the higher educational institutions provides training ground for the students for practicum or internship where the process of transferring knowledge into practice is already taking place. Industry-partners are considered customers of colleges and universities that need to be treasured and regarded as significant ingredient to the development of students' soft and technical skills in a work place.

Therefore, it is important to contextualize the customer relationship management through knowledge management system principles and concepts into practical information that would be suitable for a third world country like the Philippines. It would seek proper direction on how things could be properly incorporated and aligned in the existing quality assurance mechanisms of the institutions.

References

Abburu, S., and Babu, G. S. (2013). A framework for ontology based knowledge management. *Int. J. Soft Comput. Eng*, *3*(3): 2231-2307.

Ackerman, R. and Schibrowsky, J. (2008).A Business Marketing Strategy Applied to Student Retention: A Higher Education Initiative, J. College Student Retention, 9(3): 307-336.

Allameh, S. M., Shahin, A., and Tabanifar, B. (2012). Analysis of relationship between knowledge management and customer relationship management with customer knowledge management (case study at Azaran valve co.). *International Journal of Academic Research in Business and Social Sciences*, *2*(10), 65.

Baird, C. H., and Parasnis, G. (2011). From social media to social customer relationship management. *Strategy & Leadership*, *39*(5): 30-37.

Bejou, D. (2005). Treating Students like Customers, BizEd.

Berry, L. L., Wall, E. A., and Carbone, L. P. (2006). Service Clues and Customer Assessment of the Service Experience: Lessons from Marketing, Academy of Management *Perspectives,* DOI: 10.5465/AMP.2006.20591004

Bruning, S. D. (2002). Relationship building as a retention strategy: linking relationship attitudes and satisfaction evaluations to behavioral outcomes, Public Relations Review 28, 39–48.

Campbell, A. J. (2011). Creating customer knowledge competence: managing customer relationship management programs strategically, Industrial Marketing Management 32 (2011): 375– 383

Chalmeta, R. (2006). Methodology for customer relationship management. *Journal of Systems and Software*, *79*(7): 1015-1024.

Chan, J. O. (2005). Toward a unified view of customer relationship management. *Journal of American Academy of Business*, *6*(1): 32-38.

Chua, A. Y., and Banerjee, S. (2013). Customer knowledge management via social media: the case of Starbucks. *Journal of Knowledge Management*, *17*(2): 237-249.

Ejaz, R., Ahmed, M. A., and Ahmad, Z. (2013). Impact of CRM practices on customers' behaviors. *International Journal of Business and Management Invention*, *2*(7): 79-88.

Gibbert, M., Leibold, M., and Probst, G. (2002). Five styles of customer knowledge management, and how smart companies use them to create value. *European Management Journal*, *20*(5): 459-469.

Kuh, G. D., Schuh, J. S., Whitt, E. J., and Associates. (1991). *Involving colleges: Successful approaches to fostering student learning and personal development outside the classroom.* San Francisco, CA: Jossey-Bass.

Jayachandran, S., Sharma, S., Kaufman, P., and Raman, P. (2005). The role of relational information processes and technology use in customer relationship management. *Journal of Marketing,* 69, 177–192.

Joseph, M., Yakhou, M. and Stone, G. (2005). An educational institution's quest for service quality: customers' perspective, Quality Assurance in Education, 13 (1), pp. 66-82, DOI 10.1108/09684880510578669.

Payne, A., and Frow, P. (2004). The role of multichannel integration in customer relationship management. *Industrial Marketing Management, 33*(6): 527-538.

Petruzzellis, L., D'Uggento, A. M., and Romanazzi, S. (2006). Student satisfaction and quality of service in Italian universities. *Managing Service Quality: An International Journal, 16*(4): 349-364.

Ramachandran, S. D., Chong, S. C., and Ismail, H. (2009). The practice of knowledge management processes: A comparative study of public and private higher education institutions in Malaysia. *Vine, 39*(3): 203-222.

Rowley, J. (2000). Is higher education ready for knowledge management? *International Journal of Educational Management, 14*(7): 325-333.

Zamil, A. M. (2011). customer relationship management: A strategy to sustain the organization's name and products in the customers' minds. *European Journal of Social Sciences,* 22(3), 451-459.

Zulueta, F. M. and Costales Jr., N. E. B. (2001). Methods of Research Thesis-Writing and Applied Statistics, National Bookstore, Mandaluyong City, Philippines.

2

Global Perspective on Technical and Vocational Education and Training (TVET) School Environment and the Sustainable Development Goals (SDGs)

WORDU Chiduhiegem C. R. & SAUE Baritule P.

Introduction

Global perspective is a comprehensive lens through which one sees the world around him/her. It shapes how one perceives and understands his/her own identity and that of the people they interact with, as one begins to understand what goes into shaping culture (UNESCO, 2004). To the scholars, global perspective is when someone can think about a situation as it relates to the rest of the world. It may seem silly to see that every nation should be concerned with what goes on in another country.

Technical and Vocational Education and Training (TVET) can be described as an aspect of education which is concerned with the preparation of skilled manpower. It is a form of education, training or retraining which is directed towards developing the learner to become productive in a paid employment or in self-employment. It is therefore, the bedrock on which a country's social-economic technological and cultural advancement must be built upon. To the scholars, vocational and technical education is a means of seeking to provide solution to practically all human problems, such as industrial, economical, social, among others. Agreeing with the above, Oluwale, Jegede and Olamade (2013) put it that VTE is a vehicle for the development of marketable and entrepreneurial skills, and engine of development. Technical and Vocational Education and Training (TVET) is education that places emphasis on pragmatic attitude as a priority (for individual and community development) is technical and vocational education and training (TVET). TVET is the form of education that advocates development of the head (knowledge), training of the hand (dexterity) and enriching the heart (conscientiousness and painstaking), - the 3Hs. TVET is a total deviation from the previous emphasis on 3Rs, - reading, writing and arithmetic, which was fundamentally a form of credentializing entry into elite status with its graduates/products roaming about seeking for the non-existing white collar jobs.

Technical and Vocational Education and Training (TVET) is the education for those who need it, those who want it, and those who want to progress by it. It is a result oriented form of education. Vocational and technical education is an educational training which encompasses knowledge, skills, competencies, structural activities, abilities, capacities and all other structural experiences for securing jobs in various sector of the economy or even enabling one to be self-dependent by being a job creator. No wonder Amoor (2009) maintained that it is the core of both individuals and society's economy. He further stressed that through the acquisition of skills; individuals could explore their environment and harness the resources within it, which could serve them and the society since the wealth of any nation determines its development. Technical and Vocational Education and Training (TVET) is the type of education that prepares its recipient for the world of work and so the students are supposed to be exposed to work environment which will enable them to fit in and outside the school environment.

Technical and Vocational Education and Training (TVET) is a driving force of human capital development and a catalyst to sustainable livelihood and economic development for developing nations such as Nigeria. Uwaifo (2010) argued that technology education which is viewed as technical education and training is the training of technically oriented personnel who are to be initiators, facilitators, and implementers of technologically development of a nation. Vocational education prepares the individual in acquisition of skills and job positions in skill areas (Dokubo and Dokubo, 2013). Vocational education is an educational training which has been systematically designed to enable an individual acquires the basic skills, knowledge, abilities and understanding needed for developing skills and to be self-reliant. This type of skilled-oriented education can be achieved based on the condition and the nature of the school environment.

Therefore, school environment according to Okoro (2004) is a system within which living organisms interact with the physical elements, while educational environment is a learning place where the learners learn to interact with learning facilities in order to be socialized and face the challenges in the society. To Ehiametalor (2001), it is the operational inputs of every instructional program and they constitute elements that are necessary for teaching and learning e.g buildings, Laboratories, machinery, furniture and electrical fixtures. Infrastructure represents the empirical relevance of the totality of school environment for the realization of school business. In consonance with the above, Zais (2011) considered the school physical environment to include the school building and the surrounding grounds such as noise, temperature and the lighting as well as physical, biological or chemical agents. He further said that school environment can be seen to include material and human resources, a learning place which consists of the entire interactive setting like classroom, workshop, library, field and offices. Okwelle (2007) emphasized that environment refers to the facilities available for instruction and it possesses a strong influence in teaching – learning process. He added that there is need for adequate classroom buildings with good sitting arrangements for classroom instruction.

Development entails the full realization of the human potential and a maximum use of the nation's resources for the benefit of all (Bamgbose, 2011). If development is about human beings, then that which gives human beings the capacity to function cannot but be so important. Thus, British Council (2017) explained that since development is about sharing experiences and ideas to find better ways of working together as human beings, the languages of initiative, of education, of trade, of creative expression, of justice and of peace-building, are so crucial to sustainable development. Sustainable Development Goals (SDG) is a target as well as yardstick for every country to measure and explore its response to and business of making life conducive for her present and future citizens. It is about recreating a safe world for all through equipping of every human being with the tools for a decent and healthy living through mutual effort.

Sustainable development requires meeting the pressing needs of all people and extending opportunity to satisfy their aspirations for a better life. It ensures a developed world with secured and healthy environment for all; human beings, animals and plants alike, Ndubuisi-Okolo, Anekwe and Attah (2016). Sustainable development in terms of community projects; businessmen as effective production of goods and services; environmentalists as a means of enabling efficient and effective use of natural resources; and by the masses as a means of meeting their needs as well as a strategy for alleviating poverty (Kwasi, 2014). Sustainable development refers to the utilization of resources in order to achieve improvements in the economic outcomes of components of an economy without jeopardizing access of future generations (Oladeji, 2014). This implies intergenerational equity must be applied in all economic considerations for growth to be sustainable. According to the International Institute for Sustainable Development (IISD) sustainable development has been defined in many ways, but the most frequently quoted definitions is form Our Common Future, also known as the Brundtland Report: "Sustainable development is development that meets the needs of the present without compromising the ability of future generations to meet their own needs. It contains within it two key concepts. According to the direct Government website United Kingdom, sustainable development means a better quality of life now and for generations to come. It means not using up resources faster than the planet can replenish, or re-stock influences decision making with organizations, and therefore can go towards forming principles and business 'values'.

Since the adoption of the SDGs in September 2015, and the beginning of their implementation in January 2016, there are several concrete global plans and sector-specific strategies to achieve the set goals. This is essentially because a successful implementation of the SDGs, which replaced the Millennium Development Goals (2000-2015), would mean successful attainment of citizens' aspirations for prosperity, peace and wellbeing, as well as the preservation of the Earth's biodiversity and equitable distribution of natural resources. In other words, the SDGs generally seek to end poverty, fight inequality and injustice, and tackle climate change by 2030. The Sustainable Development Goals are a collection of 17 global goals set by the United Nations in 2015; otherwise known as Global Goals for Sustainable Development or Agenda 2030 – because the goals are expected to be achieved in the fifteen years period between 2015 and 2030. The goals are broad and somewhat interdependent yet each has a separate list of targets to achieve. In total, they have 169 targets.

The Official Agenda for Sustainable Development adopted on 25 September 2015 has 92 paragraphs, with the main paragraph (51) outlining the 12 Sustainable Development Goals and its associated 169 targets. This included the following goals:

i. **No Poverty**: End poverty in all its forms everywhere: Poverty is more than lack of income or resources- it includes lack of basic services, such as education, hunger, social discrimination and exclusion, and lack of participation in decision making;
ii. **Zero Hunger:** End hunger, achieve food security and improved nutrition and promote sustainable agriculture. Agriculture is the single largest employer in the world, providing livelihoods for 40 per cent of today's global population. It is the largest source of income and jobs for poor rural households. Women comprise on average 43 per cent of the agricultural labor force in developing countries, and over 50 per cent in parts of Asia and Africa, yet they only own 20% of the land;.
iii. **Good Health and Well-being:** Ensure healthy lives and promote well-being for all at all ages. An important target is to substantially reduce the number of deaths and illnesses from pollution-related diseases.
iv. **Quality Education:** Ensure inclusive and equitable quality education and promote lifelong learning opportunities for all. Major progress has been made for education access, specifically at the primary school level, for both boys and girls. However, access does not always mean quality of education, or completion of primary school. Currently, 103 million youth worldwide still lack basic literacy skills and more than 60 per cent of them are women.
v. **Gender Equality:** Achieve gender equality and empower all women and girls. Providing women and girls with equal access to education, health care, decent work, and representation in political and economic decision-making processes will fuel sustainable economies and benefit societies and humanity at large.

vi. **Clean Water and Sanitation:** Ensure availability and sustainable management of water and sanitation for all.
vii. **Affordable and Clean Energy:** Ensure access to affordable, reliable, sustainable and modern energy for all.
viii. **Decent Work and Economic Growth:** Promote sustained, inclusive and sustainable economic growth, full and productive employment and decent work for all.
ix. **Industry, Innovation and Infrastructure:** Build resilient infrastructure, promote inclusive and sustainable industrialization and foster innovation
x. **Reduced Inequalities:** Reduce income inequality within and among countries
xi. **Sustainable Cities and Communities:** Make cities and human settlements inclusive, safe, resilient and sustainable.
xii. **Responsible Consumption and Production**: Ensure sustainable consumption and production patterns.
xiii. Climate Action
xiv. Life Below Water
xv. Life on Land
xvi. Peace and Justice Strong Institutions
xvii. Partnership to Achieve the Goals

Components of TVET School Environment

The components of Technical and Vocational Education and Training (TVET) include facilities used for technical education programme which include among others as infrastructure (buildings-classroom blocks, administrative blocks, workshop/laboratory, farms, internal roads, pipe-borne water), equipment supplied, library facilities, communication and recreational facilities and environment. Furthermore, Ehiametalor (2001) identifies the following as components of TVET, school environment as landscape, playgrounds, buildings, library, sick bays, toilets, hostels, administrative blocks and so on, utilities such as electricity, and security facilities walls (fences) gates, telephone and information technology system.

Other components of TVET school environments are as follows;

- **Physical Environment:** The physical environment of the school include the school buildings and the school grounds which is a key factor in the overall health and safety of students, staff and visitors. These parameters must be designed and maintained to be accessible and free of health and safety hazards, and to promote learning and other school engagement. Policies and protocols must be in place to ensure food protection, sanitation, safe water supply, healthy air quality, good lightening, safe playgrounds, and emergency evacuation, among other issues that relate to the physical environment of the schools.

- **Psychological Environment:** The psychological environment of a school would refer to the stimuli that impinge up on the learner's psyche in the school. For example, the attitude of the principal and the teachers towards a learner would act as a stimulus for the learner to do or not to do certain things in the school. School is dedicated and certain anti-democratic practices and attitudes to which it is often prone, like authoritarianism in human relations, competitiveness rather than cooperation in the classroom, caste and religion based segregation and other less tangible forms of inter-group discriminations.
- **Social Environment:** The social surrounding of the school constituted its social environment. A learner is in constant interaction with the peers and teachers for a significant part of the day he spends in the school. Be it studies, playing, quarreling or simply gossiping, the learner has someone around. Every interaction and interpersonal relationship of a learner occurs in a social environment. One's interaction with others in a social environment is also known as socialization.
- **Cultural Environment:** Cultural environment includes products that are humanly produced both materials (buildings, workshop, etc.) and immaterial (ideology, value, etc.) as well as materially derived products such as social class and socio-political order. One never sees culture as such, what are seen are regularities in the behavior or artifact of a group that adhere to a common. TVET school presents to its learners an environment characterized by practices that is its cultural environment.
- **Political Environment:** Dominance of one social class over the others is called *hegemony*. Since teachers and students in a school belong to one or the other caste or community group, the practices of hegemony are also found in the school environment. This is why only certain students can attend private schools and the others, public schools. Even inside the classroom, certain students receive better attention and preferential treatment while others do not. On the other hand, a lecturer may have more courses or supervisee (research students) to teach or supervise whereas some do not have any. Thus, it is pertinent to note that every school creates a political environment for the teachers and learners.

Global Perspective on TVET

As laudable as the philosophy of TVET is, it is misconstrued by different people in the society. The parents and wards view vocational education as a form of education designed for drop-outs and those found to be less intelligent (ETF, 2005; Ladipo, Akhuemonkhan & Raimi 2013). In the vein, Okolocha (2012) deposited that TVET to some people is a low quality education suitable for the less privileged students or second class citizens. Amodu (2011) stated that the issue of negative perception of TVET is not limited to parents and ordinary Nigerians, the policy makers are equally not immune from negative impression about vocational education.

The implication of negative perception of TVET is threefold:

a) Low societal estimation of technical and vocational education and training in the society
b) Gross gender imbalance in technical and vocational education and training implementation
c) Inadequate human, material and financial resources for technical and vocational education and training institutions.

However, having explained the meaning of TVET and its socio-economic impacts on the society, it is therefore pertinent to note that a change in the global perception of Technical and Vocational Education and Training (TVET) is a stepping stone toward industrialization of leading to self-employment of the citizenry resulting in the reduction in crime rate of any society.

Relationship between TVET and SDGs

Technical and Vocational Education and Training (TVET) is crucial towards achieving the SDGs since it empowers the citizenry to make meaningful contributions towards achieving those giant goals which will in turn make the world conducive for the present and future generations while protecting the other living and non-living things are all part of creation. Sustainable development is interlinked with a broad range of TVET issues. "Sustainability is not the result of a particular technology or vocation. TVET for Sustainable Development aims at a deliberate change of behaviour; it covers all vocations and workplaces" (BMBF 2003). Nevertheless, it is useful identifying key areas of vocational activity (and, as a consequence, of TVET), the content of which carries particular potential for contributing to sustainable development. Since a broad range of vocational activities is focusing on the economic dimension anyway, it seems more appropriate focusing on the other two dimensions – the ecological and the social one.

Typically, the following areas of the SDGs are being referred to as particularly sensitive with respect to the TVET:

- Ecological dimension which includes;
    - Management of fresh water
    - Use of renewable energies to ensure continuous supply
    - Soil (e.g. agriculture, mining); impacts such as erosion and desertification
    - Livestock production and rural development

    - Management of organic substances
    - Recycling to reduce exploitation of natural resources
    - Waste management for the conservation of the environment
    - Garbage and sewage treatment
    - Life cycle analysis of products.
- Human and social dimensional areas include the following;
    - Construction and housing
    - Safety and health at work
    - Health and food standards for the prevention of pandemic
    - Teamwork in a multicultural work environment;
    - Applying ethical standards when interacting with market participants.
- Ecological and social dimensional areas include;
    - Preservation and a culture of maintenance
    - Indigenous and traditional technologies
    - Human settlements
    - Rural development
    - Transport systems
    - Management of tourism to avoid its adverse effects
    - Health and food standards for the prevention of pandemics
    - Noise emission

Close linkages have been observed between TVET and the world of work with respect to the three dimensions of sustainable development:

- TVET typically prepares for economic activities, such as the production of goods and services either individually (self-employment) or in the context of an enterprise or production unit. Frequently the products and services are delivered in a competitive market situation. Thus, the economic aspect of sustainable development is, in most cases, an integral component of any vocational activity, and needs therefore to be reflected in TVET.
- For the performance of production processes, all kinds of resources are required as inputs, such as commodities, soil, energy, fresh water, tools, transport capacities etc. These processes often do produce not only the desired products and services, but also unintended outputs such as garbage, waste, pollution, soil erosion, noise, accidents, and health risks. Thus, vocational activities do have immediate impact on ecological and environmental issues that need to be addressed in TVET.
- Vocational activities take place in work environments ranging from household and small farms and crafts shops up to multinational enterprises. Thus, work relations, teamwork, communication at the workplace, accountability, relations between employers and employees, collective bargaining as well as interaction with external

market participants, such as suppliers and customers, but also communication with public authorities, are integral part of vocational practice. Hence, the social aspect of sustainable development needs to be addressed in TVET.

Technical and Vocational Education and Training (TVET) encourages entrepreneurship development which is a panacea for achieving sustainable development goals since it serves as a means of alleviating the menace of poverty in any given society (achieving goal one (1)). It contributes to poverty reduction when it generates employment through the establishment of new industries whereby the qualified unemployed can be engaged. The jobs created via entrepreneurship activities in turn lead to equitable distribution of income which results in higher standards of living for the teeming populace. TVET activities are perceived as being capable of making tremendous impact on the economy of a nation and the quality of life of its inhabitants. In consensus with the above, Oni (2007) stressed that TVET is a specialized education designed to empower learners through the development of their technical skills, human abilities, cognitive understanding, attitudes and work habits in order to prepare learners adequately for the world of work or positioned them practically for self-employment after graduation. According to the authors, technical and vocational education and training (TVET) prepares individuals for the world of works either as employers of labour or skilled labour, thus influence the actualization of the sustainable development goals. They further reiterated that technical and vocational education (TVET) relates with SDGs to maintain and sustain a virtuous circle that links job creation and economic growth. TVET is a cross-discipline area linked to labour, industry, and employment.

Challenges of achieving SDGs in Nigeria

- **Corruption:** Corruption is difficult to define, estimate and curb. This is because most corrupt acts are carried out "off book". Corruption has been defined as the application of position of trust or authority for financial gains or other personal rewards. In corrupt climes, the rule of law, due process and equity are relaxed. Corruption is a global disease with more influence in Africa (Amadi & Ekekwe, 2014). This is because Africa faces developmental challenges and the resources meant to liberate her from sub-human living conditions are unrepentantly misappropriated.
- **Dwindling Economy:** This involve the inability to achieve a balance in all sectors of the Nigeria's economy in the form of production of goods and services be it agriculture, finance, manufacturing, health, education, etc. The Economic challenge inherent in the Nigeria economy include issues such as poverty, low per capital income, inequitable distribution of home, low capital formation, inefficiency in the

mobilization of resource, over-dependence on a singular commodity e.g. oil and gas as a major source of income, unemployment, inflation among others.

- **Infrastructure Deficits:** Sustainable development is undermined by severe infrastructure deficits that stare African development in the eye. Infrastructure deficits explain the existence of untapped productive potentials of Africa (Banerjee, Wodon, Diallo, Pushak, Uddin, Timpo, Foster, 2008).). Infrastructure is critical to significant improvements in competitiveness, domestic and international trade and global integration. Infrastructure deficit remains an undermining factor in Africa's quest for poverty reduction and sustainable development. Africa trails other developing countries in paved road density, telecommunication, electricity and water and sanitation (Oluwatayo & Ojo, 2016; Ajibefun, 2015).
- **Insecurity:** Insecurity is one of the constraints to improvements in economic activities in Africa. Terrorism has been increasing in the last few decades. Boko Haram and ISIS both account for 51 percent of all recorded global fatalities in 2014 (Nwolise, 2013). However, terrorism remains the most significant security problem in Africa. There is no universally accepted definition of terrorism but the most popular definition is contained in the UN General Assembly Resolution (Demeke & Gebru, 2014; Oche, 2014). Africa's development is currently threatened by insecurity ranging from "commercial violence", civil wars, terrorism and kidnapping. It states that criminal acts intended or calculated to provoke a state of terror in the general public, a group of persons or particular person for political purposes is terrorism (Colliers, 2003).
- Lack of qualified people to develop and implement alternative technologies due to a poor educational system and the "brain drain".
- Lack of education about finite resources. People do not know or understand the implications of over use of resources.

Conclusion

The world is faced with challenges in all three dimensions of sustainable development—economic, social and environmental. More than 1 billion people are still living in extreme poverty and income inequality within and among many countries have been rising; at the same time, unsustainable consumption and production patterns have resulted in huge economic and social costs and may endanger life on the planet. Achieving sustainable development will require global actions to deliver on the legitimate aspiration towards further economic and social progress, requiring growth and employment, and at the same time strengthening environ - mental protection. Sustainable development will need to be inclusive and take special care of the needs of the poorest and most vulnerable.

In light of the above, TVET underpins many of the proposed sustainable development goals and their achievement. TVET is crucial in reorienting society to adopt the low-carbon mentality so essential to addressing climate change. It is also impossible to think of making gains in poverty reduction, job creation and decent work provision without transforming TVET.

Way Forward

The strategies for achievement of these Sustainable Development Goals (SDGs) are identified to include: domestic and external financial resource mobilization; education and capacity development; regional integration; trade and market access; development and transfer of environmentally sound technologies; good governance and effective institutions; national cooperation; and reform of international financial and development institutions; as well as effective monitoring and evaluation at all levels (local, national, sub-regional, regional and global) with a common reporting framework for performance indicators to compare performance across countries, sub-regions and regions.

The study further suggests that nations all over the globe should also encourage the under-listed strategies toward achieving SDGs:

- Provision of soft loans to less privileged persons to promote Small and Medium scale Enterprise (SMEs).
- Address the problem of financing the real sector end mobilization of long term savings for investment.
- Job training of people in skills relevant to their immediate work environment and rural development should be incorporated.
- Agriculture and food security policies should be enhanced by strengthening research and development to improve production and enhance exportation thereby boosting income.
- Strengthen the regulation and supervisory framework of the financial sector.
- Promotion of indigenous goods and services especially through SMEs.
- Support for the Review and Development of National TVET Policies
- Capacity Building and Training Programmes
- Networking and Partnerships in TVET
- Ongoing Monitoring, Evaluation and Research. (UNESCO 2004).

References

Ajibefun, I. A. (2015). Nigeria's Agricultural Policy, Productivity and Poverty: The Critical Nexus. Inaugural Lecture Series 69 of the Federal University of Technology Akure, 1-6.

Amadi, L. and Ekekwe, E. (2014). Corruption and Development Administration in Africa: Institutional Approach. *African Journal of Political Science and International Relations*, 8, 163-174.

Amodu, T. (2011). Revamping Our National Economy through Technical Vocational Education and Training (TVET). Available online at: http://www.nigerianbestforum.com/blog/revamping-our-national-economy-through-technical-vocational-education-and-training-tvet/ (Accessed: 8 September, 2019).

Amoor, S. S. (2009). The Challenges of Vocational and Technical Education Programme in Nigerian Universities. Retrieved from: www.abu.edu.ng/publications.

Bamgbose, A. (2011). African Languages Today: The Challenge of and Prospects for Empowerment under Globalization. Retrieved November 27, 2019 from http://.lingref.com/cpp/acal/40/paper2561.pdf.

Banerjee, S. Q., Wodon, A., Diallo, T., Pushak, H., Uddin, C., Timpo, V. and Foster, S. (2008). Access, affordability and alternatives: Modern infrastructural services in Africa. Background Paper 2, Africa Infrastructure Sector Diagnostic, World Bank, Washington DC.

BMBF (2003). Berufsbildung für eine nachhaltige Entwicklung (TVET for sustainable devclopment). Erste bundesweite Fachtagung. Bundesministerium für Bildung und Forschung (BMBF), Bonn, 2003 http://www.bmbf.de/pub/berufsbildung_fuer_eine_nachhaltige_entwicklung_bundesweite_fachtagung.pdf (18.08.2005)

British Council (2017). Language and the Sustainable Development Goals. 12th International Language and Development Conference, Dakar. Retrieved November 27, 2019 from https://www.britishcouncil.com.sn/en/programmes/language.

Demeke, M. A. and Gebru, S. G. (2014). The role of regional economic communities in fighting terrorism in Africa: The case of intergovernmental authority in development. *European Scientific Journal*, *2*, 1-14.

Dokubo, C, and Dokubo, I. (2013). Identifiable problems inhibiting the effective management of vocational education programmes in Nigerian Universities. *European Scientific Journal*, *9(22):* 357-365.

European Training Foundation (2005). Integrating TVET into the Knowledge Economy: Reform and Challenges in the Middle East and North Africa. The World Bank,

Washington. DC. Available http://www.scribd.com/doc/133538720/TVET-Knowledge-Economy#download (Accessed: 14 September, 2013).

Kwasi, D. (2014). Effective leadership and sustainable development in Africa: is there "really" a link? *Journal of Global Responsibility,* 5 (2): 203 – 218.

Ladipo, M. K., Akhuemonkhan, I. A. and Raimi, L. (2013). Technical Vocational Education and Training (TVET) as mechanism for Sustainable Development (SD) in Nigeria: Potentials, challenges and policy prescriptions. Presentation at CAPA International Conference held in Banjul, The Gambia, June 3-8.

Ndubuisi-Okolo, P., Anekwe, I. E. and Attah, E. (2016). Waste Management and sustainable development in Nigeria: A Study of Anambra State Waste Management Agency. *European Journal of Management,* 8(17): 132-142.

Nwolise, O. B. C. (2013). Is Physical Security Alone Enough for the Survival, Progress and Happiness of Man? Inaugural Lecture of the University of Ibadan delivered on the 20th February, 2013, 1-10.

Oche I. A. (2014). Africa and the resurgence of terrorism-revisiting the fundamentals. *Global Journal of Arts, Humanities and Social Sciences, 2*, 1-13.

Colliers, J. (2003). Terrorism and Africa. African Security Review, 12, 1-13.

Okolocha, C. C. (2012). Vocational Technical Education in Nigeria: Challenges and the Way Forward. *Business Management Dynamics,* 2 (6): 1-8.

Okoro, C. N. (2004). School Environment and Teacher Competency Variable as Correlates of Learning Outcomes of Integrated Science Students with Hearing Impairment. Unpublished Ph.D. Thesis, University of Ibadan, Ibadan.

Okwelle, P. C. (2007). Instructional Strategies for Technology Education Teacher. Unpublished Monograph. Faculty of Technical and Science Education. RSUST, Port Harcourt.

Oladeji, S. I. (2014). Educated and Qualified but Jobless: A Challenge for Sustainable Development in Nigeria. Inaugural Lecture Series 262 of Obafemi Awolowo University, Ile Ife, Nigeria, 1-20.

Oluwale, B. A., Jegede, O. O. and Olamade O. O. (2013). Technical and Vocational Skills, Depletion in Nigeria and the Need for Policy Intervention. *International Journal of Vocational and Technical Education,* 5(6): 100-109.

Oluwatayo, I. B. and Ojo, A. O. (2016). Is Africa's Dependence on Agriculture the Cause of Poverty in the Continent? An Empirical Review. *Journal of Developing Areas*, 50: 94-102.

Oni, C. S. (2007). Globalization and Its Implications for Vocational Education in Nigeria. *Essays in Education.* 21: 30-34.

UNESCO (2004). Suggestions to UNESCO for Action Planning in TVET for Sustainable Development. Expert Meeting on Learning for Work, Citizenship and Sustainability, Bonn, October 2004. UNESCO, Paris. http://www.unevoc.unesco.org/publications/pdf/SD_ActionPlan_e.pdf (06.08.2005).

Uwaifo, V. O. (2010). Technical Education and its Challenges in Nigeria in the 21st Century. *International NGOS Journal,* 5(2): 40 – 44.

Zais, M. (2011). South Carolina School Environment Initiative. South Carolina Department of Education, Columbia. Retrieved on July 29, 2014, from *http://ed.sc.gov/agency/ac/Student-Intervention-Services/documents/SC-SchoolEnvironmentRFP-Nov2011.pdf*

3

Providing Adequate Funding in Secondary Schools Education and Teachers' Productivity in Calabar Education Zone of Cross River State, Nigeria

ANIAH Solomon A. Ph.D & EDEM Felix B. Ph.D

Abstract

Secondary education is the link between primary and tertiary education, which provides opportunity for a child to acquire additional knowledge, skills and traits beyond the primary level. In this paper, an attempt has been made to highlight the importance of education in general and secondary education in particular in the development process, and spotlight the neglect of this sub-sector of education in terms of funding. Suggestions have been made for alternative approaches to funding secondary education. These include: increased budgetary allocations to this sub-sector at federal, state and local government levels, introduction of special secondary education levies and the launching of secondary education endowment funds. The administration of secondary education funds that may be realized from these measures calls for a high sense of probity on the part of the personnel entrusted with execution of such a project, hence the need for a proper systems of accountability and auditing.

Key Words: *Funding, Education, Productivity*

Introduction

The essence of secondary education in any part of the world is to serve as the bridge between primary and tertiary education. Apart from serving as the link between primary and tertiary education, it provides opportunity for a child to acquire additional knowledge, skills and traits beyond the primary level. A major factor, that necessitates the acquisition of secondary education in Nigeria is that the education being provided at the primary level is proving to be insufficient for a child to acquire permanent literacy, communicative, and numeracy skills expected from him/her at the end of the training (Adeyemi, 2012, Adeyemi & Ajayi, 2006). Secondary education is aged in African countries including Nigeria, having developed alongside western education, which was introduced by Christian missionaries in 1842 (Adesina, 2004). At the outset, only primary education received a boost from Christian missionaries because it was used as avenue to bring the children into Christianity. Government's attention to secondary education started some decades after the development of primary education, particularly when the need for outputs of primary schools to further their education in secondary schools became paramount. This simply indicates that the rate of development in any country is dependent upon the educational attainment of her citizenry. Nigeria, since the establishment of secondary education has tried to provide equitable and sympathetic development in both her primary and secondary education, but such efforts have not been realized to its fullest perhaps due to lack of adequate fund or inadequate funding.

Consequently, successful governments in Nigeria have launched series of educational programmes such as the Science Education, Technical Education, Commercial Education Special Education, Grammar Education and so on, all to eradicate or minimize the rate of illiteracy and improve the lives of citizens in the country. All these programmes are proofs of the Federal Government's recognition that education is the key to national developments even when government was a bit slow in getting involved with few of the above mentioned education, but today, since government feels that secondary education can transform all aspects of the nation's life, it leaves no stone unturned to ensure that funds are made available for financing secondary education projects. Indeed, Adesina (2004) has observed that after major educational activities secondary education must of necessity be preventive, students at this stage are beginning to know who they are in relation to what educational programmes they are aspiring to take up in the tertiary education. The implication of this is that, secondary education should be the bedrock upon which most students have solidified their educational decision (Okoro, 2010). It is provided for children after primary education, that is, before tertiary education. It is aimed at developing a child better than the primary level, because it is obvious that primary education is insufficient for children to acquire literacy, numeracy and communication skills (Ige, 2011; Balogun, 2009). Such education is provided in secondary school, which can be owned by government (State or Federal), individuals or community. It is divided into two phases namely Junior and Senior secondary schools. A child is expected to take three years to complete junior secondary school level of education and afterward, another three years for senior secondary school.

The Federal Government of Nigeria through the National Policy on Education (2004) has defined secondary education as the education of the youths outside the primary and tertiary education (Okoro, 2010). The following objectives of secondary education are outlined by the policy:

i) To prepare individual youths for useful living within the society.
ii) To prepare individual youths for higher education.
iii) To cater for differences in talents, opportunities, and future roles.
iv) To provide trained manpower in applied science, technology and commerce at sub-professional grades.
v) To develop and promote Nigerian languages, arts and culture in the context of the world's cultural heritage.
vi) To inspire students with a desire for self improvement and achievement of excellence.
vii) To foster national unity with an emphasis on the common ties that unite us in our diversity.
viii) To raise a generation of people who can think for themselves, respect the views and feelings of others, respect the dignity of labour, appreciate those values specified under our broad national goals and live as good citizens.
ix) To provide technical knowledge and vocational skills, necessary for agricultural, industrial, commercial and economic development.
x) To give the youth citizens of the country necessary aesthetic, cultural and civil education for public enlightenment.

In addition, the recommendations of the UNESCO General Conference on the Development of Secondary Education defined secondary education as an integral part of middle life-education which contributes decisively to economic and cultural development, social progress and world peace. This implies that the aim of secondary education is essentially to enable the youth to develop his potentials economically, socially and educationally.

The third National Development Plan (1985-90) went further to bring into focus the sordid picture of secondary education in the country. It is observed that in spite of past efforts at the Federal and State levels, the literacy ratio for the country remained low. It is recognized that other adequate attention had not been paid to formal education as a necessary part of manpower and other socio-economic need of the country. Statistics revealed, that in 1989, while only 37% of the total number of people between the ages of 15 and above in sampled urban households were secondary school, as many as 63% were not (FOS, 1990). From the same source, in the rural households, while 27% were in secondary school, 73% were not. The number in secondary school students in the country by that year was estimated at 64% (FOS 1989). Since then, there has been an increasing emphasis on secondary education in all states of Nigeria. Therefore, the main purpose of this paper is to highlight the need for adequate investment in education in general and to investigate different strategies and policy options available for funding secondary education in particular. Funding of Education in General The National Policy on Education recognizes education as a tool for acquiring appropriate skills, abilities and competencies that enable the individual to live in, and contribute to the development of the Nigeria society. Education is never free, it is often paid for either directly or indirectly (Mbipom, 1998). Mbipom (1998) disclosed that the funding of education in Nigeria has been accomplished through three main sources; namely grants-in-aid from the local state and federal governments, payment of school fees and levies by cultural unions or voluntary contributions by parents, guardians and organizations, but the takeover of schools by the state governments, financial responsibilities became completely shifted to the governments. With the introduction of 6-3-3-4 system of education which involves a primary school period of six years; a secondary school period of six years which divided into three years of junior and three years of senior secondary and four year period of university education, the governments assumed full financial responsibility throughout the country.

The success of 6-3-3-4 system of education launched in Nigeria by the president Chief Mathew Olusegun Obasanjo has been a great concern to policy makers, educationists, teachers and parents alike. Their expectations are high that the programme will ensure equal educational opportunity to millions of Nigeria youths to develop their individual capabilities to the highest level and to climb out of poverty. Thus, the Federal Government set aside N300M to cover capital expenditure on primary education. to secondary education, provision was made for capital expenditure of N966.741m in respect of some additional 800 secondary schools throughout Nigeria. The funding of teacher training colleges was largely the responsibility of missions which owned most of these colleges. They however, received grants-in-aid from the various governments, but because of the UBE scheme, the federal government also accepted full responsibility for teacher training in all Federal Colleges of Education throughout the country. Before the Federal Government takeover of higher education, the Universities were financed on the basis of 30% Federal and 70% state governments. Both with the takeover of all the Universities in the country except the state Universities, the federal government now finances all the federal universities through the National Universities commission (NUC).

Problems of Funding of Secondary Education

Generally, the greatest problem in the field of education is the inability to match expansion and innovations with adequate human, material and financial resources. It is the characteristics of many West African countries, including Nigeria to pursue very ambitious educational programmes without proper planning for adequate financial requirements. This is why many African nations do not often realize their educational objectives and why the quality of instruction in schools is low. Careful examination of secondary education in Nigeria reveals the following problems that are plaguing it and undermining the achievement of its objectives:

1) Inadequate fund: The importance of adequate funding in educational development cannot be overemphasized. No organization can carry out its function effectively without adequate financial resources at its disposal. According to Obe (2009), without adequate funding, standards of education at any level will be tantamount to a mirage, that is, building castles in the air. Money is important in a school because it is used to construct buildings, purchase needed equipment, pay staff salaries and allowances, maintain the school plants and the services going. In Nigeria, secondary education derives its major fund from the annual allocation to the education sector. But for now, allocation to the education sector on which secondary education depends has been consistently low in spite of the strategic role of the sector in the training of manpower for the development of the economy. Statistics revealed that between 2000 and 2010, allocation to the education sector by Federal Government in Nigeria was not more than 14% of the annual budget, which was even low when compared to the allocation of other countries such as Kenya, Sierra Leone, South Africa, Angola, all in South Africa (Central Bank of Nigeria). Furthermore, out of the three levels of education in Nigeria, tertiary education receives the largest share of education vote, thus implying that the remaining fund is to be shared by primary and secondary education (Hinchlifee, 2002). It has been the practice of states to make provision for secondary education from the allocation to the education sector which in most cases has been in form of running grant to schools, on term or session basis and depending on the size of enrolment of each school. Unfortunately, complaints of inadequate fund for the development of secondary education in Nigeria abound in literature (Federal Ministry of Education, 2007), which is attributed to lack of fund as well as decay infrastructural facilities in secondary schools mostly in rural areas (Aluede, 2009). To worsen the situation, the limited allocation to secondary education is being threatened by increase in enrolment as a result of the rise in the demand for it (Federal Ministry of Education, 2007, Central Bank of Nigeria, 2010).

2) Inadequate and low quality of teachers: Teachers are the fulcrum on which the lever of educational system rests (Achimugu, 2005). Apart from students, they are the largest and most crucial inputs of educational output. In the National Policy on Education (2004), it is stated that no educational system can rise above the quality of the teachers. In spite of the role of teachers in educational system, issues of inadequacy and low quality teachers in secondary schools in Nigeria are prevalent (Omorege, 2005).

Obanya (2006), cited in Wasagu (2006) reported the findings of a study of secondary education in three local government areas in Cross River State in Nigeria (Akamkpa, Akpabuyo and Bakassi). There were shortfalls in the supply of secondary school teachers in the three local government areas, the shortfall affects nearly all the subjects taught at the secondary schools, to the point that even the principals and vice principals are now teaching in most secondary schools in the state. Sometimes, non-teaching staff are assigned to assist in handling a subject of their choice.

3) Inadequate and decay infrastructural facilities: School facilities are the material resources that facilitate effective teaching and learning in schools. Ige (2011) posited that they are things which enable a skillful teacher to achieve a level of effectiveness that exceeds what is possible when they are not provided. Availability of infrastructures and facilities in the right quantity and quality is germane in education provision. A school with inadequate classrooms, and facilities such as chairs, lockers, libraries, textbooks, laboratories, workshop will be uncomfortable for students to learn. Unfortunately, there are inadequate infrastructures and facilities in many secondary schools in Nigeria especially in rural schools (Central Bank of Nigeria, 2010). According to Ajayi (2006) and Ahmed (2003), in most secondary schools in the country, teaching and learning take place under unconducive environment due to lack of fund to provide a conducive environment for teaching and learning.

Strategies for Funding Secondary Education in Nigeria

Like any formal or conventional education, secondary education contributes immensely to economic growth and development. It is imperative therefore, that secondary education in Nigeria be adequately funded. Alternative strategies for funding secondary education are suggested as follows:

- **Increased budgetary allocation by the Federal, States and Local Government authorities.** It is desirable that positive attempts be made at both federal and state levels of government to redress the imbalance in funding among conventional education, especially in the educational disadvantaged states with a large population of children by increasing the subvention to secondary education. This suggestion is necessary at this time that the federal government under the regime of President Buhari appears to have taken cognizance of financial requirements for the education sector. In the 2017 budget instance, education was allocated 5.5% of the capital vote as against 10.0% in 2018 (Daily Times, Jan. 3, 2019).
- **Introduction of special levies:** Nigerians have become familiar with one form of levy or another to finance one thing or another in the spirit of self-help. One of such levies is the education levy, the proceeds of which are mainly devoted to the funding of formal education out with a little benefit to secondary education. Similarly, and without prejudice to the general education levy, it is desirable to create a special levy on a per capital basis at local government levels for financing secondary education. Administration of this levy should be in the hands of the

zonal inspectors of education of the state ministries of education with the assistance of education committees of the Local Government Areas.

- **Launching of Secondary Education Endowment Funds:** Nigerians are now used to endowment launching events, universities, for example, at one time of another, have launched endowment funds to finance their capital development projects. In the same way, it is suggested that a national secondary education endowment fund be, instead, created to which public spirited individuals and organizations could be required to generously contribute for the promotion of secondary education throughout the country. Introduction of 1 or 2% secondary education taxes on: company profits– A fixed tax to be called the secondary education similar to the higher education tax agreed between the Academic Staff Union of University (ASUU) and the Federal Government in 1992 can be made on profits accruing to industrial and commercial enterprises in Nigeria. These sources of income on education have been the practice in France for a very long time (Okereke and Mereni, 2005). Manufactured and Imported Goods. Taxes can also be made for the purposes of financing secondary education in Nigeria on manufactured and imported consumer or luxurygoods such as cars, wears, alcoholic and non-alcoholic beverages, petroleum products and industrial chemicals. These taxes can be operated like the recently introduced value Added Tax (VAT), but specifically for financing secondary education.

  Social activities such as naming ceremonies, wedding ceremonies, Silver and golden jubilee celebrations, as well as social clubs like the lion club, twin clubs, professional bodies (such as ICAN, NIFEST, etc.) and chieftaincy installations could attract some taxes to finance secondary education in Nigeria. Registrations, taxes made on birth and death registrations, car registrations and licensing, property such as land, building plans and certificates of occupancy as well as registration of business premises could generate funds that could be used to finance secondary education. Strict measures to ensure compliance must however, be adopted by the government.

- **Seeking and obtaining grants from foreign nations and international organizations:** Partnership programmes aimed at boosting secondary education programmes could be initiated between state government and some foreign nations and international organizations. For instance, the Akwa Ibom State Government entered into such a partnership programme with the United Nations Development Programme (UNDP) in 1994. (The Pioneer March 21, 1994), such partnership programmes could be entered into between either the federal, state or local governments and the foreign bodies such as the Common Wealth Commission in the United Kingdom and the Hapan Foundation Fellowship Programme in Japan etc.

- **By borrowing money through the issue of debenture of bonds:** People who have surplus money could be asked to lend some of it for the funding of secondary education at an agreed interest rate. The United States of American uses this method successfully through the local school boards (Okereke and Mereni, 2005).
- **Institution of secondary education foundation:** One of the ways by which wealthy people immortalize their names is by the creation of educational foundations such as the Nnamdi Azikiwe and Iwuanyanwu foundations. These foundations have primarily been for the promotion of formal education in which secondary education is a part through the granting of scholarships and bursaries to deserving students.

Conclusion

In this paper, an attempt has been made to highlight the importance of education in general and secondary education in particular in the development process and spotlight the neglect of this subsector of education in terms of funding. Suggestions have been made for alternative approaches to funding secondary education. These include: increased budgetary allocations to this sub-sector of federal, state and local governments, introduction of special levy and the launching of secondary education endowment funds. Since the problems of secondary education are many and varied, the government, parents and secondary schools administrators should look into the problems by ensuring that these problems are combated and that secondary education is moved forward from its form to its status quo.

References

Adesina, S. M. (2004). *The development of modern education in Nigeria.* Ibadan: Heinemann Education Books (Nigeria) Ltd.

Adeyemi, T. O. (2012). School variables and internal efficiency of secondary schools in Ondo State. *Nigeria Journal of Education Social Resources,* 2(3): 204-214.

Ajayi, I. A. (2006). Analysis of cost of spillover students' wastage in a Nigerian university. *International Student Education Administration,* 34(1): 34-35.

Aluede, O. (2009). School's counselor's roles in the Universal Basic Education programme in Nigeria. Retrieved from www.ccsenet.org/ies.

Balogun, F. A. (2009). Structure of the nine (9) year basic Education Curriculum. Paper presented at a workshop organized by Ministry of Education for Education Officers in Ondo State.

Central Bank of Nigeria (2010).

Ekezie, A. I. A. (2007). Funding of education in Nigeria with focus on adult and non-formal education. *West African Journal of Educational Research,* 1(1): 20-30.

Federal Ministry of Education (2007).

Federal Office of Statistics (1989). *Household survey report.* Lagos: Government Press.

Federal Office of Statistics (1990). *Social Statistics in Nigeria.* Lagos: Government Press.

Ige, T. M. (2011). Education and national development in Nigeria. *Journal of Student Education,* 10 (1): 35-46.

Mbipom, G. (1998). Women education in Nigeria: A necessary tool for national building. *Nigerian Education Journal,* 2(1): 77-82.

Okereke, O. and Mereni, J. I. (2005). Co-operative education and training at the Grassroot in Nigeria. *Public Administration and Development* 5(3): 219-233.

Okoro, O. M. (2010). Providing secondary education for urban and rural youths in Nigeria. Paper presented at the 5th Annual Conference of Association for Promoting Quality Education, Awka, Anambra State, Nigeria.

The Pioneer, March 21, 1994.

Wasagu, M. (2006). Resource factors as correlates of secondary school effectiveness in Bauchi State. *Nigeria Journal of Counseling and Applied Psychology,* 1(1): 109-115.

4

The Culture of Saving for Retirement Days – a Cure or Curse? A Study of Universal Basic Education Board Retirees, Akwa Ibom State, Nigeria

UDOM Cosmas A., USORO Nsidibe Ph.D & PETER Peter E.

Abstract

The study is an examination of pension administration as a correlate for retirees' wellbeing with a focus on retirees of Akwa Ibom State Universal Basic Education Board. In this study, wellbeing is measured using the OECD standard indicators of health, housing and material conditions. Related literatures were reviewed and the Social Exchange Theory was used as the theoretical framework. The study adopted the descriptive survey research design and the respondent driven sampling technique. Data was collected from 203 respondents through the use of questionnaire and determined via the Taro Yamane while the simple percentage was used as a method of data analyses. Findings from the study revealed that poor pension administration has a negative impact on the wellbeing of retirees and a majority of the retired primary school teachers have poor wellbeing a situation they slipped into post-retirement; the material condition of life of retirees is equally deplorable as reception of pension income never comes at the proper time and as such consumption pattern in most retirees households have been affected extremely. The study recommends that there should be an adjustment to the pension scheme in terms of its implementation, administration and coordination to enhance early disbursement of funds to retirees; government should encourage a stakeholder engagement forum perhaps quarterly,; the existing pension laws should be strengthened and strong disciplinary measures put in place to ensure that those who are involved in looting pension funds face the law.

Key Words: *Pension Administration, Retirees, Wellbeing, Pension Scheme*

Introduction

In recent times, pension administration as a social welfare policy has increasingly attracted the attention of policy makers in many countries as a means of facilitating privately funded retirement income savings account by an ageing work force (World Bank, 1994). The evolution of modern pension schemes has greatly altered the roles of the employer in shouldering the burden and risks of funding retirement for long-tenured workers and has consequently, given way to one in which employees are fully responsible for funding retirement themselves. According to the U.S. Department of Labour (2012) and Copeland (2012), approximately 54% of civilian workers participated in workplace retirement benefit programs with a participation rate of 79% for all civilians, 75% for private sector and 85% for states and local government areas. From the aforementioned projections, three issues can be deduced; the number of retirees in Nigeria is likely to increase; the retirees are likely to receive their pension and gratuity for a longer time because they are likely to live longer; and delay in payment or lack of payment of pension and gratuity will affect the wellbeing of retirees. Nicole and Nic (2004) posit that wellbeing is not just the absence of pain, discomfort, and incapacity. It arises from not only the action of an individual, but from a host of collective goods and relationships with other people. It requires that basic needs are met, that individuals have a sense of purpose, and that they feel able to achieve important personal goals and participate in societal activities. According to OECD (2013), understanding well-being and progress is high on the agenda of the international statistical community and this could be properly understood when we reflect wellbeing against various independent variables. On the account of this, understanding wellbeing becomes very necessary to look at in view of pension administration.

Brief History of Pension Administration in Nigeria

Nigeria started the journey of pension administration with the promulgation of Pension Decree No.102 of 1979 which took effect from April 1, 1974. It consolidated all enactments on pensions and incorporated pension and gratuity devised for public officers in the Udorji Public Service Review Concession in 1974. In the same way, Pension Act No.103 of 1979 like its counterpart Decree No.102 of 1979 on the other hand, dealt with pension benefits, liabilities and seals devised for the agreed forces. Thus, pension scheme in Nigeria was largely Defined Benefit (DB), Pay-as-you-go (PAYG) which was neither funded nor contributory but compulsory for the public sector. The scheme was characterised by massive accumulation of pension debts which made it unsustainable due to inadequate and untimely budgetary allocation; increasing number of employees and retirees; weak administration; corruption and mismanagement of pension funds; infiltration of ghost workers; lack of regulatory and supervisory agency and late release of funds for payment of outstanding pension obligations (Koripamo-Agary, 2009; Yunusa, 2009; Ahmad, 2006; Balogun, 2006). The inefficiency of the Pension Decree No.102 of 1979 gave birth to the

Pension Reform Act 2004 which was amended in 2014. The new scheme is contributory in nature, fully funded, privately managed and based on individual account for both the public and private sector employees in Nigeria.

With this reform, pension fund has witnessed tremendous growth in its total assets. It is projected that by the end of 2015, the Contributory Pension Scheme (CPS) had accumulated resources totaling N5.3 trillion ($26.9 billion) and is expected to hit N16 trillion ($100 billion) by 2034 (Okonjo-Iweala, 2018). According to the National Bureau of Statistics (2017), a total of 77.55 million pensionable workers are registered under the Contributory Pension Scheme, 1.92 million from the federal government, 1.56million from the state government and 7.82million from the private sector. It also indicated that 69.5% of the pension funds are invested in FGN bond/treasury bills, 8.94% in equity market, 8.33% in Banks, 3.55% in corporate bonds, 2.71 in real estate properties and 6.77% in other investment platforms that are not mentioned.

Challenges Facing Pension Scheme in Nigeria

Various problems can be identified that serve as challenges to the pension scheme. These include the following:

1. Dependency of the pension scheme on the erratic budgetary allocation by the Federal Government.
2. Untimely release of pension funds, which affects the payment of pension benefits and other retirement benefits.
3. Huge accumulation of pension liabilities, among several others.
4. Mismanagement and embezzlement of pension funds by officials entrusted with managing the scheme, among other issues.

As a result of these problems, the majority of retirees and pensioners do not feel the impact of this social security service put in place by the government. As such, this has led to various drawbacks for retiree's quality of life. Scholarly articles and researches on Nigeria's pension scheme suggest that for many pensioners, the reality of the pension scheme is a mix-grill of sweetness and bitterness (Stoll, 2012; Kareem and Kareem, 2010; Fabbro, 2010). Previous studies have shown that a number of retirees experience a relative wellbeing status during retirement compared to their work days (Aydogan, 2004; Mackenizie; Gerson and Cuevas, 1997; Mariger, 1987; Hammermesh, 1984). More so, other studies have equally shown that a significant number of retirees are not able to sustain their consumption pattern post-retirement (Robb and Burbridge, 1989), some of them have not even been able to lay their hands on their entitlements after many years of retirement either owing to inadequate pension funds for payment or the total omission of their names from the pension beneficiary list. Even when they are to be paid their benefits, many die in the queue owing to fatigue and deteriorating health while waiting for the payment of their pension.

The inadequacy and inefficiency of the government's public pension scheme among other things are responsible for the deteriorating wellbeing of many pensioners in Nigeria. Wellbeing can be understood as how people feel and how they function, both on a personal and a social level, and how they evaluate their lives as a whole (Thompson and Marks, 2008; Frederickson, 2001). Basically, how people evaluate their life as a whole is captured in their satisfaction with their lives, or how they rate their lives in comparison with the best possible life, especially after their working years. In this study, wellbeing is measured using the OECD (2013) standard indicators of health, housing, social connections, and life satisfaction. This study attempts to take a second look at the Pension Reform Act 2004 and examine its impact on the wellbeing of retirees, using the retirees of the Akwa Ibom State Universal Basic Education Board as a case study.

Objectives of the Study

1. To examine the impact of poor pension administration on the wellbeing of retirees of AKSUBEB.
2. To examine the effect of delayed payment of pension on the material conditions of retirees.
3. To find out how retirees support and finance their household consumption expenditure.

Research Questions

1. What is the impact of poor pension administration on the wellbeing of retirees of AKSUBEB?
2. To what extent does delayed payment of pension affect the material condition of retirees?
3. How do retirees of AKSUBEB support and finance their household consumption expenditure?

Conceptualization of Pension

A pension scheme is a transfer program that serves as a channel for redistributing income for the elderly or retirees, after a stipulated number of years in the service. Pension programs are usually put in place to serve as protection for the elderly and retirees against old age risks, poverty and other uncertainties. Moreover, in the Contributory Pension Scheme, it is also used to promote a 'savings culture' among current employees. Pension in this context is a contract for a fixed sum to be paid regularly to a pensioner by government or private company after working for specific period of time (fifteen years with effect from June, 2004) and considered too old to work or having reached the statutory age of retirement. Different scholars have used diverse definitions to describe pension. World Bank (2004) defines pension as a form of income that workers or their spouses receive after they retire, become disabled or die. It entails money paid at regular basis by government or any establishment to someone who is officially considered retired from active service after serving for a stipulated time usually minimum of fifteen years and maximum of thirty five years. Corroborating this, Fapohunda (2013) posits that pension is aimed at providing workers with security by building up plans that are capable of providing guaranteed income to them when they retire or to dependants when death occurs. Idowu (2006) conceptualizes pension as a form of social security as well as welfare package for the old or retired people who are in their years of labour inactivity. However, pension scheme is a financial package which legally specifies its organization and operation, so as to provide rest of mind to workers, sustain or spur them to more productivity and ensure that a pensioner and his dependants have a good wellbeing.

Ozor (2006) is of the view that pension consists of a lump sum payment paid to an employee upon his disengagement from active service. This payment is usually in monthly installments, which may be contributory or non-contributory, fixed or variable benefits, group or individual, insured or trustee, private or public and single or multi-employer. Amujiri (2009) identified four main classifications of pensions in Nigeria. These are:

(a) **Retiring pension:** This type of pension is usually granted to an employee who is permitted to retire after completing a fixed period of service usually 30-35 years or 60-65 years for the public service of Nigeria and 70years for professors and judges;
(b) **Compensatory pension:** This type of pension is granted to an employee whose permanent post is abolished and government is unable to provide him/her with alternative employment;
(c) **Superannuating pension:** This type of pension scheme is given to an employee who retires at the prescribed age limit as stated in the condition of service;
(d) **Compassionate Allowance:** This happens when pension is not admissible on account of an employee's dismissal from service for misconduct, insolvency, incompetence and inefficiency.

Development of Pension Administration in Nigeria

Barrow (2008) posits that the development of pension schemes in Nigeria can be traced to the beginning of organized workforces in the public and private sectors in the 20th century. Apparently, the first pension system was introduced into Nigeria by the colonial administration and this became a legislative document in the 1951 Pension Ordinance and had retroactive effect from January 1, 1946 and the pension ordinance provided both pension and gratuity to public servants (Ahmed, 2006). The law was primarily designed for the staff of the then British colony who were moved from post to post in the large British Empire, the intention was to ensure continuity of service wherever they were posted to. However, the law had limited application to indigenous staff (Nigerians) because pension was not an automatic right of Nigerians and it could be withheld at any point in time.

However, with the independence of Nigeria in 1960, the laws were codified in 1958 and the 1951 Act became known as the pension Act Cap 146 of the Laws of Nigeria. The Pension Ordinance of 1958 was amended which was replaced by the Pension Decree 102 of 1979 (now Act Cap 346 of 1990 Laws of Nigeria) retroactive from April 1, 1974. Specific professional groups were allowed to establish their pension schemes but were under Pension Decree 102 of 1979. These laws include; Pension Increase Decree No.42 of 1975; Military Pension Act Cap (Chapter or No.119); Pensions Act Cap (Chapter or No.147); War Pension Act Cap (Chapter or No.212); Pension (Special Pension) Act 1961 (Chapter or No.15); Widows and Orphans Pension Act Cap. 220; Pensions (Statutory Corporation Service) Act 1961 No. 61; Pension (Transferred Services) Act 1965 No. 28; Special Constables Decree 1966 No. 60; Police Pension Decree 1966 No. 60; Pensions (Federal Fire Service) Decree 1966 No. 74; Pensions Gratuities (War Service) Decree 1966 No. 49; Transferred Offices and Pension Liability 1971 No. 8; Military Pensions (Amendment) Decree 1975 No. 13; The Pension Act of 1979 Decree No. 102 (which awarded and united all pension Acts); The Public Services, The Recommendations Review 1974; The Armed Forces Pension Act No.13 of 1974; The Pension Rights of Judges Acts No.5 of 1988; The Amendment Act No. 51 of 1988, 29 of 1991 and 62 of 1991.

The whole of these Ordinances, Acts and Decrees are capped up in the Pension Decree No.102 of 1979 which took effect from April 1, 1974. In the case of the Pension Decree 1949, Uzoma (1993) contended that in the special case of the public pension scheme, the office of establishment and pensions acts as the trustee and constitutes the rules of the scheme. The pension scheme was for all public servants except those were on temporary or contract employment. The age of retirement for such workers was 60years for male and female except for high court judges that was 65 years and 70 years for justices of the Court of Appeal. Moreover, all government MDAs directly funded by the treasury had a unified pension scheme that was virtually managed by insurance companies and individuals who were heads of pension unit. In 1997, MDAs were allowed to have individual pension plans and arrangements for their staff and appoint Boards of Trustee (BOT) to administer same as specified by the Standard Trust Deed and rules prepared by the Office of the Head of Service of the Federation. Each BOT was free to either use an insured scheme or self-administered arrangement (Odia and Okoye, 2012). There had been about eight registered pension schemes in the country before the Pension Reform Act 2004 which were largely unfunded, self-administered and uninsured. Public organizations in Nigeria operated the

Defined Benefit (Pay-As-You-Go) pension scheme, final entitlement was based on length of service and terminal emoluments and retirees were paid pension and gratuity.

Prior to 2004, the major problem associated with pension fund administration in Nigeria was the non- payment and the delay in payment of pension and gratuity by the federal, state and local governments. In the words of Orifowomo (2006), "pension backlog was put at about N2.56 trillion as at December, 2005. In fact, pension fund administration became a thorny issue with millions of retired Nigerian workers living in abject poverty and they were often neglected and not properly catered for after retirement." Other problems associated with the old pension scheme include; demographic challenges, funding of outstanding pension and gratuities, merging of service for the purpose of computing retirement benefits, Administrative bottlenecks and bureaucracies, Corrupt tendencies and inefficiencies of the civil service, economic downturn (Orifowomo, 2006; Ezeani, 2011; Abade, 2004). It is also noted that gross abuse of pensioners and pension fund benefits which were politically motivated in some cases, coupled with extended family and other traditional ways already broken down due to urbanization, increased labour and human mobility were all problems associated with the old pension scheme (Odia and Okoye, 2012).

Moreover, according to the Statement of Accounting Standards (SAS) No. 8 on accounting for employees retirement benefits, the problems of the old pension scheme which led to the Pension Reforms of 2004 and its subsequent amendment in 2014 include; wrong investment decision, wrong assessment of pension liabilities, arbitrary increases in pension without corresponding funding arrangement, non-preservation of benefits, some were mere saving schemes and not pension schemes, and serious structural problems of non-payment and non-coverage. There was no serious adequate safeguard of the funds to guarantee prompt pension to retirees.

Considerably, the old pension scheme was Defined Benefit, unfunded, mostly Pay-As-You-Go, discriminatory and not portable. The employee was not entitled to pension benefit if he was dismissed from service. Also there was no adequate provision to secure the pension fund (Odia and Okoye, 2012). Following the unsatisfying nature of the old scheme, the unpleasant experiences faced by retirees and the huge pension liabilities, it became apparent the need for change. Therefore, the need for the federal government to guarantee workers contributions and accruing interest in the event of failure of the pension fund administrators was advocated. Besides, it was estimated that over N600 billion ($4.5billion) investible assets could be amassed annually through the pension scheme in Nigeria (World Bank, 1994).

Hence, government could not pay the retirement benefits as they become due but also utilized the saved pension fund for long-term development purposes. Okoro (2014) contended that prior to the Pension Reform of 2004 and its subsequent amendment in

2014, pension schemes was plagued by irregularities and inefficiencies both on the part of employers (public and private sectors) and pension fund managers. Suffice to say that government's budgetary allocation for pension was very poor and the most vulnerable in terms of budget implementation due to lack of resources.

The Pension Reform Act (PRA) of 2004, which is expected to be fully funded and contributory, offered more opportunities to retirees such as income stability, high labour turnover rate, greater levels of accountability (Suleiman, 2014). The 2004 Act institutionalized a framework for mandatory financial investment (of 7.5% by the employer and employee), transparency, proper management and custodianship of pension assets (Aborishade, 2012; Suleiman, 2014). According to Oke (2017), the new pension scheme allows for the maintenance of a Retirement Savings Account (RSA) by each employee, which gives the workers responsibility over their retirement savings. Pension Fund Administrators (PFAs) administered the retirement savings for employees while the Pension Fund Custodians (PFCs) held the pension funds in trust for the employees, both under strict regulation by the National Pension Commission (PENCOM), whose overriding objective is to ensure that pension matters are administered with minimum exposure to fraud and risk. Pensioners will no longer be at the mercy of their employers, and participants are assured of regular payment of retirement benefits (Aborishade, 2012; Suleiman, 2014; Oke, 2017).

Furthermore, workers could now choose how to allocate their retirement savings and diversify their investments over a range of investment instruments. Under, PRA 2004, personal accounts system also provides workers a higher rate of return than can be paid under the Define-Benefit plan. This approach also affords participants an opportunity to pass wealth to survivors in the event of death. In addition, RSA maintained by millions of workers tend to generate massive long-term funds, which are available for investment, and also, having a pension scheme that pays out benefits in the form of a life annuity affords workers with protection against longevity risk, by pooling mortality risk across others (Aborishade, 2012; Suleiman, 2014; Oke, 2017).

Empirical Literature

Many studies have been carried out to show the effects of poor pension administration on the well-being of retirees. Mackenzie, Gerson and Cuevas (1997) provide some moderately strong evidence that the introduction and development of the public pension plan in the US economy have depressed private sector savings, although it is difficult to estimate such effect. However, the most important and highly debatable issue relates to the extent to which people form expectations of future benefit. It was assumed that people expect the proportion of average replacement to be constant. Feldstein (1982) reaches similar conclusion in the later version of his work (1982, 1995) and concludes that social security program reduces private savings by close to 605%.

Hu (2005) empirically examined pension reform, economic growth and financial development. The study used panel data analysis to find a negative relationship in the short run and a positive relationship in the long run, although the results for OECD countries are not very statistically robust. Another empirical test focused on pension fund assets and the wellbeing of retirees. A positive relationship between these two variables is found by the standard economic growth specifications; in addition, evidence exist that pensions are a predicator for a good wellbeing. The Panel Granger Causality Test corroborated with this result. The final test deals with the relationship between pension assets and wellbeing. Thus, the Panel Correction Model and Panel Granger Causality Test suggest that pension fund growth leads to good wellbeing, although some sub-group estimation are not wrong.

Berkel and Borsch-Supan (2003) investigated the effects of Pension Reform on retirement decisions in Germany, and focused in particular on long-term implication of the changes implemented in pension legislation since 1992 and the reform discussed by the Germany Social Security Reform Commission. The results of the simulations indicate that the early retirement pension adjustment factors introduced by the 1992 Pension Reforms will in the long run raise the average effective age of retirement for men by somewhat less than 2 years. The across-the-board, 2year increase in all the relevant age limits proposed would raise the effective average age of retirement of men by approximately 8 months. If the actual adjustment factor is increased from 3.65% to 65%, the effective average retirement age rises by approximately 2years, thus the effects are considerably weaker for women.

Jaag, Keuschnigg and Keuschnigg (2007) investigated the impact of four often-proposed policy measures for sustainable pension: strengthening the tax benefit links, moving from wage to price indexation of benefits, lengthening calculation periods, and introducing more actuarial fairness in pension assessment. The study provided some analytical results and used a computational model to demonstrate the economic and welfare impact of recent pension reform in Australia. In addition, Stensness and Stolen (2007) studied the effects of pension reform on Fiscal sustainability, labour supply, and equity in Norway. The study used statistics of Norway's Dynamic Micro-simulation Model (MOSART). The results showed that the reform will simulate labour supply and improve public budgets, but will also lead to an increase in inequality in received pension benefits. In the same vein, Fisher and Keuschnigg (2007) evaluated the effects of pension reform on labour market incentives. They also showed parametric reform in a PAYG pension with tax benefit link affects retirement incentives and work incentives of prime-age workers in the presence of a tax benefit link thereby creating a policy trade-off in simulating aggregate labour supply. The article shows how several popular reform scenarios are geared either towards young or old workers, or indeed both groups under appropriate conditions. They also provide a strong characterization of the excess burden of pension insurance and show how it depends on the behavioural supply elasticity on the extensive and intensive margins and the effective tax rates implicit in contribution rates.

Bonin (2009) surveyed the state of the German pension system after a sequence of reforms aimed at achieving long-term sustainability. He argued that in principle the latest reforms have moved pension provision in Germany from Defined Benefit to a Defined Contributory Scheme, and that this move has stabilized pension finances to a great extent. The article further argued that the real economic consequences of the global financial crises pose threats to the core success factors of the reforms, which are cutting pension levels and raising the mandatory pension age. Finally, the paper discussed possible reform measures including the option to install a fourth pillar providing income in retirement through working after pension age.

Bruinshoofd and Grob (2006) studied how pension incentives affect retirement in the Netherlands. The study used a stated rather than a reviewed preference approach and conducted a field survey questionnaire in the Dutch De Nederlandsche Bank (DNB) Household survey to derive empirical estimates of pension adjustment and pension wealth effects. They found that retrenchments of pension arrangement to the effect of rising the standard of retirement by 1year induced people to postpone retirement by approximately half a year on average. Retirement postponement varies across people, depending prominently on earnings and non-pension wealth, wealth through earlier retirement whereas they readily accept a lower benefit in case of decrease in pension wealth.

Salen and Stahlberg (2007) studied the reason why the Swedish Pension Reform was able to be successfully implemented. They argued that governments that do not reform PAYG pension systems will eventually face a pension crisis. In a democracy, reform requires a majority support. The problem in pensions requires today's generation to bear the burden for tomorrow's generation. Sweden recently passed pension legislation that specifies a gradual transition from a public Defined-Benefit plan to a Defined Contributory Plan. They found that a political-economic perspective helps to solve this problem that there are more winners who would vote in favour of the reform than non-winners who would vote against it. The net effect (present value of remaining contributions of the working generation's aged 53years) is reduced by more than expected benefits.

Finseraas (2007) analyzed pension policies in 21 OECD countries in the period 1994-2003, using the OECDs reform intensity score in the area of early retirement with the old age pension scheme as the dependent variable. The importance of left strength parliament, institutional veto points and corporation is assessed through the use of scatter plots based on ordinary least square regression. The empirical results show that reform intensity is driven by initial conditions rather than political and institutional variables. Thus, the political elites appear to be able to overcome obstacles to reform and implement necessary changes when there is sufficient pressure for reform. Bender (2004) conducted a study on the wellbeing of retirees: Evidence using subjective data. The researcher used data from 2000 health and retirement study and found out that if individuals were forced to retire, their wellbeing is significantly lower than those who choose to retire. Additionally, health, current income and comparison retirement income have important roles in determining overall wellbeing.

Edogbanya (2013) surveyed the assessment of the impact of contributory pension scheme on Nigeria's economic development for the period 2007-2010 using the sample size of 30 and 70 for both staff and customers of Legacy Pensions Ltd. It also adopted correlation analysis for testing secondary data and ANOVA for the primary data. The study revealed that risk prevalent has positive effect on pension fund management and that the contributory pension scheme has significant positive impact on the GDP. Olanrewaju (2011) examined the Pension Reform Act 2004 and wellbeing of Nigerian Retirees and the sociological evaluation of its provisions. The study used the Marxist theory to critically analyze the 2004 pension policy of the government on the wellbeing of the Nigerian retirees and found out that the PRA 2004 has failed to contribute to basic social security in old age for the majority of Nigerians employed in the informal sector while the minority of covered workers is likely to experience problems. The implication of the findings is that forced savings for the future in a low income country characterized by large scale poverty might not be desirable for retirees especially in Nigeria where there is inadequate complementary social security system. Kareem and Kareem (2010) in their study evaluate the effects of public pension reform on civil servants in Nigeria using the error correction model. The study used an econometric model to test the long run relationship among employee's welfare and pensions, gratuity and years of service. The study discovered that there has been an inverse relationship between pensions and the welfare of employees, that the same negative relationships exist between years of service of employees and employees welfare; that many countries have adopted different pension plans that have resulted in increased social security and wealth of retired and aged employees, but that of Nigeria has been problematic owing to inadequate disbursement of pension funds and the corruption of government officials.

Nyong & Duze (2011) carried out a study on the Pension Reform Act 2004 and retirement planning in Nigeria using a survey research design and a multi-stage random sampling technique to select the sample size of 3000 from the population of serving and retired teachers and teacher pensioners in Federal and State public secondary schools between the ages of 55 and 59years. The results revealed that the objectives of PRA 2004 were yet to be achieved since retired persons still suffered trauma, pains and even death before they receive their pension packages. The study recommended e-payment of pensions to ensure easy referencing, easy up date and logistics of pension scheme system. Gunu and Tsado (2012) studied contributory pension system as a tool for economic growth in Nigeria. The study used descriptive statistics, percentages, and charts to analyze data collected. Their findings revealed that the contributory pension scheme has begun to contribute to increase in growth of the Nigerian capital market and economic growth.

Theoretical Framework

The theoretical framework adopted in this study to explain pension administration as a correlate for retirees' wellbeing is the Social Exchange Theory. Social Exchange Theory was developed by George Homans (1910-1989). Homans was a sociologist and was influenced by the works of American social psychologists such as John W. Thibant (1917-1986), Harold H. Kelley (1921-2003) and Peter Blau (1918-2002). Homans (1958) posits that social exchange is the exchange of activity, tangible or intangible, and more or less rewarding or casting between at least two persons. This definition emphasises that people are consciously incurring a cost with an expectation of receiving a reward and the reward should either produce profit or equity. The rewards we receive in social exchange can be intrinsic or extrinsic; at least one party is dependent on the other which is what prompts the social exchange (Blau, 1964).

Social exchange can be reciprocal or negotiated (Molin, 2003). Reciprocal exchanges occur when people experienced a cost while providing a reward for their partners without specifying the exact nature of repayment but usually with an expectation that some form of repayment will happen sometime (Mitchell, Cropanzana and Quisenberry, 2012). Moreover, central to the Social Exchange Theory is the idea that an interaction that elicits approval from another person is more likely to be repeated than an interaction that elicits disapproval. Thus, it can be predicted that a particular interaction will be repeated by calculating the degree of reward (approval) and punishment (disapproval) resulting from the interaction. If the reward for an interaction exceeds the punishment, then the interaction is likely to occur or continue.

Emerson (1976), Mitchell et al (2012) and Burns (1973) outline the key principles of Social Exchange Theory as follows; social behaviour can be explained in terms of cost, rewards and exchanges; people seek to maximize rewards and minimize costs in pursuit of the greatest profit; social interaction involves two parties, each exchanging a reward needed by the other person; Social Exchange Theory can be used to explain the development and management of interpersonal relationships; social exchange affects the relationship among members of groups and organizations. According to Ekeh (1974), profit is the sole economic motive that propels social interaction which is the redistribution and reciprocity system that governs socio-economic relations. Reciprocity involves a give and take relationship between persons and groups in society. When one receives, he is also expected to give in-return even though it is not necessarily an equivalent amount nor to the original giver.

The Social Exchange Theory centres on reciprocity between persons and groups in society and is about give and take relationships. To strike a balance between employers and employees, the employers are expected to reciprocate the efforts of their workers during and after their active service for having put in their most active years in the service of the organization. Moreover, the employee expects a reciprocal relationship in form of pensions in old age when he can no longer be gainfully involved in any paid employment; not withstanding that the reward may not be an equivalent of what the employee had put into the service. This becomes the motivating factor for workers to put in their best in active service.

Methodology

The study favours the descriptive survey research design because it allows the researchers to collect data from a small group which was used to describe the entire population. A multiple sampling technique was adopted in the study. The purposive sampling method was combined with respondent-driven sampling technique (RDS). Retirees among the sampling frame were purposively selected as study participants. The RDS was useful because the study population was difficult to access, small, hidden, or mobile, and largely because the targeted population were not interested in participating in the survey therefore, the researchers considered an incentive-driven sampling technique as a means of motivating them to participate in the study. The study population consist of retired primary school teachers in Akwa Ibom State between 2014 to 2019 which is a total of 489 (Pension Unit, Akwa Ibom State Universal Basic Education Board) and the Taro Yamane was used to determine the sample size from which a sample size of 203 was selected. A self-completion questionnaire was designed to measure the perception of the respondents on the efficiency of pension schemes on retiree's wellbeing. The study employed descriptive (simple percentage analysis) as a method of data analysis.

Data Analyses

Socio-Demographic Information of Respondents

As shown in Table 1 below, majority of the respondents 69% (140) are male and 31% (63) are female, a few of them 2.5% (5) are between ages 50-59, while most of them 80.3% (163) are between ages 60-69 and 17.2% (35) are above 70 years of age. The marital status of the respondents indicates that 48.8% (99) are married, while 29.1% (59) are widow and 20.2% (41) are separated, whereas a relatively few of them 1.9% (4) are not in their marriages. Educationally, majority of the respondents 51.2% (104) are holders of the National Certificate in Education (NCE), a fewer number of the respondents 39.9% (81) are holders of Teachers Grade II Certificate and 8.9%(18) are holders of Bachelor in Education (B.Ed.). Majority of the respondents 76.8% (156) have put in over 30 years of service, while 23.1% (47) have put in between 20-29 years of service.

Table 1: Socio-Demographic Information of Respondents

Variables	Frequency	Percentage (%)
Sex		
Male	140	69
Female	63	31
Total	**203**	**100**
Age		
50-59years	5	2.5
60-69years	163	80.3
70years and above	35	17.2
Total	**203**	**100**
Marital Status		
Married	99	48.8
Divorced	4	1.9
Widow	59	29.1
Separated	41	20.2
Total	**203**	**100**
Educational Qualification		
FSLC	-	-
Teachers Grade11	81	39.9
NCE	104	51.2
B.Ed	18	8.9
Total	**203**	**100**
Years of Service		
10-19 years	-	-
20-29 years	47	23.1
30 years and above	156	76.8
Total	**203**	**100**

Fieldwork, 2019

Table 2: Responses on the impact of poor pension administration on the wellbeing of retirees of Akwa Ibom State Universal Basic Education Board

Variables	Yes	No
There are improvements in the present pension administration in the payment of pension to retired primary school teachers.	96 (47.2%)	107 (52.7%)

Most of the retired primary school teachers receive their pension and gratuities within three months of retirement.	55 (27%)	148 (72.9%)
Inspite of the improvements, the new pension administration still has endemic lapses.	84 (41.3%)	119 (58.6%)
These lapses from poor disbursement of funds cause health challenges to retirees.	185 (91.1%)	18 (8.8%)
Delayed pension payment has affected family income and expenditures.	168 (82.7%)	35(17.2%)

Fieldwork, 2019

Table 2 shows that majority of the respondents - 52.7% (107) disagreed with "NO" that there are improvements in the present pension administration in the payment of pension to retired primary school teachers, while 47.2% (96) agreed with "YES". However, 72.9% (148) of the respondents disagree with "NO" that most of the retired primary school teachers receive their pension and gratuities within three months of retirement, while 27% (55) agreed with "YES". 58.6% (119) disagreed with "NO" that in spite of the improvements, the new pension administration still has endemic lapses and such lapses include the non-payment of gratuity, corruption, bureaucratic bottlenecks; while, 41.3% (84) agreed with "YES". However, 91.1% (185) agreed with "YES" that the lapses from poor disbursement of pension funds causes health challenges to retirees whereas 8.8% (18) disagreed with "NO". 82.7% (168) agreed with "YES" that delayed payment of pension has affected family income and expenditures, while 17.2% (35) disagreed. This means that the "NO" is higher in proportion of responses than "YES" implying that majority of the respondents agreed that poor pension administration impacts negatively on the wellbeing of retirees.

Table 3: Responses on what extent does delayed payment of pension affect the material conditions of retirees

Variable	**Yes**	**No**
Would you say you are satisfied with retirement life?	33 (16.2%)	170 (83.7%)
Delayed pension payment has affected payment of school fees and feeding family dependants.	145 (71.4%)	58 (28.5%)
Family feeding pattern has changed since after retirement	135(66.5%)	68 (33.4%)
And has even changed further with the irregular disbursement of pension allowances.	158 (77.8%)	45 (22.1%)
Due to irregular payment of pension, your relationship with others is reduced.	107 (52.7%)	96 (47.2%)
And you don't participate and contribute meaningfully to your community.	120 (59.1%)	83 (40.8%)
Generally, would you say that Poor Pension administration has affected your wellbeing	185 (91.1%)	18 (8.8%)

Fieldwork, 2019

Table 3 also shows that 83.7% (170) respondents disagreed that they are satisfied with retirement life, whereas 16.2% (33) of the respondents agreed. This means that majority of the respondents are not satisfied with retirement life. Similarly, 71.4% (145) agreed that delayed pension payment has affected payment of school fees and feeding of family dependants while 28.5% (58) disagreed. This is a pointer to the fact that delayed payment of pension has affected payment of school fees and feeding of family dependants. Furthermore, 66.5% (135) of the respondents agreed that family feeding pattern has changed since after retirement while, 33.4% (68) disagreed and 77.8% (158) agreed that family feeding pattern has changed further due to irregular disbursement of pension allowances whereas 22.1% disagreed. The finding indicates that retirees' family dependants can no longer eat three square meals a day due to irregular disbursement of pension allowances. Moreover, 59.1% (120) respondents agreed that they cannot participate and contribute meaningfully to their community while, 40.8% (83) disagreed and 52.7% (107) agreed that their relationship with others have reduced due to non-payment of pension funds whereas, 47.2% (96) disagreed. The finding indicates that retirees can no longer contribute to societal development due to delay in the disbursement of pension funds which makes them financially incapacitated. Generally, majority of the respondents 91.1% (185) agreed that poor pension administration has affected their wellbeing while, 8.8% (18) disagreed. The implication of this is that poor pension administration affects retirees' wellbeing.

Table 4: Responses on how retirees of AKSUBEB support and finance their household consumption expenditure

Variable	Yes	No
Spouse works and his or her income support family.	152 (74.8%)	51 (25.1%)
Rent from properties support family income.	92 (45.3%)	111 (54.6%)
Support from working children rolls away the difficulties associated with poor pension administration.	137 (67.4%)	66 (32.5%)
Do you earn extra income by working	87 (42.8%)	116 (57.1%)

Fieldwork, 2019

Table 4 further shows that 74.8% (152) of the respondents agree that their spouses work so as to support family income whereas, 25.1% (51) disagree. This finding indicates that majority of the respondents have financial support from their spouses to support family income. However, majority of the respondents 54.6% (111) disagree that rent from their properties support family income while, 45.3% (92) agree and majority of the respondents 67.4% (137) agree that support from working children rolls away the difficulties associated with poor pension administration while, 32.5% (66) disagree. This is a pointer to the fact that majority of the retired primary school teachers receive support from working children and other family members which rolls away the difficulties associated with non-disbursement of pension funds. Generally, majority of the respondents 57.1% (116)

disagreed that they earn extra income by working while, 42.8% (87) agreed. This finding indicates that due to ill-health, retirees cannot engage in extra work to bring extra income.

Findings

The findings of this study revealed that poor pension administration has a negative impact on the wellbeing of retired primary school teacher in Akwa Ibom State. The analysed data revealed that 72.9% (148) of the respondents are of the view that most of the retired primary school teachers received their pension and gratuities within three months of retirement. This study also showed that 58.6% (119) of the respondents are of the view that In spite of the improvements, the new pension administration still has endemic lapses and such lapses include the non-payment of gratuity, corruption and bureaucratic bottlenecks. This finding is in tandem with the assertion of Orifowomo (2006); Ezeani (2011); Abade (2004) and Olanrewaju (2011) who posit that despite the reforms in the pension scheme, it has failed to contribute to basic social security in old age because of the endemic challenges such as corrupt tendencies and inefficiencies of the civil service, administrative bottlenecks and bureaucracies, gross abuse of pensioners and pension funds which were politically motivated. Furthermore, a significant percentage of the respondents have poor wellbeing, this is quite contradictory as the expectation of the retirees was that a new pension administration would bring about a better social atmosphere that would enable a proper retirement life. The state of wellbeing as indicated in this study does not show any association with gender as no variation existed between the female and male retirees wellbeing.

Moreover, the study reveals that majority of the respondents agree that they are not satisfied with retirement life because delayed payment of pension affects the material conditions of retirees. Majority of the respondents 71.4% (145) are of the view that delayed payment of pension has affected the payment of school fees and feeding family dependants. The analysed data also reveal that 66.5% (135) of the research participants agree that family feeding pattern has changed since after retirement and has even changed further, as a result they can no longer eat three square meals a day due to irregular disbursement of pension funds. This finding confirms the position of Jakobsson, Hallberg and Westergreen (2007); Kareem and Kareem (2010) and Ali (2014) who noted that inconsistencies in the disbursement of pension funds is retrogression on retirees social life and impact negatively on the material condition of retirees.

Furthermore, the research also reveals that spouse of retirees work and support family income, while majority of the respondents earn extra income from farming activities such as animal husbandry, palm fruits and planting/harvesting of crops such as cassava, vegetable and fruits of all kinds. Furthermore, findings from the study also show that retirees who usually receive financial support from their children have better wellbeing than those who do not. This is because most retirees do not have the strength to work; therefore any financial assistance from the children will go a long way at easing their financial needs in the absence of their monthly pension income.

Conclusion

The study findings have demonstrated glowing evidence that poor pension administration has contributed to the decaying self-worth of retirees and other negative impacts that follow. Extant literature and findings from this study have also confirmed the general opinion on the public that despite the different reforms that had been made to Nigeria's pension scheme over the years, the scheme is yet to meet the expectations of retirees in terms of social security and risk aversion in retirement. Many countries have adopted different pension plans that have resulted in increased social security and wealth of retired persons, but that of Nigeria has been problematic owing to the inadequate disbursement of pension funds, poor management, bureaucratic bottlenecks and endemic corruption.

Generally, the material condition of life of retirees is equally deplorable as reception of pension income never comes at the proper time and as such consumption pattern in most retirees households have been affected extremely. Only those with support structure from working children and even spouses manage the time. Retirement is a period of older age as such it presupposes rest and relaxation, yet to finance family consumption, a few retirees engage in extra work or menial jobs to make ends meet. The worst case scenario of such endeavor is that some retirees have collapsed on their way to post-retirement work and even died. Thus, this study concludes that the present Nigeria's pension scheme is anything but, effective welfare-driven scheme that encourages post work life and good wellbeing.

Recommendations

In view of the findings of this study, the following recommendations are made:

1. There should be an adjustment to the pension scheme in terms of its implementation, administration and coordination to enhance early disbursement of funds to retirees. Government should re-evaluate and monitor the activities of Pension Fund Administrators (PFAs) and Pension Fund Custodians (PFCs) which will create the macroeconomic and regulatory stability within which pension funds can flourish.
2. Pension scheme should not be politicized. This can be ensured through the appointment of seasoned and proven administrators than political associates. Personnel with track record of integrity should be saddled with the task of managing the National Pension Commission (PENCOM), where possible non-government body should be saddled with the responsibility of managing the pension portfolio.

3. Government should encourage a stakeholder engagement forum perhaps quarterly, briefing the entire public and retirees of processes and progress made and challenges in the pension scheme management.
4. The existing pension laws should be strengthened, and strong disciplinary measures put in place to ensure that those who are involved in looting pension funds are severely dealt with by the law.
5. Public and private monitoring teams should be put in place to show greater commitment in monitoring and evaluating the activities of pension fund administrators and other key stakeholders involved in handling the fund.

References

Abade, R. (2004). Pension Reforms Act 2004: What's in it for you? http//www.newage-online.com. Accessed 3/1/2019.

Ahmad, M. K. (2006). The Contributory Pension Scheme: Institutional and Legal Framework. *CBN Bullion,* 30 (2): 1-18.

Amujiri, B. A. (2009). The New Contributory Pension Scheme in Nigeria: A Critical Assessment. *NJPALG, xiv (1), 137-152.*

Aydogan, U. (2004). Consumption Patterns around the Time of Retirement: Evidence from the Consumer Expenditure Surveys. Research School of Social Sciences. Canberra: Australia.

Balogun, A. (2006). Understanding the New Pension Reform Act (PRA) 2004. *CBN Bullion,* 3(2): 7-18.

Barrow, G. (2008). Pension Fund Administration in Nigeria. Pen and Pages Limited: Abuja, Nigeria.

Berkel, R. and Borsch-Supan, A. (2003). Pension Reform in Germany: The Impact on Retirement Decision.

Blau, P. M. (1964). *Exchange and Power in Social Life.* NY: John Willey & Sons.

Bonin, H. (2009). 15years of Pension Reform in Germany: Old Success and New Threats. IZA Policy Paper No.11.

Bruinshoodfd, A. and Grob, S. (2006). Do Changes in Pension Incentives Affect Retirement? A Stated Preferences Approach to Dutch Retirement Consideration. DNB Working Paper No.115.

Burns, T. (1973). A Structural Theory of Social Exchange. *Acta Sociologia,*16:188-208.

Copeland, C. (2012). Employment-Based Retirement Plan Participation: Geographic Differences and Trends. EBRI Issue Brief No.378. Employment Research Institute.

Edogbanya, A. (2013). An Assessment of the Impact of Contributory Pension Scheme to Nigerian Economic Development. *Global Journal of Management and Business Research,* 13(2): 12-22.

Ekeh, P. (1974). *Social Exchange Theory: The Two Traditions.* Harvard University Press.

Emerson, R. M. (1976). Social Exchange Theory. *Annual Review of Sociology,* 2: 335-362.

Ezeani, E. O. (2011). Planning and Managing Post-Retirement Socio-Economic Conditions: A Public Service Perspective. A Paper Presented at a Four-Day Training Workshop of Staff of Institute of Management and Technology, Enugu, Between 9-12 May, 2011.

Fabbro, G. (2010). Welfare of Pension Plans. Unpublished MSc Dissertation. University of Groningen.

Fapohunda, T. M. (2013). The Pension System and Retirement Planning in Nigeria. *Mediterranean Journal of Social Science,* 4(2):25-34.

Feldstein, M. (1982). International Differences in Social Security and Saving. *Journal of Public Economics,* 14: 225-244.

Feldstein, M. (1995). Social Security and Saving: New Time Evidence Series Evidence. NBER Working Paper 5054.

Finseraas, H. (2007). The Politics of Pension Reform: An Empirical Analysis of Pension Reform Intensity in 21OECD Countries (1994-2003). A Paper Presented at the ECPR Conference.

Fisher, N. H. and Keuschnigg, C. (2007). Pension Reform and Labour Market Incentives. Universitat St. Gallen, Department of Economics Discussion Paper No.2007-13.

Fredrickson, B. (2001). The Role of Positive Emotions in Positive Psychology: The Broaden-and-Build Theory of Positive Emotions. *American Psychologist,* 56: 218-226.

Gunu, U. and Tsado, E. (2012). Contributory Pension System as a Tool for Economic Growth in Nigeria. *International Journal of Business and Behavioural Sciences,* 2(8):6-13.

Hammermesh, D. S. (1984). Consumption during Retirement: The Missing Link in the Life Cycle. *Review of Economics and Statistics*, 66 (1): 1–7.

Hu, J. (2005). Pension Reform, Economic Growth and Financial Development: An Empirical Study. A Study Undertaken Under a Project on the Economics of Pension across OECD Countries and Emerging Market Economies. Brunel University, UK.

Idowu, K. O. (2006). Pension Reform and Public Workers Welfare in Nigeria. Paper Presented at the Asia-Pacific Regional Meeting of Economic Association, Hong Kong. Retrieved 15/12/2019.

Jagg, C., Keuschnigg, C. and Keuschnigg, M. (2007). Pension reform, retirement and life-cycle unemployment. CESIFO Working Paper No.2163.

Kareem, O. I. and Kareem, F. O. (2010). Pensions and pension reform in Nigeria. *Journal of Pensions,* 15:11-24.

Koripamo-Agary, T. A. (2009). Analytical Review of Pension System in Nigeria. http://wwwpencom.gov.ng/analytical-review-pension-system-in-nigeria. Accessed 18/12/2019.

Mackenzie, G. A., Gerson, P. and Cuevas, A. (1997). Pension regimes and saving. IMF Occasional Paper 153.

Mariger, (1987). A life cycle consumption model with liquidity constraints: Theory and empirical results. *Econometrica,* 55(3): 533 -557.

Mitchell, M. S., Cropanzana, R. S. and Quisenberry, D. M. (2012). Social exchange theory, exchange resources, and interpersonal relationships: A modest resolution of theoretical difficulties. In K. Tornblom and A. Kazemi (eds.), *Handbook of Social Resource Theory: Theoretical Extensions, Empirical Insights, and Social Applications.* NY: Springer.

Nicole, S. and Nic, M. (2004). Local wellbeing; can we measure it? In S. A. Adebowale, O. Atte, and O. Ayeni. (Eds.), Elderly Well-being in a Rural Community in North Central Nigeria, Sub-Saharan Africa. *Public Health Research,* 2 (4): 92-101.

Nyong, B. C. and Duze, C. O. (2011). The Pension Reform Act and retirement planning in Nigeria. *Journal of Economics and International Finance,* 3(2):109-115.

Odia, J. O. and Okoye, A. E. (2012). Pension Reform in Nigeria: A comparison between the old and the new scheme. *Afro Asia Journal of Social Sciences,* 3(1): 1-17.

OECD (2013), OECD Guidelines on Measuring Subjective Well-being, OECD Publishing. www.//http://dx.doi.org/10.1787/9789264191655-en.

Okonjo-Iweala, N. (2018). Fighting corruption is dangerous: The story behind the headlines. MIT Press.

Okoro, C. (2014). Pension assets. *Zenith Economic Quarterly,* 10(4): 10-32.

Olanrewaju, E. A. (2011). The Pension Reform Act 2004 and the wellbeing of Nigerian Retirees: A sociological evaluation of its provisions. *International Journal of Humanities and Social Sciences,* 1(21):315-325.

Orifowomo, O. A. (2006). A critical appraisal of pension system reforms in Nigeria. *Gonzaza Journal of International Law,* 1: 1-35.

Ozor, E. (2006). Review of factors that slowdown the processing of retirement benefits. A Paper Presented at the Workshop Organized by the Institute of Chartered Secretaries and Administration of Nigeria, Held at Modotel Enugu, 14th-16th May, 2006.

Robb, A. L. and Burbidge, J. B. (1989). Consumption, income and retirement. *Canadian Journal of Economics* 22(3): 522-542.

Salen, J. and Stahlberg, A. (2007). Why Sweden's Pension Reform was Able to be Successfully Implemented. *European Journal of Political Economy,* 23(4):1175-1184.

Stensness, K. and Stolen, N. M. (2007). Norwegian pension reform: Efforts on fiscal sustainability, labour supply and equity. A Paper Submitted to the Norwegian Ministry of Finance and the Ministry of Labour Social Inclusion.

Stoll, L. (2012). *Well-being evidence for policy: A review.* London.

Thompson, S. and Marks, N. (2008). Measuring well-being in policy: Issues and applications. Report Commissioned by the Foresight Project on Mental Capital and Well-being. Government Office for Science.

United States Department of Labour (2012). Employer survey Responses and CPS Data.

United States Department of Labour (2012). National Compensation Survey.

World Bank (1994). Averting the old age crisis: Policies to protect the old age and promote growth. Oxford University Press: New York.

World Bank (2004). Project appraisal document on a proposed credit to the Federal Republic of Nigeria for an economic reform and governance project. Washington DC.

Yunusa, A. A. (2009). An evaluation of public perception of the new pension scheme in Nigeria: A study of the perception of the academic staff of Ahmadu Bello University, Zaria. *Kogi Journal of Management,* 3(1).

5

Vocational and Technical Education, the Panacea for Multidimensional Poverty in Nigeria

IKEANYIONWU Chioma. L. Ph.D, ENWERE Judith O. &

OKAFOR Chinagolum V.

Abstract

Vocational and Technical Education (VTE) is education that provides necessary knowledge and skills for employment. VTE engenders social equity, inclusion and sustainability of development. Vocational education and technical education are commonly used interchangeably but, they are distinct and separate terminologies. Vocational education is skill based programmes designed for skill acquisition at the lower level of education while Technical education conversely designed for any particular vocation but provides general technical knowledge that prepares individuals for entry into recognized occupation at a higher level but usually lower than the first degree.A secondary data from 2017 Human Development Indices Survey for Nigeria showing multidimensional poverty indices for Nigeria as developed by United Nations Development Programme (UNDP) and National Bureau of statistics. The survey covered households in both urban and rural areas in all the 36 states of the Federation and the Federal Capital Territory (FCT), Abuja using the Enumeration Areas (EAs), which established through the National Integrated Survey of Households (NISH). A total sample 120 Enumeration Areas (EAs) were selected in each of the 36 states, and the FCT. In each EA, a sample of 15 households (HHs) was selected for the study, making a total of 1,800 households per State and a national sample size of 66,600 households. The MPI score shows the proportion of deprivation of people in a given country experience out of the total possible deprivations where everyone was poor and deprived in all indicators. According to the NG-MPI, Nigeria's poorest states are Sokoto, Jigawe and Yobe in the North, with MPI scores between 0.35 and 0.45, while the least poor states are found in the South Western part of the country with MPI scores ranging from 0.06 to 0.12. There is a nexus between multidimensional poverty and negligence of Vocational Technical Education in Nigeria. Vocational Technical Education remains the most potent tool for fighting multidimensional poverty in Nigeria. The study concluded that appropriate implementation of VTE programmes in Nigeria will go a long way in ameliorating poverty in multidimensional forms. Recommendations were also proffered.

Key Words: *Vocational and Technical Education, Multidimensional Poverty, United Nations Development Programme and Nigeria.*

Introduction

Vocational education is education designed to prepare individuals to take up career as technician or other jobs such as a tradesmen and artisans. Vocational education is also known as *career and technical education* specifically designed to provide vocational education. Vocational education takes place at the post-secondary or higher education level and interacts with the apprenticeship system. At the post-secondary level, vocational education is often provided by highly specialized trade schools, technical schools, universities, as well as polytechnics. The World Bank's 2019 World Development Report on the future of work opined that flexibility between general and vocational education particularly in higher education is necessary to ensure that workers compete in the changing labor markets where technology plays pivotal role.

Vocational and Technical Education (VTE) is education that provides necessary knowledge and skills for employment (www.unevoc.unec.org). VTE requires many forms of education such as formal, non-formal and informal learning. VTE engenders social equity, inclusion and sustainability of development. UNESCO prioritized subsectors in VTE such as literacy and higher education. According to Marope, Chakroun and Holmes (2015) the development and definition of VTE is one that parallels other types of education and training, such as Vocational Education.

Vocational education and technical education are commonly used interchangeably but, they are distinct and separate terminologies. Vocational education is skill based programmes designed for skill acquisition at the lower level of education. Technical education conversely designed for any particular vocation but provides general technical knowledge that prepares individuals for entry into recognized occupation at a higher level but usually lower than the first degree. Suffice to say that technical and vocational education is an integrated curriculum that ensures inclusion of basic technical and scientific knowledge with the skill based vocational programme

Vocational Technical Education (VTE) is understood as comprising education, training and skills development relating to a wide range of occupational fields, production, services and livelihoods. VET, as part of lifelong learning, can take place at secondary, post-secondary and tertiary levels and includes work-based learning and continuing training and professional development which may lead to qualifications. VTE also includes a wide range of skills development opportunities attuned to national and local contexts. Learning to learn, the development of literacy and numeracy skills, transversal skills and citizenship skills are integral components of VTE (UNESCO (GC) 2015, UN).

Post-compulsory education and training, excluding degree and higher level programs delivered by further education institutions, which provides people with occupational or work-related knowledge and skills. Also: Career and technical education (CTE) (USA); Further Education and Training (FET) (UK, South Africa); Vocational and Technical Education and Training (VTET) (South-East Asia); Vocational Education and Training (VET); Vocational and Technical Education (VTE) (AUS) (UNEVOC/NCVER, 2009).

Vocational Technical Education, used as an equivalent term for vocational Non-academic technical education and practical training that develop the skills and knowledge of apprentices (learners of trades or crafts) working in different sectors of industry and trainees/ students trained in different VTE Institutions (VTE Institutes, Centres & Schools). The VTE is that part of the education system that provides courses and training programmes related to employment with a view to enabling the transition from secondary education to work for young trainees / students (social objective) and supply the labour market with competent apprentices (economic objective). The VTE is used as a comprehensive term referring to those aspects of the educational process involving, in addition to general education, the study of technologies and related sciences, and the acquisition of awareness, knowledge, skills, and attitudes relating to occupations in various sectors of economic and social life (Wahba, 2013). The education or training process where it involves, in addition to general education, the study of technologies and related sciences and the acquisition of practical skills relating to occupations in various sectors of economic life and social life, comprises formal (organized programs as part of the school system) and non-formal (organized classes outside the school system) approaches. (TESDA 2010, Philippines).

Poverty is defined as the lack of money. According to the Nigeria economic report released in July 2014 by the World Bank, Nigeria had one of the world›s highest economic growth rates, averaging 7.4%. The gross domestic product (GDP) growth rate dropped to 2.7% in 2015 following the oil price collapse in 2014-2016, combined with negative production shocks the economy contracted by 1.6%.In 2016 during its first recession in 25 years, poverty remains significant at 33.1% in Africa›s biggest economy. According to (DFID, 2012) that a country with massive wealth and a huge population to support commerce, with a well-developed economy and plenty of natural resources such as oil, the level of poverty remains unacceptable. Worldbank.org noted that poverty may have been overestimated due to the lack of information on the extremely huge informal sector of the economy, estimated at around 60% more, of the current GDP figures (Yusurf, 2014).As of 2018, Population growth rate is higher than economic growth rate, leading to a slow rise in poverty. World Bank (2018) revealed that almost half the population of Nigerian citizens are living below the international poverty line of ($2 per day), and unemployment peaked at 23.1%.

Furthermore, the poor themselves consider their experience of poverty much more broadly. Poor individuals can suffer multiple disadvantages as exemplified by poor health or malnutrition, lack of clean water or electricity, poor quality of work or little schooling. Focusing on one factor such as income alone will not be enough to capture the true reality of poverty. Multidimensional poverty measures can be used to create a more comprehensive picture. They reveal who is poor and how they are poor – the range of different disadvantages they experience (UNDP, 2015). As well as providing a headline measure of poverty, multidimensional measures can be broken down to reveal the poverty level in different areas of a country and among different sub-groups of people. Amartya (1976) opined that measurement of poverty is composed of two fundamental steps, determining who is poor (identification) and building an index to reflect the extent of poverty (aggregation). The two steps have been sources of debate over time among academics and practitioners. Several decades ago, one-dimensional measures like income were used to distinguish poor from non-poor but recently new measures have been proposed to enrich the understanding of socio-economic conditions and to better reflect the evolving concept of poverty (UNDP, 2015). Multidimensional poverty measurement uses several techniques to measure poverty from a multidimensional perspective have been developed over the years. A few of the main prevailing approaches, among many others include (Alkire *et al.* 2015):

- **The dashboard approach**: an analysis of different indicators of poverty. A prominent example of which is the Millennium Development Goals;
- **The composite indices approach**: whereby deprivation indices, possibly considered in a dashboard approach, are converted into one single number. Well-known composite indices include the Human Development Index, the Gender Empowerment Index and the Human Poverty Index, all of which have been published by the United Nations Development Programme (UNDP) Human Development Report;
- **Multivariate statistical methods**: techniques to identify the poor, set indicator weights, build individual deprivation scores, and aggregate the information into societal poverty indices; iv. Fuzzy sets: mathematical technique employed to identify mathematically the poor (using fewer normative judgments);

The Global **Multidimensional Poverty Index (MPI)** was developed in 2010 by the Oxford Poverty & Human Development Initiative and the United Nations Development Programme and uses different factors to determine poverty beyond income-based lists. It replaced the previous Human Poverty Index (The Economics, 2010). The global Multidimensional Poverty Index (MPI) is an international measure of acute poverty covering over 100 developing countries. It complements traditional income-based poverty measures by capturing the severe deprivations that each person faces at the same time with respect to education, health and living standards. The MPI assesses poverty at the individual level. If someone is deprived in a third or more of ten (weighted) indicators, the global index identifies them as 'MPI poor', and the extent – or intensity – of their poverty is measured by the number of deprivations they are experiencing in this ten factors which includes education, sanitation, food and various other indicators. The MPI can be used to create a comprehensive picture of people living in poverty, and permits comparisons both across countries, regions and the world and within countries by ethnic group, urban/rural location, as well as other key household and community characteristics. These characteristic make the MPI useful as an analytical tool to identify the most vulnerable people - the poorest among the poor, revealing poverty patterns within countries and over time, enabling policy makers to target resources and design policies more effectively.

The Global Multidimensional Poverty Index(MPI) was developed in 2010 by the Oxford Poverty & Human Development Initiative and the United Nations Development Programme and uses different factors to determine poverty beyond income-based lists. It replaced the previous Human Poverty Index. The global MPI is released annually by OPHI and the results published on its website (The Economic, 2010). The global Multidimensional Poverty Index (MPI) is an international measure of acute poverty covering over 100 developing countries. It complements traditional income-based poverty measures by capturing the severe deprivations that each person faces at the same time with respect to education, health and living standards. The MPI assesses poverty at the individual level. If someone is deprived in a third or more of ten (weighted) indicators, the global index identifies them as 'MPI poor', and the extent or intensity of their poverty is measured by the number of deprivations they are experiencing in this ten factors which includes education, sanitation, food and various other indicators. The MPI can be used to create a comprehensive picture of people living in poverty, and permits comparisons both across countries, regions and the world and within countries by ethnic group, urban/rural location, as well as other key household and community characteristics. These characteristic make the MPI useful as an analytical tool to identify the most vulnerable people - the poorest among the poor, revealing poverty patterns within countries and over time, enabling policy makers to target resources and design policies more effectively.

The following ten indicators are used to calculate the MPI (MPI, 2010):

- **Education** (each indicator is weighted equally at 1/6)

1. Years of schooling: deprived if no household member has completed six years of schooling
2. school attendance: deprived if any school-aged child is not attending school up to class 8

- **Health** (each indicator is weighted equally at 1/6)

3. Child mortality: deprived if any child has died in the family in past 5 years
4. Nutrition: deprived if any adult or child, for whom there is nutritional information, is stunted

Electricity: deprived if the household has no electricity

Sanitation: deprived if the household's sanitation facility is not improved (according to MDG guidelines), or it is improved but shared with other households

5. Drinking water: deprived if the household does not have access to safe drinking water (according to MDG guidelines) or safe drinking water is more than a 30-minute walk from home round-trip
6. Housing: deprived if the household has a dirt, sand or dung floor
7. Cooking fuel: deprived if the household cooks with dung, wood or charcoal
8. Assets ownership: deprived if the household does not own more than one of: radio, TV, telephone, bike, motorbike or refrigerator and does not own a car or truck

A person is considered poor if they are deprived in at least a third of the weighted indicators. The intensity of poverty denotes the proportion of indicators in which they are deprived.

Comparison with HDI

HDI, the Human Development Index, was developed by Mahbub ul Haq and Amartya Sen, in 1990, and was also developed by the UNDP. It is calculated as the geometric mean of the normalized indices of the three dimensions of human development it takes into account: health, education and standard of living. The UNDP is trying to improve on the

HDI formula by introducing the IHDI (Inequality affected HDI). While both HDI and MPI use the three broad dimensions *health*, *education* and *standard of living*, HDI uses only single indicators for each dimension of poverty while MPI uses more than one indicator for each one. This, amongst other reasons, has led to the MPI only being calculated for just over 100 countries, where data is available for all these diverse indicators, while HDI is calculated for almost all countries.

Multidimensional Poverty Indices of Nigeria

The National Multidimensional Poverty Index for Nigeria (NG-MPI) was published by the National Human Development Report 2018 which focused on advancing development in North East of Nigeria. UNDP Nigeria in collaboration with the National Bureau of Statistics (NBS) commissioned it. The national MPI for Nigeria has a total of eleven (11) indicators covering the four equally weighted dimensions of Education, Health, Living Standards and Unemployment. The NG-MPI was computed at sub-national level using data from the 2017 Human Development Indices Survey and covered rural and urban areas in all of the thirty six (36) states and the Federal Capital Territory (FCT) of Abuja.

For calculating the NG-MPI, a household is considered multidimensionally poor if it is deprived in more than ¼ of the weighted indicators. For Nigeria, the share of multidimensionally poor people at the national level is 54% with the average intensity of deprivation standing at 42%. The indicators with the largest weighted contribution to poverty in the country are employment, years of schooling and school attendance UNDP Nigeria and NBS (2017). The NG-MPI's main focus was sub-national analysis and the report features results akin to the findings of the 2018 Global MPI, with both reports presenting stark differences in poverty levels between northern Nigeria and the rest of the country. The results from the NG-MPI show a high incidence of poverty across the North with the poorest states having over 80% of their population classified as multidimensionally poor. The intensity of deprivation in the region is above 40% for most states which means that the average household in these areas is deprived in just under half of the indicators. This is in stark contrast with the southern part of the country, especially the South West, where both the incidence and intensity of poverty is much lower UNDP Nigeria and NBS (2017).

The MPI accounts for both the incidence and intensity of poverty and its value ranges from zero to one. The MPI score shows the proportion of deprivation people in a given country experience out of the total possible deprivations where everyone was poor and deprived in all indicators. According to the NG-MPI, Nigeria's poorest states are Sokoto, Jigawe and Yobe in the North, with MPI scores between 0.35 and 0.45, while the least poor states are found in the South Western part of the country with MPI scores ranging from 0.06 to 0.12 UNDP Nigeria and NBS (2017).

The following factors contribute to the wide spread poverty in Nigeria;

They include

- income inequality
- ethnic conflict
- Political instability.

Income Inequality

By 2010, the Gini coefficient of Nigeria is rated medium at 0.43 but more rural poor than urban poor still exits and this is correlated with differential access to infrastructure and amenities. According to Aigbokham (2014) and NBS (2009), oil exports contribute significantly to government revenues; 9% to the GDP, and employs only a fraction of the population. Agriculture, however, contributes to about 17% of GDP, and employs about 30% of the population.

This incongruence is compounded by the fact that oil revenue is poorly distributed among the population, with higher government spending in urban areas than rurally. A high unemployment rate renders personal incomes even more divergent. Moreover, the process of oil exploitation has resulted in significant pollution, which devastates the agricultural sector. Additionally, agriculture growth has slowed also because of farmer-herdsmen clashes, revolts in the north-east, and floods. The majority of Nigeria's better paying jobs are in capital-intensive sectors, but they are very scarce and limited. Only the places striving with economic activity and are very capital-intensive, possess law firms, small local businesses, and the got and verging powers BBC News (2012) opined.

Long Term Ethnic Conflict and Civil Unrest

Since the return to civilian rule in 1999, Nigeria has historically experienced much ethnic conflicts, militants from religious and ethnic groups have become markedly more violent. While this unrest has its roots in poverty and economic competition, its economic and human damages further escalate the problems of poverty such as increasing the mortality rate as exemplified by ethnic unrest and the displeasure to local communities with oil companies which contributed to the conflict over oil trade in the Niger Delta, thereby threatening the productivity of oil trade (Canagrajah, Suohaesen,Thamos and Suji, 2001). Civil unrest might also have contributed to the adoption of populist policy measures which work in the short-run, but impede poverty alleviation efforts.

Political Instability and Corruption

Historic ethnic instability and large population has led to the adoption of a federal government with resultant fiscal decentralisation providing Nigeria's state and local government's considerable autonomy, including control over 50% of government revenues, as well as responsibility for providing public services (Gini index, 2010). The lack of a stringent regulatory and monitoring system has allowed for rampant corruption. Hrw.org noted that the hindered past poverty alleviation efforts to a large extent, since resources which could pay for public goods or directed towards investment to create employment and other opportunities for citizens are being misappropriated. There is a nexus between Nigerian corruption and poverty. When looking at human development, Nigeria is at the bottom of the scale and corruption scores highest. Corruption exists at all levels of government namely – Local, State and even at the Federal level. As a result of extreme corruption, even the poverty reduction programs suffer from no funding and have failed to give the needed remedy to this country. One of the reasons for the continued success of corruption is the encouragement that it receives from the government. Government shows tolerance towards corruption and to the corrupted officials to the extent that the officials facing indictment are pardoned and accepted into the society.

Vocational Technical Education could curb Multidimensional Poverty in Nigeria through the following ways;

The European Centre for the Development of Vocational Training (CEDEFOP, 2011) noted that benefits of Vocational and Technical Education can be grouped using a classical typology based on the nature of results.

- Economic
- Social

The Economic Dimension

The literature on the economic benefits from VET always showcase growth. The impacts of VTE on labour-market outcomes often reflect direct or indirect aggregate individual productivity effects. The main outcome stressed are higher participation on the labour market, lower unemployment, the opportunity to acquire a qualification for all categories for who did not previously have one, and the chance to advance in a professional hierarchy. Through lifelong learning, individuals can improve their work opportunities and qualification levels. Higher remuneration offers new opportunities which lead to further economic and social outputs, such as economic autonomy, and can also enhance psychological well- being. All these factors ultimately impact individual productivity. In the Scandinavia especially Sweden, VTE programmes outcomes resulted to a higher rate of labour-market participation coupled with lower unemployment. Two-year programmes at the upper secondary level registered lower unemployment rates than comprehensive education (nine years of schooling). VTE has been organised in cooperation with companies who emphasised the importance of on-the-job training. The programme was designated for students who finished upper secondary school but also for employees who wanted to develop their skills. The main stimulating factor was the financial support accorded to individuals who participated in the programme. Recent study showed that 83% of the former participants had a job or were running their own businesses, with a slight difference between men and women (83% to 82%). Denmark found a positive relationship between employment growth and highlighted that VTE can increase productivity in terms of hours worked but not in terms of cost reduction. VTE training has positive impact on participants' professional lives, which depend on the nature of the training. They enjoyed more stability compared to those that did not follow any VTE training.

The Social Dimension

The social benefits of VTE are more difficult to measure than the economic ones as they are embedded in the ways society functions. Economic VTE benefits can usually be considered as concrete or punctual (can be easily translated into economic units of analysis). Social benefits, compared to economic benefits, which are more tangible in quantitative terms. Social benefits are more directly related to qualitative results. Both types of benefit are interconnected. Low economic benefits can create insignificant social outcomes or even negative ones. For example, a low participation rate in VTE can result in high unemployment which creates an unstable society. A well-implemented VTE system, which connects labour-market needs to VTE and considers new challenges in terms of changing job requirements. It leads to life satisfaction which is directly linked to a stable society. Countries reported less on the social benefits than on the economic ones: it is not clear why. The social benefits reported were largely examined by studying the changes in society occurring as a result of participation in VTE programmes. The following areas were investigated: relationships between generations, health status, social cohesion, crime reduction and social integration. A common indicator for all countries is social integration, which can be defined as the movement of disadvantaged groups of a society into its mainstream.

Social integration is seen as the main return on labour market participation. Most countries also report on VTE positive effects on the integration of disadvantaged/marginalised groups which are excluded or face labour-market exclusion. Finland, Lithuania and Norway examined the integration of different disadvantaged groups on the labour market. They highlighted that specific social categories face economic and social discrimination. Lithuania pointed out the quality of life improving for those acquiring a new qualification. Besides reducing local and national unemployment, Lithuania stressed the significance of training quality in shaping professional and personal development. It also reported on a discrepancy between practical and theoretical training as theoretical knowledge is not so easily applicable in occupational activities. The UK highlighted the following social returns: positive effects on intergenerational connections, better general health, and a safer environment. Research-based evidence indicates that VET can create a stimulating environment for children if their mothers participate in VTE. At the same time, engaging youth in VTE programmes supports the prevention of unhealthy behaviour, such as smoking, alcohol or drug addiction, and reduces the incidence of delinquency. Norway emphasised that immigrants, especially non-western groups, need better grades in school to have the same opportunities as the majority population. Similar effects can be observed on the labour market when non-western immigrants want to find a job.

The differences in opportunities have been explained in terms of social capital, which is very different among migrants compared to the majority population. At the same time, VTE-trained immigrants and locally born children of immigrants suffer an income disadvantage after graduation. In Germany, VTE can function as a safety net for those that dropped out, although the opportunities for this category are dwindling over time. Other disadvantaged groups mentioned by Germany are people supported by psychological services, youths with dyslexia, people with a drug addiction history or prison record, and people in prison. People in these categories generally suffer from social stigma and are more difficult to integrate into the labour market. Portugal reported that the effects of VTE on social and civic development are not conclusive as society transformations are difficult and generally take time. For individuals, social returns are commonly measured by beneficial psychological effects on individuals in terms of motivation or attitudes, such as increasing self-esteem and self-confidence. Lithuania suggested that VTE improved the psychological state of disabled persons and increased their self- confidence and self-esteem: disability was not the central impediment to employment. Increasing employment is associated with improving economic conditions and, at the same time, reducing social exclusion, satisfying individual and family needs, qualitative free time and developing a sense of freedom, safety and optimism. Sweden considered the interconnections between economic and social returns on VTE by focusing on personal well-being: a more favourable position on the labour market is associated with better remuneration which creates further social opportunities. Iceland offered the results from one study among women with no recognized qualification. After following a two-year VTE programme, their self-confidence grew, their relationships with their families improved and the chance to find adequate work increased. For Portugal self-esteem, self-valorization, self- learning and self-knowledge are the VTE returns for individuals.

Conclusion

The impacts of Vocational and Technical Education on labour-market outcomes often reflect direct or indirect aggregate individual productivity effects. The main outcome stressed are higher participation on the labour market, lower unemployment, the opportunity to acquire a qualification for all categories for who did not previously have one, and the chance to advance in a professional hierarchy. Through lifelong learning, individuals can improve their work opportunities and qualification levels. Higher remuneration offers new opportunities which lead to further economic and social outputs, such as economic autonomy, and can also enhance psychological well- being. All these factors ultimately impact individual productivity and ultimately reduce multidimensional poverty in Nigeria.

References

The Economist. July 29, 2010. Retrieved 2010-08-04. Aided by the improved availability of survey data about living conditions for households in over 100 developing countries, the researchers have come up with a new index, called the Multidimensional Poverty Index (MPI), which the United Nations Development Programme (UNDP) will use in its next "Human Development Report" in October.

"The 2018 Global Multidimensional Poverty Index".http://www.ophi.org.uk/wp-content/uploads/Argentina.pdf

Alkire Roche Santos Seth. "Multidimensional Poverty Index 2011: Brief Methodological Note"(PDF). Oxford Poverty & Human Development Initiative (OPHI).

"Table 6: Multidimensional Poverty Index: developing countries". Table 4: Comparison between the revised and the original MPI. UNDP. March 2015. p. 54, Table 4: Comparison between the revised and the original MPI. Retrieved 22 September 2016.

Alkire, S., Foster, J., Seth, S., Santos, M. E., Roche, J. M., and Ballon, P. (2015). 'Multidimen9sional Poverty Measurement and Analysis', Oxford: Oxford University Press. Retrieved on 2 October 2015 from Oxford Scholarship Online: August 2015.

"Career and Technical Education". edglossary.org. Retrieved 2019-08-07.

World Bank World Development Report 2019: The Changing Nature of Work. Jump up to: [ab]UNESCO-UNEVOC. "What is TVET?". www.unevoc.unesco.org. Retrieved 1 April 2017.

UNESCO. "Technical and Vocational Education and Training (TVET)". www.unesco.org. Retrieved 1 April 2017.

Marope, P.T.M; Chakroun, B.; Holmes, K.P. (2015). Unleashing the Potential: Transforming Technical and Vocational Education and Training(PDF). UNESCO. pp. 9–10, 41, 43, 47–48, 80, 95, 98–100. ISBN 978-92-3-100091-1.

Asian Development Bank. "Skilling the Pacific: Technical and Vocational Education and Training in the Pacific". Asian Development Bank. 2008-09-01.

CS1 maint: others (link)

"Humboldt on Education". schillerinstitute.org. Retrieved 2018-06-29. As quoted in Profiles of educators: Wilhelm von Humboldt (1767–1835) by Karl-Heinz Günther (1988), doi:10.1007/BF02192965

"Nikil Mukerji & Julian Nida-Rümelin". St. Gallen Business Review. Retrieved 2018-06-29.

Nida-Rümelin, Julian (29 October 2009). "Bologna-Prozess: Die Chance zum Kompromiss ist da". Die Zeit (in German). Retrieved 29 November 2015.

"Learning for Jobs OECD review of Australian vocational education"(PDF). Oecd.org. Retrieved 2016-02-06.

"Australian Industry Skills Committee". www.aisc.net.au. Retrieved 2018-06-29.

Research, National Centre for Vocational Education. "Home". www.ncver.edu.au. Retrieved 2018-06-29.

Scott, Rebecca. "TAFE gears up to offer degrees" The Age July 24, 2002. Accessed August 3, 2008

Matthews, David (3 June 2017), Europeans back funding vocational training over higher education, Times Higher Education, retrieved 3 June 2017

"The German Vocational Training System - BMBF". Federal Ministry of Education and Research - BMBF. Retrieved 2018-06-29.

"RIS - Berufsausbildungsgesetz - Bundesrecht konsolidiert, Fassung vom 29.06.2018". www.ris.bka.gv.at (in German). Retrieved 2018-06-29.

"Home << IVE". www.ive.edu.hk. Retrieved 2018-06-29.

"OECD review of vocational education and training in Hungary"(PDF). Oecd.org. Retrieved 2016-02-06.

"Ministry of Skill Development And Entrepreneurship". www.skilldevelopment.gov.in. Retrieved 2018-06-29.

"National Policy for Skill Development and Entrepreneurship 2015". pib.nic.in. Retrieved 2018-06-29.

"Vocational Training in India - A skill Based Education". Vocational Training Center. 2018-05-01. Retrieved 2018-06-29.

"Overseas migration patterns from India"(PDF). Ruth Baruj-Kovarsky, Ori Figura-Rosenzweig, and Dalia Ben Rabi. MENTA – Support Program for Technical and Practical Engineering Students: Evaluation Study. Jerusalem: Myers-JDC-Brookdale Institute (2018).

OECD Policy Reviews of Vocational Education and Training (VET) - Learning for Jobs". Oecd.org. Retrieved 5 February 2016.

"Dutch vocational education in a nutshell | Education | Expatica the Netherlands". Expatica.com. Retrieved 2016-02-06.

"Industry Training and Apprenticeships | ITF New Zealand". Itf.org.nz. Retrieved 2016-02-06.

"Welcome to". Education Counts. Retrieved 2016-02-06.

"OECD review of vocational education and training in Norway"(PDF). Oecd.org. Retrieved 2016-02-06.

Ministerio de Educación y Formación Profesional. "La Formación Profesional Actual En El Sistema Educativo." TodoFP, Gobierno De España, 2019, http://todofp.es/sobre-fp/informacion-general/sistema-educativo-fp/fp-actual.html (In Spanish)

Ministerio de Educación y Formación Profesional. "Preguntas Frecuentes." TodoFP, Gobierno De España, 2019, http://todofp.es/sobre-fp/informacion-general/formacion-profesional-dual/preguntas-frecuentes.html. (In Spanish)

"humanitarian-srilanka.org". Humanitarian-srilanka.org. Retrieved 5 February 2016.

"Gold Standard: The Swiss Vocational Education and Training System"(PDF). ncee.org. Retrieved 2018-07-21.

"Vocational education and training". educa.ch. Retrieved 2018-07-21.

"Learning for Jobs OECD review of Switzerland, 2009"(PDF). Oecd.org. Retrieved 2016-02-06.

"Turkey 2012 results" (PDF). Oecd.org. Retrieved 2016-02-06. https://web.archive.org/web/20120614110134/http://ismek.ibb.gov.tr/ism/index.asp. Archived from the original on June 14, 2012. Retrieved June 15, 2012. Missing or empty |title= (help)

Owen, W. B. (1912). Sir Sidney Lee (ed.). Dictionary of National Biography – William Ford Robinson Stanley. Second Supplement. III (NEIL-YOUNG). London: Smith, Elder & Co. pp. 393–394.

Jump up to: [ab] Wolf, A. (2002) Does Education Matter? Myths about Education and Economic Growth London: Penguin. https://web.archive.org/web/20080111031753/http://www.keele.ac.uk/depts/so/youthchron/Education/9197educ.htm. Archived from the original on January 11, 2008. Retrieved June 8, 2008. Missing or empty |title= (help)

World Class Apprenticeships. The Government's strategy for the future of Apprenticeships in England. DIUS/DCSF, 2008. DFID. Retrieved 2012-03-21

"Nigeria - Country Brief". Web.worldbank.org. 2011-09-23. Retrieved 2012-03-21.

Aigbokhan, Ben. "Poverty, growth and inequality in Nigeria". African Economic Research Consortium.

Yusuf, Aremu (February 2014). "The Informal Sector and Employment Generation in Nigeria" (PDF).

Sparks, Donald. "The Informal Sector In Sub - Saharan Africa : Out Of The Shadows To Foster Sustainable Employment And Equity?" (PDF). International Business & Economics Research Journal.

[pubdocs.worldbank.org/en/848651492188167743/mpo-nga.pdf. "Nigeria›s Economy"] *Check* |url= *value (*help). Macro Poverty Outlook: Sub-Saharan Africa. World Bank: 266–277. 19 April 2018 – via Public Documents.

"Gini Index". World Bank. Retrieved 2 March 2011.

Aigbokhan, Ben E. (2000). "Poverty, Growth and Inequality in Nigeria: A Case Study" (PDF). unpan1.un.org.

"Nigerian Gross Domestic Product Report Q2 2015". National Bureau of Statistics. Archived from the original *on 15 September 2015.* Retrieved 22 September 2015.

"Nigeria 2009". comtrade.un.org.

"Labour Force Statistics, 2010". Nigerian Bureau of Statistics. 2010. Archived from the original *on 24 April 2015.* Retrieved 22 June 2015.

"Nigeria profile". BBC News. 2012-01-24. Retrieved 2012-03-21.

Canagarajah, Sudharsan; Thomas, Suji (1 August 2001). "Poverty in a Wealthy Economy: The Case of Nigeria". Journal of African Economies. 10 *(2): 143–173.* doi:10.1093/jae/10.2.143 – *via Oxford University Press Journals Current.*

"Violence in Nigeria›s Oil Rich Rivers State in 2004: Summary". Hrw.org. Retrieved 2012-03-21.

Duffield, Caroline (2010-09-28). "The illegal but lucrative trade in educational materials, for instance, cripples the work of teachers". Bbc.co.uk. Retrieved 2012-03-21.

6

Activities of the Students' Representative Council (SRC) in a Selected Higher Institution: A Case Study of University for Development Studies, Ghana

THOMPSON John D. & ANSOGLENANG Gilbert

Abstract

This paper attempted to look at activities of the Students Representative Council (SRC) in a selected higher institution, specifically, the University for Development Studies. From our interactions with past and present SRC executives, we came to realize that some SRC/NUGS executives, especially the Presidents, try to undertake over-ambitious projects in their respective institutions. When these projects are successfully executed, they are usually associated with them. The target population of this study was the four SRC Presidents of the various campuses of the University, during the 2016/2017 academic year. The method of selection was purposive sampling and the instrument used was the interview schedule. The findings of the study showed that most SRC executives come up with plans which they are unable to execute within their nine (9) months or so stay in office. Also, our investigations revealed that delayed release of funds usually accounted for the non-completion and execution of projects. Another issue that appeared disturbing to most of the executives, we interacted with, was interference by management in SRC planned activities. Also disturbing was disapproval of budgets submitted to management for consideration and subsequent approval.

Key Words: *Activities, Projects, Achievements, Students' Representative Council (SRC), University.*

Introduction

The Students' Representative Council (SRC) of every institution is the highest student leadership group with the sole aim of championing the course of all students and ensuring their general welfare. Over the years, the SRC of all institutions act as the student voice and is the legally-recognized body for student representation. Among its numerous functions, the SRC discusses issues such as accommodation, community relations, education, environment, well-being, equal opportunities that are deemed important to students with management of the institution. The SRC is able to put forward motions which are usually inspired by change that the executives and students want to see happen at the University, school or educational institution. It also has the power to lobby the institution to make changes in a number of different ways, including providing more money for students' activities, taking a public stance on a particular political or ethical issue (galamsey, legalization of same sex marriages etc.) or improving the teaching experience. All of these actions begin with the SRC, which also liaises between the student body, management and those outside the University community.

There is also the local NUGS which is responsible for taking care of the personal development of students such as organizing seminars, symposia and trainings. It draws its budget (25%) from the SRC which it uses to finance its programmes and activities. Thus when this money is not forthcoming, it usually results in agitations between the executives of the local NUGS and the SRC. Another wing of the local NUGS which is worth mentioning is the Women's Commissioner which is popularly known as WOCOM. The main target of WOCOM is women whilst the local NUGS takes care of the entire population. It is worth mentioning that all students belong to the University Students Association of Ghana (USAG). Also, the National Union of Ghana Students (NUGS) is the mother union of both the SRC and the local NUGS. According to Wikipedia, the Free Encyclopedia (n. d), a Students' Representative Council, also known as a Students' Administrative Council, represents students interests in the government of a university, school or other educational institution. Universities may have a statutory obligation to receive representation from the SRC and it is usual for students' representation from the SRC to form part of university structures including the university court, academic senate, and other bodies (Wikipedia).

The University for Development Studies (UDS) Ghana was established in 1992 following the reforms in the tertiary education system. Unlike the traditional universities, UDS has a unique mandate: to introduce new action-oriented programmes in priority areas of development to address deprivations and environmental problems, which characterize Northern Ghana and rural areas of the country. The Third Trimester Field Practical Programme (TTFPP) described in some circles as the flagship programme of the University is an innovative approach to applying acquired classroom knowledge to the solution of problems afflicting deprived communities in the catchment area of the University for Development Studies. By the Programme, students live in and interact with members of selected rural communities in all areas of their social life and activities for a period of eight weeks per year during the third trimester period for two academic years. Furthermore, the Programme is designed to enable students learn at first-hand about how community life in the selected communities is organized so that the experiences gained will serve as Livelihood Case Studies that will be useful for academic exercise and for policy direction in relation to community planning and development. The success of the Programme is contingent upon the students staying and adapting to the existing environmental and living conditions of the indigenous people by utilizing whatever facilities and resources that are available and used by the community people including, housing, water and food, among others.

Background to the Study

During electioneering campaign for the various SRC executive positions, all aspirants especially those vying for the position of SRC President come out with beautiful manifestoes. Because of the perceived benefits likely to be enjoyed by these executives when they are voted into office, aspirants go all out and try to win the elections. It is for this reason that some aspirants come out with beautiful and wonderful manifestos which normally would be very difficult to be achieved within a year. Most often than not, some SRC Presidents are unable to execute their over-ambitious projects within their period in office. Also, it would not be an understatement to say that most SRC executives, when given the least opportunity, usually have the burning desire to effect positive changes to their respective constituents. They are, however, not able to achieve their plans because of certain challenges beyond their control. Most SRC executives target areas such as students' welfare, academic, entertainment, infrastructure and security. However, in no uncertain terms, particular SRC administrations venture for the task ahead but unfortunately, one thing leads to the other and some of them (executives) are not able to execute their intended projects but rather witness major setbacks.

For these and other reasons, the researchers were interested in finding out why most SRC executives are unable to achieve successes in the projects or activities they plan to carry-out which usually are in their manifestos. Could it be the late release of funds, interference by Management in the execution of SRC projects, unclear priorities by some executives, and the limited tenure in office of executives? The above questions guided the researchers to carry out their investigations.

Methodology

We were interested in what the SRC Presidents of the various campuses were able to achieve during their tenure in office for the 2016/2017 academic year with respect to their intended activities and projects. We also wanted to know what they were unable to achieve, and why they could not achieve them. Accordingly, we first looked at the manifesto of the SRC President of the Tamale Campus after which we had an encounter with the other three SRC Presidents of the campuses. The interaction was basically to solicit from them, their achievements, what they were not able to achieve, and why they could not achieve them. It was strongly thought out that after considering all factors negating their achievements, we would be in a better position to come up with some recommendations for the SRC and also make a strong case/proposal to Management about the UDS SRC and how they could be reshaped or restructured.

Activities of the Tamale Campus SRC President for the 2016/2017 Academic Year

Termed the Synergy Agenda, the manifesto of the Tamale Campus SRC President for the 2016/2017 academic year touched on security, sanitation, academics & extra curricula, accommodation, sports and finally, on entertainment. On a scale of 1 - 10, the SRC President of the Campus scored himself 6 and indicated that he could have performed better but financial constraints resulting from delay in release of funds for projects/activities, and interference/slashing of budgets by Management accounted for his performance. He outlined the under listed as his achievements:

- ✓ Introduced Akwaaba-Amaraba newsletter for first year students of the Tamale Campus to help them get accustomed to their new environment easily
- ✓ "Name my hostel" project aimed at locating students of the Campus easily
- ✓ Procured gowns for members of the Judicial Board instead of the original plan of procuring gowns for the General Assembly (GA) leadership
- ✓ Advanced already existing programmes and projects which included water dispenser projects
- ✓ Provided security tags to taxis plying the Tamale Campus road.

He also stated that his administration was able to initiate plans for the construction of an SRC Secretariat, and indicated that the process got to the procurement stage.

He further indicated that the following programmes were not-achieved:

- ✓ The Central SRC legacy project encompassing the bore-hole at Dungu,
- ✓ Generator or power inverter at either the Lab or Library block or Faculty of Education at Choggu.

On reasons for their non-achievement, he indicated that the projects were to be carried out in consultation with major stakeholders but unfortunately, there was inadequate consultation on expert opinion. It was also because of the Central SRC crisis at the Wa campus. Another project that was not achieved was the 5-year development plan (short, medium and long term taking into consideration the resources available) which was geared towards the financial independence of the SRC. It was expected that this independence will make the SRC be in a position to sponsor the various associations where they would in-turn have viable projects to execute.

Non-achievement of the above project was because different administrations had different priorities which they intended to accomplish by themselves within a short period. Also, every administration wanted to be identified with a particular project.

Further, the SRC was not able to purchase chairs and canopies for its office, and also provide extra pavilion at Choggu where the Faculty of Education (FoE) was located (Choggu). The extra pavilion was not provided because plans were far ahead to relocate the Faculty of Education to the Tamale Campus (Dungu).

Other programmes that were not achieved under the Synergy Agenda 2016 were celebration of the `Tamale Campus SRC @ 7 with the theme "A great opportunity to assess our successes, failures and the way forward. Also not achieved was the Council's inability to renovate the main notice boards which would have given it some class and also create space for more notices. Further, the Council was not able to execute the SRC project bank because each association had its own project that it pursued annually. Nonetheless, the SRC was ever ready to support member associations raise funds and logistics for these projects.

In the area of security, the SRC intended to set-up a cadet corps at the student level, which was expected to complement the activities of the University security outfit on the campus. Concerning lighting, the Council intended to have talks with relevant stakeholders including the Metropolitan Chief Executive, Member of Parliament for the Tamale South constituency, Assembly member of the Tamale Campus area, University authorities and hostel owners to address the current lighting system and improve upon them. The Council together with Management of the University and the previous administration was able to provide security tags to taxis plying the Tamale campus.

Because cleanliness is next to Godliness, the SRC resolved to improve the sanitation situation on the campus. Accordingly, the SRC was able to increase the number of dustbins in and around the campus to minimize littering. It also organized an excellence award scheme where the best cleaner was awarded to motivate others to do their best. Further, an award scheme (name and shame) aimed at awarding the neatest class on campus as well as discouraging students from littering the lecture halls was instituted. Again, the Council intended to institute appropriate measures (i.e. employing SRC workers) to improve upon sanitation in the washrooms to enhance healthy living. Unfortunately, Management stopped the Council from embarking on this project with the reason being that this activity was purely the mandate of the University.

On academic and extra curricula activities, the SRC was able to organize four seminars for both student leaders and the general student body. It also liaised with the Transport Committee to facilitate access to bus for practical, lectures etc. outside the Campus. It was able to provide incentives (i.e. certificates, allowances etc.) for course representatives, and also build the capacity of student leaders and students via educative seminars and symposium. The Council intended to create a resource portal on the SRC website to enable students have access to lecture materials, final projects, past lecture presentations etc. online but was unable to achieve this. The Council also intended to institute the SRC "touch-a-life campaign" (disability friendly policies, reserving seats for the underprivileged and physically challenged in the various classes. The campaign was supposed to be a collaborative programme between the SRC, Course representatives and the entire students' body, but unfortunately did not materialize. Nevertheless, a level 300 physically challenged medical student was awarded to boost the morale of the physically challenged.

On accommodation, the SRC intended to establish a non-residential students' accommodation committee (NAC) which was to accredit hostels and check the pricing of hostels. The committee was to work closely with the Rent Control Board, Senior Hall Tutor and the landlords, and was to be in-charge of negotiating rents charged by landlords based on facilities provided. Unfortunately, the SRC was not able to achieve this objective.

On sports and entertainment, the SRC was able to provide the sports team with the necessary incentives and resources that were to aid the team perform well in their activities. Also, the Council was able to purchase two new sets of jerseys for the sports team, and sets of 'Jama' instruments for the supporting team. The SRC intended to institute a departmental sports fiesta in disciplines like football, basketball, volleyball etc. to help promote sports and bring about unity among the various departments. Unfortunately, this was not attainable. Also, in order to get a formidable force as far as sports was concerned, the Council planned to organize a mini gala and inter-departmental games that was to aid in the selection of sportsmen and women. It again planned to make available in-door games such as draft, scrabble, and chess for students to entertain themselves but was unable to execute this noble idea. Provision of table tennis did not also materialize.

On Internal Generation of Funds, the SRC was able to provide students with souvenirs made up of UDS-branded exercise books, stickers, book files, lapels, brochures etc. Also, the Council intended to use the SRC/NUGS website to generate funds by allowing cooperate institutions to run advertisement, but unfortunately this did not materialize.

Further, the intention to produce SRC magazines where cooperate bodies could advertise on it thereby generating funds for the SRC, did not see the light of day.

Activities of the other SRC Presidents of the Wa, Nyankpala and Navrongo Campuses during the 2016/2017 Academic Year

At this juncture, we look at activities and projects carried out by the other SRC Presidents of the Wa, Nyankpala and Navrongo campuses. We enquired from the other SRC Presidents about their planned activities and projects they intended to execute during their tenure in office for the 2016/2017 academic year. We also asked them to indicate the activities and projects that they were unable to execute or achieve and give reasons for the non-achievement.

Activities and Projects undertaken by the Nyankpala Campus SRC President for the 2016/2017 Academic Year

The SRC President of the Nyankpala Campus stated that his administration was able to carry-out the following activities and projects:

1. Purchased two large size poly tanks to increase water supply on the Campus.
2. Bought three-in-one printer for the SRC
3. Established the office of the SRC President to house only the President and got it furnished
4. Provided WiFi to the Great hall and Union hall to help increase internet access on the Campus.
5. Retrieved the SRC container which had been rented out by past executives
6. Renovated radio grin using SRC funds
7. Printed Lacoste for first year students and also provided them with eight (8) gig pen drive (which they paid for)
8. Organized carrier seminar for all students during the SRC week celebration.
9. Printed certificates for all final year course representatives and citation for all committee heads.
10. Bought a fridge for the out- gone Vice- Dean of Students of the Campus and also provided him with a citation.
11. Liaised with management for the renovation of Great hall which had just started (all funds were from management).
12. Supported many students with money us part of their welfare issues.
13. Organized games with outside institutions.

The SRC President of the Campus also indicated that his administration was not able to execute the following projects:

1. Digging of borehole to reduce water crisis on the Campus.
2. Partnering with Prudential Bank to construct an SRC hostel.
3. Organizing awards night to honor all first class and hardworking students.

On reasons for the non-achievement of the above stated projects, the SRC President of the Nyankpala Campus explained that his administration was not able to execute the borehole project because of financial challenges. He also disclosed that he and his team were not able to organize the awards night because of financial challenges. On why the SRC could not partner Prudential Bank to construct an SRC hostel, he explained that it was due to time limit to complete the process. He was however, hopeful that the current executives would be able to complete the process.

Activities and Projects undertaken by the Wa Campus SRC President for the 2016/2017 Academic Year

The SRC President of the Wa Campus outlined the following as activities and projects undertaken and successfully carried out on his campus:

1. Ensured that the radio station at the Wa Campus got accreditation as required by the National Communication Authority (NCA)
2. Introduced an electronic voting system at the Wa Campus for the first time
3. Ensured that over-paid SRC dues by affected students was refunded to them
4. Secured an office for the SRC to ease communication
5. Ensured the automation of lecture halls one and two with proper Public Address (PA) systems
6. Paid a huge sum of debt incurred by the previous administration to pave way for the incoming administration

The SRC President also indicated that his administration was not able to execute the under-listed projects which are:

1. Allowing commercial vehicles (trotro) to operate on the Campus
2. Conducting SRC elections midstream during the second trimester
3. Organizing SRC week celebration during the middle of the second trimester

On reasons for the non- achievement of the above projects, the SRC President of the Campus disclosed that his administration was unable to organize the SRC elections and SRC week celebration as planned. He said, there was the difficulty of accessing funds midstream during the middle of the second trimester. He also disclosed that interference by Management made it difficult for commercial vehicles (trotro) to operate on the Wa Campus. Considering the challenges that he faced both as SRC President of the Wa Campus and Central SRC President, he suggested the following and indicated that Management should try adopting them. They are:

1. Management should help the SRC with a legal practitioner when the SRC is faced with court suits.
2. SRC executives should either be paid monthly or given some rent or fuel allowance to mitigate them.
3. Members of the SRC executive committee should be treated differently from members of other committees. Also, lecturers should be flexible with the marking of their examination script (both mid-trimester and main examinations).
4. SRC executives should be given some incentive (popularly known as ex gratia) at the end of their tenure, as this would serve as a motivation for leading.
5. He added that there should be swift release of funds.

Activities and Projects carried out by the Navrongo Campus SRC for the 2016/2017 Academic Year

The SRC President of the Navrongo Campus indicated that his administration intended to execute projects in the area of academics, welfare, security, infrastructure and entertainment. He said, in the area of academics, the executives intended to achieve the following:

- Ensure that students receive their statement of results at the end of the trimester
- Extend the wireless internet access
- Fix new marker boards in all the halls
- Fix Public Address system in the major halls
- Empower students in entrepreneurship through lectures and symposium
- Conduct election

Under welfare and security, the SRC President of the Campus disclosed that the executives intended to:

- Complete profile of the hostels on the Campus
- Liaise with the municipal assembly for off-campus lightening
- Secure WANABIN project enhance sanitation
- Set up a unit under non-residential student representative from all hostels to bridge the gap between student and the leadership of SRC

In the area of infrastructure, he said his administration intended to:

- Provide summer hut lighting and sockets
- Rebranding of radio FAS and the SRC secretariat

Finally, under entertainment, he said the executives intended to have the following celebrations;

- Akwaaba week for fresh students
- SRC week celebrations

The SRC President of the Campus further indicated that he and his other executives were poised to make major strides in the activities they had outlined. He said, among the set goals the following were achieved by the SRC:

1. Provision of marker boards
2. Organizing of the lectures and symposium
3. Organizing of the fresher's week celebration
4. Organizing of SRC week celebration
5. Profiling of the hostels
6. Extension of wireless internet

The SRC President stated reasons that accounted for the inability of the Council to achieve its planned activities and said that the 2017 SRC was faced with lots of challenges. He outlined the following as some of the challenges:

- Late release of administrative funds
- Central administration handling projects funds
- Interference of the administration in SRC affairs
- Political interest of SRC executives compounded by the national election
- Interference of political parties in student politics.

Conclusion

All in all, we deduced from our interactions with the various SRC Presidents that they often have beautiful manifestos but are unable to execute them during their tenure in office. Late release of funds, interference by Management, and the bureaucratic processes of accessing funds accounted for this. Also, time constraints and limited tenure in office (usually nine months) made it difficult for them to accomplish their intended projects. On that score, we say that "man proposes but God disposes".

Despite the above challenges faced by the SRC executives, they deserve some commendation for their continuous support to Management in undertaking projects on the various campuses and also helping to maintain peace at the students' front. Concluding, we want to appeal to Management to assist the SRC positively to enable them deliver more.

Recommendations

From the above, we wish to make a strong proposal for the UDS SRC to be given a facelift and made more efficient. Accordingly, we wish to make the following recommendations:

1. Management should ensure that funds to the SRC are released on time to enable the SRC executives execute their intended projects.
2. The bureaucratic processes of accessing funds and information should be keenly looked at since it does not auger well for the smooth operation of the SRC.
3. As a form of motivation, SRC executives, especially the various Presidents, should be given accommodation and office space, on their respective campuses, to enable them to be more efficient.
4. Management should institute a waiver for SRC executives in terms of fees to make the position attractive to others.
5. SRC executives should be given ex-gratia allowance after leaving office. We believe this would go a long way to prevent them from all forms of corrupt practices whiles in office.
6. Scholarship for further education should be given to executives. We propose an amount of three thousand Ghana cedis (GHC 3000.00) to be given to any junior member as suggested by one of the executives.
7. Insurance cover should be put in place for SRC executives and heads of committees against any unforeseen contingency/ circumstance befalling any of them whiles in office.
8. We recommend that monies to the SRC should be released quarterly.
9. Management should consider giving each SRC executive a certificate after his/her tenure in office
10. We again recommend the SRC to quit the national mother unions (NUGS) if the need be. This is because the current impasse between the two factions resulting from political infiltration is yet to be resolved.
11. Apathy on the part of students to programs/events should end. Example was the orientation for final year students of the Tamale campus in April 21, 2017 by the National Service Scheme. Patronage by students to programmes is often very low and sometimes, this delays the start of such programmes and almost gets the exercise called off. The SRC needs to do more in that direction because of the tendency to incur extra cost on such programs.

12. Management should stop interfering in students electoral issues. Example is when electoral policies are imposed on the SRC without prior notice to the student's front.
13. Projects started by previous executives should be completed by the new executives and should not be discontinued. Since resources have already gone into such projects, there is the need to complete them so that they do not become white elephants.

References

Wikipedia, the Free Encyclopedia (n. d). Definition of Student Representative Council (SRC). In https://en.wikipedia.org/wiki/Students%27_representative_council. Cited June 20, 2017

7

Healthful School Environment: A Sine-Qua-Non for Sustainable National Development

GEORGE S. T. Ph.D, UDOKOP C. A. Ph.D & UZOH U. V. Ph.D

Introduction

Environment is a critical factor in any form of development, be it human, economic, political, social or cultural. It can make or mar any process, illiteracy inclusive. It comprises both the visible and invisibles; tangible and the intangibles such as structures, layout, equipment, people, the ambience (comprising temperature, noise, radiation, air quality – level of carbon dioxide). These variables, in one way or the other affect the quality of learning, hence quality of development.

School is believed to be the only universal entitlement of the child and school is the only institution that allows access to almost all students from age 5-17 years throughout the world (Idowu, 2017). According to Idowu, apart from preparing pupils or students academically, the school is relied upon to transit culture and socialize the children and youths so that they can adjust better in the society.

A growing body of literature, for example, Tanner (2006) and Jones, Axelrad and Wattigney (2007), has proved that improved physical environments in schools (e.g. indoor air quality, lighting and acoustic conditions) can enhance learners health outcomes as well as academic achievements. In order to achieve these laudable outcomes, the idea therefore, is to design buildings, including facilities that are more sustainable in reducing energy consumption, lessening environmental impact, as well as creating healthier spaces for occupant. The environment is a key factor in all matters relating to human and animal health (Moronkola, 2017). Thus, a conducive learning environment is a sine qua non for excellent academic performance.

The health of learners at all levels of education is very important, if they are to benefit from the school offering. Learners' health can be taken care of at home, school or community.

Hence it becomes appropriate to prepare a good and healthy school environment to enhance the health of learners based on the premises that, it may be very difficult to study in an environment that works at variance with the stipulated environment (Ekpu and Egwuasi, 2011). Moreover, it is a general knowledge that the relationship of human beings and their environment have profound influence on them. Udoh (1999) averred that the school is mandated to provide opportunities which should have favourable influence on knowledge, attitude and behaviour. Such opportunities are channeled through formal health instruction, provision of health services and a conducive environment.

Healthful school environment, also known as healthful school living is a part of school health programme which include: school environment, school feeding and skill-based education. Healthful school environment is an environment that include things which may also be sub-divided into: physical (air, soil, water, wastes, waste disposal, lightening, ventilation, noise, climate, among others); biological (micro-organisms like bacteria, viruses, fungi and various forms of plants and animals); social environment (relationship as determined by culture, customs, norms, habits, occupation and family) and spiritual environment (the way people worship, faith, belief system). Thus, healthful school environment is that which takes care of the health and wellbeing and the safety of learners and other members of the school community (Federal Ministry of Education, 2006). Healthy, educated, disciplined, well informed and skilled people form the bedrock of development in any nation.

Education brings forth literacy; hence the importance of literacy which is mostly obtained through schools cannot be over emphasized. Oladapo as cited in Adedokun and Adeyemo (2011) emphasized that the role of literacy in the development of any society is necessary and indispensable for economic, social, political and technical growth and advancement of any nation. Education/literacy is regarded as human right, and an essential ingredient for achieving equity, development and peace (UNESCO, 1997). Adenrito, Akande and Ogunrin as cited in Adedekin and Adeyemo (2011) posited that literacy creates condition for the acquisition of critical consciousness on the contradictions of the society in which man lives. This means that, literacy stimulates initiates and enhances promotion in any society. According to the authors, literacy is also known to be key to various human developments over the ages. The authors averred that education/literacy has also been viewed as a tool which enables citizens to take their rightful place in the community.

The Sustainable Development Goals (SDGs), or Global Goals, formulated and adopted by all United Nations member states in 2015 is a universal call to exploit, end poverty, protect the planet and ensure that all people live and enjoy peace and prosperity by 2030. The SDGs are integrated – that is, an action in one area will affect outcomes on others and that development must balance social, economic and environmental sustainability.

Education/Literacy

Education in the Nigerian contemporary society is viable when it is focused on societal needs and aspirations, as well as international competitive standards. Education for work, self survival, self-reliance, values and skills for improving the society is in vogue (Mezieobi, 2011). According to Bello as cited in George and Ekpu (2018), education is the bedrock of any nation development, and no nation can rise above the quality of its education system, as quality of its workforce will be determined by the system of education. Education therefore is generally accepted as the leading avenue through the challenging needs of any society should be met.

Aderinoye described a literate, as a person who has acquired the knowledge and skills indispensable to perform all activities for which literacy is necessary in order to play an effective part in his/her community and whose achievement is reading, writing and arithmetic, such that, they are enabled to continue the development of the community and participate actively in the life of his/her community. Thus literacy is a tool that helps and equips one to face his/her challenges without any bias mind. Everyone therefore needs to be literate in order to function properly in the society.

In Nigeria, as well as other countries, education is perceived as a tool for socio-economic and political development and as such, education is accorded the necessary attention. This position is amplified in the Nigerian National Policy on Education which stated that, education is an instrument peer-excellence for effective national development (The National Policy on Education, 2011). Education/literacy, according to Hornby and Wehmecier as cited in Ajibola et al. (2011) is the ability to read and write. It empowers people to develop reading culture and depending on the types of books and reading materials available to them, exposes them to new and scientific information, values and practices, other than what tradition has laid down for them. Ajibola et al. (2011) also posited that Education/literacy serves to remove their attitude against obnoxious cultural practices. This makes room for cultural adjustments and reformations.

Similarly, education/literacy, according to Hilleerich in Oyinloye (2007) is the demonstration of competence in communication skills which enables the individual to function appropriately in his/her age independently in the society. Oyinloye stated that education/literacy no longer looks as the ability to read and write, but the ability to read, write and use computer. Hence, literacy influences and determines to a large extent the growth and development of individuals and this culminates in national development. Education therefore is a veritable tool for national development. To meet the demands of modern life, people need a combination of different forms of literacy, as literacy is not an unborn human characteristic but an ability that is taught, learnt most often in school.

According to Wager (2000), literacy is an individual's ability to understand printed text and to communicate through print. Literacy could be seen as a life skill and the primary learning tools for personal and community development and self-sufficiency in a rapidly changing and increasingly interdependent world. Literacy therefore is seen as a vital tool for communication which makes a person independent of personal contact. This involves reading, writing and arithmetic. According to Archer and Fleshman as cited in Ekpu and Egwuasi (2011), the school has been traditionally known to be an institution where knowledge is being imparted to learners. It is composed of individuals organized into different organizational structures, with specific and defined functions. According to the authors, it is considered a social system because the participants are interdependent and their actions are socially organized or directed towards achieving specific goals.

Accordingly, Ekpu and Egwuasi (2011) posited that there are a number of characteristics which are common to school systems and other formal organizations. One of such is that, a school system, like a business or hospital, has an organizational objective. Another is that it contains a network of interrelated and interdependent roles within an organizational environment. The business of the school therefore is to educate children and adults likewise, and those who occupy positions in schools are involved in achieving this goal. The school authorities therefore can only achieve this goal which is educating children/adults for excellent performance by providing an enabling environment. The school administration is expected to harness the available resources within the school, that is, man, material and money for the betterment of the health and well-being of students and staff.

One of the most important targets of education in a developing and changing world is to raise individuals to think, explore, question, produce, decide by themselves, undertake the responsibility of learning, control their learning processes, take part actively in such processes, and have self-confidence in their capabilities and correctly use their capabilities instead of individual raised with traditional education involving mechanical learning (Tait-McCutocheon, 2008). Similarly, Moronkola and Ogunmola (2015) asserted that the main purposes of the school as a social institution is to ensure that learners acquire knowledge and are socialized so as to be knowledgeable social beings. By so doing, learners will be able to relate well with fellow learners and staff and live in harmonious way in the larger society by blending with prevailing positive social values. The importance of school is enormous as it helps learners to develop their social skills (analytical mind, communication, confidence, personal organization, teamwork, obedience, ability to face challenges) and reduce violence in well-ordered societies among others.

Healthful School Environment

Gold (2002) as cited in Anspaugh and Ezeli (2013) stated that the Joint Committee and Health Education Terminology sees health "as an integrated method of functioning which is orientated towards maximizing the potential of which the individual is capable. It requires that the individual maintains a continuum where he/she is functioning". Sunderlal, Adarsh and Pankaj (2009) attested that health is difficult to define but easier to understand as many people see it as absence of disease or infirmity and to many it may mean sound body and sound function of the body.

Moronkola (2017) believed that health is the ability of a person to live a life that is socially and economically acceptable to self and others at a particular period and within the context of one's environment and genetic make-up. Health may also be viewed as that ability and capacity of an individual to cope with all daily demand to effectively function physically, mentally, emotionally, spiritually and in line with the person's genetic make-up. According to Moronkola, it is an individual personal asset that enables one to meet normal needs and challenges of life. It is therefore a means to an end in achieving one's desires in life e.g. excelling in academics, industry, governance, sports and commerce among others.

Generally, a school is regarded as a place or institution where teaching-learning takes place. Schools are of different types – depending on the age of the learners, the emphasis on what type of learning should take place and reason for its establishment. Thus a school has a definite location(s), is well-structured, and manages to provide learning spaces. The school is also an avenue for socialization, acquisition of necessary evidence-based knowledge and skills for the good of the learner, the community and the whole world at large (Moronkola, 2017). Schools, because of their location and prominence in societies, and because of the significant high percentage of children that attend them at some stage in their lives, are considered the ideal avenue, through which most education can be achieved. According to Bello as cited in George and Ekpu (2018) schools also have the obvious advantage of reaching all sectors of society regardless of their gender, social status, religion, ethnic or physical fitness skill, level and age.

The concept of healthful school was developed over a century ago. The aim was to achieve healthy lifestyle for the total school population by developing conducive environment to the promotion of health. The following are ten basic components of the healthful school:

I. Investment in schooling must be improved and expanded.
II. The full educational participation of girls must be expanded.
III. Every school must provide safe learning environment for students and safe working place for staff.

IV. Every school must enable children and adolescents of all levels to learn critical health and life skills.
V. Every school must serve as an entry point for healthy promotion and a location for health intervention.
VI. Policies, legislation and guidelines must be developed to ensure the identification, allocation, mobilization and coordination of resources at the local, national and international levels to support school health.
VII. Teachers and school staff must be properly valued and provided with the necessary support to enable them promote health.
VIII. The community and the school must work together to support health and education.
IX. School health programme must be well designed, monitored and evaluated to ensure their successful implementation and outcome.
X. International support must be further developed to enhance the ability of member states, local communities and schools to promote health and education.

According to Lucas and Gillas (2003), a man's total environment includes all the living and non-living elements in their surroundings. It consists of three major components: the physical, biological and social. Thus, Healthful School Environment is that environment where the physical, biological and social environment is working optimally.

1. The Physical Environment

Physical entails air, soil, water, wastes, waste disposal, lighting, ventilation, noise, climate, among others. Ajala (2002) averred that to promote the physical environment, there is need to prevent accidents in schools and that this can be done through safety education and proper environmental management. School healthful environment must be addressed as the situation is getting worse especially in public school from primary to universities. Hence, Moronkola (2017) posited that it is open secret that most public schools are without chairs, tables, windows, doors, toilet facilities, overcrowded classrooms, ill-equipped laboratories, lack of simple first aid boxes, unkempt school compounds, schools without gates or less security, leading to kidnapping of students and staff.

Ademuwagun and Ajala (2002) emphasized that prevention does not lie primarily in devising more and more safety devices, however, important as this may be, it's in improving man's knowledge, skills, attitude and habits. Safer livings does not require freedom from all potentially hazardous conditions, for this is neither possible nor desirable; rather it requires the ability to function at optimum level in the presence of necessary hazards, therefore there is need for safety education in an enabling school environment for academic achievements. One of the physical determinants of an enabling school environment is the location of the school. Adepoju and Akinwumi (2002) observed that some schools are built near highways or near markets or industrial centers, and does not favour learning. According to Ekpu and Egwuasi (2011), one needs some basic things like desk or table and a chair, enough light, a place to store paper, pencils, pen, books and other study materials. According to the authors, most importantly one must try to avoid noise and other visual distraction. Similarly, Udo (2005) posited that if one is to study successfully, one needs a conducive atmosphere to work in as well as suitable tool. Most importantly try to avoid noise and other visual distraction.

2. The Biological Environment

Lucas and Gilles (2003) viewed this as all the living things in an area: plants, animals and micro-organisms. Since plants have been listed as one of the biological components of the school environment, the idea therefore is to provide the environment with the beautiful plants/flowers, plant trees to check erosion where applicable and also provide shade. Ekpu and Egwasi (2011) posited that efforts should be made to ensure that there is no stagnant water within the school environment. This, according to the authors, is to discourage the breeding of mosquitoes, insects and rodents. This preventive strategy is to ensure that children do not contact diseases from school environment. Moreover, school environment with beautifully planted flowers, trees and shrubs raise aesthetic values of the school, attract children, boost their ego and promote learning.

3. The Social Environment

The aspect of the school environment is entirely made by the people. It basically concerns the relationships between the students, staff, community and within the students themselves. A healthful school community is a school that promotes the health of the community. The psychological or emotional environment in educational institutions involves relationship between staff and staff, students and staff and students and students in their day to day activities. Hence, Moronkola (2003[a]) noted that for effective learning to take place, both the teachers and students must be psychologically ready to perform the task. Most Nigerian schools of today are persistently repeatedly exposed to many evils and distractions that negatively affect the social, psychological and mental health of both staff and students, including the host community.

Moronkola (2003[b]) listed such evils like strikes by staff, violent demonstration, sexual malpractices including sexual harassment, cultism, bullying, drug abuse, dilapidated buildings, poor electricity and water supply, poor sitting arraignment and reading facilities which do not promote academic excellence. Thus, Moronkola and Oginmola (2015) contended that school location, leaderships, policy, size, amenities, facilities for teaching and research all affect the well-being of staff and students, and to some extent the host community.

Objectives of Healthful School Environment

The Federal Ministry of Education (Nigeria) (2006) listed the following as objective of healthful school environment:

(i) to provide a safe and conducive living and learning condition that maximizes the benefits from educational programmes;
(ii) to promote healthy practices among learners and staff in order to prevent water and sanitation related illnesses and diseases;
(iii) to bring about positive change in hygienic behaviour of learners and the community at large;
(iv) to provide safe recreational facilities in the school;
(v) to organize school health days;
(vi) to establish interpersonal relationship within the school community and
(vii) to encourage compliance with approved environmental health and sanitation standard for schools.

Hence the characteristics of healthful school environment or conditions required for healthful school include:

(i) location of the schools away from potential environmental hazard;
(ii) protection of the school community from excessive noise, heat, cold and dampness;
(iii) provision of adequate buildings, constructed in line with approved standards, with particular emphasis on facilities for learners with disabilities;
(iv) provision of an appropriate and adequate and adequate number of furniture for learner and staff;
(v) provision of an adequate number of gender sensitive toilet facilities;
(vi) provision of adequate safe water supply and sanitation facilities for the school community;
(vii) provision of proper drainage and water disposal facilities;
(viii) provision of safe recreation and sports facilities;
(ix) permanent fencing of the school;
(x) observation of annual school health day.
(xi) promotion of healthy human relationships in the school community.
(xii) promotion of health related school policies and
(xiii) promotion of maintenance culture (Moronkola, 2017).

Health Promoting Schools

A health promoting school can be described as a school that is constantly strengthening its capacity as a healthy setting for living, learning and working. A health promoting school;

i. Strives to improve the health of school personnel, family and community members as well as students.
ii. Fosters health and learning with all the members at disposal.
iii. Engages health and education officials, teachers, teachers' union, students, parents, health providers and community leaders in effort to make the school a healthy place.
iv. Strives to provide a healthy environment, school health education, school health services along with school/community projects, health promotion programmes for staff/students, nutrition and food safety programmes, opportunities for physical education and recreation and progorammes for counseling, social support and mental health promotion.
v. Implements policies and practices that respect an individual wellbeing and dignity, provide multiple opportunities for success and acknowledges goal effort and intention as well as personal achievement.

Four main strategies were used by the World Health Organization (WHO) to disseminate this framework and these include;

i. Consolidating researchers and experts opinion to describe the nature and effectiveness of school health programme.
ii. Building capacity to advocate for Healthy Promoting School (HPS). Priority health issues e.g. helminthes infection, violence, nutrition, tobacco use HIV/STIs were tackled.
iii. Strengthening collaboration between the ministries of education and health and other relevant organizations and national capacities to improve school health.
iv. Creating network and alliance. This is demonstrated by network among which are WHO, Education International, UNESCO, USAID, CDC to strengthen the capacities of teachers union to prevent HIV/STIs (Idowu, 2007).

Sustainable Development Goals

In 2015, the United Nationals General Assembly formally adopted the Universal Integrated and Transformation 2030 Agenda for Sustainable Development, a set of 17 Sustainable Development goals (SDGs). The goals are to be implemented and achieved in every country from the year 2016 to 2030. The broad goals were interrelated though each has its own target to achieve. The total number of target is 169. The SDGs cover a broad range of social and economic development issues. These include poverty, hunger, health, education, climate change, gender equality, water, sanitation, energy, environment, social justice, among others (United Nation (UN), 2014). The 17 SDGs are:

1) End poverty in all its forms everywhere
2) End hunger, achieve food security and improved nutrition, and promote sustainable agriculture
3) Ensure healthy lives and promote wellbeing for all at all ages
4) Ensure inclusive and equitable quality education and promote lifelong learning opportunities for all
5) Achieve gender equality and empower all women and girls
6) Ensure availability and sustainable management of water and sanitation for all
7) Ensure access to affordable, reliable, sustainable and modern energy for all
8) Promote sustained, inclusive and sustainable economic growth, full and productive employment, and decent work for all
9) Build resilient infrastructure, promote inclusive and sustainable industrialization, and foster innovation
10) Reduce inequality within and among countries
11) 1Make cities and human settlements inclusive, safe, resilient and sustainable
12) Ensure sustainable consumption and production patterns
13) Take urgent action to combat climate change and its impacts (taking note of agreements made by the UNFCCC forum)
14) Conserve and sustainably use the oceans, seas and marine resources for sustainable development
15) Protect, restore and promote sustainable use of terrestrial ecosystems, sustainably manage forests, combat desertification and halt and reverse land degradation, and halt biodiversity loss
16) Promote peaceful and inclusive societies for sustainable development, provide access to justice for all and build effective, accountable and inclusive institutions at all levels
17) Strengthen the means of implementation and revitalize the global partnership for sustainable development

These 17 Sustainable Development Goals (SDGs) are designed to bring the world to several life-changing 'zeros', including zero poverty, hunger, AIDS and discrimination against women and girls. Although, few developed countries had advocated pruning these robust ideals, some countries have committed to fast-track progress for those furthest behind first, through the pledge to 'Leave No One Behind'. In line with this, involvement of every individual is required to attain these ambitious targets. The creativity, knowhow, technology and financial resources from all of society are necessary to achieve the

SDGs in every context and schools are cognate partner in this campaign (United Nations Development Programme, 2020).

Healthful School Environment and Sustainable National Development

A school is an institution for educating learners. School also provides exposure to activities, ideas, and fields of knowledge that one might never encounter otherwise. School is important because it is a tool to help prepare one for life. Not only can one learn the basic skills to read, write, and do arithmetic but can also learn about peoples, places, and nature (Pennsylvania State University, 2015).

A positive school environment is defined as a school having appropriate facilities, well-managed classrooms, available school-based health supports, and a clear, fair disciplinary policy. These are some of the many hallmarks of schools with a positive climate. With this type of environment, healthy, skilled and productive citizens are produced. Citizens that know and value development will surely develop policies to implement and sustain them.

What catches the sight and the mind of any individual when entering a new place is, the physical environment - the layout plan, the lawns, the flowers, the structures and the pathways. It could be repulsive or attractive. An environment with high aesthetic values creates a positive psychological impression on individuals, which in turn triggers the brain to release pleasure hormone (dopamine)which in turn gives individuals positive boost and drive to quest and achieve worthwhile objectives and goals that environment can provide. Physical structures constitute the basis of educational environment. A critical point, which should be borne in mind at the design stage of every structure, is their ability to deliver their intents and their compatibility with the physically challenged learners and teachers. This group of special people forms part of the nation's economic force and should be properly and adequately integrated into the learning system.

Learning infrastructure includes suitable spaces to learn. This is one of the most basic elements necessary to ensure access to education. School classrooms are the most common place in which structured learning takes place with groups of learners. Apart from buildings, fixtures and equipment are necessary for effective and efficient operation of the program of public education. These include libraries, rooms and space for physical education, space for fine arts, restrooms, specialized laboratories, cafeterias, media centers, building equipment, staff rooms, among others.

The quality of school buildings can help or hinder learning and teaching. Well-designed buildings and pleasant surroundings can lead to better attendance and concentration as well as motivation and self-esteem - factors which can improve performance. Studies have demonstrated that facilities themselves have a huge impact on student behavior, grades, teacher tenure and even community satisfaction, (Okcu, Ryherd and Bayer, 2011; Zippin, 2014).

Student Behavior – studies show a relationship between the physical learning environment and student behavior. Broken Window Theory states that physical disorder, such as broken windows, run-down buildings, among others, leads to bad behavior and disorderly conduct. School facilities that are not in great condition could be the cause of poor student behavior and conduct in the classroom (bullying and truancy). This negates the philosophy of SDG 4; Student Achievement – facilities have the power to weaken or improve the teaching and learning environment. Higher grades have been associated with the design and condition of school facilities (Tanner, 2006). Studies in different geographic areas have even shown a link between facilities and teacher tenure. Teachers are more likely to stay in their job if the school is in good condition. All these attributes, aggregate in the making of well informed and productive people, who would inadvertently embrace sustainable development as well as execute them.

It is obvious that, as the world's population grows, more resources and policies are needed to ensure that learners everywhere get a good education. The world needs two million teachers and four million new classrooms to make sure every student can get an education. Full access to quality education is the first step to achieving sustainable development, poverty eradication, gender equality and women's empowerment. There are five primary facets of physical environmental impact as predisposed by school facilities, such as: acoustics/noise, air quality, lighting, temperature, and space. These are addressed as follows;

(i) Noise levels greatly affect teacher and student performance. In fact, excessive noise causes dissatisfaction and stress in both teachers and students. Research has found that schools that have classrooms with less external noise are positively associated with greater student engagement and achievement compared to schools with classrooms that have noisier environments. Thus, building schools that buffer external noise from classrooms can improve student outcomes and achievements (Krüger and Zannin, 2004).

(ii) Indoor air quality is also a concern because poor air quality is a major contributor to absenteeism for students with asthma. Research also indicates that many schools suffer from "sick building syndrome" which affects the absenteeism and performance of all students. Moreover, bacteria, viruses, and allergens that contribute to childhood disease are commonly found in schools with poor ventilation systems. Indoor pollutants are also emitted from office equipment, flooring materials, paints, adhesives, cleaning products, pesticides, and insects.

All of these environmental hazards can negatively affect children, particularly in schools with poor ventilation systems (Mendell & Heath, 2005).These can affect the development of the total man and productivity negatively.

(iii) Research has shown that artificial lighting has negative impacts on those in schools while natural lighting has positive impacts (Hathaway, 1995). The author stated that not only does classroom lighting boost the morale of teachers and students, appropriate amounts of natural lighting also reduces off-task behavior and improves test scores. Hathaway in his study found that students with the most exposure to natural daylight progressed 20% faster in math and 26% faster in reading than students who were taught in environments with the least amount of natural light.

(iv) One consistent research finding across individuals of all ages is that the temperature in which a person works affects engagement levels and overall productivity, including student achievement. The ideal temperature range for effective learning in reading and mathematics is between 20°C and 23.3°C.To maintain such a temperature in every classroom within a school, teachers typically need to be able to control the temperature in their own classroom. At the very least, teachers should be able to control the temperature of small blocks of classrooms that receive the same amount of sunlight and have similar exposures to outside temperatures (Pennsylvania State University, 2019).

Studies by the Pennsylvania State University (2019), affirmed that overcrowded classrooms and schools have consistently been linked to increased levels of aggression in students. Overcrowded classrooms are also associated with decreased levels of student engagement and, therefore, decreased levels of learning. Alternatively, classrooms with ample space are conducive; providing appropriate learning environments for students and is associated with increased student engagement and learning. Classroom space is particularly relevant with the current emphasis on 21st century learning such as ensuring learners can work in teams, solve problem and communicate effectively; classrooms with adequate space to reconfigure seating arrangements and facilitate the use of different teaching methods that are aligned to contemporary skills. Creating private study areas as well as smaller learning centers reduces visual and auditory interruptions, and is positively related to student development and achievement (Duncanson, 2003).

According to the Pennsylvania State University (2019), policymakers, educators, and business people are now focused on the need to ensure that the students learn contemporary skills such as teamwork, collaboration, effective communication, and other skills. As noted above, older buildings simply are not conducive to the teaching of 21st century skills. This is particularly true with the respect to reconfiguring seating arrangements to facilitate various modes of teaching and learning and the use of technology in the classroom as a mode of teaching and learning. Conducive school environments enhance quality teaching and learning which in turn produces educated and well informed individuals who will understand and appreciate the need for sustainable development and likewise implement them.

School age children for basic education are between the ages of 5 to 15 years of age, and they form ¼ of the world's population with about half of them in schools. They undergo rapid physical and mental development at this age. They are very moldable at this age. They are tomorrow's leaders. They are the survivors of the high childhood mortality and so may bear the squeal of these diseases. Higher education age in Nigeria starts from 16 years legally. Learners spend about seven to eight hours in school. So, there is no denying the fact that school has an important and lifelong impact on their socialization developmental process. Apart from teaching children to read and write, and commencing them in subjects such as math, languages and science (which is schools' main function), they also have a latent function of nurturing within the learners, the value of teamwork, punctuality and following a set schedule (to make them responsible citizens). In other words, a lesson stressing on the necessity for discipline in carrying out one's daily activities is pinpointed.

Schools also play a major role in fostering the values of national pride and citizenship in the children. For instance, school children in Nigeria and some other nations, have to take the Pledge of Allegiance. In schools, children also learn about concepts such as gender and race, not only through their textbooks but also practically. For example, segregating the seating arrangements of boys and girls may affect their behavior with the opposite sex thus elevating gender differences; thus affecting SDG 4 negatively. Also, learners' formal learning environment is technically the institution wherein a child is first exposed to a hierarchical bureaucratic setup under which everything takes place within a set framework of rules and regulations. This means that a child, in order to get something done, has to follow a certain procedure and that makes this kind of setup a basic factor for making the child understand the importance of social rules and regulations (Balogun, 2010).This setting will also create or improve in them the sense of social equity and gender equality and the need to implement and sustain such values.

Healthy students not only excel academically but are more likely to be positively engaged in social, community, and extracurricular activities. The benefits of supporting student health and wellness are far-reaching and beneficiary to economic growth and sustainable development of the nation. Zippin (2014) reported that student achievement is often purely looked at from the perspective of the strength of the curriculum and the quality of the teachers. However, study after study demonstrates that facilities themselves have a huge impact on student behavior, grades, teacher tenure and even community satisfaction.

The role of teachers and other staff members in a healthy school environment is to impress upon the children the primary hygienic requirements like cleaning of teeth, eyes, ears, combing, cleaning and cutting of hair, nails, wearing clean clothes etc., which should be according to the prevailing season. If any abnormal symptoms are detected then priority should be given to inform the parents promptly.

Often times, general administration or management of a learning facility could be quite palpable; and feasibly felt, thus, giving it a sense of a felt-environment. Policies, rules and regulations that will nurture learners into responsible, productive individuals, who sustainably build a nation are introduced and taught.

Adequate security of school environment provides safe and conducive learning and teaching environment for all parties in the facility. Teachers have a sense of freedom and relaxed mind to concentrate on knowledge and skills impartation, while the learners, with the sense of a safe atmosphere are readily open to assimilation and understanding. Secure environment precludes fears of kidnap or harassment, hence the enhancement of teaching and learning. With good physical and mental health, learners are bound to develop good attention and concentration in their lessons; thus supporting SDG 3 & 4.

Aside from influencing and building the occupants, the physical condition of facilities can also affect community members. Housing prices change based on the quality and appearance of schools, which can in turn affect incoming student population, the number of community events held in school facilities, community involvement with school activities, and more. It is worthy of mention that, the social and cultural attributes of the community contribute in no small measure - positively or negatively on the school or its learning outcomes and goals

In a healthy school environment, learners, parents, staff, administration and community support the learners wellness policy, nutrition education and school meals programs with the shared values of healthy eating, active living and sustainable environmental practices; all in a bid to support the nurturing of quality and productive minds. A healthy school environment implements the viable policies and practices consistently, every day, in the schools, before and after school programs. Healthy bodies and brains translate into improved academic performance and attendance. It develops learners that make informed healthy choices, establishing a positive example for the health and longevity of the community and the environment. A healthy school environment is a commitment; thus supporting SDGs in particular and SDGs 1, 2, 3 and 4 in general.

Conclusion

A healthful school environment is that which takes cares of the health as well as the safety of learners and other members of the school community. It has implications in all areas of school health. It addresses physical and aesthetic surrounding, psychological climate and culture of the school community, so that maximum benefits of/from education can be achieved. Hence the provision of healthful school environment guarantees productivity of students and staffs. Thus, services, facilities and tools need for the physical, social and emotional well-being of the school community members must be addressed, safeguarded and maintained. The long standing sub-optimal physical, mental and emotional environments of schools of all level have resulted in graduates with non-productive aptitudes.

Schools are the bastions of development. Education is a key fact in sustainable development goals' implementation and sustainability. Information, knowledge and training are composites of development. People and nations can only develop through training and research. This is the reason advocates call for improved funding for education; stressing that, illiteracy and poverty are obstacle to SDGs. Observation and analysis suggest or seem to place SDGs 3 and 4 at the center of the goals' achievement. This is based on the fact that with a healthy body, sound information, knowledge and training, individual and nations are well equipped to do the right things and implement worthwhile policies that SDGs stand for, which will lead to sustainable development. It is roundly acknowledge that, the level of educational standard of any nation determines the principles and focus on which such nations are run. Making a sound investment in quality education by ensuring that primary and secondary schools are free for every child, in order to produce well educated human beings, have great potentials sustainable development in their nations.

Recommendations

Based on the discussions above, it is recommended that:

(1) Bullying/violence/cultism should be stopped in schools.
(2) To ensure buildings within schools are of modern standard, especially classrooms and staff rooms.
(3) Schools should ensure adequate lightening within the classrooms and buildings.
(4) Schools should be well sited as most eager proprietors of private schools just establish schools with utter disregard to the rules governing the location of schools.
(5) Facilities should be adequately provided for learners so that they can always study with relative ease.
(6) Learners should not be allowed to go to school hungry, as they cannot study properly or assimilate when hungry.

(7) Prospective proprietors should consider the aesthetic aspect of the school when planning to establish a school knowing that this attracts children and also facilitates learning.

(8) Finally, school authority should endeavour to provide basic learning/ICT facilities to make teaching and learning more convenient for both staff and students.

References

Adedokim, M. O. and Adeyemo, C. W. (2011). Literacy and women development in Nigeria. In B. O. Ogundele, O. A. Moronkola and J. F. Babalola (Eds.), *Education, Health and Sports: the Way forward.* Ibadan: Department of Human Kinetics and Health Education, University of Ibadan, Nigeria, pp. 1-12.

Adepoju, T. L. and Akinwumi, F. S. (2002). Location of secondary schools as a factor in determining academic performance of students in senior schools certificate examination in Oyo State, Nigeria *Ibadan Journal of Educational Studies,* 2 (1): 462-469.

Ajala, J. A. (2002). Safety education. In Ademuwagun, Z. A., Ajala, J. A., Oke, E. A., Moronkola, O. A. and Jegede, A. S. (Eds.). *Health Education and Health Promotion.* Ibadan: Royal People Ltd., pp. 142-149.

Ajibola, C. A., Akpan, S. C., Ogunjimi, L. O. and Emeribe, V. C. (2011). Literacy for cultural reformations: its perspective in the control of HIV/AIDS. In B. O. Ogundele, O. A. Moronkola and J. F. Babalola (Eds.), *Contemporary Issues in Education, Education, Health and Sports: the Way forward.* Ibadan: Department of Human Kinetics and Health Education, University of Ibadan, Nigeria.

Akan, N. A., Nkangineme, K. E. O. and Oruamabo, R. S. (2000). The school health programme: A situational revist. *Nigerian Journal of Paediatric,* 28 (1): 1-6.

Akani, A. O. and Nkanginieme, K. E. O. (2006) National school health policy by the Federal ministry of education. Policy guidelines on school sanitation by the federal republic of Nigeria, 2005. Available atwww.healthiersf.orgwww.who.int Accessed on 02/12/2019

Anspaugh, D. J. and Ezele, G. (2013). *Teaching today's health.* (10th ed.). Boston: Person.

Balogun T. M. (2010). Available at http://www.authorstream.com/Presentation/premalatha.v-1400495-21-school-health-services/Accessed on 02/12/2019

Baron, R. A. (1972). Aggression as a function of ambient temperature and prior anger arousal. *Journal of Personality and Social Psychology, 21*(2), 183.

Duncanson, E. (2003). Classroom space: right for adults but wrong for kids. *Educational Facility Planner,* 38(1): 24-8.

Ekpu, F. S. and Egwuasi, P. I. (2011). Enhancing academic excellence through an enabling school environment. In B. O. Ogundele, O. A. Moronkola and J. F. Babalola (Eds.), *Contemporary Issues in Education, Education, Health and Sports: the Way forward.* Ibadan: Department of Human Kinetics and Health Education, University of Ibadan, Nigeria.

Federal Ministry of Education (2006). *Implementation guidelines on national school health programme.* Abuja: Federal Ministry of Education, Nigeria.

Federal Republic of Nigeria (2011). *The national policy on education*, Lagos: Federal Government Press.

George, S. T. and Ekpu, F. S. (2018). Social predictors of contents of school health education in secondary schools. In I. P. E. Eyam, D. A. Aboho and P. I. Egwuasi (Eds.), *Nigeria Education Curriculum: Issues, Challenges and Prospects.* Onitsha: West and Solomon Publishing Company Ltd.

Hathaway, W. E. (1995). Effects of school lighting on physical development and school performance. *The Journal of Educational Research, 88*: 228-42.

Idowu, B. B. (2017). An overview of school health programme. In O. A. Moronkola (Ed.). *Health Education for Tertiary Institution Student.* Ibadan: Royal Publishers, pp 101-118.

Jones, S. E., Axelrad, R., and Wattigney, W. A. (2007). Healthy and safe school environment, part II, physical school environment: Results from the school health policies and programs study 2006. *Journal of School Health,* 77(1): 544-556.

Krüger, E. L., and Zannin, P. H. (2004). Acoustic, thermal and luminous comfort in classrooms. *Building and Environment*, 39(9), 1055-1063.

Lucas, A. O. and Gilles, A. M. (2003). *Short textbook of Public health medicine in the tropics* (4th ed.) London: Edward Arnold.

Mendell, M. J., and Heath, G. A. (2005). Do indoor pollutants and thermal conditions in schools influence student performance? A critical review of the literature. *Indoor Air*, 15(1): 27-52.

Mezieobi, D. I. (2001). Repositioning social studies for sustainable life long education in Nigeria Universities. In B. O. Ogundele, O. A. Moronkola and J. F. Babalola (Eds.), *Contemporary Issues in Education, Health and Sports: the Way forward.* Ibadan: Department of Human Kinetics and Health Education, University of Ibadan, Nigeria, pp 136-156.

Moronkola, O. A. (2003). Health promoting school: our precious need. In Ayodele-Bamisaiye, O., Nwazuoke, I. A. and Okediran, A. (Eds.) *Education this millennium; Innovations in theory and practices.* Ibadan: Macmillan.

Moronkola, O. A. (2003). *School health programme*. Ibadan: Royal People Nig. Ltd.

Moronkola, O. A. (2017). *School health programme in Nigeria: A Jewel in Search of True Love.* An Inaugural lecture. Ibadan: University of Ibadan, pp 46-52.

Moronkola, O. A. and Ogunmola, P. O. (2015). School violence in Nigeria. Aetiological factors and preventive. *Nigerian School Health Journal,* 27 (2): 104-112.

Okcu, S., Ryherd, E. and Bayer, C. (2011) The role of physical environment on student health and education in green schools. *Reviews on Environmental Health,* 26(3):169-179.

Pennsylvania State University (2019) The Importance of School Facilities in Improving Student Outcomes. Available at https://sites.psu.edu/ceepa/2015/06/07/the-importance-of-school-facilities-in-improving-student-outcomes/ Accessed on 05/12/2019.

Sunderlal, Adarsh and Pankaj. (2009). *Textbook of Community Medicine* (2nd ed.) New Delhi: CSB Publishers and Distributors.

Tait-McCutcheon, S. L. (2008). *Self-Efficiency in Mathematics: Affective, Cognitive, and conctive Domains of functioning.* Proceedings of 31st Annual conference of the Mathematic Education Research Group of Australia, Brisbane, 28 June -1 July, 2008.

Tanner, C. K. (2006). Effects of the school's physical environment on student achievement. Educational Planning, 15 (2): 25-44.

Udoh, C. O. (1999). *Teaching health education.* Ibadan: Kiitams, pp 31-38.

Udoh, I. I. L. (2005). Maintaining a healthy study habit in secondary school. *Journal of Applied Literacy and Learning,* 2:91-98.

United Nation (UN) (2014). *Press-release-UN – General assembly Open working Propose Sustainable Development Goals.* Sustainable development un.org.

UNESCO (1997). *The Hamburg declaration of adult learning (CONFINITEAV) Agenda for the future of adult education and development.* Paris: United Nations Educational Scientific and cultural organization.

United Nations Development Programme (2020) Sustainable Development Goals: Deadline 2030. https://www.undp.org/content/undp/en/home/sustainable-development-goals.html

Wager, D. A. (2010). *Literacy and Adult Education executive summary.* Adult Education Development, Germany: Thenec Druck, pp. 129-139.

Zippin, S. (2014). Community Blogs: How does your school's physical environment affect students? Available at https://www.dudesolutions.com/community/discover/blogs/how-does-your-schools-physical-environment-affect-students. Accessed on 05/12/2019.

8

Blended Learning: An Innovative Approach to Learning in Nigerian Higher Institutions

AJOKU Lawrence I. Ph.D & CHINDAH Worokwu Ph.D

Introduction

The search for an effective and viable system of education in Nigeria that will address the high unemployment rate of Nigerian youths, has led to curricula reforms at various levels of education. This development as observed by Onyia (2011) is not only peculiar to Nigeria but also in developed countries like Russia and America. Education is viewed as an effective tool that can be used to respond rapidly to the changing needs and aspirations of any nation. An innovative curriculum will therefore seek to accommodate what is needed in the education system in order to create employment and eradicate poverty in the nation. Implementing this innovative curriculum will demand innovative approaches hence the need for blended teaching and learning.

Blended learning, which is the focus of this paper, is seen as an innovative approach to learning. For many educators and trainers, a blended learning approach provides innovative educational solutions through an effective mix of traditional classroom teaching with mobile learning and online activities. The need for blended learning is to promote efficient teaching and learning toward enhancing the academic performance of both teachers and students. The traditional model has not been good enough in enhancing students' involvement and improving better performance. One very obvious challenge of the traditional method of teaching and learning is that it is teacher-centred, making the students less involved in the process of learning. With advances in technology however, a more efficient method has been evolved to balance the involvement in the process of learning, of making students part of their process of learning. The big difference is that students can teach themselves and learn according to their own time, space, methods and pace. It is to this end of corporate involvement of teachers and students in the learning process, their active, conscious and fuller participation that the concept of blended learning finds its relevance. The traditional educational system considers a teacher as the main player and the whole learning operation depends completely on him. In the blended learning, teachers represent one of the tools provided by the educational corporation.

Blended learning environment integrates the advantages of e-learning method with some advantageous aspects of traditional method, such as face-to-face interaction. According to Finn and Bucceri (2004), blended learning brings traditional physical classes with elements of virtual education together. Similarly, Thorne (2003) described blended learning as a way of meeting the challenges of tailoring learning and development to the needs of individuals by integrating the innovative and technological advances offered by online learning with the interaction and participation offered in the best of traditional learning. The integration of e-learning environment and traditional learning environment may combine ideally the useful aspects of both methods. Therefore, blended learning is essentially a combination of face-to-face and web based environment.

The Concept of Blended Learning

Blended learning as a concept is elusive and so lacks consensus definition. There is this idea that it is a fusion or merger of the traditional classroom model of teaching and learning with modern means of technology – aided model to drive home the teaching – learning process for a better performance of students. It is a style of education in which students learn via electronic and online media as well as traditional face to face teaching. It is the blend of computer-enhancing and face-the -board-and-teacher-model. This technological model is more task-oriented, all engaging, paced at students time, employed at the very comfort of students in and outside of the classrooms. Its assumption is that students perform better compared to the classroom setting which is monological, confrontational and based on the whims and caprices of the school teacher. In blended model, students confront more with the materials either in groups, individually or in the class as directed by teachers. These engage them since anything about using computers attracts the complete attention of the students of this age.

The term "blended learning", "hybrid learning", "technology-mediated instruction", "web-enhanced instruction", and "mixed-mode instruction" are often used interchangeably in research literature. However, Bonks & Graham (2006) defined blended learning as learning systems that combine face-to-face instruction with computer mediated instruction. Currently, the use of the term blended learning mostly involves combining internet and digital media with established classroom forms that require the physical co-presence of teacher and students (Friesen, 2012). Most people agree that blended learning combines teaching and learning methods from face-to-face, mobile and online learning and that it includes elements of both synchronous and asynchronous online learning options.

According to Garrison and Vaughan (2008), blended learning is defined as the thoughtful fusion of face-to-face and online learning experiences. Therefore, the basic principle is that face-to-face oral communication and online written communication are optimally integrated such that the strengths of each are blended into a unique learning experience congruent with the context and intended educational purpose.

Blended learning is used to describe learning that mixes various event-based activities: self-paced learning, live e-learning and face-to-face classrooms. Self-paced learning is what the learner does by executing the e-learning process. Self-paced activities can be taken at the learner's leisure irrespective of time and place. The important thing these days is not only to access knowledge but timely access of relevant and interesting knowledge. The value of self-paced learning is not only that it can reach everyone at anytime and anywhere, but that it can teach the learner appropriately, providing the right skills at the right time. Live e-learning takes place in a virtual classroom at a scheduled time at which learner undertakes to attend. Thus, it enables learners to collaborate with one another, share ideas, and ask questions in real time.

The concept of blended learning is rooted in the idea that learning is not just a one-time event; rather, it is a continuous process. Blending provides various benefits over using any single learning delivery medium alone (Singh, 2003). According to Dziuban, Hartman & Moskai (2004), blended learning should be viewed as a pedagogical approach that combines the effectiveness and socialization opportunities of the classroom with the technologically enhanced active learning possibilities of the online environment, rather than a ratio of delivery modalities. The picture being painted here is that of a traditional classroom environment on one end of the spectrum and on the other end of the spectrum is the student learning at a computer at home. Blended learning is somewhere in the middle (see figure 1).

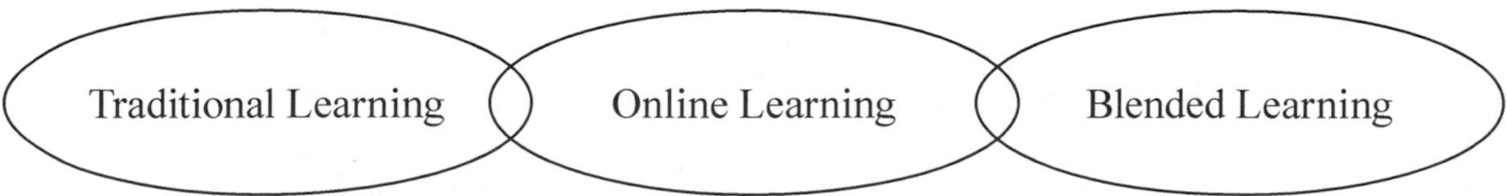

Figure 1: Blended Learning

Education Connection (2013) defines blended learning as computer-mediated instructional strategy that leverages technology and focuses on the student-teacher relationship to enhance independence, engagement and achievement. Basically, blended learning is just a combination of teaching or facilitation methods, learning styles, resource formats, a range of technologies and a range of expertise. Blended learning takes the best from traditional learning and online learning (e-learning). From classical classroom learning, it takes the teacher driven presentation and selection of relevant content; social interaction and the dialogue between the student and teacher. From online learning (e-learning), it benefits from the advantages of self-paced learning, which is, learning anytime everywhere; students can work through a specific task or problem, as often as they want, until they reach their learning goal. In classroom training, this would be impossible. Also, there is the possibility to form virtual groups for specific topics or specific levels of competence. It should be noted that applying blended learning concepts does not mean a radical change, as elements of traditional training are still present. Blended learning is the concept that includes framing teaching and learning process that incorporates both face-to-face teaching and learning supported by information and communication technology (ICT). It incorporates direct instruction, indirect instruction, collaborative teaching and individualized computer assisted learning. In essence, students are learning from their computers as well as they get instruction from their teachers. Blended learning is an instructional methodology that leverages technology to provide a more personalized approach to learning, giving students control over the time, place, path and pace. It is a formal education programme in which the student learns in part through online learning, and partly in a supervised brick – and – mortar location away from home. From an educational perspective, blended learning means courses that integrate online with traditional face-to-face class activities in a planned pedagogically valuable manner; and where a portion of face to face time is replaced by online activity. It is primarily focused on integrating two separate paradigms, the classroom-synchronous and online-asynchronous (Laster, 2005). According to Osgathorpe & Graham (2013), blended learning is the combination of face-to-face with distance delivery systems so that the benefits of face-to-face and online methods can be maximized. Similarly, Owston, York & Murtha (2013), viewed blended learning as the integration of classroom face-to-face learning experiences with online learning experiences. So, it is a combined instructional environment where face-to-face learning and online learning are mixed within a single teaching and learning environment. Furthermore, face-to-face learning refers to the traditional classroom instruction where instructors and learners teach and learn face-to-face in physical classrooms. Online learning, then, refers, to web-based and self-directed learning either synchronously or asynchronously at computers. This involves the use of various virtual resources and tools such as online learning materials, charts, message boards and net meetings. We can simply say that blended learning is an approach to education that combines online educational materials and opportunities for interaction with traditional place-based classroom methods. It requires the physical presence of both teacher and student, with some elements of student control over time, place, path or pace.

Components of Blended Learning

There are three main components of blended learning as shown in figure 2 below.

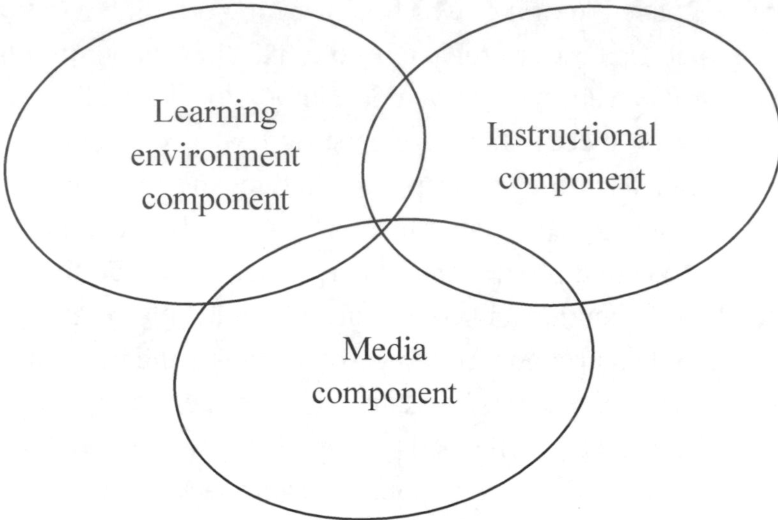

Figure 2: Components of Blended Learning

- **Learning Environment Component:** A learning environment can either be synchronous or asynchronous. Each learning environment has a distinct set of advantages and disadvantages. The goal of blended learning is to leverage the specific positive attributes of each environment to ensure the optimum use of resources to attain the instructional goal and learning objectives.
- **Media Component:** Media refers to vehicles that simply deliver content. Some instructional media, however, may be more appropriate than others in supporting either a synchronous or asynchronous learning environment, but no single medium is inherently better or worse than any other. Whereas a given delivery medium might not alter the desired content, the selection of a particular medium may affect how you design the content to take advantage of unique attributes of that specific medium. Nevertheless, when the most appropriate media are selected, learning outcomes will not be affected – it is the instructional strategies employed that does.
- **Instructional Component:** This component is used to select the most appropriate instructional strategies that support the learning objectives. Such strategies are the products of learning objectives and serve to ensure the transfer of learning. When developing blended learning, maintaining instructional quality is paramount.

Models of Blended Learning

Blended learning comes in a wide variety of implementation models. This part summarizes the range of suggested models of blended learning. It may help to understand the many ways in which online learning blends with and supports traditional learning strategies. According to Wilson (2013), blended learning can be categorized into six models in terms of their delivery.

1) **Face–to–face Model:** This model allows teachers to use technology in the classroom in particular situations to help those students who have capacities more than their peers to advance ahead and achieve better learning. This model will also be used to help students who face problems with keeping up with the class pace-especially in language learning classes.
2) **The Rotation Model:** You have some students who get instruction from their teacher, some students work together in collaboration and some students work on their computers. They rotate throughout those stations throughout the day. So, this approach entails students working in a number of different activities or centers, including whole-group instruction, small group instruction, peer-to-peer activities, pencil and paper assignments, as well as individual work on a computer or tablet. Within the rotation model, there are several different implementation settings:
    - o **Station Rotation:** Similar to the classroom center rotation, students work through a circuit of activities in the classroom (or classrooms) during one or more class periods,. With at least one of these activities involving instruction via technology.
    - o **Individual Rotation:** Students work through some or all of the classroom centers based on an individualized prescription determined by the teacher with the help of a technology-driven assessment tool.
    - o **Lab Rotation:** Students work on individualized, online instruction in a computer lab. Then, typically, the teacher will use data from students progress in the lab session to inform whole – or small – group instruction in the classroom.
    - o **Flipped Classroom:** Students receive the primary instruction (similar to the whole group instruction) in the form of online learning outside of the school day. The core lesson is provided via technology as "homework", and then students apply the skill through assignments and projects during class time with the teacher's support.

3) **The Flex Model:** This is introduced for those students who have behavioural, academic and social challenges and involves full online learning under the supervision and help of the teacher. It provides the students with a safer learning environment. Students learn on-site in a brick – and – mortar setting using an online instructional tool as the back bone of the course or subjects, with the teacher providing support as necessary. Students' instructional paths are customized and fluid, and the depth, frequency and manner of teacher support can vary based on each school's implementation model.

4) **Online Lab Model:** In this model, students are expected to go to online laboratory in order to take some courses that are not offered in their school. The students' work in the laboratory goes under the supervision of adults but not teachers. In addition to having courses that are not offered by the school, students can work in a pace that suits them. The entire curriculum is delivered via a digital platform but in a consistent physical location.
5) **The Self-blend Model:** In this model, students choose to augment their traditional learning with online course work. The self-blended model, which involves self-selected subjects to learn, meets the demand of high school students who look for extra courses to help them in university admission or getting a job.
6) **Online Driven Model:** Students here complete an entire course through an online platform with possible teacher check-ins. All curriculum and teaching is delivered via a digital platform and face-to-face meetings are scheduled or made available if necessary. The students with their limited time can meet their teachers online and selectively come to have face-to-face classes or attend meetings. This model offers a high level of flexibility.

It is important to note that even blended learning models can be blended together and many implementations use some, many or even all of these as dimensions of larger blended learning strategy. These models, for the most part, are not mutually exclusive.

Characteristics of Blended Learning

The main features of blended learning are:

Students have the option of the two modes: Students in blended learning can select either the traditional mode of classroom teaching where they can get personal interaction with the teacher and their classmates or they can choose ICT supported learning. This largely depends on the nature of content and objectives being targeted. Sometimes, course designers or teachers themselves decide on the mode appropriate for topics being dealt with.

Teachers are well versed with both modes: It is an important feature of the blended learning that teachers are very dynamic, technologically competent and fully trained to work efficiently in both formats – traditional classroom format and ICT supported format. They should be well equipped in using traditional methods and other modern technologies.

Students get face to face interaction as well as interact in virtual space: Students get ample time to interact with other students pursing same course. They can interact with them inside the university or college campus and also in virtual space. Thus, their group can become very large and with much diversity so that the student's knowledge becomes wide and they also develop a feeling of understanding, love and harmony with students of other cultures and countries.

Students get full experience in using new technology: The present century is the century of ICT. Today, the illiterate is not only the one who cannot read and write but a person who is not well versed with modern technologies is also an illiterate. Today, all professions demand expertise in ICT and so blended learning help to make students ICT experience rich. Students involved in blended learning gain capability to exploit available technologies to the fullest of their benefit.

Students get training in different life skills: Life skills are those skills that are needed to lead a happy peaceful and successful life. They include empathy, decision making capability, love, patience, communication, self-management and critical thinking. Blended learning helps students to practice these skills. Students get acquainted with such life skills as empathy, love, patience in the classroom through their teachers and classmates, self-management, decision making, critical thinking and communication through the online experiences.

All round development of personality is targeted: In blended learning, the students get full opportunity for all round development of their personality. All the aspects of personality (cognitive, affective and psychomotor) are developed through blended learning which is difficult to achieve in traditional mode or ICT approach if followed in isolation.

Students get wide exposure and new perspectives of the course content: Due to a variety of experiences, students get wide exposure and their content knowledge is enriched as they get to see various new dimensions of the content and gain practical useful knowledge.

It provides multicultural approach to teaching and learning: Blended learning provides students the opportunity to communicate and share their views and feelings with other students all over the world thereby making teaching and learning process multicultural in nature.

Makes teaching and learning process child centred: Blended learning is designed to provide maximum gain to students and this reaches the goal of child centred education.

Diverse role of the teacher: The teacher in blended learning plays diverse roles. In the traditional classroom, the teacher acts as a motivator, resource person, and an organizer. When he develops the content to be provided through ICT, he acts as a guide to the students.

Students construct knowledge rather than just consuming it: Blended learning also includes constructivism. Students construct their own knowledge rather than depending on others to design teaching and learning strategies for them.

Basic Requirements for Implementing Blended Learning

Implementing blended learning is not an easy task. It requires certain fundamental preparations in all the elements of teaching and learning process. The following are the basic requirements for implementing a successful blended learning.

1) **Well trained teachers:** Though child centred, teachers are very important factors in the implementation of blended learning. Teachers should be well acquainted with the concept of blended learning and be fully trained and skilled to blend both types of approaches – traditional and technological. They should be trained to develop content in digital form so that it could be available to students online. They should be well versed with internet browsing and internet terminology; should be aware of all the websites that can be useful for the students while learning online. The teachers should know how to utilize blogs, YouTube facility, software like Skype, google and others for video conferencing and social networking sites for educational purposes.
2) **Teachers with scientific attitude:** It is very important that teachers have scientific attitude. They should have good observation skills; they should be optimistic and should have problem solving skills. Scientific attitude will help the teachers to deal positively with failures they will get while working on the innovative concept of blended learning. This right type of scientific attitude will automatically filter from teachers to students.
3) **Teachers with wider outlook and positive approach towards change:** As it is the case for the success of any innovative idea, blended learning process also needs teachers that have a wider outlook and should be flexible. They should be ready to accept changes and be innovative and dynamic.
4) **Complete facilities like well-furnished computer laboratory, internet connection and provision for video chatting:** Blended learning largely depends on infrastructure. The school should not only have good classrooms but also well-furnished computer laboratories with sufficient number of computers to cater for all the students. There is also need for steady power supply in the school for effective use of the computers and other facilities.
5) **Students have access to internet at their private computers:** In addition to well-furnished computer laboratories in the school, the students should have their personal computers for basic hardware support to learn online and offline at their

residence. The government can procure computers for students and this will make them cultivate positive attitudes towards their studies.

6) **Flexibility in the system:** The school should be flexible; flexible lecture time table and examinations. This is very crucial for the successful implementation of blended learning.
7) **Parents should be fully involved:** The parents should be made well aware of this innovative approach to teaching and learning so that they can fully support their children and wards especially in the area of providing personal computers. The parents should be made to see the benefits of blended learning as against the traditional approach to teaching their children.
8) **Formative evaluation and continuous internal assessment:** The school authorities and higher educational bodies should be ready to completely implement continuous internal assessment and other tools of formative evaluation. Provision should be made for online examination which makes the system more flexible.

Advantages of Blended Learning

When properly implemented, blended learning has a lot of benefits; blended instruction is more effective than purely face-to-face or purely online classes. Blended learning methods can also result in high levels of student achievement more than face-to-face learning. By using a combination of digital instruction and one – on – one face time, students can work on their own with new concepts which frees teachers up to circulate and support individual students who may need individualized attention. Rather than playing to the lowest common denominator, as they would in a traditional classroom, teachers can now streamline their instruction to help all students reach their full potential. Blended learning facilitates a simultaneous independent and collaborative learning experience for university students. The use of information and communication technologies has been found to improve students' attitudes towards learning. By incorporating information technology into class projects, communication between lecturers and students has improved, and students were able to better evaluate their understanding of course material via the use of computer-based qualitative and quantitative assessment modules.

Blended learning also has the potential to reduce educational expenses and lower costs by putting classrooms in the online space and it essentially replaces pricey textbooks with electronic devices. Blended learning gives the opportunity for data collection and customization of instruction and assessment as two major benefits of this approach. It includes software that automatically collects students' data and measures academic progress, providing teachers, students and parents detailed students' data. Often, tests are automatically scored, providing instantaneous feedback. Student logins and work times are also measured to ensure accountability. Schools with blended learning programmes may also choose to reallocate resources to boost student achievement outcomes. Students with special talents or interest outside of the available curricula use educational technology to advance their skills or exceed grade restrictions. Blended learning allows for personalized education, replacing the model where a teacher stands in front of the classroom and everyone is expected to stay at the same pace. It allows students to work at their own pace, making sure they fully understand new concepts before moving on. A classroom environment that incorporates blended learning naturally requires learners to demonstrate more autonomy, self-regulation, and independence in order to succeed.

A learning management system or federation of systems, helps develop a better feel for an online community where discussions can be held to better aid students. This virtual learning environment help connect teachers with students without physically being present, thus making this a 'virtual café'. Many schools use this online tool for online classes, class work, question and answer forums and other school related work. The advantages of blended learning are dependent on the quality of the programmes being implemented. Some indicators of excellent blended learning programmes are: facilitating student learning, communicating ideas effectively, demonstrating an interest in learning, organizing effectively, showing respect for students and assessing progress fairly.

Disadvantages of Blended Learning

Unless successfully planned and executed, blended learning could have disadvantages in technical aspects since it has a strong dependence on the technical resources or tools with which the blended learning experience is delivered. These tools need to be reliable, easy to use and up to date, for them to have a meaningful impact on the learning experience. Information technology (IT) literacy can serve as a significant barrier for students attempting to get access to the course materials, making the availability of high-quality technical support paramount. Another aspect of blended learning that can be challenging is group work because of difficulties with management in an online setting. The use of lecture recording technologies can result in students falling behind on the materials. In a study performed across four different universities by Gosper et al (2008), it was found that only half of the students watched the lecture videos on regular basis, and nearly 40% of students watched several weeks' worth of videos in one sitting.

From an educator's perspective, most recently, it has been noted that providing effective feedback is more time-consuming (and therefore more expensive) when electronic media are used, in comparison to traditional (e.g. paper-based) assessments. Using e-learning platforms can be more time consuming than traditional methods and can also come with new costs as e-learning platforms.

Another critical issue is access to network infrastructure. Although the digital divided is narrowing as the internet becomes more pervasive, many students do not have access to the internet, even in their classrooms. Any attempt to incorporate blended learning strategies into an organization's pedagogical strategy needs to account for this. This is why learning centers are built with good Wi-Fi connections to make sure this issue is addressed.

Conclusion

One single teaching and learning approach is no longer enough for 21st century students. To improve information retention, engagement and teaching, blended learning is more important than ever. A good blend of learning formats goes a long way in offering efficient training to your workforce, curtailing costs and extending the training accessibility. With blended learning, trainers are better positioned to bridge the knowledge gap and help learners reach their maximum potential. Collaboration is one of the key factors necessary for effective learning. Everyone is motivated to actively participate, which leads to much better learning outcomes. Blended learning enables the course participants to work together, engage in discussions and provide useful feedback to one another, which undoubtedly leads to improvement and higher engagement. Blended learning as a teaching model is currently gaining more and more recognition and acceptance and thus appears as an alternative teaching approach that help students improve their performance. Blended learning breaks down the traditional walls of teaching and offers flexible time frames that can be personalized to each person, offering them the ability to learn at their own pace. In conclusion, it could be said that blended learning, to a reasonable extent, is the solution to the problems prevailing in our educational institutions especially at the higher level. If implemented in a well-planned and organized way and with the right type of attitudes, it can become the future of our educational system.

References

Bonk, C. J. and Graham, C. R. (2006). *Handbook of blended learning: global perspectives, local designs.* San Francisco: Jossey-Bass/Pfeiffer Publishing.

Diziuban, C., Hartman, J. and Moskai, P. (2004). Blended learning. *EDUCAUSE,* vol. 2004, Issue 7. Retrieved December 16, 2019 from http://net.educause.edu/ir/library/pdf/ERB0407.PDF

Education Connection (2013). Blended instruction: exploring student-centred pedagogical strategies to promote a technology – enhanced learning environment. Litchfield: Center for 21st century skills at education connection.

Finn, A. and Bucceri, M. (2004). A case study approach to blended learning. Retrieved December 2, 2019 from http://www.centra.com/download/whitepapers/casestudy-BlendedLearning.pdf.

Friesen, N. (2012). Report: defining blended learning. Retrieved December 4, 2019 from http://www.learningspaces.org/papers/definingBlendedLearningNF.pdf

Garrison, D. R. and Vaughan, N. D. (2008). Blended learning in higher education: framework, principles and guidelines. The Jossey-Bass higher and adult education series. San Francisco: Jossey-Bass.

Gosper, M., Green, D., McNeill, M., Philips, R. A., Priston, G. and Woo, K. (2008). Final report: the impact of web-based lecture technologies on current and future practices in learning and teaching. Australian learning and teaching council. Sydney.

Laster, S. G. (2005). *Redefining blend learning.* San Francisco: Jossey – Bass.

Olelewe, C. J. (2014). Challenges facing effective utilization of blended learning model in teacher education programmes in Nigeria. Paper presented at 10th Annual National Conference of Quality education in Nigeria, held at the Benue State University Makurdi, 12th – 16th May, 2014.

Onyia, U. A. (2011). Job creation and entrepreneurship education: challenges for the 21st century. *Nigerian Journal of Research Production,* 19(1), 48 – 55.

Osyathorpe, R. E. and Graham, C. R. (2013). Blended learning environment: definitions and directions. *The Quarterly Review of Distance Education,* 4(3), 227 – 233.

Owston, R., York, D. and Murtha, S. (2013). Student perceptions and achievement in a university blended learning strategic initiative. *Internet and Higher Education,* 18: 38-46.

Singh, H. (2003). Building effective blended learning program. *Issues of Education Technology,* 43(6), 51-54.

Thorne, K. (2003). Blended learning: how to integrate online and traditional. London: Kogan.

Wilson, J. W. (2013). 6 models of blended learning. Retrieved December 16, 2019 from dream box. http://www.dreambox.com/blog/6-models-blended-learning#sthash.6vnmJzcZ.dpuf.

9

School Environment and the Sustainable Development Goals (SDGs) for Greater Performance among Staff and Students

ALLISON B. R. & PAUL A. H.

Abstract

Education is the process of facilitating learning or the acquisition of knowledge, skills, values, beliefs and habits. Educational methods include discussion, teaching, training and directed research. The school is a formal and planned social institution with rules and regulations specifically charged with the responsibility of preserving, improving and extending the culture by showing appreciation to it and adherence to its norms. The basic function of the school in the socialization of the child is the development of cognitive abilities. The school environment is surrounded by disciplinary policies and a practice which sets the stage for the external factors that affect students. Environment is everything that is around us. It can be living (biotic) or non-living (abiotic) things. It includes physical, chemical, and other natural forces. The new Sustainable Development Goals ensure that both genders (girls and boys) complete free primary and secondary schooling by the year 2030, the goals emphasize that global efforts in education must give central importance to quality and learning, ensure equal access for all women and men to affordable and quality technical, vocational and tertiary education, including university.

Key Words: *School, Environment, Sustainable, Development, Goals, Performance*

Introduction

Achieving inclusive and quality education for all, reaffirms the belief that education is one of the most powerful and proven vehicles for sustainable development. These goals ensure that all girls and boys complete free primary and secondary education by 2030. The new Sustainable Development Goals emphasize that global efforts in education must give central importance to quality and learning. The aim of the Sustainable Development Goals is to end extreme poverty, achieve decent work for all, promote justice, peace and prosperity and protect the natural environment from human caused harms (Holborn, 2014)

The school environment should be conducive for effective teaching and learning. The school environment is one of the most important factors affecting teachers and students performances. A positive environment provides relevant, content, clear learning goals and feedback, opportunities to build social skills and strategies to help students succeed (Weimer, 2009). School environment can be positive on the health of learning environment or a significant barrier to learning. It can affect many areas and people within schools. For instance, a positive school climate has been associated with fewer behavioral and emotional problems for students.

Amerald (2016) opined that an ideal school environment embraces the idea that all students can learn. It works to build safe learning spaces for students. It attracts teachers who are knowledgeable, care about students learning and adapt their instruction to meet the needs of their learners. It makes sense that students would do better when they learn in positive environment. Most people would agree that some environments are more conducive to learning and academic performance. This is significant because teacher's turnover has been linked to increased costs and poor student achievement. The physical environment of school buildings and school grounds are the overall health and safety of students, staff and visitors. School buildings and grounds must be designed and maintained to be free of health and safety hazards to promote learning. A healthy school environment entails good nutrition, physical activity, basic safety, clean air and water, access to care. In a healthy school, students learn through lessons and by example, to value their own health and that of the environment (Baas, 2013).

The school environment is one of the most important factors affecting learning goals and feedback, opportunities to build social skills and strategies to help students succeed(Lancer,2013).It can be positive on the health of learning environment or a significant barrier to learning. It can affect many areas and people within schools, for instance, the school climate can be associated with fewer behavioral and emotional problems for students. The school environment includes a variety of factors such as the physical environment, instructional environment, student wellness, and discipline practices.

As Martin (2002) explains, 'the hierarchy of design-ability is a construct that measures the degree of control of change that teachers have over the physical elements of the classroom setting. In examining teacher's use of the classroom space, architectural elements have been classified in terms of hard (fixed features) and soft architecture (semi-fixed, semi-flexible and flexible features)'. Teachers generally manipulate the environment for their students in changing the arrangements of desks and chairs to improve their teaching and the students' learning. Martin (2002) shows there is a strong relationship between the pedagogical ideas of the teachers and their dealing with the classroom conditions, but often the teachers have no ideas about how to change classrooms to improve their teaching. Higgins, Hall, Wall, Woolner and McCaughey (2005) point out that, despite the fact that we still find traditional classrooms in use, 'at the same time, our understanding of learning itself is changing. Research on learning styles, formative assessment, multiple and emotional intelligences, constructivism and so on have combined with the rapid development of technology enabled, peer-to-peer and self-directed learning to facilitate very different approaches to the 30-students-in-rows model. But despite these changes, we do not yet have a robust research base for integrated and personalized learning environments' (Higgins, *et al.* 2005). As a result, teachers have to deal with traditional room settings while at the same time they often want to teach in a modern and future-centered way.

One of the SDG and targets, we are setting out is a supremely ambitious and transformational vision. We envisage a world free of poverty, hunger, disease and want, where all life can thrive. We envisage a world free of fear and violence; a world with universal literacy. A world with equitable and universal access to quality education at all levels, to health care and social protection, where physical, mental and social wellbeing are assured. A world where we reaffirm our commitments regarding the human right to safe drinking water and sanitation and where there is improved hygiene; and where food is sufficient, safe, affordable and nutritious. A world where human habitats are safe, resilient and sustainable and where there is universal access to affordable, reliable and sustainable energy.

The Concept of School

According to Nwama (2016), the school is a formal and planned social institution with rules and regulations specifically charged with the responsibility of preserving, improving and extending the culture by showing appreciation to it and adherence to its norms. The basic function of the school in the socialization of the child is the development of cognitive abilities. The school is designed to use its curriculum as a major instrument to transmit on to the child and possibly reinforce the skills, practical knowledge, important cultural values, norms, patriotism, and loyalty, lesson of obedience, ambition, concern for all and so on. Ajala (2014) added that it is in the school that the child extends the range of his human contacts and prepares himself to deal with a world infinitely more complex than his own family.

Teaching is necessarily interactive and people-centered. This interaction is frequently mediated by equipment and materials and teachers adapt their teaching to supplies and equipment available. In traditional classrooms, teachers have only limited space for their movement and their interaction with their students. As illustrated by Müller (2008), even within bad room conditions there exist some possibilities to activate and to motivate students; for instance, the teacher's movement can produce interaction with and between the students.

The Concept of Environment

Environment is everything that is around us. It can be living (biotic) or non-living (abiotic) things. It includes physical, chemical, and other natural forces. In the environment, there are different interactions between animals, plants, water and other living and nonliving things (Edelman and Booth, 2014). From the above concepts, a school environment is broadly characterized by the facilities, classrooms, school based health supports, and disciplinary policies and practices. It sets the stage for the external factors that affect students. Whiteford and Chichi (2013) identified some ways teachers can create positive learning environment. The importance of school buildings and classroom spaces for teachers' and students' practice had been ignored for many years (Martin, 2002). Most teachers do not think about their school and their classrooms as a built environment for teaching and learning. Rather, they focus on the restrictions of their school building and their classrooms (Walden 2009; Weinstein 2007, 2011). Students also see the bad conditions in their classrooms and their schools. However, when asked in more detail – for example in the studies of Woolner *et al.* (2007, 2011, 2012, 2013) – teachers and students were able to communicate the school buildings and classrooms they desired. If we thought about better conditions for teaching and learning in our schools and classrooms, we would realize that a focus on the constructed environment and its possibilities would support teaching and learning.

Henry Sanoff (1994, 1996) discusses school design and the possibilities of designing a responsive school and shows that the school building is an important factor for successful schools. Walden (2009), in writing about schools for the future, outlines the main aspects for 'a positive educational quality of the learning environment', such as, color scheme, form design, lighting, heating, cooling and ventilation, acoustics and noise, furniture, and equipment. Her work also corresponds to Steele's (1973) findings which state that physical settings serve a number of basic functions. As outlined by Gislason (2011), there are many studies on building quality and academic outcomes, which focus on indoor air quality, lighting, noise and acoustics, occupant density and thermal comfort. The importance of these environmental factors is recognized by architects and building engineers. However, these empirical studies have only considered the surroundings as important factors for well-being in schools, and do not provide any detailed evidence of their importance for teaching and learning. Research has also shown that the quality of facilities influences the citizens' perceptions of schools and thus can serve as a point of community pride and increased support for public education (Uline, Tschannen-Moran and DeVere, 2008).

School design influences school culture and changes the way of teaching and learning. Or is it the other way round – have the changes in teaching and learning over the past two hundred years changed the school design and school culture? Most of the research in this field postulates changes in teaching and learning which have influenced the school building and classroom design (Gislason 2011). Both for Europe and for the United States, Gislason finds two developments in school history which have a strong effect on school design and school culture: first, 'the single-grade classroom replaced the multi-grade school-room' (Gislason, 2011: 1) and second, 'a growing interest in non-traditional educational practices has prompted architects to develop a variety of experimental design solution (Gislason, 2011: 1).

Woolner (2010) describes three principles for understanding how schools are judged over time: the value of community recognition, the importance of good design and the importance of evaluation continuing over time. Little is known about how teachers and students deal with the school and classroom environment for their teaching and learning (Stadler-Altmann 2013). To describe ideal learning environments, this section will illustrate some relationships between the constructed environment of the classroom and the educational processes that take place within them. Most of the educational research is based on the work of Steele (1973), who illustrated the function of various classroom settings. He states that the physical environment can influence the way teachers and students feel, think and behave. Following his considerations, Weinstein (2007, 2011) argues that five of Steele's functions - security and shelter, pleasure, symbolic identification, task instrumentality, and social contact - are especially important for teaching and learning in classes:

Security and shelter: These are the most fundamental functions of all built environments. Physical security is a precondition that must be satisfied, at least to some extent, before the environment can serve students' and teachers' other higher-level needs. Additionally, psychological security is also an important precondition; that is, the feeling that school and classrooms are safe and good, comfortable places to be.

Pleasure: Equally important is the fact that teachers and students find their classrooms attractive and pleasing. Some educational studies demonstrate that an aesthetically pleasing environment can influence behavior: attractive classrooms have a positive effect on attendance and feeling of group cohesion (Horowitz and Otto, 1973) and on participation in class discussions (Sommer and Olson, 1980).

Symbolic identification: This is the so called personality of classrooms and schools, when they are designed by teachers and students in a daily routine.

Task instrumentality: This function describes the ways in which the environment helps us to carry out the tasks teachers want to accomplish.

Social contact: The arrangements of desks, for example, promote social contact or give space for individual work. So teachers could plan clusters for student interaction. The way students are arranged can also affect the interaction between teachers and students.

A number of studies have found that in classrooms where desks are arranged in rows, the teacher interacts mostly with students seated in front and in the center of the classroom. Students in this 'action zone' participate more in class discussions and initiate more questions and comments. These functions of the classroom settings discussed above provide the background theory for many studies and research projects. Other studies concern the design of classroom environments and the effect of these environments on the practice of teachers (Martin, 2002).

There is little on the use of the classroom in the empirical educational research. Where it has been considered, one focus has been on the questions of how teachers deal with classroom conditions, how they position themselves in the classroom, how they move through the classroom and how the teacher's body language, expressed therein, influences lessons. A second focus has been whether changes in classroom architecture (Buddensiek 2008; Rittelmeyer 2010) affect the level of classroom activity (Steele 1973; Weinstein 2007; Weinstein *et al.* 2011). The following discussion examines whether teachers change their teaching in school or classroom spaces that have been changed according to their wishes, on the basis that the classroom, as a constructed environment, influences both well-being and classroom activities (Forster 1997; Rittelmeyer 2010).

However, before crucial aspects of teacher's practice and students' response are outlined, consider the environmental situation in German and English. Most of the European and American classrooms are planned in the same way. As a consequence of the fact that most of our schools are planned and built in the nineteenth century (Buddensiek 2008; Tanner and Lackney 2006), the governmental guidelines for school architecture are still often based on these traditions (see Rittelmeyer 2010). As Tanner and Lackney (2006) have shown in their History of Education Architecture, there was and still is a relevant discussion and critique on school building and classroom design. The progressive movement of the late nineteenth century has had a strong influence on school architecture, with new forms of school buildings being designed. These schools are often private schools; for example the Laboratory School of John Dewey, the Waldorf School of Rudolf Steiner and the schools in the tradition of Maria Montessori. One can also find influences of the progressive movement in public schools (Tanner and Lackney 2006). In general, though, traditional classrooms and traditional furniture still prevails, in that most of these traditional classrooms were planned as rooms for teaching in front of the class and for teacher-centered instruction (Buddensiek 2008; Montag Stiftung 2011). Methods by which teachers can create positive learning environment include:

1. Address students' needs.
2. Create a sense of order
3. Let students get to know you
4. Get to know your students
5. Provide feedback
6. Avoid judging
7. Employ class building games and activities
8. Be vulnerable
9. Establish a supportive learning culture
10. Celebrate success

Address students' needs: Students, like adults, have not only physical needs but also important psychological needs for the security and order, love and belonging, personal power and competence, freedom and novelty, fun. Students are driven to meet all of these needs all the time. When teachers internally address these needs in the classrooms, students are happier to be there.

Create a sense of order: Students need structure and want to know that their teacher not only knows his content area but also knows how to manage his classroom. It is the teacher's responsibility to provide clear behavioral and academic expectations.

Your students should know you: there is nothing wrong for your students to know and communicate with their teachers. This creates a healthy school environment.

Get to know them: educate yourself about their culture, talk to them, assign journal prompts, read and respond to them, attend extra-curriculum events, have student's complete learning style and personality assessments, hold regular class meetings.

Provide feedback: this is the great way to connect with learners and to set their learning efforts in the right direction. Feedback is important for learners as it helps them in tracking their progress and in changing their learning strategies accordingly. It helps them recognize their weak areas while improving the developed skills.

Avoid judging: the human brain has its own reward system. When students succeed at a challenging task, be it academic or not, praise them, talk to them on how it feels to achieve proficiency, strategies and processes that led them to successes. Then talk about what they learned this time that will help them achieve their next successes.

Employ class building games and activities: this can be done by using the best way of encouraging group activities. Introduction of non-competitive games and active breakdown of the cliques within a learning environment, also assists the new and shy students to have a sense of belonging.

Be vulnerable: always be vulnerable

Establish a supportive learning culture: each member of the learning community should have the feeling of connectedness, they must feel that they are contributing to the environment while being bigger and important part of a supportive learning culture.

Celebrate success: when learner's achievements are recognized and shared by the instructors with other learners, it creates a sense of achievement and fosters healthy learning behavior.

Improving the School Environment

We can improve the school environment by;

1. Making it a collaborative atmosphere. If teachers were to sit behind their classroom doors, all day teaching by themselves, this would make for a terrible place to work.
2. Getting social with your colleagues
3. Taking on a leadership role.
4. Keeping focused
5. Staying positive

Sustainable Development Goals

Goal 1. End poverty in all its forms everywhere

Goal 2. End hunger, achieve food security and improved nutrition and promote sustainable agriculture

Goal 3. Ensure healthy lives and promote wellbeing for all at all ages

Goal 4. Ensure inclusive and equitable quality education and promote lifelong learning opportunities for all

Goal 5. Achieve gender equality and empower all women and girls

Goal 6. Ensure availability and sustainable management of water and sanitation for all

Goal 7. Ensure access to affordable, reliable, sustainable and modern energy for all

Goal 8. Promote sustained, inclusive and sustainable economic growth, full and productive employment and decent work for all

Goal 9. Build resilient infrastructure, promote inclusive and sustainable industrialization and foster innovation

Goal 10. Reduce inequality within and among countries

Goal 11. Make cities and human settlements inclusive, safe, resilient and sustainable

Goal 12. Ensure sustainable consumption and production patterns

Goal 13. Take urgent action to combat climate change and its impacts

Goal 14. Conserve and sustainably use the oceans, seas and marine resources for sustainable development

Goal 15. Protect, restore and promote sustainable use of terrestrial ecosystems, sustainably manage forests, combat desertification, and halt and reverse land degradation and halt biodiversity loss

Goal 16. Promote peaceful and inclusive societies for sustainable development, provide access to justice for all and build effective, accountable and inclusive institutions at all levels

Goal 17. Strengthen the means of implementation and revitalize the Global Partnership for Sustainable Development

Goal 4. Ensure inclusive and equitable quality education and promote lifelong learning opportunities for all

4.1By 2030, ensure that all girls and boys complete free, equitable and quality primary and secondary education leading to relevant and effective learning outcomes

4.2 By 2030, ensure that all girls and boys have access to quality early childhood development, care and pre-primary education so that they are ready for primary education

4.3 By 2030, ensure equal access for all women and men to affordable and quality technical, vocational and tertiary education, including university

4.4 By 2030, substantially increase the number of youth and adults who have relevant skills, including technical and vocational skills, for employment, decent jobs and entrepreneurship

4.5 By 2030, eliminate gender disparities in education and ensure equal access to all levels of education and vocational training for the vulnerable, including persons with disabilities, indigenous peoples and children in vulnerable situations

4.6 By 2030, ensure that all youth and a substantial proportion of adults, both men and women, achieve literacy and numeracy

4.7 By 2030, ensure that all learners acquire the knowledge and skills needed to promote sustainable development, including, among others, through education for sustainable development and sustainable lifestyles, human rights, gender equality, promotion of a culture of peace and non-violence, global citizenship and appreciation of cultural diversity and of culture's contribution to sustainable development

4. a Build and upgrade education facilities that are child, disability and gender sensitive and provide safe, non-violent, inclusive and effective learning environments for all

4.b By 2020, substantially expand globally the number of scholarships available to developing countries, in particular least developed countries, small island developing States and African countries, for enrolment in higher education, including vocational training and information and communications technology, technical, engineering and scientific programmes, in developed countries and other developing countries

4. c By 2030, substantially increase the supply of qualified teachers, including through international cooperation for teacher training in developing countries, especially least developed countries and small island developing States

Conclusion and Recommendation

The school environment should be healthy. A healthy school environment brings about good nutrition, physical activity, basic safety, clean air and water, access to care and education about making healthy choices allow students to thrive. In this environment, students learn through lessons and by examples, to value their own health and that of the environment. Schools should provide students with a safe environment in which they can be nurtured and grow emotionally, behaviorally, and academically and developing relationships with others. The school as well as the environment is important because it provides exposure to activities, ideas and fields of knowledge that one might never encounter. It is a tool to help prepare one for life. Not only can one learn the basic skills to read and write, but also learn about people, places, and nature.

References

Ajala, O. S. (2014). Effect of socio-emotional climate of the school on the adjustment of students. *Psycho-lingua* 36.

Amerald, M. S. (2016). *School climate. Measuring, improving and sustaining healthy learning environment.* Philadelphia, P.A.: Falmer Press.

Buddensiek, W. (2008) 'Lernräume als gesundheits- & kommunikationsfördernde Lebensräume gestalten. Auf dem Weg zu einer neuen Lernkultur' [Schoolrooms supporting health and communication. A Way to a new Learning-Culture], in: G. Brägger, N. Posse and G. Israel (eds.), *Bildung und Gesundheit – Argumente füreine gute und gesunde Schule* (pp. 1–28), Bern: h.e.p. Verlag.

Clark, J., Laing, K., Tiplady, L. and Woolner, P. (2013). *Making Connections: Theory and Practise of Using Visual Methods to Aid Participation in Research.* Newcastle, UK: Research Centre for Learning and Teaching, Newcastle University.

Edelman, P. H., and Booth, M. L. (2014). Promoting physical activity among children and adolescents. The strengths and limitations of school based approaches.

Holborn, H. A. (2014). *The school environment and society.* 7th edition.

Higgins, S., Hall, E., Wall, K., Woolner, P. and McCaughey, C. (2005). The Impact of School Environments: A Literature Review. London: Design Council.

Gislason, N. (2011). *Building Innovation: History, Cases, and Perspectives on School Design.* Big Tancook Island, Canada: Backalong Books.

Horowitz, P. and Otto, D. (1973). *The Teaching Effectiveness of an Alternative Teaching Facility.* Alberta, Canada: University of Alberta.

Lancer, J. K. (2013) *School climate.* Bloomington. Phi. Delta Kappa

Martin, S. H. (2002). The classroom environment and its effects on the practice of teachers. *Journal of Environmental Psychology,* 22: 139-156.

Montag Stiftung Urbane Räume, Montag Stiftung Jugend und Gesellschaft (2011). (eds.) Vergleich usgewählter Richtlinien zum Schulbau – Kurzfassung [Comparison of selected guidelines for School Buildings], Heft 1, Reihe: Rahmen und Richtlinien füreinen leistungsfähigen Schulbau in Deutschland.

Müller, W. (2008). 'Der Lehrer auf der Bühne des Klassenraums. Wirkungen der Raumregie' [Teacher on Stage of the Classroom. Effects of the Stage Directions], Pädagogik, 60: 26-30.

Nwama, T (2016). *Principles and practice of Education.* Tenth impression Singapore, Longman.

Rittelmeyer, C. (2010). 'Wie wirkt Schularchitektur auf Schülerinnen und Schüler? Ein Einblick in Ergebnisse der internationalen Schulbauforschung' [Do School Buildings Affect Students? Results of the International Research on School Buildings], in Gestaltung von Schulbauten. Ein Diskussionsbeitrag aus erziehungswissenschaftlicher, Zürich: Stadt Zurich, Schulamt.

Sommer, R. and Olson, H. (1980). The soft classroom. *Environment and Behavior,* 12: 3-16.

Stadler-Altmann, U. (2010) Das Schülerselbstkonzept. Eine empirische Annäherung [Students Self-Concept. An empirical Approach], Bad Heilbrunn: Klinkhardt.

Stadler-Altmann, U. (2013) 'Lehren und Lernen in gebauter Umgebung. Anmerkungen zur medialen Nutzung des Klassenraums' [Teaching and Learning in a Constructed Environment], in K. Westphal and B. Jörissen (eds) Vom Straßenkind zum Medienkind. Raum- und Medienforschung im 21 (pp. 176–196), Jahrhundert: Juventa.

Steele, F. I. (1973). *Physical Settings and Organisation Development,* Reading MA: Addison-Wesley.

Tanner, C. K. and Lackney, J. A. (2006). *Educational Facilities Planning, Leadership, Architecture, and Management.* Boston, New York, San Francisco: Pearson.

Uline, C. L., Tschannen-Moran, M. and DeVere Wolsey, T. (2007). The walls still speak: The stories occupants tell', paper presented at the annual meeting of the American Educational Research Association, Chicago.

United Nations: Transforming Our World: the 2030 Agenda for Sustainable Development. Available online at sustainabledevelopment.un.org.

Walden, R. (2009) Schools for the Future. Design Proposals from Architectural Psychology, Cambridge, Göttingen: Hogrefe & Huber.

Weimer, M. (2009). Teacher effectiveness in the school. *Journal of Teacher Education,* 30 (52).

Weinstein, C. S. (2007). *Middle and Secondary Classroom Management. Lessons from Research and Practice.* New York: McGraw-Hill.

Weinstein, C. S. and Romano Mignano, A. J. (2011). *Elementary Classroom Management. Lessons from Research and Practice.* New York: McGraw-Hill.

Whiteford, G. S., and ChiChi, B. (2013). *Issues and Perspectives in Sociology.* Ibadan: Sam Bookman.

Woolner, P. (2010). *The Design of Learning Spaces.* London, New York: continuumbooks.com.

Woolner, P., Clark, J., Hall, E., Tiplady, L., Thomas, U. and Wall, K. (2010). Pictures are necessary but not sufficient: using a range of visual methods to engage users about school design. *Learning Environments Research,* 13: 1-22.

Woolner, P., Clark, J., Laing, K., Thomas, U. and Tiplady, L. (2012). Changing spaces: preparing students and teachers for a new learning environment. *Children, Youth and Environments,* 22: 52–74.

Woolner, P., Clark, J., Laing, K., Tiplady, L. and Thomas, U. (2013). Teachers preparing for changes to learning environment and practices in a UK secondary school. Paper presented at the European Conference on Educational Research conference, Istanbul.

Woolner, P., Hall, E., Wall, K. and Dennison, D. (2007). Getting together to improve the school environment: user consultation, participatory design and student voice.

10

Achieving Stable Secondary School Environment through Sustainable Development Goals in Nigeria

DUNU Benson T. Ph.D & NWOSU Nancy Ph.D

Abstract

Development trajectory has been the bane of the African societies generally known as third world countries or underdeveloped countries. Nigeria was one of the African countries that had acquired notoriety as an underdeveloped country. In the credence to this notion the country is now ascribed as the world's poor capital. Attempts by various governments had adopted and implemented diverse developmental policies both at the national and international level, but have not yielded the results. The little or no success stories of all these developmental polices gave rise to an international policy for development known as "Millennium Development Goals" which recorded a minimal success at the end of its fifteen-year gestation period. The desire for development led to the adoption of another international policy for development known as "Sustainable Development Goals" with seventeen key goals. This paper is an examination of the environmental component goal in secondary schools in Nigeria for a sustainable development. The study is going to use secondary data to analyze, evaluate and project the plausible and possibility of success in the SDGs. In conclusion, the study suggested a very effective way the environment of the secondary school could be managed for a sustainable development. The study also highlighted diligent implementation and prioritization of secured school environment to achieve quality education.

Key Words: *Underdeveloped Countries, Developmental policies, Millennium development goals, Sustainable development goals*

Introduction

The issue of development in Nigeria is a paradox in juxtaposition with other climes in Europe, America, Asia and even some African countries that have recorded sustainable development strides far above Nigeria. Laying credence to this notion is to juxtapose Nigeria with countries such as South Africa, Ghana, Malaysia, Indonesia etc. that were in the same pace with Nigeria but have outpaced the country virtually in all spheres of developmental trajectory known in the 21st century. According to Oshewolo (2010), the richly endowed country which was one of the wealthiest 50 countries in the world in the 1960s and 70s has retrogressed in trading shoulders with the poorest countries.

This affirmative situation is largely attributed to so many self-inflicted circumstances. Utomi (2008) attributed this to the unmitigated and primitive accumulation of wealth of our political leaders who are corrupt neck deep. This has created a vicious circle of self-aggrandizement of politicians with no interest of the masses at heart. According to Eshalomi (2010), China, which was seen as a non-aligned developing country in the 1960s is now one of the largest exporters of manufactured goods. This development is attributed to reforms, policies, commitment, visionary and innovative attributes of committed leaders through pragmatic educational policies and reforms.

Incidentally, these innovative government policies and reforms such as creation of diversified economy, fiscal decentralization and collectivized agriculture diligently implemented with apt commitment made countries like Indonesia, Malaysia etc. that had the same GDP size grow considerably. Indeed, while Indonesia policy led to 40% increase in total export, Nigeria's export was less the same in the 1920s (Anaduagwon, 2005; Chukwuemeka, ibid). The grave consequences have created more dangerous and breathtaking situation of uncertainties such as poverty, unemployment, insecurity, underdevelopment, environmental insecurity, dwindling economy and falling standard of education. Recently, amnesty international adjudged Nigeria as the 40th most unsafe country in Africa and 14th in the world. National and individual life threatening symptoms and signs need to be frontally attacked with all the seriousness it deserved.

To ameliorate the grave consequences of poverty and development disorder, successive governments have put some mechanisms in place and implemented a number of policies and projects. Maduato (2005), identified 35 of such developmental programmes that were embarked upon by various states and national government. Some of the programmes include; Operation Feed the Nation (OFN) in 1978, Green Revolution in 1980, Directorate of Foods, Road and Rural Infrastructural (DFRRI) in 1986 to construct good roads, provide rural water and electrification supply for those in rural areas, National Directorate of Employment (NDE) 1986 aimed at, providing finance, training and guidance for unemployed youths, Poverty Alleviation Programme (PAP) which was introduced in (2000) to address the problems of rising unemployment in the society and provide the basic necessities of life such as affordable health care, quality education, sanitized secured environment amongst others. In spite of all these developmental strategies, Adebayo (2009),

Chukwuemeka (2012), Igwe (2015) are of the opinion that the level of poverty increased and unemployment in the country increased to an astronomical height incomparable to her contemporaries.

Similarly, Greg (2019) identified recent government developmental and poverty alleviation programmes to include "You Win" programme design to empower small scale farmers and entrepreneurs; the Amnesty Programme in 2007 that pays money and salaries to repentant former agitators in the Niger Delta oil rich volatile region. Other specific initiatives targeting the poor are National Social Investment Project (NSIP) comprising of cash transfer investment programmes, Home-grown school feeding programme; Government Enterprise and Empowerments, Development Scheme (GEEDS); Women's Entrepreneurship Development Scheme (WEDS), and N-Power programme for skills development especially the youth.

Diametrically, all these past strategies did not translate into tangible development and this has resulted to high unemployment rate of 14.2%. Almost two third e.g. (62.6%) of the population is classified as poor, 27.9% of the population classified as multi-dimensionally poor with deepening inequality, poor education outcomes which has an estimated 10 million children out of school (Waziri, 2015; Usman, 2015; Shittu, 2015; Omoh, 2014 and Onyekpere, 2016).

Conceptual Context: School Learning Environment

The School learning environment is where learning, instruction and skill acquisition is carried out. In view of the school as the milling house that transforms minds who will contribute to the development of the nation, the security of the learning environ is a sin-qua-non. Owolabi and Aleyomi (2013), considered service and learning environment as a broader concept that embodies the overall quality of services, social, physical, psychological and pedagogical that learning institutions offer and which would have a direct influence on student's expectations, perception and academic achievement, behaviour and attitudes. Similarly, Oduyemi (2015), opined that the school or learning environment include students and teachers perception in classroom interaction, educational innovations including on-line, audio visual aids where teaching takes place. This also includes the place, space in the design of the environment, problem-based learning and cultural diversity.

From the above analogy, the school/learning environment has psychosocial and physical dimensions. The school environment strongly influences student outcome and the more conducive the environment, the better students' achieving an attitude towards learning. It is a valuable resource for those wishing to improve the effectiveness of school. According to Durokifa and Abdul (2019), the nature of the learning environment is influenced by its psychosocial dimensions in terms of degree of students, cohesiveness, self-esteem and self-confidence. Giving the above, the school/learning environment should be conducive, cordial, secured and motivating for students, staff and other workers in the school environment to achieve educational goals.

Sustainable Development

The concept of sustainable development is all embracing and quite multifaceted in nature. It stands as progress, advancement and improvement in several aspects of human endeavour. The concept has a deluge of credence to the notion of development. Igbuzor (2017) defined sustainable development as the development that can be maintained, sustained, persistent and lasting for a long time. The Brutrant Commission (1987) also known as the World Commission on Environment and Development also stated that Sustainable Development Goals meet the needs of the present without compromising the ability of future generation to meet their own needs. Similarly, the United Nations Development Programme (UNDP) (2015), explain sustainable development to mean a better standard of living for people and for the future generations to come (Reid 2013, Rogers, Jalal 2012, Boyd, 2012). In the same vein, Adejumo and Adejumo (2014) and Emas (2015) conceptualize, sustainable development as not using up resources faster than the earth could replenish or decision making that could degenerate the future. Stating further, they agreed that sustainable development is mainly achieved through the integration and acknowledgement of economic, environmental and social factors.

From the avalanche of definitions of sustainable development, the environmental dimension stands out more critical. The environment is central to all development goals to be achieved. The environment has to be secured, maintained and sustained as long as life exists. To that end, development should be gradual and futuristic minded in order to accommodate for future generations yet unborn.

Perspectives of Sustainable Development Goals

The world is fast becoming a global community and world powers and leaders are desirous and concerned about challenges anywhere in the global village. In a bid to address most of these daunting challenges, the global community adopted a post 2015 development agenda known as Sustainable Development Goals (SDGs). This was launched in September 25, 2015; operations and implementation of the (SDGs) commenced in 2016. Prior to the launching of the SDGs, the Millennium Development Goals (MDGs) was launched and implemented in 2000 for a period of fifteen years. The dire need for development made Nigeria to key into the agenda and immediately operationalize the Millennium Development Goals.

Regardless of these developmental programmes, expected development is yet to take place. According to Banwo and Ohiranti (2013), instead poverty, unemployment, child mortality, corruption, lopsided income and environmental degradation etc. have been on the increase. Thus, Nigeria only recorded a pyrrhic success over the implementation of the MDGs. Nonetheless, MDGs during its 15 years benchmark made some remarkable success and some of the goals achieved include reduction in poverty, hunger, disease, gender inequality, child mortality. However, so many African countries, especially those in sub-Sahara were not able to measure up. In order to address these myriad of challenges associated with MDGs and to sustain the positive results achieved by the programme, the global community adopted a post 2015 development agenda known as the "Sustainable Development Goals" (SDGs). It was launched on 25/9/2015 and commenced operation in 2016. The programme identified 17 targets with the aim to improve stability of the economy and environment, improve livelihood and protect the planet for future generations (Emas, 2015 and Waziri, 2015).

The Sustainable Development Goals (SDGs) are as follows:

1) End poverty in all ramifications
2) End hunger, food security and promote sustainable agriculture
3) Good health and wellbeing
4) Quality education and life-long opportunities
5) Gender equality and women empowerment
6) Clean water and sanitization for all
7) Accessible, affordable, reliable and sustainable energy for all
8) Promote decent work and economic growth
9) Promote sustainable industrialization
10) Reduce inequalities within and among countries
11) 1Build inclusive safe and sustainable cities and communities
12) Promote sustainable consumption and production pattern
13) Urgent action to address climate change
14) Conservative and sustainable use of marine resources, oceans and seas
15) Protect, restore and promote terrestrial ecosystem and halt biodiversity loss
16) Promote peaceful and inclusive society, rule of law, effective and accountable society while ensuring sustainable development
17) Strengthen the means of implementation and global partnership for sustainable development

These goals are in tandem with Spangenberg (2005), the Rio Earth Summit (1992), climate change and environmental education which will serve as a companion to the child-friendly school manual. To this end, the emphasis of the SDGs is on the economic, environmental, social and institutional issues of the society.

Priorities in Achieving Prospects of SDGs and School Environment in Nigeria

Implicitly, all the SDGs are inexplicably interwoven. The concern of this paper which focuses on the environment and indeed the school environment deserves prominence. The environment component which embodies all other component is elucidated in goals 6, 13, 14 and 15. According to Odunyemi (2015), the safety of the school environment through the environment sustainability and safety school environment is predicated on almost all the other goals. Environmental sustainability is now a topical global issue. The issues such as urgent action to address climate change, clean water and sanitation for all; accessible, affordable, reliable and sustainable energy for all, and sustainable use of resources, oceans and seas; and protect, restore and promote terrestrial ecosystem and halt biodiversity loss are global concerns and views for school environment security.

According to Odwusi (2015), the smooth implementation of the environment component goal is tantamount to healthy and safe learning school environment, which is translated to quality education that will lift one out of poverty, avert hunger, reduce inequality and give one access to good health. Ihejirika (2015) therefore opined that the achievement of quality education through school environment safety and productivity outcome is implicitly linked to the achievement of the rest Sustainable Development Goals. To that end, priority should be given to safe and sustainable school environment to boost quality education.

Nigeria has whole heartedly adopted the pursuant and attainment of SDGs which are prerequisites for Nigerian development and have been integrated in domestic National pre developmental interventionist programmes such as NEEDS, Vision 2020 and the Transformation Agenda (Igbuzor, 2015; Odunyemi 2015). In the light of the above, some of the emerging priorities in achieving Sustainable Development Goals in Nigeria in general and the school environment in particular will suffix as follows:

Early Commencement in the Implementation: The early commencement to implement the Sustainable Development Goals in Nigeria should be given the priority it deserves. Unlike the Millennium Development Goals, that was inaugurated in 2000 for a timeline of 15 years, the actual implantation started in 2015 due largely to financial constraints and lack of will power. This impacted on the success of the programme.

Funding is another crucial area that necessitated early and smooth implementation of developmental programmes in Nigeria. In realizing the intrinsic value of these goals, adequate funding is unequivocal. For these lofty goals to be achieved, enough financial and other resources should be pumped into the programme. Similarly, the government should provide separate budget estimate to fund the programme. This is in addition to donors from friendly international communities. Impliedly, when monies are voted for, there should be monitoring and evaluation system in place to ensure judicious use of such allocations.

Good, Open and All-Inclusive Governance: Good, corrupt free and accountable governance is the hallmark for achieving developmental programmes. Igbuzor (2012) attributed good governance as a prerequisite to development; good governance, which requires the provision of basic social amenities that accounts for the welfare of the people. Terungwa and Akwen (2014) also stated that qualities of good governance entail engaging the people in the conduct and management of affairs as well as accountability and transparency in the mobilization and utilization of resources.

Application of Reliable and Accurate Data: The utilization of available data is essential in planning developmental programmes and policies. According to Ejemudo (2013), a country that does not have accurate data will not be able to put in place necessary strategies and policies. The lack of accurate data in a country like Nigeria has been the bane of developmental programmes. For lack of inaccurate data, the Nigeria MDGs report (2015) on data report on the poverty level of Nigerians by NBS contradicts that of the World Bank even though same measuring stick was used (Nigeria MDG Report, 2015). Similarly, the data report of the level of unemployment by the presidential committee for the assessments and monitoring of the MDGs also contradicts that of the World Bank (Ejemudo, 2013).

Political Will and Policy Ideas: This is a very good strategy towards development: a strong and committed will and policy idea towards the actualization of such programmes or goal would eradicate poverty and enthrone sustainable development. The political will power of the government and the total commitment is paramount to a sustainable development of any country.

Implementation Strategies of SDGs on School Environment

Since the adoption of the SDGs in September 2015, and the beginning of their implementation in January 2016, there were several concrete global and sector specific strategies to achieve the goals. This is essentially because a successful implementation of the SDGs, which replaced the Millennium Development Goals, would mean successful attainment of goals. Considerations for prosperity, peace and wellbeing as well as preservation of the earth's biodiversity and equitable distribution of natural resources are well enshrined in the goals. According to Greg (2019), one of such global alliances and sector driven strategic interventions is known as "Women 2030". This is a 5-year strategic agreement signed on 18th March 2016 in Brussels by five global and regional women organizations with the European Commission for the project titled, women CSOs, networking to realize the sustainable development goals. The partnering women organizations that signed the women 2030 include the "Women Environmental Programme". The women 2030 project is being implemented in 52 countries of the world across Eastern Europe, Asia, Africa, Latin American regions. Women Environmental Programme (WEP) taking the lead for Africa, Ghana, Burkina Faso, Togo, Senegal etc.

The Federal Government of Nigeria has also put some mechanisms in place to ensure hitch free implementation of SDGs. There is also a House Committee on SDGs at the lower chamber, while there is a counterpart senate committee in the upper chamber to provide oversight functions that make appropriation for the SDGs. There is an inter-ministerial committee on the SDGs establishment to guide the coordinated engagement with ministries, departments and agencies. There is also a private sector advisory group on SDGs, a platform for different stakeholders to discuss Nigeria's SDGs plans, policies and programmes and make necessary recommendations that would help the country realize the SDGs.

The Women Environmental Programme (WEP), which made a preliminary assessment of the SDGs in Nigeria, was released. As part of the activities under the project and to establish baseline information against selected SDGs and targets, WEP undertook the assessment to ascertain how issues relating to the selected SDGs affected women, men, youth, the physically challenged, the aged and what were their needs and how to be addressed in order to realize the SDGs. The programme also put mechanisms in place to ensure that school environments are protected, safe for quality learning. The aim of the Women Environment Programme was to gather objective information to be used to engage the government and other development actors so that they could come up with relevant programmes, projects and policies that would address the issues towards the realization of the sustainable school environmental development goals.

An assessment was undertaken in ten states in Nigeria between May and December 2017 namely; Lagos, Delta, Anambra, Rivers, FCT Abuja, Nasarawa, Plateau, Kano, Benue and Yobe. According to Greg (2019), the data presented in the assessment however, only covered the quantitative data on goals 1, 4, 6 and 7. Goal 6 seeks affordable and clean energy for all. Highlights of the assessment report revealed troubling revelations that there are very few schools that have drinking water and toilet facilities and very few schools with internet facilities. Unequivocally, if these concerns are not tackled, we may still be a long way off from achieving the SDGs of a secured school environment.

The issue of funding for the SDGs was a central point. Adequate funding has always been the bane of developmental policies and programmes. At the event of Women Environment Programme 2016 in Abuja, the senior special assistant to the president on the SDGs. Princess Adejoke Orelope-Adefulire, whose office is charged with the responsibility of inter-governmental coordination of the SDGs planning, implementation, multi-stakeholders' partnership and resource mobilization as well as ensuring a seamless and robust strategic communications and advocacy around the SDGs agenda, disclosed that the office was working with the Ministry of Budget and National Planning, and United Nations Development Program (UNDP) on the SDGs Needs Assessment and Costing. Princess Adejoke (2017) identified enhanced partnership groups for a seamless implementation of SDGs. These include:

- ✓ Private sector advisory group on the SDGs;
- ✓ Development partners' forum on the SDGs anchored by the UNDP;
- ✓ Civil Society Organizations (CSOs) Advisory Groups on the SDGs
- ✓ Partnership with the National Youth Service Corps;
- ✓ And Conditional Grants Scheme (CGS) – incentives, states and local government to set aside and utilize 50% and 20% of the cost of select SDGs related projects in their annual budgets.

Importantly, due to the keen implementation strategy earmarked, Princess Adejoke further identified some notable achievement to include:

- ✓ Integrating the SDGs into the (ERGP) especially its implementation plan.
- ✓ SDGs Needs Assessment and Policy and Scenario Analysis;
- ✓ Data completion of SDG's data mapping;
- ✓ SDGs data supply framework and 'Data Bond' developed
- ✓ SDG's Baseline Survey Completed
- ✓ National Social Register developed to ensure that 'no one is left behind'
- ✓ Public awareness and advocacy (continuous and ongoing) – general high level of awareness and political support for the SDGs.

Likely Implementation Problems of SDGs in School Environment

Although, implementation process is ongoing, however, this paper through document analysis and opinion survey has envisaged some likely implementation challenges. The challenges not limited to the following, include;

- ✓ Lack of transparency and accountability.
- ✓ Poor governance;
- ✓ Corruption/diversion of funds.
- ✓ Limited economic diversification and continued vulnerability to both internal and external economic shocks.

- ✓ Limited financial resources for investments in SDG and school environment-related activities.
- ✓ Huge infrastructural and technological deficits in schools.
- ✓ Humanitarian crises in the North East through the activities of Boko-Haram and insecurity in the Niger Delta, the North Central through the activities of militancy and youth restiveness and Fulani and farmers' crises that have made the school environment vulnerable to attacks.
- ✓ Weak public sector institutional capacity.
- ✓ Lack of reliable and accurate data, (Aziken and Nwabughiogu 2016), Mail and Guardian Africa, 2016; Vanguard 2016; princess Adejoke 2017)
- ✓ Poor education outcome – an estimated 10 million children out of school, low participation rate of youths in formal and non-formal education.

Conclusion

The Sustainable Development Goals (SDGs), which commenced operation in 2016, are aimed to improve livelihood, stability of the economy and environment. As Nigeria embarked on this development programme, it is instructive that holistic policies and programmes be formulated and accurate plan is needed to promote an inclusive economic development for environmental sustainability. To achieve this awful enterprise, the areas of resource mobilization, technology transfer, continuous capacity development for reliable data collection, processing as well as putting in place institutional mechanism for monitoring and evaluation in accessing progress towards sustainable development over space and time be put in place. Undoubtedly, the patriotism of the entire Nigerian citizenry alongside moral and kind support from the international community is highly critical for a sustainable secondary school environment.

Suggestions for Improving SDGs on School Environment

Having been a member-country committed to the United Nations Sustainable Development Goals, the following suggestions are highlighted with a view of implementing strategies and policies to achieve sustainable school environmental goals;

1) Create and maintain smart and effective partnership with committed stakeholders nationally and internationally;
2) Develop the SDGs through wide consultative process by involving all strata of the society.
3) Build on previous plans and programmes that are aligned to the SDGs goals. For example, MDGs to some extent recorded some successes and the SDGs could be built on those areas of successes and analyzing some of the challenges with a view of overcoming those challenges.

4) To achieve the SDGs, the diversification of the economy is crucial. To this end, seven cardinal areas are imperative and these are; Agriculture, Manufacturing, Solid Minerals, Services, Construction and Real estate, Oil and Gas, Tourism and by leveraging Science, Technology and Innovation.
5) Investing in infrastructure in the school environment would provide the basic facilities in the school environment. This will enhance and sustain school environment sustainability where students will stay and learn without fear or danger.
6) Adequate funding, openness and accountability. In order to avoid the pitfalls of the Millennium Development Goals, which was due largely to inadequate funding and lack of transparency, concerted and committed efforts should be made towards provision of adequate funding of the programme and judicious use of those funds to realize the Sustainable School Environmental Development Goals.

References

Adebayo, S. (2014). Achievement of Millennium Development Goals in Nigeria: A critical examination. *International Affairs and Global Strategy*. 25:24-26.

Adejumo, V. and Adejumo, O. (2014). Prospects for achieving sustainable development through the Millennium Development Goals in Nigeria. *European Journal of Sustainable Development*, 3 (1): 33 – 40.

Boyd, O. (2007). Africa Development: Imperatives of Indigenous Knowledge and values. PhD Thesis, University of South Africa.

Banwo, A. and Oluranti, O. (2012). Isolating and understanding its Health component (456) for successful action and sustainability in Nigeria. *Mediterranean Journal of Social Sciences*, 5: 441 – 451.

Chukwuma, U. (2012) Millennium Development Goals and poverty reduction in Nigeria. *International Journal of Basic and Applied Sciences*, 1 (3): 504 – 540.

Durokifa S. and Abel, D. (2019). *Good, effective and equitable governance and the SDGs. In Governance for Sustainable Development: ideas for the post 2015 Agenda* (online) Available at jilellie:/users/201316769/downloads/full-SD Governance- book- July, 2019 pdf. Accessed 19 Nov. 2019.

Durokifa, A. A. and Abdul-Wasi, B. M. (2019). Evaluating Nigeria's Millennium Development Goals (MDGs): Determinants, Deliverables, and shortfalls (online) Available at http://www.researchgate.net'/publication/312642009 Accessed 7 December 2019.

Ejumudo, K. B. (2013). The problematic nature of development planning in Nigeria. A critical discourse. *Developing Country Studies,* 3 (4): 67 – 80.

Emas, M. (2015). The Millennium Development Goals. Milestones or millstones? Human Rights priorities for the post – 2015 Development Agenda. *Yale Human Rights and Development Journal*, 15 (1): 55 – 74.

Eshalomi, S. (2008). *Corruption: Bauchi freezes MDGs accounts* (online) Available at http://www. Thisdayonline.com/nviewphp?id=122662. Accessed 15 November.

Greg, O. (2019). *Accessing SDGs implementation in Nigeria*. Online University Degree. Atlantic int'l University.

Guardian Africa (2016). *Nigeria: & 2 trillion looted from the treasury. 55 officers charged.* (online) Available at http://mgaAfrica.com/article/2016-02-04-nigeria (Accessed 30 July 2019).

Igwe, E. (2015). Towards achieving Millennium Development Goals in Nigeria: Prospect and challenge. *Journal of Economics and Sustainable Development,* 3(9): 74 – 82.

Igbuzor, O. (2017). Review of MDGs in Nigeria: Emerging Priorities for a Post-2015 Development Agenda. In: *The National Thematic Consultations for the Post-2015 Development Agenda.* Abuja: Ladi Kwali Hall, Sheraton Hotel. 18 – 19 February.

Ihejirika, P. H. (2015). SDGs: *Will Nigeria overcome extreme poverty, hunger by 2030 leadership* (online) Available at: leadership.ng./news/472659/sdgs-will-nigeria-overcome-extreme-poverty-hunger-by-2030 (Accessed 19th December 2019).

Maduagwu, E. and Mullings, L. (2014). *On our own terms: Race: Race, Class, and gender in the lives of African-American women.* Routledge.

Nwabughiogu, I, (2016). *Buhari makes u-turn says he won't pay ₦5000 stipend money for unemployed* (online) Available at: http://www.vanguardngr.com/2016/02/614925/ (Accessed 1 December 2019).

Odunsi, W. (2016). *Budget Breakdown of Sums allocated to presidency.* MDGs, others. (online) Available at: http://dailypost.ng/2015/12/26/2016-budget-breakdown-of-sums-allocated-to-presidency- mdas-others/

Oduyemi, J. (2015). *The age of sustainable development.* Ibadan: University Press.

Omoh, G. (2014). *Nigeria third on world poverty index. World Bank.* Vanguard (online) 16 October Available at: http://www.vanguardngr.com 2014/04/440695/#sthash.eorw55.dput (Accessed December 2019).

Onyekpere, E. (2016). *Buhari's 2016 budget of frivolities* (online) Available at: Jimidisu.com/buharis-2016-budget-of-frivolities-2-by-eze-Onyekpere.

Oshelowo, S. (2011). Poverty reduction and the attainment of the MDGs in Nigeria: problems and prospects. *International Journal of Politics and Good Governance*. 2(2): 1-22.

Owolabi, A and Adeyimi, E. (2013). Economic crossroads: the experiences of Nigeria and lessons from Malaysia. *Journal of Development and Agricultural Economics,* 3(8): 368 – 378.

Princess Adejoke, O. (2017). *Nigeria's voluntary National Review on the implementation of the 2030 Agenda and SDGs.* A presentation to the United Nations High Level Political Forum. Conference Room UN HQS.

Reid, O. (2013). *Sustainable development: an introductory guide.*

Routledge R. (2012). An *introduction to sustainable development.* Earthsean.

Shittu, J. (2015). *Towards delivering sustainable development for all prioritizing targets for implementation.* Lagos: Centre for Public Policy Alternatives.

Spangenberg, J. H. (2005). Economic sustainability of the economy concepts and indicators. *International Journal of Sustainable Development* 8(2): 47 – 64.

Ferungwa, P. J. (2014). The attainment of Sustainable Development in Nigeria: A Good Governance Perspective. *Journal of Sustainable Development in Africa.* 16(3): 113 – 129.

The Millennium Development Goals Report, 2015.

Utomi, C. (2006). *Can Nigeria be the China of Africa?* In University of Benin Founders' Day Benin City, Nigeria: University of Benin.

Usman, S. (2015). *Improving the lives of Girls and Women in Nigeria issues, policies and action.* British Council, Nigeria.

Vanguard, (2016). *Recovered Loots: FG releases interim reports.* (online) Available at: http.//www.vanguardngr.com/2015/12/2016budget-and-poverty-alleviationmattersarising. Accessed 1st December 2019.

11

Work Engagement of Non-Academic and Academic Department Heads in Lyceum of the Philippines University

MENEZ Norma L. Ph.D & BADILLO Elmer

IIINTRODUCTION

Employee engagement concept is not very ancient for it is how positively the employee thinks about the organization, feels about the organization and is proactive in relation to achieving organizational goals for customers, colleagues and other stakeholders (Cook (2012). An employee, who is highly engaged, works with passion with satisfaction and with enthusiasm for the work one does (Robbins and Judge 2013).

Work engagement has been defined as job engagement which is an employee's interest in, enthusiasm for and investment in his or her job. Further, empirical studies have revealed that job engagement is associated with various positive behaviours and outcomes for both employees and the organization (Kirkpatrick, 2007). In a different construct, work engagement, according to Scaufelli *et al* (2002), is a positive, fulfilling, work-related state of mind. It is characterized by vigour at its high levels of energy and mental resilience while working and the willingness to invest effort in ones work and persistence in the face of difficulty; dedication as to its sense of significance, enthusiasm, inspiration, pride and challenge and absorption as a highly concentrated and happily engrossed in works so that one feels time passes quickly. Truly engaged employees is a powerful instrument that will aid every organization to keep their people which is considered the most valuable and if properly handled and engaged cannot be replicated by competitors (Anitha, 2014).

In the study done on employee engagement and how employees as teachers are engaged in their respective work, Laguador, Bay and An (2014) posted significant results such as services provided by their university as contributory for teachers to be engaged in their work and that engagement of employees is their commitment in their organization, how hard they work, and how long they intend to stay.

Relative to the same university research, Menez and Laguador (2015-2016) also posted results on employee engagement which is characterized by their willingness to do their best in the tasks assigned to them. Most of the LPU employees are very determined in finishing the demands of their work specifically during accreditation visits, quality assurance and other related activities of the university. This very high result of their work engagement as to dedication, is a product of the employee's long stay in the University. How LPU leaders manage their employees is a result of the kind of engagement levels they demonstrate in their respective workplaces. Such engagement influences their work performance thereby contributing to LPU's success in the area of accreditation, student board performances and other quality assurance activities.

To conclude, employees who stay longer become more dedicated, involved, enthusiastic, inspired and challenged to their workplaces. The results of this research are useful data in the conduct of continuous improvement of the organization as a result of work engagement and identified significant variables contributory to the possible seminars by the Human Resource Department of the university; it is in this context that researches were inspired to conduct this study.

Objectives of the Study

This study is an attempt to identify the work engagement of non-teaching and teaching personnel in terms of vigour, dedication, and absorption; to determine if the level of respondents' work engagement significantly differs when they are grouped according to their demographics and if relationship exists between work engagement when they are grouped according to non-teaching and teaching personnel.

Review of Literature

Engagement can affect employees' attitudes, absence and turnover levels and various studies have demonstrated links with productivity, increasingly pointing to a high correlation with individual, group and organizational performance, a success measured through the quality of customer experience and customer loyalty. (Hemsley Fraser, 2008, cited in The HR Director, 2008; The Conference Board, 2006).

Organizations with higher engagement levels tend to have lower employee turnover, higher productivity, higher total shareholder returns and better financial performance (Baumruk, 2006). Also, Towers Perrin (2007) found that organisations with the highest percentage of engaged employees increased their operating income by 19 per cent and their earnings per share by 28 per cent year to- year. Highly engaging organisational cultures may also have an attractive talent (Martin and Hetrick, 2006).

By building a culture that enables employees to engage in their work, organisations may benefit from staff who are willing to go the extra mile and achieve better financial performance (Baumruk, 2006). However, despite the potential gains of improved engagement levels, Gallup found that more than 80 per cent of workers are not truly committed to their work, and a quarter of these are dissatisfied and 'actively disengaged', putting no passion into their work (Flade, 2003). Gallup (2006) proposed that employees could be divided into three types with regards to their level of engagement, the engaged, not-engaged and the actively disengaged, with the latter being of most concern to the employer brand as a result of sharing their discontent with their co-workers and the wider world.

Engaged employees will stay with the company longer and continually find smarter, more effective ways to add value to the organization. The end result is a high performing company where people are flourishing and productivity is increased and sustained'. (Catteeuw et al., 2007 p. 152). Employee engagement is 'a combination of attitudes, thoughts and behaviours that relate to satisfaction, advocacy, commitment, pride, loyalty and responsibility'. It is 'broader than the more traditional concept of employee satisfaction and relates to the extent to which employees are fully engaged with the company and their work'. (BT, 2008) Barclays suggests a formal definition of employee engagement might be 'the extent to which an employee feels a sense of attachment to the organisation he or she works for, believes in its goals and supports its values". People Management(2008) research results may manifest in various ways such as through increased productivity, customer loyalty, increased sales or better retention levels (Cleland et al., 2008). Gallup found that employees are more productive and contribute more financially to the organisation if they feel involved in, and are committed to the organisation (Gallup cited in Levinson, 2007).

If colleagues influence each other with their work engagement, they may perform better as a team. Bakker et al. (2006) conducted a study on engagement and performance among 105 school principals and 232 teachers. Their study showed significant and positive associations between school principals' work engagement scores and teacher-ratings of school principals' performance and leadership. More specifically, results of structural equation modeling showed that engaged principals scored higher on in-role and extra-role performance. In addition, engagement was strongly related to creativity; the higher school principals' levels of work engagement, the better they were able to come up with a variety of ways to deal with work-related problems. Finally, engaged school principals were seen as transformational leaders – being able to inspire, stimulate and coach their co-workers.

Results showed that engaged employees are highly self-efficacious; they believe they are able to meet the demands they face in a broad array of contexts. In addition, engaged workers believe that they will generally experience good outcomes in life (optimistic), and believe they can satisfy their needs by participating in roles within the organization (organizational-based self-esteem; see also Mauno et al., 2007).

These findings were replicated and expanded in a 2-year follow-up study (Xanthopoulou, Bakker, Demerouti, & Schaufeli, 2008). The findings indicated that self-efficacy, organizational- based self-esteem, and optimism make a unique contribution to explaining variance in work engagement over time, over and above the impact of job resources and previous levels of engagement. As a final example, Bakker, Gierveld, and Van Rijswijk (2006) in their study among female school principals found that those with most personal resources scored highest on work engagement. Particularly resilience, self-efficacy, and optimism contributed to work engagement, and were able to explain unique variance in engagement scores (in addition to social support from team members and colleague principals, opportunities for development, and social support from the intimate partner). Thus, resilience is another personal resource that may facilitate work engagement.

Truly, as organizations has been gaining significant importance on engaged employees, it will pose as a challenge to every organization considering that today's workforce is composed of a diversified pool of employees from different cohort groups that differentiate them emotionally, personally, and cognitively (Ashipaoloye, 2016). It is becoming more productive, vigorous, dedicated and enthusiastic to perform duties and responsibilities as part of the dynamic organizations are results of a higher level of work engagement of its people.

Engagement is a measurement of how happy employees are with their respective jobs, working environment (Mehta, N.K. (2013); thus, it has become the top most priority of business leaders for they know that high performing workforce is very important for the development and survival of a dynamic economy. (Right Management Group, 2012). With the entry of new generations, and their differences, a study was done on work engagement using Utretch Work Engagement Scale (UWES) among educational institutions (Alvaro, 2017).Her findings show that dedication is their number one engagement dimensions. What motivates them to work hard and be dedicated is the recognition of their multi-tasking abilities and committee works. People empowerment, recognition and the feeling of belongingness are truly for these generations' factors to stay long in their respective universities.

Method

Research Design

The researchers used the descriptive type of research method to determine the work engagement of non- academic and non- academic department heads in LPU.

Respondents of the Research

Since there is already a computerized encoding of the results, based on the records forwarded from the Management Information System (MIS) office, the total participants recorded for this 2015-2016 is 397 which is 297 for non- academic and 100 for academic department heads.

Data Gathering Instrument

The standardized instrument of Utrecht Work Engagement Scale (UWES) was used to measure work engagement. Using the short form of the Utrecht Work Engagement Scale (UWES 9) developed by Schaufeli et al (Scaufeli *et al,* 2002). This measure is a three-factor scale consisting of nine items aiming to measure the three dimensions of work engagement- vigour; dedication and absorption. Three items were used to measure each of the dimensions. Items used to address the vigour dimension of work engagement include statements like (V1) At my work, I feel bursting with Energy, (V2) At my job, I feel strong and vigorous, and (V3) When I get up in the morning, I feel like going to work. Participants'' dedication to the job of teaching was measured using items such as, (D1) I am enthusiastic about my job, (D2) My job inspires me, and (D3) I am proud of the work that I do. Absorption aspect of the teachers was also measured using a three-item subscale consisting of statements like (Ab1) I feel happy when I am working intensely, (A2) I am immersed in my work, (A3) I get carried away when I am working. All nine items were anchored in a seven-point Likert-type scale ranging from 1 (never) to 7 (always). Cronbach alphas ranging from 0.75 to 0.82, dedication (five items) with Cronbach alphas ranging from 0.88 to 0.90 and absorption (six items) with Cronbach alphas ranging from 0.70 to 0.75 (Schaufeli& Bakker, 2003).

Data Gathering Procedure

Upon approval of the president for the study to be conducted, the researchers sought permission from the HRMDO and MIS to access the data online Work Engagement results for 2016. This approval led the researchers to conduct the study.

Data Analysis

Statistical tools used to analyse data include percentage distribution, weighted mean, T-test and Analysis of Variance.

Results and Discussion

Table 1: Percentage Distribution of the Respondents' Profile

Profile Variables	Frequency	Percentage (%)
Gender		
Female	150	37.8
Male	247	62.2
Category	397	
Non academic	297	74.8
Academic Department heads	100	25.2
Department	397	
Administrative	87	21.9
CBA	36	9.1
CEAS	49	12.3
CCS	19	4.8
CITHM	18	4.5
DENT	25	6.3
LIMA	32	8.1
MSCCJ	12	3.0
COE	19	4.8
CON	10	2.5
CAMP	38	9.6
Length of Years		
Below 1 year	13	3.3
1 – 10 years	230	57.9
11 – 20 years	110	27.7
21 – 30 years	39	9.8
31 years and above	5	1.3

Table 1 presents the profile of the respondents as to their gender, job category, department and length of years in the university. This is a system generated results of the online survey conducted by the Human Resources management of the University. Much that the researchers would like to get a 100% results; only 397 responded to the survey. They are those who willingly share their thoughts on work engagement. Profile results show that most of the respondents are male with 62.2%, non - academic personnel is 74.8% while academic is 25.2%. Each college is represented very well ranging from 10-49 teaching staff which varies depending on full time category only. The non-academic personnel is 87 fair enough to represent their department as there are mostly 2 - 4 personnel per department. The length of years in service presents a good number of academic department heads who are from 11 years and above working in LPU, meaning respondents who will rate their work engagement are working for longer period of time.

These variables used by researchers served as an avenue to understand their contribution to LPU as an organization. Using a standardized Utrecht Work Engagement Scale (UWES) of which most academic researchers also use this instrument which is a brief, valid and reliable questionnaire. As organizations has been gaining significant importance on engaged employees, it will pose as a challenge to every organization considering that today's workforce is composed of a diversified pool of employees from different cohort groups that differentiate them emotionally, personally, and cognitively (Ashipaoloye, 2016).

It has to be accepted that dynamic people in an organizations are becoming more productive, vigorous, dedicated and enthusiastic to perform duties and responsibilities. This resulted into a higher level of organizational productivity and in the academe institutional success. By building a culture that enables employees to engage in their work, organisations may benefit from staff who are willing to go the extra mile and achieve better financial performance (Baumruk, 2006).

Table 2.1: Work Engagement as to Vigour

Vigour	Weighted Mean	Verbal Interpretation	Rank
1. At my work, I feel bursting with energy	4.73	Very Often	6
2. At my job, I feel strong and vigorous.	5.29	Very Often	1
3. When I get up in the morning, I feel like going to work	5.22	Very Often	3
4. I can continue working for very long periods at a time	5.15	Very Often	4
5. At my job, I am very resilient, mentally	5.07	Very Often	5
6. At my work, I always persevere, even when things do not go well	5.26	Very Often	2
Composite Mean	5.12	Very Often	

Legend: 5.50 – 6.00 = Always; 4.50 – 5.49 = Very Often; 3.50 – 4.49 = Often; 2.50 – 349 = Sometimes; 1.50 – 2.49 = Rarely; 1.00 – 1.49 = Almost Never; 0 = Never

Table 2.1 reveals how non-academic and academic departments rated their work engagement in terms of vigour. Work engagement is defined as a concept in its own right: "a positive, fulfilling, work related state of mind that is characterized by vigour, dedication, and absorption" (Schaufeli, Salanova, González-Romá, and Bakker, 2002: 74). In terms of vigour dimensions, very often, that academic and non-academic department heads feel strong in their work that they are doing (5.29) with perseverance even when things do not go well (5.26) and feel like going to work when they get up in the morning (5.22).

Such kind of work engagement from being persistent in the task assigned to them or the experience of "being fully there, is a dimension of their feeling attentive, connected, integrated, and focused in their role performance. Thus, this is a manifestation of positive outcomes which is attested by the various accomplishments of Lyceum as a university. Vigour as the word defines is the ability to do things with powerful strength; when non-academic department heads were interviewed, they claimed how they are working harder to achieve the vision of becoming a recognized university in the Asia pacific region by 2022. The efforts are truly worth recognizing when they were doing the teamwork with academic department heads in the preparation of statutory and regulatory requirements of all certifying bodies encompassing the need of the university. For Xanthopoulou, Bakker, Demerouti, & Schaufeli,(2008), these findings indicated a unique contribution of vigour to work engagement over time over and above the impact to their job. Vigour is a valid way to think about engagement. If employees appear peppy, energetic, and interested in the work they do, they are likely engaged.

Table 2.2: Work Engagement as to Dedication

Dedication	Weighted Mean	Verbal Interpretation	Rank
1. I find the work that I do full of meaning and purpose	5.54	Always	2
2. I am enthusiastic about my job	5.42	Very Often	4
3. I am proud of the work that I do	5.66	Always	1
4. To me, my job is challenging	5.43	Very Often	3
Composite Mean	5.51	Always	

Legend: 5.50 – 6.00 = Always; 4.50 – 5.49 = Very Often; 3.50 – 4.49 = Often; 2.50 – 349 = Sometimes; 1.50 – 2.49 = Rarely; 1.00 – 1.49 = Almost Never; 0 = Never

Table 2.2 is a work engagement measured by dedication to work which posted grand mean of 5.51 rated as always. Respondents claimed they are always proud of the work that they do (5.66) and found full of meaning and purpose in what they are doing. Very often that they are enthusiastic about their job (5.42), and found it very challenging (5.43). This describes how in LPU, it is their degree of concentration and happiness which might vary; thus showing strong feeling of support and loyalty to the management, and the university they served depends upon the colleges and other demographic variables.

As an organization, it is very important to understand why your employees are emotionally connected and dedicated to their respective work assignments; which at times, dedicated employees of LPU claimed it's generally much more than salaries, training, or benefits but the familial culture that counts. Not surprisingly, for engaged and dedicated employees that working is fun, which is precisely the reason why they work so hard (Schaufeli, LeBlanc, Peeters et al., 2001); however, the reverse is not true; not all employees who work hard are engaged and committed. Although there are various reasons to work hard, variables such as financial needs, promotion prospects, or perhaps a poor marriage, some do so because they are driven by an obsession to work. These so-called workaholics are not pulled towards their work because they like it, but they are pushed by a strong inner drive they cannot resist. Some non-academic department heads show dedication not obsession because they love LPU much, they are even engaged in its very unique familial culture thus turning them to be productive and feel validated and appreciated.

Similar to the engaged school principals (Mauno et al., 2007), they are also productive as they believe they are able to meet the demands they face in their work. For them as engaged workers, they believe that they will generally experience good outcomes in life (optimistic), and they can satisfy their needs by participating in roles within the organization.

It has to be accepted that dynamic people in an organization are becoming dedicated to perform duties and responsibilities which may result into a higher level of organizational productivity and in the academe institutional success like LPU. By building a culture that enables employees to engage in their work, organisations may benefit from staff who are willing to go the extra mile and achieve better financial performance (Baumruk, 2006).

Table 2.3: Work Engagement as to Absorption

Absorption	Weighted Mean	Verbal Interpretation	Rank
1. Time flies when I am working	5.01	Very Often	4
2. When I am working, I forget everything else around me	4.23	Often	7
3. My job inspires me	5.47	Very Often	1
4. I feel happy when I am working intensely	5.28	Very Often	2.5
5. I am immersed in my work	5.28	Very Often	2.5
6. I get carried away when I am working	4.62	Very Often	6
7. It is difficult to detach myself from my job	4.72	Very Often	5
Composite Mean	4.94	Very Often	

Legend: 5.50 – 6.00 = Always; 4.50 – 5.49 = Very Often; 3.50 – 4.49 = Often; 2.50 – 349 = Sometimes; 1.50 – 2.49 = Rarely; 1.00 – 1.49 = Almost Never; 0 = Never

Table 2.3 is on work engagement as to absorption which obtained grand mean of 4.94 interpreted as very often. Non - academic department heads posted that absorption feeling is manifested very often with their inspiration in their job (5.47), they are carried away by their job (5.28) and they feel immersed in their work. Least in their absorption dimension, is that when they are working, they forget everything else around them (4.23). Inspiration is a product of reward; non-academic department heads felt they are inspired for they are part of the success of LPU. Whatever accomplishments of the organization; they also feel their importance as the tag line" LPU power team and their strength is their people". There are the employees who are still serving LPU for more than 20 years as they are still inspired and carried away by their jobs to continually be a meaningful employee in spite of their age. This contributes to an employee's sense of self-actualization and is extremely self-rewarding.

Theoretically, when employees are engaged in their work it is linked to all kinds of positive outcomes for organizations. Engaged workers are full of energy, committed to the organization and work hard, without developing work-related stress complaints. They are not only productive, but their positive work attitude creates a positive atmosphere at work as well. This is the same results on the research done by Bay et al (2014) that in terms of absorption, LPU faculty members were very often immersed in their work and they feel very often that time flies when they are working. They feel happy when they are working intensely and they very often get carried away when they are working However, they also very often feel difficult to detach themselves from their work and when they are working, they forget everything else around them which obtained the least weighted mean scores. This is an implication that LPU just like non- academic department heads possessed high work engagement. No. 4, 2014

Table 3 presents the comparison of responses on work engagement when a grouped according to profile as gender, department and years of service. It was observed that there was a significant difference on vigour when grouped according to department (0.000) and years of service (0.000) since the computed p-values were less than 0.05 alpha level.

Table 3: Difference of Responses Work Engagement when grouped according to Profile Variables

	Vigour			Dedication			Absorption		
Profile Variables	F-value	p-value	I	F-value	p-value	I	F-value	p-value	I
Gender	1.210	0.227	NS	2.169	0.031	S	1.055	0.292	NS
Department	3.475	0.000	HS	2.150	0.016	S	2.913	0.001	S
Years in Service	6.249	0.000	HS	4.068	0.003	S	6.181	0.000	HS

Legend: Significant at p-value < 0.05

This means that the responses vary significantly and was found out from the post hoc test conducted, employee from CCS and those who are in the institution for more than 31 years are more engaged in their work. With these results, it was very notable how the College of Computer Studies employees are very vigorous in the task assigned to them. As they are accredited under Accreditation Board for Engineering and Technology (ABET), non-academic and academic employees who are serving the university for long under this program are in full force and with extra efforts in meeting the international quality standards that produce graduates prepared to enter a global workforce.

The value of an ABET-Accredited School provides assurance that a college or university program meets the quality standards of the profession to have a solid educational foundation and is capable of leading the way in innovation and emerging technologies. With such demands, their responses to work loads are truly commendable. Even research suggested that the level of work engagement in general is affected by the work place (Brown, 1996; Kahn, 1990, in Kirkpatrick, 2007) and the characteristics of the work, including job status and job demands (Mauno *et al.,* 2007). In this university, workloads and job statuses are contributory for each department undertaking accreditation, ISO, ABET, Center of Excellence and other standards for they are preparing more documents than other departments/ colleges. People are more likely to be engaged if their jobs and the culture of the organization match both their abilities and skills, and their motivation and values.

As to dedication, result reveals that the responses when grouped according to gender (0.031), department (0.016) and years in service (0.003) differ statistically. This means that the null hypothesis was rejected and implies that female employees who are in the academic department heads working for more than 31 years and under College of Nursing are more dedicated and engaged in their work.

It is very much expected that there would be differences in work engagement between male and female, however; highly engaged employees regardless of their demographics seems to give extra effort because in their work they feel they are being cared for. People's recognition send powerful message to employees that the organization understands and appreciates that they are doing their work well. Parallel to the result of the research done by Bay et al (2014) on Work Engagement, it is not surprising that for faculty members of LPU, dedication was found to be part of the characteristics towards teaching profession. They commit themselves to share their utmost knowledge for the benefit of the students and welfare of the university. They always look forward to the transformation of attitude and behavior of the learners through their unwavering effort of giving motivation and encouragement to pursue higher goals and objectives.

For non-.teaching, the more years of service that employees whether academic or non-academic are dedicated in the task assigned to them. Their dedication is characterized by the last to leave work for they love what they do so much. This isn't because they are workaholics or toiling long hours out of fear for losing their jobs but they genuinely love what they do.

With regards to the respondents' engagement in terms of absorption, it was found out that there was a significant difference when grouped according to years in service (0.000) and department (0.001). This was observed because the resulted p-values were less than 0.05 alpha level. The result only shows that the level of engagement varies and it was disposed that non- academic employees from College of Nursing and working in the institution for 31 years and above are more fascinated in their work compared to others.

Table 3: Difference in the Responses on Work Engagement when Grouped according to Category (Non- Academic and Academic Department Heads)

	Vigor			Dedication			Absorption		
Profile Variables	F-value	p-value	I	F-value	p-value	I	F-value	p-value	I
Category	1.919	0.056	NS	2.784	0.006	S	3.523	0.000	HS

Legend: Significant at p-value < 0.05

Table 3 presents the differences in the responses regarding work engagement when grouped according to category as non- academic and academic department heads. They are not significant in terms of vigour (p=.056) greater than .05, significantly related to dedication and highly significant to absorption.

Vigour results posted a grand mean of "very often" (5.12) for both academic and non-academic department heads. This measures an equal footage on how they persevere, and feel the strength every morning to go to their work. Their dedication is significant for there are varying category of their profile variable dimensions as gender, department and length of service. Dedication is showing loyalty to the management and university they served and thus individual differences in this is at par to be taken into consideration. Although there are various reasons to work hard, variables such as financial needs, promotion prospects, or perhaps a poor marriage, some do so because they are driven by an obsession to work.

The high differences on absorption as to years in service (0.000) and department (0.001). Absorption posted highly significant among rating of non-academic and academic department heads as to years of service and department; non- academic employees from College of Nursing and working in the institution for 31 years and above are more fascinated in their work compared to others. Thus; it connotes high concentration in work and parameters of a happily engrossed employees; that individual varies. Therefore, they are differently rated since it is a manifestation of their motivation to work, and their productivity. Employees have different motivations for working at a job. What people want from work is situational, depending on the person, his needs and the rewards that are meaningful to him.

Conclusion

The profile results show that most of the respondents are male, non - academic personnel represented very well by their respective departments and working for longer period of time. These variables used by researchers served as an avenue to understand their contribution to LPU as an organization. Academic and non-academic department heads' work engagement is characterized in their sense of dedication, vigour and absorption. As a dynamic people in LPU, they manage to be dedicated to perform duties and responsibilities which resulted into the many academic blessings of institutional success.

The gender as male and female is not contributory to the respondents' work engagement only in dedication; further, the department and years in service of the respondents show significant and highly significant in their feeling of dedication, vigour and absorption. Thus, dedication of the non-academic and non-academic department heads varies significantly on how they are being engaged. Absorption posted highly significant rating of non-academic and academic department heads as to years of service and department high concentration in work and parameters of a happily engrossed employee varies. Therefore, they are differently rated since it is a manifestation of their motivation to work, and their productivity to their job.

Recommendations

1. LPU management may consider other innovative forms of incentives for those who have been working and stay long in the institution. This may not be financial but sustainable for them.
2. Intrinsic motivation may also be done by HRMDO in order to improve their vigor and absorption work engagement dimensions.
3. The MIS office may offer other means of improving work engagement variables in order to improve healthy work environment in Lyceum of the Philippines University.
4. LPU alumni may also be part of this work engagement instrument for future use of this valuable data.

References

Bay, A. B., An, I. and Laguador, J. M. (2013). Organizational Satisfaction And Work Engagement Of Filipino Teachers In An Asian University. *International Journal of Multidisciplinary Academic Research* Vol. 2, No. 4, ISSN 2309-3218S.

Bakker, A. B., Gierveld, J. H., and Van Rijswijk, K. (2006). Success factors among female school principals in primary teaching: A study on burnout, work engagement, and performance. *Diemen the Netherlands: Right Management Consultants.*

Bakker, A. B., Hakanen, J. J., Demerouti, E. and Xanthopoulou, D. (2007). Job resources boost work engagement particularly when job demands are high. *Journal of Educational Psychology,* 99, 274-284.

Bakker, A. B., Schaufeli, W. B., Leiter, M. P., and Taris, T. W. (2008). Work engagement: An emerging concept in occupational health psychology. *Work & Stress, 22*(3): 187-200.

Baumruk, R. (2006). Why managers are crucial to increasing engagement: Identifying steps managers can take to engage their workforce. *Strategic HR Review,* 5(2), 24-27.

Catteeuw, F., Flynn, E., and Vonderhorst, J. (2007). Employee Engagement: Boosting Productivity in Turbulent Times. *Organization Development Journal, 25*(2).

Cleland, A., Mitchinson, W., and Townend, A. (2008). Engagement, assertiveness and business performance–A new perspective. *Ixia Consultancy Ltd.*

Crush, P. (2007). 'Rules of engagement', Human Resources, October 2007.

Flade, P. (2003). Great Britain's workforce lacks inspiration. *Gallup Management Journal, 11*, 1-3.

Johnson, M. (2004). The new rules of engagement: life-work balance and Employee commitment, The Chartered Institute of Personnel and Development.

Gallup Organization. (2006). Gallup study: Engaged employees inspire company innovation. *Gallup Management Journal.*

Hetrick, S., and Martin, G. (2006). Corporate reputations, branding and people management. Routledge.

Johnson, M. (2004). *The new rules of engagement: life-work balance and employee commitment.* CIPD Publishing.

Madina, M. (2017). Employees Engagement across the Generations.

Mauno, S., Kinnunen, U. and Ruokolainen, M. (2007). Job demands and resources as antecedents of work engagement: A longitudinal study. *Journal of Vocational Behavior,* 70, 149_171.

Pech, R., and Slade, B. (2006). Employee disengagement: is there evidence of a growing problem? *Handbook of Business Strategy,* 7(1): 21-25.

Schaufeli, W. B., Taris, T. W., and Bakker, A. B. (2008). It takes two to tango. Workaholism is working excessively and working compulsively. *The long work hours culture: Causes, consequences and choices*, 203-226.

Schaufeli, W. B., Bakker, A. B., and Salanova, M. (2006). The measurement of work engagement with a short questionnaire: A cross-national study. *Educational and psychological measurement*, *66*(4): 701-716.

Schaufeli, W. B., and Taris, T. W. (2005). The conceptualization and measurement of burnout: Common ground and worlds apart. *Work & Stress*, *19*(3): 256-262.

Westman, M. (2001). Stress and strain crossover. *Human relations*, *54*(6): 717-751.

The intended outcome of the research is for the improvement of the Human Resource Management in terms of improving its incentives thru the identified work engagement among significant numbers of employees who participated in the conduct of the research.

The management considers an Innovation in as far as Succession planning is concerned. A new University policy was installed during the very recent planning on giving value for those employees who are qualified and been staying long in the University to be promoted and be the next in rank department Heads. This will surely improve their vigor and absorption work engagement dimensions.

A discussion with Alumni Director, Dr. Evangeline Mendoza, was also done for Work Engagement to be incorporated in her "Sinsay Muna Alumni "wherein visiting alumni will be asked to have a 2 minutes online of their Work Engagement which will be a potential research data of the University.

12

The Role of Chemistry Education for Sustainable Transformation

EGHAGHA, Patricia N.

Abstract

The Paper examined the role of chemistry education for sustainable transformation. It focused on the meaning of chemistry, its origin, branches, chemistry and other disciplines, chemistry for human development, in food processing, preservation, medicine and agriculture, Chemistry Education for industrialization; and in cottage industries. Challenges of chemistry education, industrialization in Nigeria were also examined. Among the way forward suggested include: encouraging development of cottage industries, banning of importation of foreign goods, promoting the development of our local goods and services and government dialoguing with organizations like United Nations Educational, Scientific and Cultural Organization (UNESCO), Science Teachers Association of Nigeria (STAN) and Institute of Chartered Chemists of Nigeria (ICCON), etc. in other to achieve industrial restructuring of our nation using chemistry in particular and science education in general.

Key Words: *Chemistry, Education, Sustainable, Transformation*

Introduction

Chemistry is as old as man and began when man started using certain substances capable of relieving aches, pains and hunger. It is involved in daily human activities such as cooking, baking, brewing, mining, washing, dyeing and medicine. Chemistry is an aspect of science which deals with chemical elements, their compounds (e.g composition, Properties and structures) and the changes they undergo which leads to inter- conversions of substances, the chemical reactions (Busev and Edimov, 1984).

The alchemical period corresponds to the span of human history that preceeded the era in which fundamental understanding in the chemical sciences began to be acquired by mankind. Most scholars believed that alchemy has its roots in ancient Egypt. China has also emerged as a possible source of alchemical thought. Thus, alchemy was the practice of chemistry such as it existed over the approximately twenty–five centuries before the time of Robert Boyle (1627 – 1691) and Antoine Lavoiser (1743 – 1784), when chemistry began to develop into the science we know today. Alchemy was an early precursor to science and included many of chemistry–related processes. That has become known as the chemicals arts – The working of metals and alloys, glass making and glass colouring, the preparation and use of pigments, dyes and therapeutic agents.

Man's interest in chemistry is essentially a practical one. He is interested in the way materials in the universe behave and react under different conditions and the ways in which he can use these materials for his own purposes. Complementary to this practical approach is a logical scientific method of writing, the discovery of law to summarize information and the development of ideas and theories to interpret and explain observations (Hill and Holman, 1983).

Branches of Chemistry

The three main branches of Chemistry are organic chemistry concerned with carbon compounds, inorganic chemistry concerned with the compounds of all other elements; and physical chemistry which deals with the study of the physical properties of compounds and the physical changes that occur during reactions.

Chemistry and other Disciplines

Chemistry plays an important role in both pure and applied sciences. Chemistry in biological sciences gave birth to a branch of science named bio-chemistry. This is due to the fact that chemical reactions occur in the living system and the knowledge of these reactions in the living system is very important to man. It is also of interest to know that physicists use many chemistry concepts to explain their theories. Application of chemistry in orthodox medicine e.g. diagnosis and drug prescription has resulted in orthodox medicine being preferred to traditional medicine in some parts of the world. Merging chemistry and geography gave rise to geology and geological studies have led to the discoveries and identification of large mineral deposits which are being exploited for human use. Carbon dating in Archeology is a chemical technique used in age determination of object of historical importance (Okecha, 1989). Chemistry is applicable in engineering in the study of properties of materials especially metal to determine their suitability for fabricating machine, construction of bridges, road and building. Cartography (an aspect of surveying), use Chemistry in the area of azo compounds in printing maps. All ICT materials are made of chemical compounds. The application of chemistry in other fields of knowledge cannot be exhausted, because of the important place of chemistry in human life.

Chemistry for Human Development

Since chemistry is the study of man and the world around, its role in the development of mankind cannot be over–emphasized. The following are the major areas of application of chemistry in human development.

Chemistry in Food Processing and Preservation

According to SciTechnol (2017), food preservation includes preventing the growth of bacteria, fungi or other micro – organisms as well as retarding the oxidation of fats that cause rancidity thus promoting longer shelf life and reduced hazard from eating the food. Food processing is the process of transformation of raw ingredients into food by the means of physical and chemical means. It is the process of producing raw food ingredients into marketable food products which can be easily prepared and used by the consumers. Example of food processing includes preparing space food for consumption under zero gravity. It is easy to keep processed food for a long time, canned and frozen fruits and vegetables; food fortified with nutrients such as fiber, vitamin D and Omega-3 fatty acids. Lack of appropriate technology for processing and preserving abundant agricultural products resulted in huge wastage of food materials in the past. About 50% of the food materials perish after harvest but the discovery that chemical substances such as the one's mentioned above are good for preserving food materials has brought an end to the post harvest loss previously experienced (Gara, 1976).

Chemistry in Medicine

According to National Institute of General Medical, (NIM, 2011), Chemistry plays such a role in tweaking molecules to interact appropriately with the body. Most important medical progress in recent history has come from the development of powerful antibiotics and vaccines to treat infectious diseases caused by bacteria, viruses and parasites. The misuse of antibodies is the most common reason why antibiotic resistance is such a significant public health problem. Making matters worse, methicillin resistant staphylococcus aureus or MRSA has become resistant to most disinfectants and antiseptics used in hospitals. Chemists are working hard to outwit microbes that develop resistance. New forms of antibiotic drugs are currently in the pipeline, and researchers are trying to design them to target vulnerable molecular regions of enzymes within bacteria.

Chemistry in Agriculture

The rapid growth in population coupled with only small percentage of the population engaged in farming has resulted in acute shortage of food. The discovery of chemical substances (i.e. fertilizers and hormones) for crops resulting in rapid growth and high yields has revolutionized the agricultural sector and has increased food production. Also, herbicides, the most effective tool for weed control developed by the chemical industries, has considerably reduced human labour in weeding.

According to Creative Common (2017), knowledge in Agricultural Chemistry - the study of both Chemistry and Biochemistry has enhanced agricultural production, the processing of raw products into foods and beverages, and in environmental monitoring and remediation. These studies emphasize the relationship between plants, animals and bacteria and their environment. It is the science of chemical compositions and changes involved in the production, protection, and use of crops and livestock.

Chemistry Education for Industrialisation

The distinction between the developed, developing and under-developed nation is the level of technological advancement. Science and technological knowledge is an important tool for industrialization. Steel and petro–chemical industries are bed–rock for rapid industrialization of any nation. Steel industries serve as a gate-way for other industries for casting and fabrication of machines, tools and spare parts can be established based on availability of steel products. Converting iron ore into steel and allied products is essentially a chemical process. Sound knowledge of chemistry is a compulsory requirement for people who aspire to be trained as metallurgical and chemical engineers. Also man-power in petro-chemical industry requires sound knowledge of chemistry for effective training. Quality control laboratories personnel deal with chemical analysis of raw materials, intermediate products and finished products to ensure that they conform to set standards for production. So, skilled personnel of quality control laboratories are trained chemists and other chemistry related disciplines. With these few examples, the relevance of chemistry education in industrialization cannot be over-emphasized.

Chemistry in Cottage Industries

India for example is undergoing rapid industrialization because of her involvement in cottage industries. This is because cottage industries are inexpensive and do not require the use of complicated machines required by giant industries resulting in job creation as more hands may be required to carryout some manual processes in the absence of machineries; thereby making the products cheap. There are living evidences to show that people with sound chemistry education do well in cottage industries e.g. in the area of soap and cosmetics. Even crude petroleum can be refined at the backyard with the knowledge of chemistry of fractional distillation to monitor and collect the products.

Challenges of Chemistry Education in Nigeria

No country in the world aiming at rapid industrialization takes Chemistry Education in particular and Science Education in general so lackadaisically as Nigeria does (Modupe, 1995). Most secondary schools lack functional science laboratories; especially those located in the rural areas. Proper teaching of chemistry cannot be done without well equipped laboratories. Also is the lack of qualified and experienced chemistry teachers some schools use teachers who do not major in chemistry to teach the subject resulting in poor performance of students.

Another challenge is the low level of awareness in the society concerning the relevance of science and chemistry in particular for rapid industrialization. Instead, emphasis is on professions such as Medicine, Accounting, Engineering, Management, ICT etc. without knowing that science is the basis for meaningful industries where these other professions take their root. Students do not know what to do with chemistry; because the relevant practical training that would have made the subject relevant to the society is missing.

Challenges of Industrialisation in Nigeria

The challenges of Science and Chemistry Education in particular having no serious impact on the nation's industrial development can be traced to the poor and wrong pattern of our industrial development since independence. Our leaders in the past pursued rapid industrialization by way of importing machineries, scientific equipment and technical manpower for the establishment of industries. This type of industrialization that depended solely on importations does not allow industrial development as it lacked indigenous contributions in the form of local design and manufacture of machineries, processing equipment, local sourcing of raw materials, and adaptation or upgrading of technologies (Ufaruna, 1991). The foreigners that dominated the Nigerian industries were not interested in local inputs in terms of raw materials and technical manpower.

This problem eventually resulted in most industries in Nigeria becoming producers of secondary products and importers of primary raw materials from abroad. The few Nigerian scientists employed by these multinational companies were only involved in routine duties and as a result the Nigerian scientists or technologists cannot impact his/her knowledge or improve on it because of limitation to routine duties. This was a calculated attempt by foreign based companies operating in Nigeria to put the nation in perpetual dependence on importation of semi-processed products from their parent companies abroad. This factor generated the notion among Nigerian under-graduate studying science and technology courses that what one learns in school has no direct application after graduation and as a result, no conscious effort is made to acquire the proper skills required during training. The effect of this problem is that most Nigeria scientists and technologists are not able to establish a small scale industry on their own, resulting in high rate of unemployment in Nigeria.

Way Forward

1. Cottage industries should be encouraged seriously by the government by empowering interested persons especially chemistry and science personnel's with soft loans, machines etc.
2. Government should match policies with action by ensuring the effective implementation of science curriculum at all levels.
3. Serious funding of Science and well equipped science laboratories should be a combined effort of both government and non-governmental agencies to ensure the practice of science in all level of education.
4. Importation of local goods should be banned and our indigenous industries and goods should be encouraged to develop.
5. Government and educational boards should ensure that only science teachers should teach science based on their area of specialization
6. Government should mount awareness programmes that will popularize chemistry and other sciences for industrial development
7. More workshop and seminars should be organized periodically for chemistry teachers at various levels for updating and acquisition of knowledge about latest development in chemistry.
8. Government should always dialogue with chemistry and science agencies. e.g. UNESCO, STAN and ICCON, etc., in other to achieve industrial restructuring of our nation.

References

Busev and Edimov (1984). *Chemistry.* Moscow: Mir Publishers.

Creative Common (2017),Wikipedia, Attribution–share Alike 3.0.unported (CC by – SA 3.0) Edited 2017

Gara, I. D. (1976). *Introductory food chemistry.* West Post, Connectial: Avi Publishing Company Inc.

Hill, G. O. and Holman, J. S. (1983). *Chemistry in Context*, 2nd Ed. Edinbungh: Thomas Nelson and Sons Ltd.

Modupe, O. (1995). "Evolution of and National Policy of Technology Education in Nigeria" (ASUP) Kaduna Polytechnic, Kaduna.

NIM, (2011), National institute of General Medical Sciences 45 Center Drive MSC 6200 Bethesida. MD 20892.6200.

SciTechnol, (2017). Immunology and Microbiology Journal of food and nutritional Disorders 5716 corsa Ave, Suite110, Westlake, Los Angeles C.A I.P. 91862 – 7854, USA

Ufuaruna, I. N. (1991), Technological Research and Industrial development - the missing Link convocation week Lecture delivered at the Federal Polytechnic, Idah, Kogi State.

13

Restructuring the Nigerian State: Problems and Prospects

ADEDAYO Temitayo G. & SENUGA Mabayoje A.

Abstract

The study investigated the problems and prospects of restructuring the Nigerian state. The study adopted a survey research design, where two sampling techniques were used. Purposive sampling technique was used to select respondents in Ijebu-Ode and Odogbolu Local Governments, accidental sampling technique was used to select students, market women, civil and public servants as well as members of the civil society in the two selected local governments. A self-designed questionnaire tagged 'Restructuring The Nigerian State: Problems and Prospects (RTNSPP) was used. Three research hypotheses were formulated and tested using Student "t" test at 5% level of significance to guide the study. The result of the study indicated that there is a significant relationship between sharing of national resources and call for restructuring in Nigeria; there is a significant relationship between power sharing and call for restructuring in Nigeria and there is a significant relationship between ethnicity and call for restructuring in Nigeria. The study, therefore, recommended that various federating units should develop according to their resources and at their own pace without being slowed down by others, the issue of over- centralization of power and resources in Nigeria need to be revisited and the principle of Federal Character aimed at creating equity in appointment, representative positions, allocation of resources and location of social infrastructure among component units should be revisited and reviewed such that it can correct imbalances in the body polity when implemented properly as most Nigerians do not believe in the ability of the commission, as it is presently, to correct the imbalance and preponderance of some units over others.

Keywords: *Restructuring, Prospects, Problems, Federal character, Over-centralization and Imbalances*

Introduction

Before colonialism, the area that is now known as Nigeria comprised of different kingdoms, empires, caliphates and chiefdoms, that evolved complex systems of government independent of contact with Europe. Most of these kingdoms were heterogeneous in culture, traditions, norms and religions. There were great Kingdoms such as the Kanem-Borno Empire, with known history of more than a thousand years as well as the Sokoto Caliphate which existed for nearly a century before it was conquered by Britain. It had ruled most of the Savannah area of Northern and part of Western Nigeria. There were also kingdoms of Ife and Benin; the Oyo Empire, the City-States of Niger-Delta and the Igbo of South-East (Crowther, 1976; Ibezute, 1999). As part of these empires, caliphates and kingdoms, there existed small City-States or Chiefdoms who agreed to live within the Kingdoms with submissive allegiance. There was also commercial and cross-cultural contact between the diverse groups (Rodney, 1972). Similarly, a symbolic inter-group relationship also persisted which was hinged on respecting the norms and values of each other as the case may be (Rodney, 1972).

Structurally, Nigeria is a heterogeneous society, made up of different ethnic nationalities with diverse belief systems, customs and institutions. Though the exact number of ethnic groups is not known, some scholars put the number at 250, while others believe that it has more than 350 ethnic groups (Obikeze and Anthony, 2003). Professor Okwudiba Nnoli, a leading expert on ethnic politics in Africa attributed this uncertainty to lack of agreement on the criteria used in identifying ethnic groups (Nnoli, 2008). According to him, some analysts who relied on linguistic factor identified 394 ethnic groups in Nigeria, while others put the figure at between 550 and 619. Based on these ethnic configurations, the country is governed by a system of government that operates in accordance with the provisions of a Federal Constitution except during military regimes where the Constitution is often suspended.

According to Wheare (1964), federalism is the method of sharing powers so that the central and regional governments are each within a sphere coordinate and independent. This definition has remained the benchmark for the practice of federalism in all states structured along its principles. Its principles of coordinate, independent and on different levels of government promote the concept of separation of powers between the central government and the component units within a given territory. This means that federalism is a system of arrangement that promotes the sharing of governmental powers within a country. The definition of federalism as given by Tamuno (1998) is, however, all-embracing and underscores its raison d'etre. According to him, federalism is "a form of government where the component units of a political organization participate in sharing powers and functions in a cooperative manner through the combined forces of ethnic pluralism and cultural diversity among others, which tends to pull people apart". This implies that federalism is a device for dealing with the problem of unity in a plural society.

No wonder, the 1954 Lyttleton Constitution, which first provided for the division of powers between two levels of governments, namely: Federal and Regional governments, marks the beginning of federalism in Nigeria. In the said division of power and function, each level was autonomous in its own area of jurisdiction. The promulgation of 1954 constitution marks the actual take-off of formal inter-governmental relations and interaction between levels of governments within Nigerian polity. The federal principle introduced since 1954 in Nigeria survived to present day despite contemporary political development in terms of crises and restructuring.

In the Nigerian federal system of government, there have been series of agitations from the component units that make up the federating units. As pointed out by Adeyeri (2010), Nigeria's federal system has oscillated between the excessive regionalism that marked the First Republic (1960 -1966) and the excessive centralization of the military, and relatively the post-military era. Contradictions in Nigeria's federal system such as the colonial factor, military rule, structural imbalance, over-centralization of power in the central government, among others, have overtime perpetuated various thorny issues and challenges within the Nigerian federation. Other contending issues in the Nigerian federalism include but are not limited to resource control, revenue allocation, state creation, federal character question, leadership crisis, enmity, divisions and hatred with a sense of sectionalism, ethno-tribal chauvinism, geographical polarizations and imbalance.

In fact, from the pre-colonial to post-independence era and up to the present democratic dispensation, resource control has remained the most contentious issue among the tiers of government. The situation in Nigeria is such that the federal government harnesses the natural resources and shares revenue with the States and Local Governments, which is a clear departure from an ideal federal constitution in which, the regions or states are the federating units and control resources located in their territories (Tambuwal and Gbajabiamila cited in Agbaje, 2013) and this promote agitations and calls for resource control and restructuring.

In an attempt to address these challenges facing Nigerian federalism, various policies and programmes had been put in place by previous regimes in Nigeria ranging from Niger Delta Development Commission (NDDC); Reconciliation, Reconstruction and Rehabilitation after the Civil War, derivation fund for oil producing state and above all creation of states and local governments. Nigeria presently consists of 36 states and a Federal Capital Territory which in almost everything enjoys the status of a state. Also among the federating units are 776 local government councils being government at the grassroots (Constitution, 1999). Despite this number of sub-national unit, there exists agitation for more states and local government areas to be created due to observed imbalance (Bassey, Omono, Bisong and Bassey, 2013). Agitation also exists in terms of allocation of resources (revenue), political restructuring, allocation of social infrastructures and amenities, occupation of presidential and other representative positions, ethnicity problems and national unity, minority issues, state creation problem, resource control controversy, secession, boundary disputes, dual loyalty, principle of federal character controversy amongst other challenges which have really denied Nigeria the opportunity of becoming a strong and united nation. Thus, the need for this study aimed at examining the current trends and agitations calling for the restructuring of the Nigerian state.

Statement of the Problem

The word "restructuring" is not new in Nigerian polity as a word like 'resource control' has previously been used to express disenchantment over marginalization especially by the ethnic minority. In the last two years, the agitation for restructuring has gained momentum across the country and has nearly torn the country apart. The proponents of restructuring based their argument on the imbalance in political appointment, ethnicity, dominance of one region over the other in leadership/governance of the federation, marginalization, lop-sidedness in resource allocation amongst others. The agitation has also taken its toil on the National Assembly members as they shared divergent opinion on the issue of restructuring. The Nigerian citizens have also expressed their opinion on national newspapers and social media on restructuring but much attention has not been given to the outcry of the minority on restructuring, especially as it relates to resource control, occupation of presidential and other representative positions, ethnicity problems and national unity, state creation, secession, boundary disputes, amongst others. This calls for an investigation into the problems and prospects of restructuring the Nigerian State.

Research Hypotheses

The following hypotheses were formulated:

$H0_1$: There is no significant relationship between sharing of national resources and call for restructuring in Nigeria

$H0_2$: There is no significant relationship between power sharing and call for restructuring in Nigeria

$H0_2$: There is no significant relationship between ethnicity and call for restructuring in Nigeria.

Concept of Federalism

The concept federalism has numerous and multifaceted definitions. According to Tamuno (2003), "Federalism is that form of government where the component units of a political organization participate in sharing powers and functions in a co-operative manner through the combined forces of ethnic pluralism and cultural diversity, among others". In the words of A.V. Dicey, "Federalism is a political invention which is intended to reconcile national unity and power, with the maintenance of the rights of the separate member states" (Elaigwu and Akindele, 1996). Jega in his own view said federalism is "essentially about the distribution of political and economic decision-making power among constituent units or levels of governments" (Elaigwu and Akindele, 1996).

Sills (1993) defines federalism as:

> "mode of political organization which unites separate politics within an overarching political system so as to allow each to maintain its fundamental political integrity, which is achieved by distribution of power among general and constituent governments in a manner designed to protect the existence and authority of all the governments, where all policies are reached and implemented through negotiation"(pg.23).

Nigeria is a federal state with the federal government as general unit, while state and local governments are federating units. Wheare (1963) saw federalism as a constitutional arrangement which divides the lawmaking powers and functions between two levels of government in such a way that each within its respective spheres of jurisdiction and competence, is independent and coordinate (Wheare, 1963). Federalism is derived from the Latin word "foedus" meaning covenant. It is a political concept in which a group of members are bound together by covenant with a governing representative head. The term is also used to describe a system of the government in which sovereignty is constitutionally divided between a central governing authority and constitutional political units (like states or provinces). The classic definition of a Federal Government, as provided by Sir Kenneth Wheare, is a system of government in which sovereignty is divided between the central and state governments.

According to Elaigwu (1996),

> "Federalism is essentially a mechanism for managing conflicts in a multicultural state between two types of self-determination and

> natural self-determination which guarantee security for all in the nation state, on the one hand, and the self determination of component groups to retain their identities on the other hand" (pg.96).

According to Appadorai (1982), a federal state is the one in which there is a central authority that represents the whole and acts on behalf of the whole in external affairs and on such internal affairs as are held to be of common interest and in which there are also provincial or state authorities with powers of legislation and administration within the sphere allotted to them by the constitution. A federal system of government often arises from the desire of the people to form a union without necessarily losing their identities. Federalism would, therefore, seem to provide an attractive system of government especially in the context of ethnic pluralism found in many African states. Federalism is generally accepted by many as necessary for managing the country's ethnic diversity as reflected in the adage "unity in diversity". Federalism in principle implies the construction of a system where consensus is reached between current demands of the union and the territorial diversity within an emerging society, by the creation of a single political system within which central and provincial governments are assigned coordinated authority in a manner defining both the legal or political limits of equality or subordinate functions (Agbu, 2004).

Babalawe (1998) explained federalism as one in which there is an explicit and constitutional demarcation of powers and functions among national and sub-national units. Moreover, the powers and responsibilities are distributed in such a manner as to protect the existence of authority of both levels of polity, each of which is independent within its own sphere. It refers to the doctrine which advocates and promotes the form of organization of a state in which power is dispersed or decentralized by contract as a means of safeguarding local identities and individual liberties. From an operational perspective, Ojo (2002) points out that federalism is reputed to be an effective political-cum-constitutional design for managing complex governmental problems usually associated with ethnic and cultural diversity.

Generally, federalism connotes the existence of two levels of government, each constitutionally or jurisdictionally empowered to make decision independent of each other within the legislature sphere assigned to it. In his own submission, Mazrui (1971) claims that federalism is an institutionalization of compromise relationship. It is not only democratic, complete with the institutionalization of most essential ingredients; it is also creative and flexible enough to incorporate several accommodation formulas. Federalism is a system in which the power to govern is shared between national and state governments, creating what is often called a federation (Akindele and Olaopa, 2002).

Theoretical Framework

The paradigm guiding analysis in this study is the Bassonian Theory of National Integration and Development. It is a model of analysis which explains society as being composed of competing and conflicting forces. Each force is an autonomous entity which can foster integration or disintegration. The combination of these forces makes for the development or destruction of a system. This theory viewed society as a dynamic system.

Bassey (2000) identified the following forces: eco-centric, ethno-centric, theo-centric and natu-centric. Eco-centric force resides at the individual domain and it is the force that propels a person towards achievement and accomplishment. Eco-centric force controls individuals to strive for self-preservation and accomplishment. This same eco-centric force compels a person to attempt to outshine another person. It promotes personal and private accumulation of wealth, private capital formation, security and protection. Eco-centric force operates at individual level and it accounts for why individuals compete with one another, even among siblings. The success of one person at the expense of others is due to high degree of eco-centric force. People with high eco-centric force controlling them tend to be more successful in business and professional vocations.

Ethno-centric force operates within a group. Such groups share characteristics of both secondary and primary group in the sense that, though relationship is formal, degree of solidarity and integration are comparatively very high. The type of group this force exists is the ethnic or tribal group. Ethno-centric force is the force that binds together members of ethnic or tribal groups as homogeneous entity. This force differs in its effect from society to society. In ethnically homogeneous society, this force promotes strong unity and ensures that the society exists as one indivisible entity with high rate of social solidarity and integration. In ethnically heterogeneous society, ethnocentric force draws dividing line between and among ethnic groups, acting as a divisive force.

Theo-centric force is the force that is controlled by religious sentiments occasioned by indoctrination and belief system. This force exists among and binds together members of the same religious faith, for example, Moslems. In a society with mono-belief system, just like ethno-centric force, theo-centric force is a uniting element. In a society with religious heterogeneity, it is a divisive force as theo-centric force puts members of different religions apart, while it brings members of the same religion together.

Eco-centric force operates in every society as society is made up collectivity of individuals. In this sense, individuals are the fundamental units of interaction at inter-personal level, and such interaction is guided by eco-centric force. Ethno-centric force exists in almost every society or community. From societies that are homogeneous, to those that are heterogeneous, ethnocentric force permeates, exerting different consequences as noted earlier. Theo-centric force also exists in every society in varying dimension, within members of same religious faith. Since ethnocentric and theo-centric forces exert divisive consequences in heterogeneous society, another force is needed to bind such societies together in terms of eliminating the divisive consequences of ethnocentric and theo-centric forces. This emergent force in highly heterogeneous society is natu-centric force.

Natu-centric force is the force that ensures stability in the society. Just like ethno-centric force that pulls members of the same ethnic or tribal group together, natu-centric force fosters integration and solidarity among members of the same nation, especially when the nation is ethnically and tribally heterogeneous. This force is required in every federal state and other systems of government which there is remarkable diversity and pluralism in ethnic and tribal composition. In a country which is racially or ethnically homogeneous, natu-centric force equates ethnocentric force. Natu-centric force is not natural to every ethnically plural society, but must be invoked through conscious advocacy, indoctrination and deliberate public policy formulation and implementation.

United States of America is a good example of a country that is able to invoke natu-centric force in the course of her development. Natu-centric force brings with it a sense of national unity, patriotism and commitment to national goals and value. This force once invoked dislodges the preponderance of other forces and redirect the citizens to work towards achievement of national values and goals. An American Indian Jew is primarily concerned with the success of America as a nation without focusing on acquiring power, wealth and fame for self or place of origin and indigeneship. This is so because natu-centric force produces sentiment which erases other prebendal and primordial sentiments associated with other forces which are natural to every individual and society. For a federal state to be stable and balanced, natu- centric force is required as a stabilization element and balancing strategy.

Governmental agency should be created to perform the function of re-orientation towards pursuing national values represented by equal right of every citizen in every part of the country, the citizen locates his or herself despite place of origin or indigeneship. Such agency should be strategized with advocacy and indoctrination of citizens. There should be legislation and policy directed at playing down on ethnic sentiment and consciousness. Ethnic affinity should rather be maintained through preservation of cultural heritage, as practiced in United States of America.

This theoretical model fosters unity of societies characterized by ethnic diversity. This is the reason for its development and adoption as a guide in this study. Nigeria is a plural society in terms of ethnic composition, with well over 374 ethnic groups, over 400 distinct languages, diverse belief systems, customs and institutions (Tamuno, 1998). This diversity impacts negatively on federal balance in Nigeria, resulting in power tilt and imbalanced structure, allocation of resources, location of infrastructure etc. It is in view of this that this research work expounds on and adopted Bassonian Theory of National Integration and Development as a theoretical guide. In this regard, the creation of natu-centric force in Nigeria is expected to erase all structural and systemic distortion occasioned by Nigeria diversities which produces imbalance and distorts the practice of true federalism.

Restructuring since the Return to Democratic Rule in 1999

The return to civil rule on May 29, 1999 following the re-establishment of democratic governance did not lay to rest the agitation for a Sovereign National Conference. The weaknesses of the 1999 Constitution had become more evident with various peoples of Nigeria expressing concerns about its operation. From May 1999 when the Constitution came into effect, many had challenged as a lie, the preamble to the Constitution which states:

> *"We the people of the Federal Republic of Nigeria having firmly and solemnly resolved, to live in unity and harmony as one indivisible and indissoluble sovereign nation under God, dedicated to the promotion of inter-African solidarity, world peace, international co-operation and understanding; and to provide for a Constitution for the purpose of promoting the good government and welfare of all persons in our country, on the principles of freedom, equality and justice, and for the purpose of consolidating the unity of our people; do hereby make, enact and give to ourselves the following Constitution."*

The proponents of a Sovereign National Conference continued to insist that this lie about "we the people..." must be resolved through a national conference in order to have a People's Constitution. In which case, the national conference should be seen as a constitution-making arrangement and a platform for the fundamental definition of our nationhood and citizenship. They also pointed out that rather than classify the proponents of national dialogue as agents of balkanization, Nigerian leaders must seize the opportunity presented to work towards redesigning the foundation of the nation to enable it achieve its potentials as a strong, prosperous and proud nation.

Against the backdrop of widespread pressures and agitation by Nigerians for opportunities to rethink the historical evolution, context and basis of their continued existence in one Nigeria, President Olusegun Obasanjo convened a National Political Reform Conference from February-July 2005. Among the issues of political reforms were: the federal structure, fiscal federalism (especially in relation to resource control), form of government, citizenship, accountability and ethics in government, the Independent National Electoral

Commission, political parties, reform of the electoral system, the economy, foreign policy and the environment.

Although the convocation of the conference provided the platform for national dialogue on important national issues, prominent leaders of civil society organizations argued that the National Political Reform Conference was similar to the late General Sani Abacha's National Constitutional Conference of 1995, and that it was not based on systemic people-determined structure. The leadership of the Conference of Nigerian Political Parties also questioned the rationale for the conference. As the debate intensified, a new group known as the Pro-National Political Reform Conference Organization (PRONACO) organized a parallel Conference. The PRONACO conference produced a report, including a model Constitution. But as it turned out, it lacked the capacity to implement or enforce its decisions and recommendations.

With the skepticisms about the value of the National Political Reform Conference and its possible breakup before commencing sitting, the civil society organizations continued their agitation for a Sovereign National Conference. In the end, the Conference deliberated and treated more than 700 memoranda submitted by Nigerians, and arrived at near unanimity on 187 recommendations out of 189 subjects decided upon. There was serious disagreement on only one subject, "Resource Control" and a sharp disagreement on the tenure of the President and Governors.

The proponents of Sovereign National Conference continued their agitation for a National Roundtable. To them, the 2005 National Political Reform Conference was not the kind of national dialogue they have been advocating. The Committee of Patriots, a group in the forefront of the agitation for convening a National Conference called on some personalities labelled, "Fathers of the Nation" to lend their voices and appeal to the Presidency and members of the National Assembly to yield to the call for a National Conference. The group strongly believed that "a National Conference will enable Nigerians from across ethnic and religious groups to deliberate and agree on the terms and conditions on which they are to live together in peace and unity." The group also emphasized that a National Conference would help "to work out a programme for ensuring development, progress, justice, equality and freedom for all Nigerians, and to adapt a Constitution whose source of authority, as the supreme law of the land, is the people, acting in a Constituent Assembly (i.e. National Conference) and a referendum, otherwise called a People's Constitution." What the group considered worrisome was the trend of events in the country and the nature and character of the political campaigns already mounted for the 2015 elections, This in itself, should inform the basis for the convocation of a national conference so that the future might not lead to chaos in the country.

Methodology

This study adopted a survey research design. Two sampling techniques were used in the study. Purposive sampling technique was used to select respondents in Ijebu-Ode and Odogbolu Local Governments, accidental sampling technique was used to select students, market women, civil and public servants as well as members of the civil society in the two selected local governments. A self-designed questionnaire tagged 'Restructuring the Nigerian State: Problems and Prospects (RTNSPP)', was used. The instrument had two sections, Section A contained items that elicited demographic information of the respondents while Section B contained structured items relating to the research hypotheses that necessitated the research study. The instrument was validated by two Senior Lecturers in Political Science and one English Language specialist from Tai Solarin University of Education, Ijebu-Ode and their comments /suggestions were reflected in the final production of the instrument. Also, a reliability coefficient of 0.82 was established using Cronbach alpha.

Presentation of Results

Analysis of Research Hypotheses

Hypothesis 1: ($H0_1$): There is no Significant Relationship between Sharing of National Resources and Call for Restructuring in Nigeria

Table 1: Student 'T' Analysis of the Relationship between Sharing of National Resources and Call for Restructuring in Nigeria

SUBJECT	Mean (X)	SD	No	df	t-cal.	t-critical	Decision
AGREED	3.28	0.50	104	118	22.72	1.65	Reject HO_1
DISAGREED **Source: Field Research, 2016**	2.94	0.21	16				

Level of significance – 0.05 N=120

Since "t" calculated is greater than the table/critical value (i.e. 22.72 > 1.67), it therefore implies that the null hypothesis which stated that there is no significant relationship sharing of national resources and call for restructuring in Nigeria is rejected while the alternative hypothesis which stated that there is a significant relationship between sharing of national resources and call for restructuring in Nigeria is upheld/retained.

Hypothesis 2: ($H0_2$): There is no Significant Relationship between Power Sharing and Call for Restructuring in Nigeria

Table 2: Student 'T' Analysis of the Relationship between Power Sharing and Call for Restructuring in Nigeria

SUBJECT	Mean (X)	SD	No	df	t-cal.	t-critical	Decision
AGREED	3.03	0.49	97	118	14.69	1.65	Reject HO_2
DISAGREED	2.47	0.44	23				

Level of significance – 0.05, N=120

Since "t" calculated is greater than the table/critical value (i.e. 14.69 > 1.65), it therefore implies that the null hypothesis which stated that there is no significant relationship between power sharing and call for restructuring in Nigeria is rejected while the alternative hypothesis which stated that there is a significant relationship between power sharing and call for restructuring in Nigeria is upheld.

Hypothesis 3 ($H0_3$): There is no Significant Relationship between Ethnicity and Call for Restructuring in Nigeria.

Table 3: Student 'T' Analysis of the Relationship between Ethnicity and Call for Restructuring in Nigeria

SUBJECT	Mean (X)	SD	No	df	t-cal.	t- crit.	Decision
AGREED	4.02	0.64	85	118	6.19	1.65	Reject HO_2
DISAGREED	3.16	0.14	35				

Level of significance – 0.05, N=120

Since "t" calculated is greater than the table/critical value (6.19 > 1.65), it therefore implies that the null hypothesis which stated that there is no significant relationship between ethnicity and call for restructuring in Nigeria is rejected while the alternative hypothesis which stated that there is a significant relationship between ethnicity and call for restructuring in Nigeria is upheld.

Discussion of Findings

Research hypothesis one stated that there is no significant relationship between sharing of national resources and call for restructuring in Nigeria. The testing of this research hypothesis indicated that there is a significant relationship between sharing of national resources and call for restructuring in Nigeria. In Nigeria, resource control has remained the most contentious issue among the tiers of government. With the discovery of oil in the South-South Region with its attendant challenges of environmental degradation which are either not attended to or sturdily addressed by the federal government, the issue of control over the resource becomes the order of the day. Despite the 13% derivation given to the oil producing state, the issue of agitation over resource control in Nigeria is still a recurring decimal. According to Tambuwal and Gbajabiamila cited in Agbaje (2013), the situation in Nigeria is such that the federal government harnesses the natural resources and shares revenue with the States and Local Government which is a clear departure from an ideal federal constitution in which, the regions or states in the federating units exercise control over resources located in their territories. According to him, this promotes agitations and calls for resource control and restructuring.

Research hypothesis two stated that there is no significant relationship between power sharing and call for restructuring in Nigeria. The result of this research hypothesis revealed that there is a significant relationship between power sharing and call for restructuring in Nigeria. Some ethnic groups in Nigeria are aggrieved over the continued domination of political power by some ethnic groups who believe that the power to rule belongs to them and this often results to the call for zoning and rotation of power amongst the geo-political zones in the country. Onwudiwe (2004) opined that the impetus for zoning and rotation of power was ostensibly derived from efforts to create a sense of belonging amongst ethno-national elite groups in the face of the inadequacies of federal character principles. According to him, zoning can rescue minorities from political obscurity and at the same time guarantee majority interests, foster national stability and ensure the success of democracy. In the same vein, Elaigwu (1997) positioned that there was a relatively delicate division of power between the North and the South. The North's control of political power was counter-balanced by the South's monopoly of economic power in the country.

Research hypothesis three stated that there is no significant relationship between ethnicity and call for restructuring in Nigeria. The result of this research indicated that there is a significant relationship between ethnicity and call for restructuring in Nigeria. Ethnic bickering and rivalry in Nigeria has become an incessant and regular occurrence. There is hardly any day that passes without news of killing, maiming, arson etc. between two or more ethnic groups. At each election, census, recruitment, etc., an issue of where the candidate comes from becomes the burning national issue or the struggle to have the highest or a bigger population for economic advantage.

Conclusion

The study established that the call for restructuring in Nigeria is predicated amongst other thing on sharing of national resources amongst the constituents, power sharing and ethnicity. Therefore, the study concluded that the country and its leaders have failed for too long to accept that they can only live in a widening sea of troubles while they continue to operate a convoluted system that is unitary but claims to be federal, and thus breeds injustice, antagonism and discontent. Only a true federalism through a regional autonomous political configuration will be an alternative strategy to quench the yearning and aspiration of the secessionists in Nigeria while ethnicity in appointment into position and recruitment should be jettisoned in order to reduce to the barest minimum ethnic bickering and rivalry in Nigeria. Besides, zoning of political power especially the presidency amongst the geo-political zones can rescue minorities from political obscurity and at the same time guarantee majority interests, foster national stability and ensure the success of democracy while the states should be empowered to exploit natural resources found in their area and remit the approved rate to the central government.

Recommendations

1. Various federating units should develop according to their resources and their own pace without being slowed down by others. The process of restructuring should involve changes in the distribution of power, responsibility and resources. The implementation of the recommendation of the 2014 National Conference will be a useful guide in this respect. The implementation of the report will not only move power, revenue and resources away from the Centre to the federating units to decimate the states from mere consumers of oil rent to auto-viable, productive and co-equal components of the Nigerian federation.
2. Concerted and deliberate efforts by leaders at all levels should be made with a high sense of patriotism and selflessness to ensure that discrimination against any ethnic group in terms of employment, holding position of responsibilities or appointment into board of federal parastatals and agencies is jettisoned such that the interests of all diverse segments of Nigeria are protected and promoted in the present federal structure.
3. The issue of over centralization of power and resources in Nigeria needs to be revisited. There is need to decentralize power and resources among the levels of government as federalism implies. A federal structure with weak center and little concentration of power and resources will greatly reduce the clamour by any particular region/ethnic group/geo-political zone to hold on to power in perpetuity. A system where central government claims ownership of local resources and decide how much of earnings from the resources goes to the state and local government

will continue to result in threat to national unity and agitation for restructuring in Nigeria.

4. The principle of Federal Character aimed at creating equity in appointment, representative positions, allocation of resources and location of social infrastructure among component units should be revisited and reviewed such that it can correct imbalances in the body polity when implemented properly as most Nigerians do not believe in the ability of the commission, as it is presently, to correct the imbalance and preponderance of some units over others.

References

Adeyeri, O. (2010). Federalism and the challenges of nation-building in Nigeria. *International Journal of Research in Arts and Social Sciences,* 2: 1-9.

Agbu, O. (2004) Re-inventing federalism in post-transition Nigeria: Problems and prospects. *African Development,* Vol. XXIX, No. 2, 2004, 26-52.

Akindele, S. T. and Olaopa W. O. (2002). Fiscal federalism and local government finance in Nigeria: An examination of revenue, rights and fiscal jurisdiction. In F. Omotoso (ed.). *Contemporary issues in public administration.* Lagos: Bolabay Publications, 46-64.

Babalawe, T. (1998). *The impact of the military on Nigerian federalism, Re-inventing federalism in Nigeria: Issues and perspectives.* Kunle Amuwo and Tunde Babalawe (eds.) Ibadan: Spectrum Books.

Bassey, A. (2000). My vision of Nigeria in 2050. An essay presented to African Leadership Forum. Lagos, Nigeria. Unpublished.

Bassey, A., Omono, C., Bisong, P. and Bassey, U. (2013). State and local government areas creation as a strategy of national integration or disintegration in Nigeria. *Journal of Educational and Social Research* 3 (1). January. Mediterranean Centre for Social and Educational Research, Italy.

Crowther, M. (1976). *The Birth of Nigeria.* Lagos: Mimeo.

Iaigwu, J. I. and Akindele, R. A. (1996). (eds.) Foundation of Nigerian federalism: 1960-1995. Vol. 3: National Council on Intergovernmental Relations, Abuja.

Ibezute, C. (1999). *Nigerian leadership, political development and democracy.* Owerri: Cel – Bez and Co. Publishers.

Mazrui, A. (1971). Pluralism and national integration. In L. Kuper, and M. G. Smith, (eds.) *Pluralism in Africa.* Berkeley: University of California Press.

Nnoli, O. (2008). *Ethnic politics in Nigeria.* Revised second edition.Enugu; SNAAP Press Ltd.

Obikeze, O. and Anthony, O. (2003). *Government and politics of Nigeria: The struggle for power in an African state.* Onitsha: Bookpoint Ltd.

Ojo, E. O. (2002). The New Federal Capital Territory as an integrative mechanism in Nigeria. *Indian Journal of Politics.* 27(1 and 2).

Onwudiwe, E. (2004). Geopolitical zones and the consolidation of democracy. In A. Agbaje, I. Diamond and E. Onwudiwe (eds.). *Nigeria's Struggle for Democracy and Good Governance,* pp. 267–276. Ibadan: Ibadan University Press.

Rodney, W. (1972). *How Europe underdeveloped Africa.* London: BoglehL'ourverture Publishers.

Sills, D. (eds.) (1993). *International encyclopedia of social sciences.* Vol. 18. New York: Macmillan Company and the Free Press.

Tamuno, T. (1998). Nigerian federalism in historical perspective. In: K. Amuwo *et al.* (eds.) *Federalism and political restructuring in Nigeria.* Ibadan: Spectrum Books.

Tamuno, T. N. (2003). Nigerian federalism in historical perspective". In K. Amuwo, *et al* (eds.) *Federalism and political restructuring in Nigeria.* Ibadan: Spectrum Books Limited.

Wheare, K. C. (1963). *Federal Government.* New York: Oxford University Press.

Wheare, K. C. (1964). *Federal Government.* Oxford: Oxford University Press.

14

The Transformation of Energy System for Sustainable Development: Challenges for Poverty Eradication

DANIA Clement M. Ph.D & OTI Elizabeth C.

Abstract

This paper was aimed at examining the transformation of energy system for sustainable development and the challenges for poverty eradication. To achieve this, the paper examined the outline of Sustainable Development Goals (SDGs) in which SDGs 7 aims to ensure access to affordable, reliable, sustainable and modern energy for all. The paper also examined the sources of energy and its utilization, the energy system, transformation of energy system for sustainable development and the challenges. The paper concluded that at the centre of transformation lies the revamping of the world energy system. The paper recommended among others that there should be, reliable, adequate and quality electricity supply and linkages between energy and the pillar of sustainable development: social progress, economic development and environmental sustainability.

Key Words: *Transformation, Energy System, Sustainable Development, Poverty Eradication*

Introduction

Sustainable development has occupied a place in the global agenda since the Brundtland commission's 1987 report "our common future". According to the report, sustainable development is the development that meets the needs of the present without compromising the ability of the future generation to meet their own needs. Then, United Nations (UN) Secretary General Kofi Annan reflected when he wrote in his Millennium Report to the General Assembly that "freedom from want, freedom from fear, and the freedom of future generations to sustain their lives on this planets" are the three major challenges facing the international community at the dawn of the last century (Udoye, Ettte and Onyenso, 2016). Sustainability has become an issue in an international affair. This is why in September 2015, the heads of state and government of the 193 member nations of the united Nations (UN) converged in the city of New York in the United States of America to formally flag off a new goals and targets to be pursued worldwide for the next 15 years beginning from January 01, 2016 for the overall good of mankind and planet earth. These universal goals and targets code-named Sustainable Development Goals (SDGs) aimed to achieve sustainable development for humanity and a well safeguard planet earth by the year 2030.

Thus, United Nations (UN), open working group came up with 17 goals and 169 targets under the new agenda. According to Udoye *et al* (2016), the 17 SDGs which came into effect on 1 January 2016 are:

1. End poverty in all its forms everywhere
2. End hunger, achieve food security and improve nutrition and promote sustainable agriculture
3. Ensure healthy lives and promote well-being for all at all ages
4. Ensure inclusive and equitable quality education and promote life-long learning opportunities for all
5. Achieve gender equality and empower all women and girls
6. Ensure availability and sustainable management of water and sanitation for all
7. Ensure access to affordable, reliable, sustainable and modern energy for all
8. Promote sustained inclusive and sustainable economic growth, full and productive employment and decent work for all
9. Build resilient infrastructures, promote inclusive and sustainable industrialization and foster innovation
10. Reduce inequality within and among countries
11. Make cities and human settlements inclusive, safe, resilient and sustainable
12. Ensure sustainable consumption and production pattern
13. Take urgent action to combat climate change and its impacts
14. Conserve and sustainably use the ocean, sea, and marine resources for sustainable development
15. Protect, restore and promote sustainable use of terrestrial ecosystems, sustainably manage forests, combat desertification and halt and reserve land degradation and halt biodiversity loss.
16. Promote peaceful and inclusive societies for sustainable development, provide access to justice for all and build effective accountable and inclusive institutions at all levels
17. Strengthen the means of implementation and revitalize the global partnership for sustainable development.

The UN adoption of the 2030 Agenda for Sustainable Development and its Sustainable Development Goals (SDGs) include a dedicated and stand-alone goal on energy. The SDG 7, calling to "ensure access to affordable, reliable, sustainable and modern energy for all". Energy lies at the heart of both the 2030 agenda for Sustainable Development and the Paris Agreement on climate change. Ensuring access to affordable, reliable, sustainable and modern energy for all will open a new world of opportunities for billions of people through new economic opportunities and jobs, empowerment of women, and youth, better education and health, more sustainable, equitable and inclusive communities and greater protection from and resilience to climate (UNESCO, 2006).

The only way to build sustainability in the energy system is to introduce sustainable management of those economic, social and environmental interactions. The transformation of the energy system should be a core element in any agenda for sustainable development that aims at improving the living standards of the people with the framework of equity and environmental sustainability.

Energy Sources and Utilization

The first time humans used energy according to Bowman, Balch and Artaxo (2009), is the discovery of fire which dated back to about 400,000 – 500,000 years ago. The fire was derived mainly from wood (Biomass) and was used for cooking, heating and warmth. They also stated that the discovery of fire by man led to invention of ovens which was used for cooking, crafting, pottery and refining metals from ore.

The second source of energy utilization by man was the agricultural revolution (Heinsberg, 2011). This has led to increase in food production thereby increasing human population. Animal derives its power from chemical energy in food that is released during digestion. Thereafter, the animal is effectively being used for transportation and ploughing the farm.

The guest for energy by man later led to the discovery of water and wind powers that were invented about 2,000 and 5000 years ago respectively (Lucas 2006). The energy derived from these mills was used in operating grinding machines to crush grains into flour, olives into olive oil, tanning of leather, smelting of iron, sawing wood, raise water from well and so on (Reynolds 1983). The era of fire and agricultural revolution is referred to as the Organic Energy Economic (Daniel, 2018). This is because energy source is basically derived from plants (Biomass), thus, the organic energy economy depends on the rate of solar energy that is converted into useful work.

The industrial revolution emerged due to invention of the steam engine by James Watt, a Scottish Mechanical Engineer. The steam engine is an external combustion type which converts chemical energy (coal-off-fossil origin) into heat and then into mechanical energy (motion). The engine was also used in extracting coal, moving of ships and trains (locomotives). The invention of steam engine laid the foundation for the present complex and energy intensive for human economic system.

Another source of energy was developed in the early 19th century. It does not require combustion engines. It is known as the electric generator or dynamo. This device which works by the principle of electromagnetic induction was propounded by Michael Faraday. The device is capable of converting mechanical energy into electrical energy.

The recovery of energy from waste was another form of energy utilization that came into existence in the late 19th century. The first incinerator was built in United States in 1885. The water discharges and emission of air were later discovered to be detrimental to the environment. Based on this, the incinerator technology has been improved upon with high efficiency in recovering energy from waste at very insignificant air emissions (United state Environmental Protection Agency (EPA), 2017).

Following the discovery of atom towards the end of 19th and early 20th centuries, physicists focused on how to harness the energy from the nucleus of an atom. This form of energy was later called nuclear energy. The period between 1939 and 1945 marked an intensive study on how to harness the energy from atoms for the generation of electricity (World Nuclear Association, 2014). This was achieved through nuclear fission process and later nuclear power plants or rectors. Nuclear waste remains radioactive and is hazardous to health; however, technologies have been developed for safe handling and storage of nuclear waste.

Energy can either be renewable or non-renewable. Renewable energy is that energy that is not depleted when used as well as naturally replenished on a human time scale. It includes solar, wind, waves and tides, geothermal, hydro and biomass. The renewable energy is sustainable and will never run out. On the other hand, non-renewable energy is one that comes from sources that will run out or that cannot be replenished in our life time. Most non-renewable sources are fossil fuels. There are three types of fossil fuels. They are petroleum, natural gas and coal. Radioactive fuel e.g. uranium is also non-renewable energy.

The Energy System

The energy system constitutes the ensemble of production, conversion and use of energy and thus closely linked to the earth's carrying capacity and to the economic social and cultural organization of human life. This is shown in the figure below. The energy system comprises of primary energy sources (e.g. coal, oil, and gas) which are converted into energy carriers (e.g. electricity, gasoline, and liquefied gas). These then serve in end-use applications for the provision of various energy forms (e.g. heat, transport, and light), require delivering final energy services (e.g. thermal comfort, transportation and illumination) (International Energy Agency, 2012).

The energy system can be characterized by the dominant set of technologies used to convert primary energy resources into useful energy (secondary energy). Energy can be further differentiated into the energy supply sector and the end-use energy sector. The energy supply sector encompasses the extraction of energy resources (involving so-called up stream activities), their conversion into suitable forms of secondary energy and their delivery to the locus of demand (involving so-called downstream activities). The end-use energy sector, in turn, handles with the provision of services such as cooking, information processing, illumination, thermal comfort, transportation food production and refrigerated storage. The ultimate goal of the energy services required is to satisfy human needs.

Schematic Diagram of the Energy System Illustrative Example of the Energy Sector and Energy End Use and Services

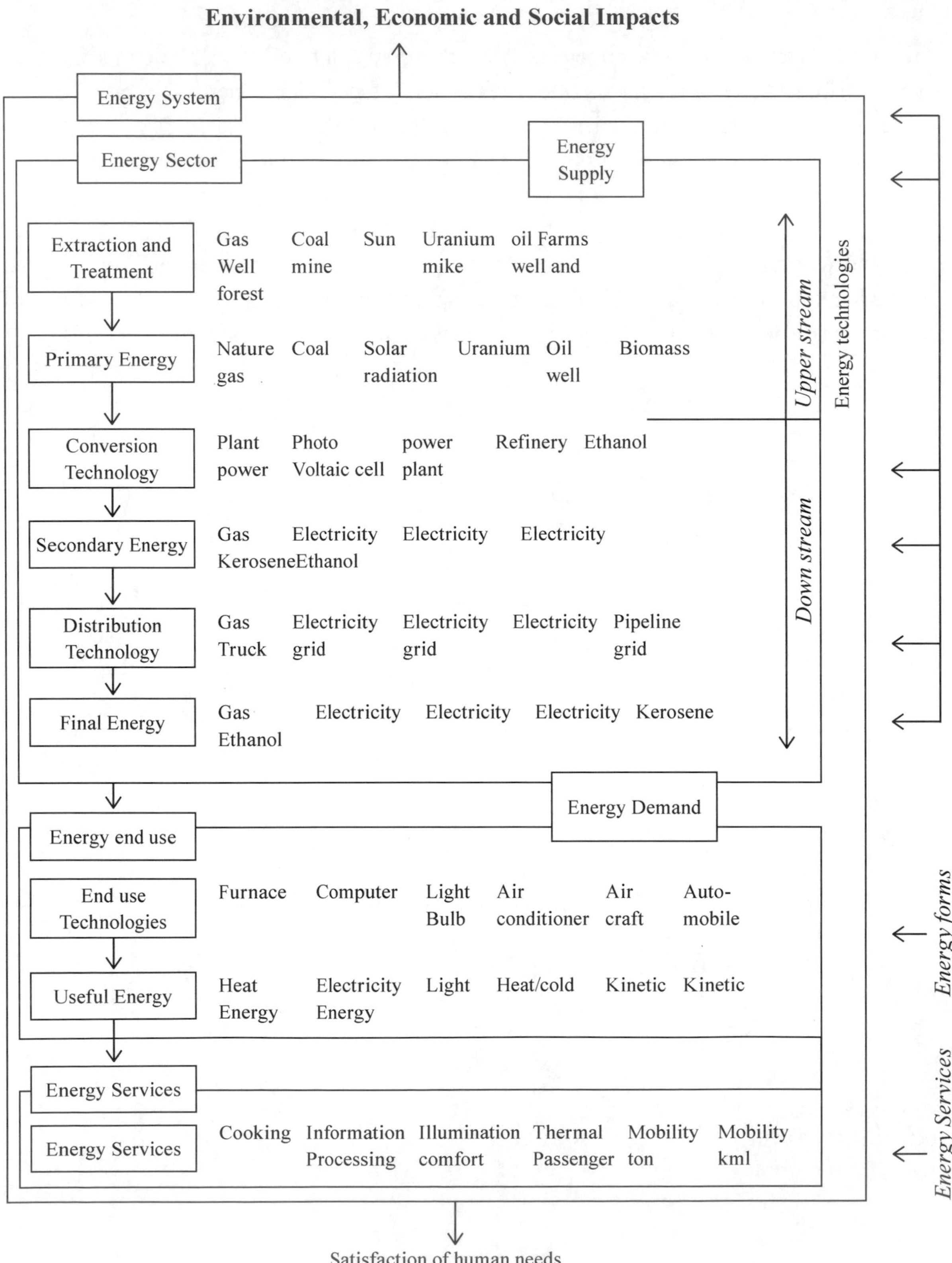

Source: Glubler et al (2012)

Transformation of Energy System and Sustainable Development

Energy has always been one of the most essential resources that facilitates human development and general survival of all living things (Daniel, 2018). The transformation of the energy system needs to be a major element of the sustainable development agenda, in order to improve the living standards of people with equity and environmental sustainability. Under the Secretary General's Sustainable Energy for all initiative and in other contexts, explicit energy goals have been suggested to end the dependence on traditional biomass as a source of thermal energy; to improve access to reliable, adequate and high-quality electricity, to facilitate convergence to best practices in the provision of energy services, and to ensure that unreliable or low-quality energy sources do not compromise the opportunities of the working poor who are self-employed or run household enterprises.

The economy system of our country and the world in general is calling for transformation so that there could be a balance relation with the earths boundaries while accommodating the legitimate development aspirations of the billions of people who would like to have access to quality and nutritious food, decent clothing and shelter, health, good-quality education, water, and sanitation, and modern amenities (Ange, 2010). At the heart of this transformation lies on the revamping of the world energy system as it is energy that underpins the production of the goods and services that sustain human life. The energy system harnesses natural resources and transforms them into energy carriers to be used by the appliances and machinery that provide energy services, such as heat, refrigeration and transport. Providing energy services to current and future generations requires energy systems that are sustainable in terms of both the use of natural resources, and the disposal and absorption of the pollutants associated with the generation and use of energy. The transformation of the energy system should therefore be a core element in any agenda for sustainable development that aims at improving the living standards of people within a framework of equity and environmental sustainability.

Sustainable Energy and Poverty Eradication

With a rapidly soaring population of 170million inhabitants, Nigeria is urgently in need of sustainable solutions to the many socio economic challenges that confront her development. Leading among these are the rampant corruption, endemic poverty and inadequacy in social infrastructure (Ojoko, Abubakar, Ojoko and Ikpe, 2016). These challenges manifest basically in poor energy with resultant effect on development.

Sustainable energy influence people's lives and is engine for poverty eradication, social progress, women and youth empowerment, equity, enhance resilience economic growth, and environmental sustainability (Anger, 2010). Over the centuries energy has helped transform economies and societies, spurning industrialization and thereby raising living standards. Around our locality, energy is needed for running a borehole, grinding, melting and welding irons, heating substances, cooling system and so on.

Energy is indispensable for fulfilling numerous basic human needs including nutrition, warmth and light, and directly impacts people, communities and nations. It helps to realize human rights, including the right to work, the right to education and the right to better health. The global trends towards an electricity-based economy in modern society where governments, business and citizens rely heavily on electricity, makes energy all the more relevant for accessing modern forms of communication and information technology (i.e. internet, computers, mobile phones) and engaging in economic activities such as online commerce and market places (United Nations, 2012).

Despite these clear benefits, the energy challenges faced by developing countries and Nigeria in particular, are complex and pervasive, affecting every aspect of life. UNDP describes these challenges through the linkages between energy and the three pillars of sustainable development: social progress, economic development and environmental sustainability.

Challenges in Transforming Energy System for Sustainable Development

A technically feasible large scale plan that intended to supply energy from solar sources to millions of people in Nigeria will require an expanse of solar farms. The economic, social and political challenges associated with changing land use policy so that such large extensions of land can be allocated to the generation of solar energy attest to the magnitude of the obstacles that need to be overcome when setting up renewable energy alternatives.

Another challenge is the substitution of fossil fuel – driven automobiles with electricity-propelled cars. Even if technically feasible and environmentally sound, Mbalisi and Offor (2015) observed that such a change will not occur unless the retail network required significant investments and might be strongly resisted by vested interests.

Another challenge is the investment challenge. Despite the six fold increase in global investments in renewable energy in the period 2004 – 2011, investments leading to sustainable development still fall short of what is needed.

Couple with declining oil revenue and lack of viable economic alternative, it is clear that though the Nigeria government will do its best, it may not be good enough and consequently will pose a problem in ensuring access to affordable, reliable, sustainable and modern energy for all by 2030.

There is also the challenge of ensuring that people and policy makers learn from scientific and factual evidence and current consumption patterns.

It is widely acknowledged that many of the technologies necessary for supporting sustainable development are already available. The challenge is how to improve these technologies, how to accelerate cost reduction and achieve meaningful changes, how to integrate them along coherent development paths that respond to specific local and sectional needs and how to provide incentives and mechanisms for rapid innovation, diffusions and knowledge sharing (United Nations, 2011).

More challenges are the unavoidable economic social and cultural obstacles that will need to be overcome in order to implement new technologies that are to replace the currently dominant fuel-based technology. Obstacles include not only the entrenched interests of the energy industry but also challenges associated with shifts in land and changes in the economic structure and its associated consumption patterns.

Finally, one should not forget that implementation challenges are exacerbated by the fact that changes need to take place in a short period of time.

Conclusion

The world economic system is in need of transformation which will enable billions of people living on earth planet to have access to facilities such as quality and nutritious food, decent clothing and shelter, health, good – quality education, water and sanitation, and modern amenities. At the centre of this transformation lies the revamping of the world "energy system" as it is energy that underpins the production of goods and services that sustain human life.

Recommendations

For the transformation of the energy system to be used for sustainable development and consequently poverty eradication, the following recommendations are hereby proffered.

- Transformation of the energy system needs to be a core element of the sustainable development agenda so as to improve the living standards of the people within the framework of equity and environmental sustainability.
- Sustainable development should be inclusive and take care of the needs of the poorest and most vulnerable.

- An energy system is engaged in multiple interactions with the economy, society and the environment. To build sustainability in the energy system is to introduce sustainable management of those economic, social and environmental interaction.
- Policies should be made to explore possible synergies with other development goals by promoting for example health, education, training and employment creation through improvement of workers skills in the area of design, deployment, and maintenance of sustainable energy system.
- There should be reliable and adequate quality electricity supply so as to eradicate dependence on traditional use of biomass as a source of thermal energy.
- There should be linkages between energy and the three pillars of sustainable development. Social progress, economic development and environmental sustainability.

References

Anger, E. O. (2010). Poverty Eradication Millennium Development Goals and Sustainable Development in Nigeria. *Journal of Sustainable Development,* 3 (4): 138 – 145.

Bowman, D. M., Balch, J. K. and Artato, P. (2009). Fire in the Earth System. *Science,* 324 (5926): 481-484.

Daniel, T. A. (2018). *Fundamental of Environmental Physics.* Kontagora: Unique Press.

Environmental Protection Agency (EPA) (2017). The History of Energy Recovery from Combustion.https://www.era.giv/smm/energy-recovery-combustion-municipal-solid-wastemgwttistory. Retrieved on April 27 2018.

Glubler, A. et al (2012). Energy Primes. In International Institute for Applied Systems Analysis: Global Energy Assessment: Towards a Sustainable Future. New York. Cambridge Universal Press: Laxenburg, Austica 11 ASA 99-150.

Heisberg, R. (2017). *The End of Growth: Adapting to our New Economic Reality.* Gabriola Island Bc. New Society Publishers.

International Energy Agency (2012). *World Energy Outlook* (2012).Paris OECD/IEA.

Lucas, A. (2006). *Wind, Water, Work.Ancient and Medieval Milling Technology.* The Netherland Brill Academic Publishers.

Mbalisi, O. F. and Offor, B. O. (2015). Energy Crisis and its effects on National Development. The need for Environmental Education in Nigeria. *British Journal of Education,* 3(1): 21 – 37 available at www.egournals.org.

Ojoko, E. O., Abubakar, H. O., Ojoko, O. and Ikpe, E. O. (2010). Sustainable Housing Development in Nigeria: Prospects and Challenges. *Journal Multidisciplinary Engineering, Science and Technology* (JMEST), 3 (5): 4851 – 4873.

Reynolds, L. G. (1983). The Spread of Economic Growth to the third world: 1850 – 1980. *Journal of Economic Literature,* 21 (3): 941 – 980.

Udoye, R. N., Ette, M. U. and Onyenso, A. K. (2016). Achieving United Nations Sustainable Development Goals in Nigeria by 2030.*Global Journal of Academic Research Forum,* 4 (1): 123 – 150.

UNESCO (2006). Education for Sustainable Development. United Nations Decade of Education for Sustainable Development (2005 – 2014).

United Nations (2012). Sustainable Energy for All. Available from http://www.un.org/en/envents/sustainable/energyfora//background.sh+ml. Retrieved 12/03/2019.

15

Motivation, Students' Engagement and Civic Achievement of Secondary School Students in Agbowo Community, Ibadan

OLUBELA Afolabi Ph.D & OGUNSANYA Adeola Ph.D

Abstract

Civic Education is one subject that is specifically designed in content and function, to produce healthy, good and active citizens, wherein a good citizen is seen as patriotic, responsible, disciplined and conscientious; morally sound with love for his/her country. While many studies have shown positive correlation between motivation and academic performance, very limited have been reported on the roles of students' engagement in civics achievement, or the combination of the two variables – motivation and engagement on students' academic achievement in civics. Hence, this study examined the relative and composite contributions of motivation and students' engagement on secondary school students' academic achievement in Civics in Agbowo Community, Ibadan, Oyo State, Nigeria. This study adopted a descriptive survey research design where simple random sampling technique was used to select 450 male and female students from the 5 selected secondary schools. The participants responded to Students' Motivation Scale (SMS, $r = 0.73$), Students' Engagement Scale (SES, $r = 0.84$) and Students' Civic Achievement Test (SCAT, $r = 0.77$). Pearson Correlation and Multiple Regression analyses were used to test hypotheses at 0.05 level of significance. Results showed a significant positive relationship among: motivation ($r = 0.407$, $P<0.05$) engagement ($r = 0.239$, $P<0.05$) and students' civics achievement. Also, the factors have a positive moderate multiple relationship with students' achievement ($R = 0.319$). The result also reveals an adjusted R^2 value of 0.094, which implies that the factors contributed 9.4% to the variance of students' achievement. Furthermore, motivation made the higher contribution ($\beta = 0.235$) to students' civics achievement while students' engagement ($\beta = 0.116$) made the least contribution. The study concluded that motivation is a key predictor of students' achievement and active engagement of students in classrooms effectively enhanced their achievement in civics. It *was recommended that school teachers and parents should adequately provide varieties of motivation for students' achievement. Students-centred methods and activities should also be employed in order to efficiently engage students in teaching-learning processes, for an enhanced achievement.*

Keywords: *Motivation, Civics, Students' Engagement, Civic Achievement*

Introduction

Civics as one of the emerging trends in social studies curriculum, occupies a prominent position in solving the problem of incivility and political ignorance in the society. Citizenship Foundation (2014) avers that civics increases learners' knowledge and skills to understand, challenge and engage with the pillars of democracy: politics, economy and law. In its own submission, the American Sociological Association (2009) describes civics as the teaching of knowledge, skills and dispositions needed to become a responsible and effective citizen of a country. Kerr (2009) explains that civics increases students' knowledge, skills and values. To Akinlaye (2003), civics also prepares students to take appropriate democratic actions as individuals or as members of groups devoted to societal improvement. Merrifield and Mutebi (1991) further reveal that Civics enables students to understand, appreciate, and apply knowledge, processes, and attitudes from academic disciplines. Civics is one subject, according to VanSledright (2011) that is specifically designed in content and function to produce healthy, good and active citizens, wherein a good citizen is seen as patriotic, responsible, disciplined and conscientious, morally sound with love for his/her country.

The shortfall in students' civics knowledge, values and practices according to Ogunsanya, Ajiboye and Olubela (2010) contributes largely to an unending gap between the aspirations and dreams of the founding fathers of the Nigerian nation and the current socio-political realities. Lamenting this trend, Nduka (2004) remarks that many Nigerians exhibit unethical attitudes in every aspect of lives. To him, indiscipline is common in the country and it is exemplified by uncivil behaviour in public places, recklessness in driving, violent crimes, lack of respect for law and order, rampant avarice, exploitation of fellow citizens, poor attitude to work, lack of commitment to sound ethical values, cheating, cybercrimes, and fraud including the notorious advance fee fraud called '419'. Amosun and Ige (2010) also reveal that, youths in Nigeria, like many countries of the world, are developing addiction to psychoactive substances, which has significantly increased the number of accidents and untimely deaths. More worrisome, according to Egegbulem (2013), is the situation whereby students are finding it increasingly difficult to live desirable ways of life, particularly in the areas of human relationships, responsibility, obedience, respect, and orderliness. Yussuf (2005) and Oyeleke (2011) observe that students' level of civility could be said to be low, a phenomenon attributable largely to the lapses of the school and home. Students show political lassitude and obvious flagrant display of indifference to voting and electoral matters in Nigeria. This trend must be discontinued, if Nigeria is to experience a transformation from the current socio-political oblivion.

Adesoji (2008) emphasizes that many factors contribute to students' knowledge, attitude and skills. Such factors include; the teaching methods, teacher's attitude, influence of parents, motivation, gender, age, cognitive styles of pupils, students' engagement, career interest, amongst others. However evidence has shown that socio-demographic variables such as school location, motivation, family income and students' engagement could also predict students' academic performance (Abubakar, 2010).

Motivation is a zest and determination with a kind of excitement that leads one to persevere to reach greater heights, in all avenues of life; be it personal or professional. The drive may come from an internal or external source; the factors that motivate an individual keep changing as one climbs the ladder of age and maturity. Also, achievement of one goal sets the ball rolling for another one to be achieved. Thus, to be motivated is a constant need. There are times when one faces a period of de-motivation and everything seems bleak. It is then that they need to find what would motivate them back into action.

Psychologists believe that motivation is a necessary ingredient for learning (Biehler & Snowman, 2006). Satisfactory school learning is unlikely to take place in the absence of sufficient motivation to learn. Denhardt (2008) defined motivation as what causes people to behave as they do. Lawler (2004) stated that motivation is goal-directed. Motivation outlines the achievement and pursuit of goals. Pettinger (1996) defined motivation as environmentally dependent. Motivation is not directly observable, not the same as satisfaction, always conscious, and not directly controllable.

Students' motivation to choose which courses that best suits them can bring great effect on their performance in the first year (Byrne & Flood, 2008). Motivation theory is student main priority focus in the long term future prospect where they will put more effort forcing them to complete the task given to them persistently (Habibah, 2011). The achievement need of a person became the main drive to succeed in academic level. Hence, motivation plays an important role in students' interest in study and pushes them to learn and achieve their target progressively.

Intrinsic motivation refers to the behaviours that are done out of pleasure or for the sake of enjoyment (Clark & Schroth, 2010). In the studies done by Moneta and Spada (2009), high intrinsic motivation correlated positively with students' preparedness before examinations and coping with the stress as well. Besides that, when intrinsic goal are prioritized by students, they are more likely to put a lot of effort and show persistence when acquiring detail information about the given task which eventually leads to better academic performance. Students with extrinsic goals on other hand, do not generate similar results with those with intrinsic motivation (Lee, 2010). Further evidence of intrinsic motivation being positively correlated with academic performance is from Walker (2006) who found that intrinsic motivation, self-efficacy and cognitive processing correlated positively with students' achievement of academic success in terms of Grade Point Average.

Motivation is viewed as a dynamic, situated and social construct (Norton, 2010) and closely related to learners' identity construction (Dornyei, 2005). According to Yumei (2009), motivation is one of several important factors that may influence students' civics achievement. Learners' motivation has been widely accepted as a key factor which influences the rate and success of school learning (Ellis, 2004). Among the factors influencing students' learning, motivation is thought to be an important reason for different achievement. Motivation is a very important factor which determines the success or failure in learning because motivation can directly influence the frequency of using learning strategies, willpower of learning, goal setting, and the achievement in learning (Li & Pan, 2009).

In a research comprising several field studies and laboratory experiments, Boggiano (2012) revealed that motivation positively influenced academic performance, and it was found that motivational orientation predicted children's standardized achievement scores. Children with an intrinsic motivation orientation had higher scores and higher overall achievement scores compared to their extrinsic counterparts. There is a significant correlation between academic achievement and motivation (Sikwari, 2014).

Furthermore, students' engagement in school is a factor that influences students' achievement. Research has shown that students' engagement and attachment to school is an important predictor of education success. Students who have more positive feelings about their school and about their teachers tend to do better in school – and students who lack these feelings are likely to become estranged with the education process (Finn, 2009). In spite of evidence that students' perceptions about their schoolwork and people at school are an important determinant of performance in school, student engagement largely has been neglected in research and policy. Students who are more engaged with aspects of their schooling are less likely to leave high school before graduating and have lower levels of problem behaviours while in school (Newman, 2012). Students' engagement has been identified as a decisive requirement for students' achievement and persistence in many studies (Libbey, 2004). A report by the National Research Council and Institute of Medicine (2004) draws attention to how engagement with school can improve academic achievement and reduce student disaffection and dropout rates. Mills and Blankstein (2000) also discovered that students who are self-oriented and high standard setters have higher scores in examinations. Eventually, the assessing factor portrays extrinsic motivation as their benchmark in their academic goal has then proven to be positively correlated with the students resort to be competitive and also gain recognition by the public from their success (Mills & Blankstein, 2000).

Students' engagement is also an important field of study in educational psychology. Engagement requires not only being active, but also feeling and sense making (Harper & Quaye, 2009). Bomia and colleagues (2007) defined student engagement as students' willingness, needs, desire motivation and success in the learning process. Hu and Kuh (2011) and Kuh (2009) referred to students' engagement as the time allocated by students to education activities to contribute to the desired outcomes and as the quality of their related efforts. According to Stovall (2003), students' engagement includes not only the time students spend on tasks but also their willingness to take part in activities. Krause and Coates (2008) associated students' engagement with the high quality in learning outcomes.

Engagement involves students' sense of connection with the school environment, the teachers and the learning processes. Diminishing levels of students' engagement play a central role in the explanation of dropout processes in various education systems. Students who have a sense of attachment to the school are much less likely to leave before completing their degree, a relationship found in several other studies (Newmann, 2012). Recent work has shown that students' engagement is one of the most promising theoretical models for explaining school dropout processes and, possibly, for intervening to prevent students from dropping out (Appleton, Christenson, Kim, & Reschly 2006).

A study using national data from the United States found that students who work hard in schools and pay attention in class have significantly higher scores on achievement tests in high school (Ainsworth-Darnell & Downey, 1998). Eighth graders who have a greater sense of belonging to the school also have higher grades (Roeser, Eccles & Freedman-Doan 1999). A range of empirical studies, using data from a variety of samples, have found a generally consistent relationship between students' engagement and academic achievement.

Marks (2010) shows that more engaged students have higher grades and fewer disciplinary problems than those who are less engaged. Other studies have found the same relationship between engagement and a series of school discipline troubles (Murdock, Anderman & Hodge 2006). Overall, students' engagement with school work is a proximate determinant of school performance. Students' sense of connection with teachers has also been shown to benefit students' performance (Finn, 2009). When students feel supported by and connected with their teachers, they are more likely to behave in ways sanctioned by their teachers and perform up to teachers' expectations (Davis, 2003). Research has shown these relationships to be present and important in both elementary and secondary schools

(Murdock, 2009). Fredricks (2004) also investigated studies that analyzed the relationship between engagement and students' achievement, and found that students' engagement is the strongest predictor of academic success.

Social Learning Theory

The social learning theory places great emphasis on the events that take place in the individuals' environment. The theory regards the environment as a potentially powerful factor in the development of various behaviours and personality traits. In this sense, social learning theory is sometimes considered an environmental approach because it specifies the nature of the relationship that exist between a child's evolving behaviour and the environmental factors that facilitate or inhibit the behaviour. The history of the child's interaction with the environment is, of course, considered to be a highly important aspect of a child's current behavioural capacities and/or limitations. According to Sears, the child is born with basic drives (such as hunger, protection) that become "socialized" through interaction with parents, slowly evolving into motivational systems within the child's personality.

Sears' major research interests have been in the area of aggression and dependence on children, and yet these studies have always been part of a broader interest in the effects of social interaction between the child and the parent on the child's developing personality. He described these interactions as the mechanics of interpersonal influence. For Sears, the study of a child development is essentially the study of the most fruitful conditions under which learning takes place, namely the consistent interactions or interpersonal influences between the child and significant others. It is these interactions, Sears concludes, that motivating good social environments are most central in the formation and maintenance of the child's personality. Sears clearly notes two distinct stages of socialization; the learning in which the family is the initial agent of socialization, and the learning that occurs through interaction with social agents beyond the family, such as peers and teachers. Development is thus understood to be an orderly process in which the child's evolving behaviour meets with certain types of social responses, or reinforcements, so that consistent patterns of reinforcements produce consistent patterns of behaviour.

Statement of the Problem

While many studies have shown positive correlation between motivation and academic performance, very limited have been reported on the roles of students' engagement in civics achievement, or the combination of the two variables – motivation and engagement on students' academic achievement in civics. Hence, this serves as the rationale of this study.

Objective of the Study

This study seeks to examine relative and composite contributions of motivation and students' engagement on secondary school students' academic achievement in civics in Agbowo community, Ibadan.

Hypotheses

In view of this, the following hypotheses were tested at 0.05 level of significance:

Ho1: There is no significant relationship among secondary school students' motivation, engagement and civics achievement in Agbowo community, Ibadan.

Ho2: There is no significant joint impact of motivation and students' engagement on secondary school students' civics achievement in Agbowo community, Ibadan.

Ho3: There is no significant relative effect of motivation and students' engagement on secondary school students' civics achievement in Agbowo community, Ibadan.

Methodology

This study adopted a descriptive survey research design. A simple random sampling technique was used to select 450 male and female students from the 5 selected out of 18 secondary schools in Agbowo community, Ibadan. Three self-designed and validated instruments were used for data collection and these were Students' Motivation Scale (SMS, r = 0.73), Students' Engagement Scale (SES, r = 0.84) and Students' Civic Achievement Test (SCAT, r = 0.77). Social studies teachers in the five schools served as the research assistants, who administered the questionnaire to the students. The instruments were analyzed using correlation coefficient and multiple regression analysis to test the hypotheses at 0.05 level of significance.

Results

Ho1: There is no significant relationship among each of students' motivation, engagement and students' Civics achievement

Table 1: Relationship among students' motivation, engagement and students' Civics achievement

		Motivation	Engagement	Students' achievement	Significance (p)

Pearson correlation	Motivation	1.00	.348	.286	0.000*
	Engagement	.348	1.00	.218	0.000*
	Students' achievement	.286	.218	1.00	0.000*

* *P<0.05*

Table 1 reveals that there is positive significant relationship among: motivation (r = 0.407, <0.05), engagement (r = 0.239, P<0.05) and students' Civics achievement.

Ho2: There is no significant composite effect of students' motivation engagement on students' civics achievement

Table 2: Composite effects of students' motivation and engagement on students' Civics achievement

	R	R Square	Adjusted R Square	Standard Error of the Estimate
1	.319[a]	.102	.094	6.524

a. Predictors: (constant), motivation, engagement

Table 3: ANOVA Table of students' motivation and engagement on students' Civics achievement

Model	Sum of Squares	Df	Mean Square	F	P	Remark
Regression	2092.591	2	523.148	12.288	0.00[b]	Sig
Residual	18434.852	446	42.575			
Total	20527.443	448				

a. Dependent Variable: students' achievement
b. Predictors (constant), motivation, engagement.

Table 2 shows that the factors have a positive moderate multiple relationship with students' achievement (R = 0.319). The table also reveals an adjusted R^2 value of 0.094, which implies that the factors contributed 9.4% to the variance of students' achievement. Table 3 indicates that the R value obtained in table 4.2 is not by chance but as a result of the joint effect of the independent variables ($F_{(2, 446)}$ = 12. 288, P<0.05).

Ho3: There is no significant relative effect of students' motivation and engagement on students' civics achievement.

Table 4: Relative contributions of students' motivation and engagement on students' Civics achievement

Model	Unstandardized Coefficient		Standardized coefficient	t	sig
	B	Std. Error	Beta		
(Constant) Students' civic achievement	10.538	3.970	-	2.654	.008
Motivation	0.262	0.058	0.235	4.523	.000
Engagement	0.083	0.037	0.116	2.220	0.027

Table 4 shows that motivation made the higher contribution (β = 0.235, p <.01) to students' civics achievement while students' engagement (β = 0.116, p <.05) made the least contribution.

Discussion of Findings

The result of hypothesis 1 showed that there was a significant positive relationship among students' motivation, engagement and students' achievement. The finding showed a significant positive relationship between motivation to learn and students' achievement. This finding conforms to the position of Biehler and Snowman (2006) which emphasized that motivation is a necessary ingredient for learning satisfactorily. This means that school learning is unlikely to take place in the absence of sufficient motivation to learn. Roderick (2003), Appleton, Christenson, Kim and Reschly (2006) show that students who have a sense of attachment to the school are much less likely to leave before completing their degree, a relationship found in several other studies. Newmann (2012) has shown that students' engagement is one of the most promising theoretical models for explaining school dropout processes for intervening to prevent students from dropping out.

The result of hypothesis 2 showed that the factors have a positive moderate multiple relationship with students' achievement. This corroborates the findings of Denhardt (2008) who argued that motivation is not directly observable. Motivation is an internal state that causes people to behave in a particular way to accomplish particular goals and purposes. The study also showed that students' engagement is significantly positive on students' achievement in English reading comprehension. This study conformed to the finding of Roeser, Eccles and Freedman-Doan (1999) which found a generally consistent relationship between students' engagement and academic achievement. A number of studies have documented the association between level of engagement and achievement in school.

Analysis of hypothesis 3 showed that motivation for reading made the highest contribution to students' achievement, followed by students' engagement. This finding supports the earlier study of Moneta and Spada (2009) who opined that motivation correlated positively with student preparedness before exam and coping with the stress as well. Besides that, when intrinsic goals are prioritized by students, they are more likely to put a lot of effort and show persistence when acquiring detail information about the given task which eventually leads to better academic performance. Marks (2010) found that more engaged students have higher grades and fewer disciplinary problems than those who are less engaged. Murdock, Anderman and Hodge (2006) have also found the same relationship between engagement and a series of school discipline troubles.

Conclusion

Motivation and engagement were found to be positively related to students' achievement in Civics. They are essential in the learning and teaching of civics. Teachers should, therefore, adopt methods and strategies that enhance students' motivation and engagement.

Implications of Findings

The findings of this study have a lot of implications for teachers, students and the government. Teachers should improve learners' participation in lessons and enhance their academic performance. Students should be encouraged to embark on wide reading and exchange books amongst themselves to increase their understanding. Students should also make and adopt different learning experiences to enhance their academic achievement. There is need for the curriculum developers and the government to put into considerations factors such as motivation and engagement in civics curriculum. Also, civics texts and activities that are relevant to leaners' background, social and cultural environment should be recommended, in order to improve their achievement.

Recommendations

Based on the findings of the study, the following recommendations are made:-

1. Teachers should increase motivation activities for the learners and actively engage them in the teaching-learning experiences.
2. Teachers should be resourceful in their teaching by providing materials that will stimulate learners' civic background knowledge.
3. Varieties of motivation should be provided for the learners at all stages of education.

References

Adesoji, F. A. (2008). Managing students' attitude towards science through problem – solving instructional strategy. *Kamla-Raj Anthropologist.* 10(1)

Ainsworth, I, Darawell, K and Downey, F. (1998). Interrelations of behavioral, emotional, and cognitive school engagement in high school students. *Journal of Youth and Adolescence,* 42, 20-32.

Akinlaye F. A. (2003). Fundamentals of social studies curriculum planning and instruction. Pumark Nigeria Ltd. (Educational Publishers).

American Sociological Association. (2009). *21st Century Careers with an Undergraduate Degree in Sociology.* Washington DC

Appleton, C., Christenson, B., Kim, H. and Reschly, P. (2006). *Facilitating student engagement: The importance of life satisfaction.* Unpublished doctorate thesis, South Carolina University.

Biehler, M. and Snowman, J. (2006). Engaging students at school and with learning: A relevant construct for all students. *Psychology in the Schools,* 45, 365-368.

Boggiano, I. (2012). The Value of Student Engagement for Higher Education Quality Assurance. *Quality in Higher Education,* 11(1), 25-36.

Bomia, J. (2007). What motivates children's behavior and emotion? Joint effects of perceived control and autonomy in the academic domain. *Journal of Personality and Social Psychology,* 65,781-791.

Brine, M and Flood, L. (2008). Classroom belonging among early adolescents students' relationships to motivation and achievement. *Journal of Early Adolescence,* 13(1): 21-40.

Citizenship Foundation. (2014). *Understanding Citizenship Education.* Citizenship Foundation (UK) www.citizenshipfoundation.org.uk/main

Clark, O. and Schroth, N. (201). Student engagement scale: Development, reliability and validity. Assessment & Evaluation in Higher Education, DOI: 10.1080/02602938.2014.938019.

Denharat, C. (2008). *Student engagement in the middle years of schooling (years 7-10): A literature review.* Wellington: Ministry of Education.

Dornyei, L. (2005). The impact of teaching strategies on intrinsic motivation. Champaign, IL: ERIC Clearinghouse on Elementary and Early Childhood Education.

Egegbulem, V. (2013). *Amending constitution will not solve Nigeria's problems*. www.thisdayonlineng.com

Ellis, A. H. (2004). An in-depth investigation of students' engagement throughout their first year in university. UK National Transition Conference, University College London, April 24th.

Finn, J. D. (2009).. *School engagement and students at risk*. Buffalo, NY: U.S. Department of Education, National Center for Educational Statistics (ERIC Document Reproduction Service No. 362-322.)

Habibah, K. (2011). Determining the role of technology in student engagement and examining of the relationships between student engagement and technology use in class. (Unpublished doctorate thesis). Anadolu University, Turkey.

Harper, G and Quaye, F. (2009). Student engagement and classroom variables in improving mathematics achievement. *Asia Pacific Education Review, 6*(1): 87-97.

Hu, J. and Kuh, T. (2011). Early adolescents' perceptions of the classroom social environments, motivational beliefs, and engagement. *Journal of Educational Psychology, 99*(1), 83-98.

Kerr, D. (2009). *Citizenship and values education to the rescue! Making the case for call to action. Executive summary of the ninth conference*. London: Institute for Global Ethics/Gordon Foundation.

Krause, U. and Coates, E. (2008). Flow in schools: Cultivating engaged learners and optimal learning environments. R. Gilman, E. S. Huebner, & M. Furlong (Ed.), Handbook of Positive Psychology in Schools İcinde (s.131-145). New York: Routledge.

Kuh, T. (2009). First and second-generation college students: A comparison of their engagement and intellectual development. *Journal of Higher Education, 76*, 276-300.

Lawler, C. (2004). Sense of relatedness as a factor in children's academic engagement and performance. *Journal of Educational Psychology, 95*,148–162.

Lee, H. (2010). A Phenomenographic Investigation of Teacher Conceptions of Student Engagement in Learning. *The Australian Educational Researcher, 5*(1): 57-79.

Li, L. and Pan, T. (2009). Student engagement and student learning: Testing the linkages. *Research in Higher Education, 47*(1): 1-32.

Libbey, G. (2004). School Engagement: Potential of the Concept, State of the Evidence. *Review of Educational Research, 74*(1): 59-109.

Marks, T. (2010). Social learning spaces and student engagement. *Higher Education Research & Development, 30*(2): 105-120.

Mills, B. and Blankstein, P. (2000). Students' engagement in first-year university. *Assessment and Evaluation in Higher Education, 33*(5), 493-505.

Murdock, A. (2009). Assessment of student engagement: An analysis of trends. *Tertiary Education and Management, 18*(2), 171-191.

Nduka, O. (2004). Value Education. *A Key note address proceeding of the 19th Annual Congress of The Nigerian Education Academy*, Lagos.

Newman, K. (2012). School characteristics related to school engagement. *Journal of Negro Education 62*(3), 249–268.

Noneta, A and Spada, M (2009). *Student Engagement in Higher Education.* New York and London: Routledge.

Norton, B. T. (2010). Student involvement: A developmental theory for higher education. *Journal of College Student Development,* 40(5): 518-529.

Ogunsanya, M., Ajiboye, J. O. and Olubela, R. A. (2010). Deepening teaching effectiveness of Human Rights Education Concepts in Social Studies through Transformative Learning Perspectives. *Journal of Contemporary Issues in Education*. Special Edition, 2 (1).

Oyeleke, O. (2011). The Democratization Process and Classroom Teachings in Nigeria. *Journal of Citizenship, Social and Economic Education*, 10 (1).

Pettinger, L. J. (1996). *School motivation, engagement, and sense of belonging among urban adolescent students.* Paper presented at the Annual Meeting of the American Educational Research Association, San Francisco, CA.

Roderick, V. (2003). What student affairs professionals need to know about student engagement. *Journal of College Student Development. 50*(6): 683–706.

Roeser, D., Eccles, H. and Freedman-Doan, L. (1999). Student Engagement in Instructional Activity: Patterns in the Elementary, Middle, and High School Years. *American Educational Research Journal, 37,* 153-184.

Sikwari, J. (2014). *Finding flow: The psychology of engagement with everyday life*. The masterminds series. New York: Basic Books.

Stovall, R. (2003). The relationship between institutional mission and student's involvement and educational outcomes. *Research in Higher Education, 44*(2): 241-261.

VanSledright, B. (2011). *The challenge of rethinking history education: On practices, theories, and policy.* New York: Routledge.

Walker, G. (2006). Being (Dis) Engaged in Educationally Purposeful Activities: The Influences of Student and Institutional Characteristics. Paper presented at the American Educational Research Association Annual Conference. Seattle, WA, 10–14 April.

Yumei, C. (2009). The role of engagement in inspiring teaching and learning. *Innovations in Education and Teaching International, 44*(4), 349-362.

16

Transformation and Sustainable Development Goals through Science and Technology in Nigerian Schools Environment

KANU Chikaodili L. & AGU Bartholomew O. (Rev. Fr. CSSp)

Abstract

This paper discussed transformation and Sustainable Development Goals through science and technology in Nigerian School environment. The concepts of transformation and Sustainable Development Goals were highlighted. Challenges facing achieving Sustainable Development Goals were outlined and discussed and way forward was suggested. Recommendations on how government will help to achieve transformation and Sustainable Development Goals through science and technology in Nigerian schools environment were also made.

Key Words: *Transformation, Sustainable Development Goals, Science and Technology*

Introduction

Transformation could be described as a process through which human and material resources can best be utilized to achieve a dependable standard of living for the people of a community of nation. It implies a basic change of character and little or no resemblance with the past configuration or structure. It could also be described as uplifts from existing situation to a better one. According to Rundell (2007), transformation is a change into someone or something completely different or the process by which this happens. It is a process of profound and radical change that orients an organization in a new direction and takes it to an entirely different level of effectiveness unlike 'turnaround' (which implies incremental progress on the same plane). For transformation to take place in any developing country like Nigeria, there must be a reliable education process that inculcates into her citizens the right knowledge, skills and attitudes to enhance good standard of living.

Science is a way of finding out a lot about our environment and interpreting events which occur therein. By this definition, science can then be viewed in two perspectives – process and product. It is a process because, it involves investigative study during which observation, classification, measurement, communication, prediction, inference, making operational definitions, formulating hypothesis, interpreting data and experimenting are made. The product aspect results in the outcome of all the above exercises involved in the process aspect, in the form of verification and testable knowledge which form facts, the theories, principles and laws in science (Eze, 2012).

Technology is the application of scientific principles, skills, devices and materials to the task of solving human needs (Nwokolo, 2002). The word 'technology' encompasses tools and instruments to enhance human ability to shape nature and solve problems; knowledge of how to create things or how to solve problems and culture. According to Rundell (2007), technology is an advanced scientific knowledge used for practical purposes, especially in industry. Technology is also an applied science. It is the means employed by man to solve his needs. It encompasses all the processes or techniques and skills in solving human needs. It is methodological ideas, principles, laws and general procedures which are further made to assume a definite form made real into practical tools and machines. Science and technology are intimately interrelated, each relying on the other. Science has contributed immensely to modern technology and technologies developments.

Sustainable development is actually a very broad concept to define because it is continuously evolving. It tends to investigate and emphasize the development of the present without compromising the future of the upcoming generations. Sustainable national development can be seen as a process of improving the range of opportunities that will enable people to achieve their aspirations and full potential over a period of time while maintaining the resilience of economic, social and environmental systems, basically, it is knowledge based and revolves round three basic concepts, the economy; the environment; and the society. The members of a society are financially empowered and responsible to not damage the environment so that our children's future is not compromised (McKeown, 2002).

Science is a way of finding out a lot about our environment and interpreting events which occur therein. By this definition, science can then be viewed in two perspectives - process and product. It is a process because it involves investigate study during which observation, classification, measurement, communication, prediction, inference, making operational definition, formulating hypothesis, interpreting data and experimenting are made. The product aspect results in the outcome of all the above exercises involved in the process aspect, in the form of verification and testable knowledge which form facts, the theories, principles and laws in science (Eze, 2012).

Technology, according to Rundell (2007), is an advanced scientific knowledge used for practical purposes, especially in industry. The word "technology" encompasses tools and instruments to enhance human ability to shape nature and solve problems; knowledge of how to create things or how to solve problems and culture. Technology is also an applied science. It is the means employed by man to solve his needs. Technology is the application of scientific principles, skills, devices and materials to the task of solving human needs (Nwokolo, 2002). It encompasses all the processes or techniques and skills in solving human needs. Technology is methodological ideas, principles, laws and general procedures which are further made to assume a definite form made real into practical tools and machines. Science and technology are intimately interrelated, each relying on the other. Science has contributed immensely to modern technology and technological developments. Engineers through their endeavours apply scientific ideas into inventions.

Transformation through Science and Technology

In today's world, science and technology are undoubtedly vehicles for socio-economic development. Decades ago, developed nations were more or less as undeveloped as developing nations today. They are now transformed from rural, peasant communities into highly urbanized industrialized countries through the development of their science and technology. In the process, they became rich and politically powerful (Ezeagwu, 2013). The Nigerian educational system took its root from the pre-colonial era. This was a period of indigenous education in which education activities were practiced in various vocations like farming, weaving, blacksmithing, pot making, traditional medicine, hunting, etc. learning at that time was characterized by apprenticeship and much of unexplained science and technology. There was no formal curriculum, but the training was relevant to the needs of the society. Some authors described the training as somehow primitive and localized (Ajeyalemi, 2008) because it was informal.

Traditional method transfers knowledge to students by inactive exchange or rote learning which leads to the acquisition of low level facts and knowledge that is far below what is required in this current complex technology era. The traditional method is a contrast to active participation of the students in their learning process through oral discourse, asking questions, making contributions and role play (Bonwell and Elson, 2003). Traditional method emphasizes only surface learning, instead of deep learning. According to Gordon and Debus (2002), surface learning is characterized by a study behavior that enables students to reproduce information in a required form without analysis or integration, leading to low quality learning outcomes. This means that the traditional science classroom learning environment emphasizes the objective pedagogy and is reproduction oriented, subject matter oriented, or teacher centered. For Nigeria to achieve her age-old goal of crossing the borderline, between being a developing country and a developed country, she must develop scientifically and technologically. It should be added that science and technology have become integral parts of the world's culture and to lag behind is to be out of place. However, science and technology have continued to have a largely low status in developing or under-developed societies including Nigeria (Ezeagwu, 2013).

The foundation necessary to develop science and technology in the country is obviously education – elementary, secondary and tertiary education. Adequate science teaching and learning environment such as well equipped laboratories, functional libraries, classroom and the use of modern materials for teaching, create more concrete knowledge and positive attitudes towards the discipline. It also encourages the application of imaginative thinking and science reasoning skills as well as link classroom science to everyday life in society. Momeke, (2007) says "exposure to technological equipment in learning, such as computers and Internet, video automated teaching, etc. will expose learners and teachers to think in the same direction as their counterparts in other nations of the world". For transformation to occur, web-based training is more convenient for students, administrators and instructors. This is because e-learning uses the Internet for delivery of training content and allows students to access course materials, reference information and examinations anywhere and anytime their schedule permits. The student uses her own computer at home, school or at work. Students often correspond and share ideas with other students taking the same course via e-mail and correspond with instructor or mentor for clarification of concepts. It allows instructors to concentrate on clarifying specific concepts one-on-one rather than delivering lecture to the audience. It allows administrators to focus on delivering a broader range of educational products and consistently high-quality educational experiences for student rather than the burdens of scheduling and allocating resources.

Science and technology have to be taught and studied systematically and purposefully respectively at all levels of education including, at least, first years of tertiary education for arts and the humanities. It is evident that science and technological transfer and development is solely dependent on science and technology education in the country. Scientists and technologists are definitely required for economic infrastructure of the society before any science and technological development and industrialization will occur. Such scientific literacy will equip the citizens' contribution to our country's development in an increasing competitive and rapidly changing world.

Recent analysis shows that economic growth over the period of 1950 to 2010 is indebted to the innovations, incentives and productivity gains arising from technological advancements. Advances in science and technology can help to diversify the economy, by improving productivity in sectors like agriculture, while defining new ones. Look also at the relatively recent development of the hybrid engines that harness solar power and batteries (for cars and more recently for ocean liners and ship); one of science and technology's responses to the challenges of carbon emission and exclusive reliance on fossil fuels like diesel and petrol. There is a technological advancement in the ICT sector. It also plays a key role in improving the quality of life. For instance, research in healthcare has proven vital to prevention, diagnosis and treatment of various killer diseases. In the education sector, particularly higher education, there is an emerging paradigm shift in the world today (Okonjo-Iweala, 2012).

Science, Technology and Sustainable Development

Sustainable development is probably the most daunting challenge that humanity has ever faced, and achieving it requires that the fundamental issues be addressed immediately at local, regional and global levels. At all scales, the role of science and technology is crucial; scientific knowledge and appropriate technologies are central to resolving the economic, social and environmental problems that make current development paths unsustainable. Science and technology has been one of the main driving forces of the economic growth of nations. Most developed countries have generated new technologies with potential to result in dynamic economic performance. This, however, has not been the case with most of the developing countries and their developmental plans have not given adequate emphasis and importance to science and technology and in particular to research in the science and technology aspects. Countries like India, South Korea and Taiwan in the region have achieved much through science and technology, and stand out as having demonstrated the absolute importance of science and technology for economic growth. These countries are examples for the developing countries. The impact of technology on society, without doubt, is going to be even more marked in the future. It is then of paramount importance to generate and develop new knowledge in science and technology for application nationally through our own research capability (Nalini, 2006). Science and technology can be used to attain sustainable development when education in science for your child can also mean better things for the society by helping students develop into more responsible citizens who will help to build a strong economy, contribute to a healthier environment and bring about a brighter future for everyone.

Science and technology should be able to transform the typical teacher-centered classroom lecture into a discovery and problem-solving arena. This encourages creativity and originality. In order to achieve this, the students have to be actively engaged in finding problems and looking for the solutions (Renner, Stafford and Ragan, 1973). The introduction of the New Senior Secondary School Curriculum (NSSSC) in the secondary schools in Nigeria is a fresh initiative which according to Nigeria Education Research and

Development Council (NERDC, 2011) aims at ensuring that graduates from secondary schools are, among other things professionally trained in entrepreneurship skills and posses relevant Information Communication and Technology (ICT) skills that will equip them for challenges of the labour market. Hence, every student, irrespective of his or her field of study, is expected to study five (5) core subjects viz: English language, General Mathematics, Civic Education, Computer Studies and One (1) trade Entrepreneurship subject, out of thirty (33) subjects, which include: Auto body repair and spray painting; auto electrical work; auto mechanical work; air condition/refrigeration; electrical installation and maintenance work; brick laying and concrete work; painting and decoration; carpentry and joinery; upholstery; garment making; cosmetology; key boarding; leather goods manufacturing and repair; animal husbandry; marketing; tourism; GSM maintenance and others. The aim is to ensure the attainment of National Policy objective of 'preparation for useful living within the society' (Federal Republic of Nigeria, 2004). It is meant for every Nigeria citizen to be equipped to break the façade of unemployment through the development of self, as a precursor to a meaningful contribution to the development of the society. The skills of science and technology may be learned easily if the students are given opportunities to explore and tensions surrounding evaluation are relaxed in their minds. Hands on activities must be encouraged as it makes learning of science more real and practical to the students, encouraging critical thinking and exploration, leading to a sustainable development.

Science and technology can help to build a strong economy through the communication, research, reporting and collaboration skills that science provides. This can produce a generation of individuals who are better prepared for any career and can make greater contribution to society. Students who have a solid knowledge base in science will later be more open to emerging technologies and ideas that can boost business and stimulate the economy. It has been noted that the difference between developed and developing countries is based on the quantity and quality of science and technology they possess (Ochu, 2007). Effective and consistent implementation of science and technology curriculum will lead to poverty alleviation, increase in productivity, rapid economic growth, and sustainable development.

Challenges of achieving Sustainable Development Goals through Science and Technology in Nigerian Schools Environment

1. **Quality of teacher:** Inadequate teaching has been advanced as one of the problems of science and technology in Nigerian schools. Quality science teaching is effective science teaching. Effective teaching occurs when students learn and achieve many scientific goals and not just being able to repeat scientific knowledge (Omoifo,

2012). Enhanced science teaching at both the primary and secondary levels is central to scientific and technological capacity building, and to a better public understanding of sustainable development issues. During effective learning, student develops conceptual understanding and thinking skills, thus helping students change their intuitive, everyday ways of explaining the world around them to incorporate scientific concepts and ways of thinking into their personal frame works. Therefore, students' ability to solve problems and enhanced learning occurs. Quality teaching lies at the teacher's capacity to transform written knowledge into forms that are pedagogically powerful and yet adaptive to the students' abilities and backgrounds.

2. **Teachers' incompetency:** Poor quality of science teachers in terms of adequate knowledge base and pedagogic skills is another factor identified to influence students' performance. The teacher's academic qualifications and knowledge of subject matter, competencies and skills, and the commitment of teacher, have a great impact on the teaching-learning process. An effective science teacher should be a master of his subject, as well as grounded in methods of teaching, and be able to relate the science concepts to real life experience. According to Nada (2008), the status of competency in secondary school science education in Nigeria appears very low.
3. **Lack of instructional materials:** Lack of instructional materials for science and technology teaching and learning in Nigerian schools has been a major issue of concern. The quality of education a student receives largely depends on the quality of teaching or learning resources provided. Teaching or learning resources are all the things used by the teacher during teaching, to aid understanding and make teaching successful and effective. They include: modern textbooks, equipments, consumables like chemicals and reagents, models, charts etc. and the physical learning environments which include; the science classrooms and laboratories. Majority of the schools in Nigeria, lack essential resources for imparting the knowledge of science concepts. They have empty rooms labeled laboratories. To worsen the problem, few available ones are not properly maintained, protected and cared for. Majority of students do not have textbooks and the school libraries have outdated textbooks.
4. **Inadequate funding:** Due to lack of fund, there is inadequate provision of equipment in the laboratories, ill-equipped libraries, low number of teachers needed and others. These work against sustainable development.
5. **Corruption:** Corruption has eaten deep into Nigeria system and it is manifesting in every sector including education. When money is provided to purchase the instructional materials, they neither supply the required specification, nor the required quantity. At times, they don't even supply anything. Employment is no

longer based on merit, those who are qualified for teaching science and technology are not given employment, because they don't have 'godfather' in the government.

6. **Teachers' salary:** It is very important, because it has a capacity to uplift the other aspects of teacher quality. If a teacher gets suitable salary that covers the basic living costs, he may be able to live comfortably and thus be more effective as he is motivated to use his abilities, competencies and skills. Poor remuneration affects the morale of teachers, distracts and hinders their commitment and effectiveness.
7. **Unavailability of machine for educational purposes:** Computer is an expensive machine, therefore to purchase it and distribute to schools as teaching and learning machine and aid, imposes problem to the educational exercise in tertiary institutions.
8. **Irregular power supply:** Many tertiary institutions that use machines and light, will be hindered from achieving their aim, due to inconsistency of power supply. If they cannot purchase a standby generator set for their own use. They have to rely wholly on power holding electricity for their source of power, hence jeopardizing e-learning of science.
9. **Lack of relevant software:** Software developers and publishers in the developed countries have been trying for long to develop software and multimedia, that have universal application, but due to the differences in education standards and requirements, these products do not integrate into curriculum across countries. Software that is appropriate and culturally suitable to the Nigerian education system is in short supply.

Conclusion

There is no alternative to science and technology for sustainable development of our nation. For this to be achieved, the government has to provide quality science teachers, instructional materials and fund, to run schools. Then Sustainable Development Goals will be achieved.

Recommendations

1. The government should ensure that employment is based on who is most qualified, not minding whom you know. This will help to curb corruption and more competent teachers who have the quality should be engaged in the system.
2. The government should provide fund in order to purchase modern instructional materials. They should equip the libraries and science laboratories appropriately.
3. The government should pay teachers well and regularly, this will enhance teachers output.

References

Ajeyalemi, D. (2008). Curriculum reforms in the Nigerian educational system. How sustainable in development and sustainability in Nigeria education system. Proceedings of the 2nd National Conference of the Institute of Education, Olabisi Onabanjo University.

Bonwell, C. C. and Elison, J. A. (2003). Active learning; creating excitement in the classroom. Retrieved on 4/5/2015 from www.gwu.edu/-erichie.

Eze, A. E. (2012). Indigenous science and technology education for entrepreneurship development. A Lead Paper presented at the 7th National Conference of the School of Science, Federal College of Education, Eha -Amufu.

Ezeagwu, E. (2013). Relevance of science and technical education in Nigeria's development. http://risenetworks.org/2013/08/14/relevanceofscienceandtechnic. Retrieved on 15-03-2015.

Federal Republic of Nigeria (2004). National Policy on Education, Abuja. Nigeria Education Research and Development Council NERDC Press.

Gordon, C. and Debus, R. (2000). Developing deep learning approaches and personal teaching efficacy within a pre-service teacher education context. *British Journal of Educational Psychology,* 72(4): 483-511.

Mckeown, R. (2002). Environment society economy education for sustainable development, Toolkit version 2. http://www.esdtoolkit.org (Accessed Feb. 13, 2016).

Momeke, C. D. (2007). "Effects of the learning cycle and Expository Instructional Approaches on Students' learning outcome in secondary Biology". An unpublished Ph.D Thesis submitted to the School of Post Graduate Studies, University of Benin: Benin City.

Nada, T. (2008). The Reality of innovation in government. http://www.innovationpeer-revive reality pdf. Retrieved on 20-3-2015.

Nalini, R. (2006). The role of science and technology in nation building http://www.jnsfsl.sljol.infolarticle/download/3640/29341. Retrieved on 2/11/15.

Nwokolo, M. I. (2002). *Philosophy of Technology and Nigeria*. Owerri: Claretian Institute of Philosophy Inc.

Ochu, A. N. O. (2007). Evaluation of undergraduates chemistry Education programme in the universities in North Central Education Zone in Nigeria. Unpublished Ph.D Thesis, University of Nigeria, Nsukka.

Okonjo-Iweala, N. (2012). Science and Technology-The key to Nigeria's Transformation. http://www.walemicaiah.blog.com/.../Science-and-Technology-the-key-to-Nigeria's....... Retrieved on 02-04-2015.

Omoifo, C. N. (2012). Dance of the limits, reversing the trends in Science Education. Inaugural Lecture, University of Benin, Benin City.

Renner, S. and Ragan, W. (1973). Teaching Science in the elementary school. In O. C. Ohunene, and B. E. Ozoji, *Science Education and Sustainable Development in Nigeria.* http://www.pubsscienpub.com/education/2/8/6/byocohunene-2014. Retrieved 30-01-2015.

Rundell, M. (2007). *Macmillan English Dictionary for Advanced Learners 2nd Edition,* Malaysia: Macmillan Publishers Limited

17

Using Factors Analyses Approach in Conservation of Historic Sites in Ijebu Region, Ogun State, Nigeria

LAWAL M. O., SENUGA M. A., ADEDAYO T. G. & OBAKOYA T. T.

Abstract

This paper analysed the relationship among 21 variables that affect the conversation of historical sites in Ijebu Region, Nigeria using factor analysis. The study covered the traditional areas in towns. The study area was divided into seven zones in which a reconnaissance survey was carried out. During this survey, 337 historical sites were identified and classified into six groups. Out of these sites, 189 were selected to form the sample size. Data were collected through field survey and administration of questionnaire on curators of the 189 sites. Factor analytical technique was used to analyse the data collected. The analysis revealed five principal factors having eigenvalues greater than 1.0: conservation needs (6,981); site accessibility (2.421); building design (1.581); residential location (1.3 17); and CBD accessibility (1.079). The study further revealed that the five factors had 63.7% of the total variance loading on factor 1, which is need for conservation. The result of the analysis also showed that there is a significant relationship between conservation needs and the physical planning characteristics of historical sites. The study concluded that important factors for effective conservation of historical sites are conservation needs and physical planning characteristics of the sites.

Key Words: *Conservation, Historical Sites, Cultural Heritage, Correlation, Factor, Analysis, Eigen value.*

Introduction

The physical environment of most towns in developing countries has been experiencing a multidimensional growth particularly in the last few decades. This is evident in the surge of the population of such cities resulting in a myriad of problems. The problems include scarcity of land for development, inadequate transportation facilities, acute housing shortage, rapid development of slums, human health hazards and high incidence of violent crimes (Onibokun, 1973). Also, green areas and open spaces are among the first casualties of urbanisation, as such areas are often appropriated for the provision of essential social and infrastructural facilities to update the old parts of the towns (Mabogunje,1968). The demolition of historical sites of local and national interests comprising architectural buildings, archaeological sites, shrines, grooves and monuments are desecrated or demolished in the misguided pursuit of modernization. Obviously, our environment is historic because people responding to the surroundings they inherit have shaped it. Towns and cities contain unique and dynamic record of past human activity, which reflect the aspirations, skills and investment of successive generations (English Heritage, 2007).

Historical sites, as cultural and natural heritage of the people, reflect the knowledge, beliefs and traditions of communities. They give distinctiveness, meaning and quality to the places in which we live, providing a sense of continuity and identity. They are economic assets and source of learning and enjoyment (English Heritage, 2007). However, the prevailing modernisms of religion and advancement in technology have undoubtedly eroded the regard for historical sites where conservation has been thrown to the back stage. The fact that conservation of natural and cultural heritage is imperative cannot be denied. It is the process of managing change in ways that will best sustain the significance of a place in its setting, while recognizing opportunities to reveal or reinforce its values for present and future generations.

It is equally significant to mention that Islam and Christianity, being the most popular religions, have taken precedence over the traditional belief system in the country. Originally, the Yoruba people of Southern Nigeria believed in the worship of 'Olodumare' (god) through some deities that were offered sacrifices in the forms of animate and inanimate objects. However, the people of the different religions now look down on such practices as barbaric. Gradually, the deities lost their pride of place in the hearts of the people, and several sites of historical, archaeological and architectural importance were abandoned to the mercy of inclement weather and vandals. Worse still, such sites on daily basis face the danger of encroachment by urban land developers. This is coupled with the apparent lack of interest on the part of the government, corporate bodies and individuals on the need to converse these historical sites.

This paper examined the characteristics of historical sites in Ijebu Region in Southwestern Nigeria. It analysed those factors that are important for effective conservation of historical sites in order to secure a serene environment by adopting physical planning techniques. Ijebu is one of the principal towns in Ogun State of Nigeria. It lies within Ijebu East Senatorial District of Ogun State. During the study, it was observed that worshippers visited most of the traditional religious sites during the dry and raining season. The people living in the study area are predominantly Yoruba. Hence, they share identical notions about birth, death and reincarnation. Among the people, the choice of burial sites after death is often influenced by age, social status, religion and circumstance of death (Omisore and Ajala, 1999). In their study, they found that important persons were often deified after death and worshipped. Over time, their burial places become religious and historical sites.

Literature Review

The most relevant theoretical basis for this study revolves around the three programmes of urban renewal. They are rehabilitation (bringing substandard structure up to a prescribed standard); conservation (process of upgrading) and redevelopment (the demolition, clearance and reconstruction of an entire area) (Warren and Goldsmith, 1974). Out of the three concepts, the most germane to this study is the conservation concept. Scot (1971) argued that citizens were mainly interested in visual arts and the aesthetic beauty of urban renewal programmes, but were less concerned with the socio-economic and political relevance of such sites.

Conversation is a popular concept that has been declared suitable and highly relevant in the sustenance of resources, both natural and human. It is the technology by which preservation is achieved (The Canadian Encyclopedia, 2008). In particular, conservation of heritage has been considered as placing value on our communities, our future and ourselves (Kingston and Arthur's Vale, 2004). Effective heritage conservation, which involves preservation, rehabilitation, or restoration, considers many perspectives to determine heritage value. This is based on various factors including appearance, historical or spiritual significance and use.

Heritage and conservation have become important themes in current discussions on place, cultural identity, and the preservation of the past (Matero, 2008). In America, historic conservation has been part of the conser-programme of the Department of Interior since 1906 and of the National Park Service since its establishment, which considered historic conservation as an important responsibility of the organisation (National Park Service, 2003). However, current concerns with the escalating destruction of historical sites can be attributed to the perception among the public and professionals alike that represent finite non-renewable resources deteriorating at an increasing rate (Matero,

2008). This deteriorating at an increasing rate causes issues, ranging from neglect and poor management to increased visitation and vandalism, from inappropriate past treatments to deferred maintenance. This destructive tendency towards heritage has been the reason to preach conservation.

According to Oliver, Shutter and Minns (2005), everyone should be able to participate in sustaining the historic environment. Everyone should have the opportunity to contribute to understanding and sustaining the historic environment. Judgements about the value of places and decisions about their future should be made in ways that are accessible, inclusive and informed. In the words of UNEP-WCMC (2006), learning about conservation is central to sustaining the historic environment. It raises people's awareness and understanding of heritage, including the varied ways in which different generations and communities perceive their values. It encourages informed active participation in caring for the historic environment. In the same vein, English Heritage (2007) stressed that in order to identify the values of an heritage site, it is necessary to understand its fabrics, and how and why it has changed over time; and then to consider:

- Who values the heritage site and why they do so;
- How those values relate to its fabric
- Their relative importance;
- Whether they are enhanced by associated objects;
- The contribution of the setting and context of the site to its values;
- How well the site compares with other sharing similar values.

Historic places should be well managed to sustain their values. A change in the historic environment is inevitable, whether caused by natural processes, through use, or by people responding to social, economic and technological advances. Therefore, its inevitability depends on utility and continuity. English Heritage (2007) further stressed that conservation is achieved by people that are concerned with managing a significant place, sharing an understanding of its significance, and using it to:

- Judge how its heritage value are vulnerable to change;
- Take the actions and impose the constraints necessary to sustain, reveal and reinforce those values;
- Mediate between conservation options, if action to sustain one heritage value could conflict with action to sustain another ;
- Ensure that the place retains its authenticity-those attributes which most truthfully reflect and embody the heritage values attached to it.

Considering conservation as the ideal concept, Olaore (1987) posited that three broad groups of theories have been found to exist on the subject. The theories are Economic,

Spatial Allocation and Behavioural Models. Of these three groups, the economic theory group is considered relevant to this study. It has been argued that the main lines of the economic theory have been developed particularly by Davis and Whiston (Richardson, 1974). The basic tenet of this theory is that most buildings can be maintained in a good state of repair if their owners are willing to provide the maintenance expenses required. The argument here is that structures decline in quality because their owners permit them to do so. This could be through the inability to meet the cost of maintenance.

Another variant of the Economic Theory is the so-called aggregate analysis of cumulative income decline in core areas. Baumol (1963) argued that blight is associated with a decline in the income of residents in central areas with a tendency for the decline to become cumulative. This trend often displays itself in the familiar bright phenomenon such as failure to maintain property. This shows a wide gap between neighbourhood tax receipts and expenditure on services, outmigration of high-come residents in developed countries had been the abandonment of central areas to the less congested periphery of these towns. Consequently, Baumol (1963) argued that buildings become derelict, dilapidated and ruined.

The Economic Theory as the basis of explaining the concept of conservation seems weak when applied to the Nigerian situation. Its major weakness is based on the assumption that deterioration is mainly an equity consideration, based on social cost and benefits. The theory never considered the socio-economic factors compelling resident not to move out of such areas even when the buildings are dilapidated. In an attempt to make up for the deficiencies of the Economic Theory, town planners and geographers introduced the Spatial Allocation Models. For examples, transportation modelers would assign lower income people to places in and around the core area of an urban centre (Herberts and Stephens, 1960). It is argued that as an urban area grows and develops, the tendency is for people in the central area to move into the surroundings districts with the resultant deterioration in the environment.

Another issue of importance is the control of development or land. The ability to control development lies within the power of the public sector and could therefore be used as a concept of conservation. In particular, the appropriate town planning authorities where the properties to be renewed are located could evoke the power of compulsory accusation. Hence, such properties could be acquired for public use. In this case, such power could be enforced to acquire historical sites and utilize them publicly (Nigeria, 1992). This could be an effective method of ensuring the conservation of historical sites for cultural heritage purpose.

Methodology

The study was conducted using both primary and secondary data. The primary data include questionnaire administration and physical survey. For the purpose of data collection, a reconnaissance survey of the study area was made. This involved a comprehensive physical assessment of historical sites, administration of the structured questionnaire, personal observation and oral interviews.

Stratified random sampling technique was adopted at two levels which include:

1. The spread of the samples among the existing sites in Ijebu Region urban area.
2. The spread of the samples among the various categories of historical sites

The stratification involves the spread of the samples selected among the existing seven sites in Ijebu Region: Ijebu-Ode, Ijebu-Remo, Ijebu-Igbo, Ijebu-Waterside, Ijebu-Imushin/Ijebu-Ife, Odogbolu and Ago-Iwoye. Apart from dividing the study area into wards, the historical sites were categorized using a stratification factor (Moser and Kalton, 1971). Stratification is a means of increasing the precision of a study, meaning that before any selection takes place, all the sites are divided into a number of strata, then a random sample is selected within each stratum. The selection of the historical sites was carried out in wards by adopting the criterion used by David (1995) in a similar study on historical sites in United Kingdom. The criterion was based on selecting each sites from each category listed below:

- Natural history attraction
- Science based attraction
- Socio-cultural attraction
- Attractions associated with historic persons
- Pleasure gardens
- Stately and central homes
- Religious attractions
- Villages and hamlets
- Festivals and pageants

By adopting the above listed criteria, 337 different historical sites were identified as shown in Table 1. The breakdown is as follows: Ijebu-Ode 60, Ijebu-Remo 39, Ijebu-Igbo 39, Ijebu-Waterside 41, Ijebu-Mushin/Ijebu-Ife 71, Odogbolu 59 and Ago-Iwoye 28. An evaluation of the sample frame shows that some categories of historical sites were available in limited numbers. These include monuments, museums, squares and grooves. In view of this, all of them were included in the sample size to be studied. From the remaining two categories that have high representation in all the zones (architectural buildings and shrines), one out of every two historical sites was randomly selected using the ballot system. This yielded 189 sites. This is shown in Table 2.

From the questionnaire, information about variables such as: building, age of historical site, number of floors, materials of construction, condition of the building, area occupied and the infrastructural facilities on the site were obtained. The last sets of questions were about accessibility to site, maintenance and reasons for conservation.

Table 1: Sampling frame of historical sites

Ward	Monument	Building	Museum	Square	Shrine	Groove	Total	%
Ijebu-Ode	1	18	1	1	8	5	34	18.0
Ijebu-Remo	2	8	1	1	9	1	22	11.6
Ijebu-Igbo	-	12	1	-	7	-	20	10.6
Ijebu-Waterside	2	8	-	-	11	-	21	11.1
Ijebu Imushin/ Ijebu Ife	5	15	1	2	16	1	40	21.2
Odogbolu	5	17	1	-	6	3	34	18.0
Ago iwoye	5	6	1	2	4	-	18	9.8
Total	20	84	6	6	63	10	189	100.0

Table 2: Sample size of historical sites

Ward	Monument	Building	Museum	Square	Shrine	Groove	Total	%
Ijebu Ode	1	36	1	1	16	5	60	17.8
Ijebu Remo	2	16	1	1	18	1	39	11.6
Ijebu Igbo	-	24	1	-	14	-	39	11.6
Ijebu Waterside	2	16	-	-	22	-	41	12.2
Ijebu Imushin/ Ijebu Ife	5	30	1	2	32	1	71	21.0
Odogbolu		34	1	-	16	3	59	17.5
Ago Iwoye	5	12	1	2	8	-	28	8.3
Total	20	168	6	6	126	10	337	100.0

Source: Author's Field Survey (2019)

The 21 variables listed in Table 3 are measures of the different attributes of the historical sites. These variables can be categorized into four groups:

i. Variables 01, 02, 03, 04, 05, 06 and 07 are measures of the characteristics of these historical sites;
ii. Variables 08, 09,10 and 20 are measures of the physical planning dimension of each historical sites as regards their spatial distribution;

iii. Variables 11, 12, 13, 14, 15, 16, 17, 18, 19 and 20 are measures of the services available on these sites that would encourage their patronage and consequently influence the decision to conserve them or otherwise;
iv. Variable 21 relates to the cost of maintenance of each site by direct method of project execution.

The collection of secondary data were through an inventory of existing historical sites from existing documents, government publications such as gazettes, decrees and by-laws. Other sources of secondary data include newspaper and periodicals.

Table 3: Variables used in factor analysis

Variables No	
01	Needs for conservation
02	Site use
03	Building style
04	Building age
05	Floor number
06	Material of construction
07	Site condition
08	Area condition
09	Distance from curators residence
10	Distance of historical site from town centre
11	Footpath with the site
12	Electricity
13	Water
14	Telephone
15	Toilet
16	Security
17	Guest accommodation
18	Parking space
19	Refuse bin
20	Access
21	Estimated cost of maintenance

Source: Author's Field Survey (2019)

Analytical Techniques

Factors analyses technique was used to subject the 21 variables from relating to 189 historical sites to assess the significance of each of the variables while at the same time, taking cognizance of the significance of the other variables in the data sets. This is important in that a variable, which is significant, when treated as an individual in a multivariate analysis, may, in reality, be insignificant because of its strong relationships with some other variables in the same data set (Mather, 1976; Johnson, 1984). The factors analyses also makes it possible to assess the internal relationships among the various historical sites (cooley and Lohnes, 1971; Tatsuoka, 1971; Kim and Mueller,1978; Field, 2005).

Data Analyses

The result of the analysis shown in Table 4 revealed that five factors with eigenvalues > 1 accounted for about 64 percent of the total variance in the original data. Factor 1 (conservation needs) accounted for the highest eigenvalue of 6.981 in all the variables. The variance accounted for by other factors are factor 2- site accessibility (2.421), factor 3- building design (1.581), factor 4- residential location (1.3 17) and factor 5-CBD accessibility, accounted for 1.079 of the variance. These five factors were selected for further analyses as shown in Table 5.

Table 4: Factor Analysis Result

Factor Number	Eigenvalue	Percentage of Variance	Cumulative % of Variance
1	6.981	33.2	33.2
2	2.421	11.5	44.8
3	1.581	7.5	52.3
4	1.317	6.3	58.3
5	1.079	5.1	63.7
6	0.92	4.4	68.1
7	0.82	3.9	72
8	0.711	3.4	75.4
9	0.631	3	78.4
10	0.611	2.9	81.3
11	0.508	2.4	83.7
12	0.497	2.4	86.1
13	0.466	2.2	88.3
14	0.408	1.9	90.2
15	0.377	1.8	92.1
16	0.364	1.7	93.7
17	0.339	1.6	95.3

18	0.309	1.5	96.6
19	0.248	1.2	98
20	0.222	1.1	99.1
21	0.191	0.9	100

Source: Author's Field Survey (2019)

Table 5: Factor Analysis Result and the Generic Name

Factor 1	Conservation Needs
Factor 2	Site Accessibility
Factor 3	Building Design
Factor 4	Residential Location
Factor 5	CBD Accessibility

Source: Author's Field Survey (2019)

The Component Loading

Table 6 shows the components for each primary variable on each of the five factors. The loading provide the basis for a detailed examination of both (1) the structure of the five components and (2) the behaviour of each primary variable across the five components. It must be noted that the sign either (+ve) prefix or (-ve) prefix of the loading is usually ignored if selected for consideration are not below +1-0.60. This is to avoid duplicity of variables.

The five factors selected are: (1) conservation needs (2) site accessibility, (3) building design, (4) residential location and (5) CBD accessibility. These five factors are those that were rotated using varimax program, which tends to produce. The loadings are as shown in Table 6. These five factors are the reasons for conservation of historical sites and will be determined by the degree of use and age of those structures.

Discussion of Results

The first factor on Table 4 accounts for 33.24 percent. In Table 6, the remaining four factors were also examined to underscore their relationship. Table 6 indicates that factor 1 loads highly on the measure of need for conservation (0.70), building age (-0.69), floor number (0.68), site condition (0.72), electricity (0.82), water (0.78), telephone (0.70) toilet (0.74), parking space (0.74), and refuse bins (0.82). It should be noted that 10 of the 21 primary variables considered in the analysis load to the required +/-60 on factor 1and that 6 of these have factors load above 0.70 (Table 7).

Factor 1 suggests that the characteristics of the historical and infrastructural facilities are significant with conservation. This was further strengthened by the fact that no factor loadings on other variables are selected because they are below the required value +/-0.60. For instance, it depicts that the need for conservation cannot be associated with the site (-0.30), distance of residence curator to site (-0.69), the availability or non-availability of footpath within the historical sites (-0.15) and that accessibility to these historical sites has nothing to do with their conservation (-0.41) Thus, factor 1 depicts those factors that influence the need for conservation. The indices of material construction (-0.49) and cost of maintenance (0.38) are significantly associated with the need for conservation. This is because the material of construction of an historical site should correlate significantly with the age of the buildings and the physical condition of the historical site. This will determine the cost of maintenance when decision to conserve has been made.

Table 6: Loadings of Variables in Five Factors

		Factors				
	Loading Variables	**1**	**2**	**3**	**4**	**5**
01	Need for Conservation	0.70	-0.31	0.08	-0.15	0.03
02	Site Use	-0.30	0.61	-0.28	-0.32	0.36
03	Building Style	0.16	-0.02	0.73	-0.14	0.36
04	Building Age	-0.69	0.26	0.02	-0.05	0.07
05	Floor Number	0.68	-0.32	-0.22	0.12	-0.09
06	Material	-0.49	0.34	0.48	-0.11	0.41
07	Site Condition	0.72	-0.16	-0.24	-0.09	0.03
08	Area Occupied	0.37	0.50	0.25	0.06	-0.38
09	Distance from Residence	0.11	0.36	0.44	-0.05	-0.61
10	Distance from Town Centre	0.01	0.11	0.24	0.79	-0.12
11	Footpath	-0.15	0.64	-0.19	-0.28	-0.00
12	Electricity	0.82	-0.19	0.01	-0.01	-0.01
13	Water	0.78	0.06	0.06	0.09	0.08
14	Telephone	0.70	0.29	0.06	0.01	0.16
15	Toilet	0.74	-0.07	-0.01	0.20	0.06
16	Security	0.59	0.39	-0.15	-0.33	0.06
17	Guest Accommodation	0.57	0.52	-0.07	0.17	0.23
18	Parking Space	0.74	0.41	-0.12	0.03	0.13
19	Refuse Bin	0.82	0.21	0.04	0.06	0.01
20	Access	-0.41	0.31	-0.46	-0.10	0.03
21	Cost of Maintenance	0.38	0.08	0.13	-0.47	-0.34
	Eigen Value	6.98		1.58	1.32	1.08
	% of Total Variance	33.24	11.53	7.58	1.32	1.08
	Cumulative % of Total Variance	33.24	44.77	52.30	58.57	63.71

Table 7: Loading considered on Factor 1

Variable Number	Variable	Loading (*)
01	Need for conservation	0.70
03	Building Age	-0.69
04	Floor Number	0.68
07	Site Condition	0.72
12	Electricity	0.82
13	Water	0.78
14	Telephone	0.70
15	Toilet	0.74
18	Parking space	0.74
19	Refuse Bin	0.82

(*) All figures are rounded up to 2 decimal points
Source: Author's Field Survey (2019)

Further consideration of Table 4 shows that factors 2, 3, 4 and 5 seem to be more of physical planning factors than factor 1. An examination of the variables on factor 2 suggests that this factor is indexing physical planning factors as depicted by combination of site use (+0.61) and footpath (+0.643). In fact, all the loadings on their variables on this factor are very low. This is also confirmed on the loading of factors 3,4 and 5 that have high loadings on building style (factor 3), distance from town centre to site of historical site (factor 4) and the distance of the residence of the curator to the historical site (factor 5).

Conclusion

The study revealed that five factors were very significant. These factors included conservation needs, site accessibility, building design, residential location and CBD accessibility. The result showed that there was a correlation between conservation needs and the condition of historical sites. The study showed that there were five principal factors with eigenvalues > 1. These factors were; conservation needs, site accessibility, buildings design, residential location and CBD accessibility. The factor analysis of data showed that the physical characteristics and infrastructural facilities were significant on factor 1 and that the remaining four factors (2, 3, 4 and 5) were significant on physical planning features of the historical sites.

In addition, the study revealed that there was a correlation and significant relationship between conservation needs and the physical planning characteristics of historical sites. This outcome from the analysis of data suggests the significance of structural condition and physical planning characteristics of historical sites towards achieving the overall goal of conserving the historical sites.

Recommendations

As a result of these findings:

- There is need for all levels of government in Nigeria to take urgent steps towards the conservation of historical sites to prevent their total collapse and to enhance their patronage. The intervention should be in the areas of funding and provision of relevant facilities.
- The Federal Government of Nigeria should set up agencies and strengthen existing agencies for the identification, listing, rehabilitation and maintenance of historical sites.
- The roads leading to these historical sites should be rehabilitated to enhance patronage by tourists.
- The facilities within the historical sites and around their environment should be improved.

References

Adejuyigbe, O. (1975). *Boundary problems in Western Nigeria: A geographical analysis.* Ile Ife: Ife University Press.

Askari-Krapf, E. (1969). *Yoruba and Cities.* Oxford: Claredon Press. 37-38.

Baumol, W. J. (1963). Interactions of Public and Private Decision. Public Expenditure Decisions in the Urban Community Research (italics). Schaller H. Ed. John Hopkins Press.

Cooley, W. W. and Lohnes, P. R. (1971). *Multivariate Data Analysis.* New York: John Wiley.

David, T. H. (1995). Heritage, tourism and society. England, Tourism and Recreation Services. English Heritage.2007. Conservation Principles: Polices and Evidence for the Sustainable.

Field, A. P. (2005). *Discovering Statistics Using SPSS,* 2nd Ed, London Sage.

Gruffydd, B. (1977). Protecting historic landscapes. Cheltenham.

Hobert, J. O. and Stephens H. B. (1960). "A model for the distribution of residential activity in urban areas. *Journal of Regional Science,* 2:21-31.

Johnston, R. J. (1984). *Multivariate Analysis in Geography.* London: Longman.

Kim, J. and Mueller, C. W. (1978). Factor Analysis Sage: University Publication.

Kingston and Arthur's V. (2004). Historic area conservation management plan for Kingston and Arthur's Vale historic area management board. Norfolk Island.

Mabogunje, A. L. (1972). *Yoruba Towns.* Ibadan: University of Ibadan Press.

Mabogunje, A. L. (1968). *Urbanization in Nigeria.* London: University of London Press. 42.

Marther, P. M. (1976). *Computational Methods of Multivariate Analysis in Physical Geography.* London: John Wiley.

Matero, F. G. (2008). Heritage Conservation and Archaeology: An Introduction. A1A site preservation programme.

Moser, C. A. and Kalton, G. (1971). *Survey Methods in Social Investigation.* London: Heineman Educational Books.

National Park Service (2003). A Brief History of National Park Service. http!/www.cr.pps.gor/history/online-books!kielv!kiely5.htm

Nigeria, Federal Republic. (1992). The Nigeria Urban and Regional Planning Law. Decree 88 Lagos. Federal Government Printer.

Olaore T. (1987). Theoretical framework of urban renewal. Urban renewal in Nigeria. Onibokun et al. Ibadan. NISER.

Oliver, C. K., Shutter, B. J. and Minns, C. K. (2005). Toward a definition of conservation principles for fisheries management. *J. Fish. Aquart. Sci.* 51:2115-2125.

Omisore, E. O. and Ajala A. O. (1999). Location Analysis of Tombs Cemeteries in South-Western Nigeria. Unpublished Manuscript.

Onibokun, A.G. (1973). Forces shaping the physical environment of cities: the Ibadan case. *Land Economics,* 49: 424-481.

Richardson, H. W. (1974). *An introduction to town planning techniques. The Built Environment Series.* London: Hutchinson. 94-95.

Scott, C. (1961). Research on mail Surveys. *Journal of the Royal Statistical Society* 124.

Tatsuoka, M. M. (1971). *Multivariate analysis technique for educational and psychological research.* New York: John Wiley.

Warren, A. and Goldsmith, F. B. (1974). *Conservation Practice.* London: John Wiley.

18

Relationship between the Learner and the School Personnel in Nigeria Education

OSARO Christiana A. Ph.D & OBINDAH Fortune Ph.D

Abstract

The work examined relationship between the learner and school personnel in Nigeria education. The work found that change of behaviour takes place in three domains of learning. Quality education is featured first at hours and at the three levels of education. Parents being the first teacher of the child should maintain good relationship with their children and care givers at home, at early childhood education, and at all levels of education. Servants are to be respectful to their masters, obey instruction and perform their tasks effectively with the fear of God. Day care workers should be trained, certificate issued to them for special performance which will make them unique in their job. The head of schools is to protect lives of teachers, students and those working for the progress of the school from intruder who may come to abuse or destroy them at school. Regular meetings with staff, and students give opportunity to solve problems that boarder them. Employ counsellors at all levels of education to assist individuals solve their problems; a stich in time saves mine.

Keywords: *Relationship, Learner, School Personnel, Nigeria*

Introduction

Education is the instrument for national development, aim to equipped students toward effective integration into the society. This aim is achieved through the school system where learning and teaching take place. Njama-Abeng (2006) in Fortune and Osaro (2019), stated that education is a process where learners work in co-operation with each other. The school should be a sort of living situation where teachers and students work with mutual and social spirit of cooperation. The learner is the child and the individual who assist the learner to acquire knowledge is the teacher, tutor or lecturer. Teaching and learning in the school system take place in the class room. Achuonye (2019), opined that the teacher is someone who carries out the activity of teaching engages in the act of helping people to learn. The individual that plans and involves the learner in the various activities that brings about the desired change in behaviour.

The change of behaviour takes place in three domains of learning; the cognitive, affective and the psychomotor domains.

- The cognitive domain is all about knowledge and skills.
- The affective domain deals with emotions and feelings.
- The psychomotor domains involve physical skills and manual work.

All these develop and prepare the child to be useful to self and to the society. Amaele (2019) explained that education is the reflection of the holistic man, must have all the functional components. It must develop the mind, the body and the soul of individuals. Professionally, education must address the three main domains; cognitive, affective and psychomotor domains. Hence, no domain should be neglected if quality education must be realised.

Quality education brings about change of behaviour. It is nurtured in the three levels of education. The primary education which is the foundation of all education, the Post Basic Education, is the education children receive after a successful completion of ten years of Basic Education Certificate Examination (BECE) and Junior Arabic and Islamic studies certificate Examination (AJISCE) (National Policy on Education, 2013). Tertiary Education is the education given to students after Post Basic Education. Tertiary education is the education given at the university, polytechnics, and Colleges of Education, Colleges of Technology, and Advanced Teacher Training Colleges. It is also the education after secondary education (Uzoeshi, 2013). These three levels of education need guidance and counselling to assist the learner focus on the academic work and to resolve problems that affect them.

The Learner and Home Relationship

Parents are the first educators of children at home. As the first teacher, they teach language, counting identification and writing of numbers and alphabets. They are the first to teach the child how to use pencil to write. At home, there are relatives and friends who also take part in early child care. In some home where parents go to work in order to make food available at home, they employ the service of nanny, to care for the child at home. The nanny becomes the second mother of the child and other children, and also performs most house chores in some homes. In most cases, payment is made for the services rendered or going to school with other children (Bruce and Meggitt, 2005). There can be no equality in early childhood services unless there is equality of opportunity. Equality of opportunity means opening up access for every child and family to full participation in early child services. Lack of access causes poor self-esteem, misunderstanding stereotyping and discrimination, lack of respect and lack of confidence.

Relationship between Parents and Members of the Family

Parents are the centre of love and peace in the home, caring for one another maintaining peace and happiness between members of the family. The child learns basic facts of life from home such as respect for elders, the fear of God, obedience, honestly and hand work from parent. When parent recognise that all the children are important they give them equal attention and assistance in education; being fair to provide their needs, equal attention and teaching them to know their responsibilities in house chores. Mezuebi and Opara (2007) stated that if children live with acceptance, tolerance, fairness and love in their formative years, they will learn to love and be compassionate when they grow up.

Relationship between Parents and Nannies/Servants

Parents' inability to care for their children, perform all the house chores and also to work in an organization, perceive employing the service of assistance (nanny) will relieve them of much work load. The nanny is a member of another family brought into another family to assist in performing household chores and care for the child or children. The nanny or servant is a human being who needs parental care; treat him or her as a member of your own family by showing love, and attending to his/her needs. Reduce the work load by allowing your children to participate in house chores, so that they will also learn to perform tasks. The house chore is not the responsibility of only one person. Members of the family should take part in washing clothes, dishes, cleaning, sweeping, bathing the children and other activities at home.

When parent are back from work, they should create time to ask about how the children faired at school and in the house when they were absent and try to resolve whatever problems they encountered. Make them feel happy, but do not promise what you cannot give, that will create mistrust and unhappiness. Show love to your servants so that they will love your children. Do not belittle yourself by making love with your nanny, it is illegal and sin before God and man.

Servants or nannies; be obedient to your masters. Obey instructions; perform your task diligently with fear of God. When you are good to them, they will assist in your education and progress in life. Ephesian 6:5-7 posited that servants should be obedient to them that are your masters according to the flesh, with fear and trembling in singleness of your heart as unto Christ. Not with eye service as men pleasers but as the servants of Christ, doing the will of God from the heart; with good will doing service, as to the Lord and not to men.

Early Childhood Education/Pre-primary Education (0-4) Years

Early Childhood Education is education given to children prior to primary education, situated in educational institutions. It includes the crèche, the nursery and the kindergarten. Federal Government of Nigeria, in its National Policy on Education (2013) presents Early Childhood Care, Development and Education (ECCDE) as the care, protection, stimulation and learning promoted for children from age 0-4 years in a crèche or nursery. The purpose of early childhood care, Development and Education shall be to effect a smooth transition from home to school, prepare the child from the primary level of education, provide adequate care, supervision and security for the children while their parents are at work, among others. These purposes prepare them into primary education.

Relationship between Parents and the Day Care Management

It is obvious that the management of Daycare, arranges with parents on specific amount to be paid for services rendered. When this money is paid on time, it ensures a good relationship; it gives the care giver happiness for work well done. When parent go for the children after work, they ask the nanny how the child faired, since the child cannot explain anything or what happened better. If there be any health challenge, they ask the health worker how the child faired, such as feeling the temperature and relaxation; proper observation by the parents is needed for the child.

The nanny, who cares for the child at school, should ensure adequate care and protection from injury and hurt from other children, electric shock from phone, or socket. When the child is in good health, the parents feel happy and may appreciate the care worker. Bruce and Meggitt (2005) stated that it is important for early childhood worker of all kinds to work according to principles of equality and inclusivity. This is at the heart of early hood work in every kind of setting. The Daycare workers are untrained for the job. They require training for effective job. This will guide who should work as a day care worker. The certificate at the end of the training will actually specify who is a Daycare worker or not. The government should encourage such training with specific number of years for the programme.

The Primary Education (Basic Education) 5-6 years

The primary Education is the foundation to all education programme. It is the first formal education that a child attends, the duration is from 6 to 11 years. As the foundation, children are taught alphabets and numbers, how to perform four operations in mathematics and how to make simple sentences, reading and writing are built at this level. A child that graduates from early childhood class into primary education usually performs better than a child that attends school for the first time. The teacher needs to understand the child before effective teaching and learning can take place. Teaching is from known to unknown for the child to learn effectively (Nwamadi-Wosu, Ordu, Nwamadi-Wosu and Osaro, 2014). For any learning to be effective, the learner must be able to use the knowledge and skills in other situations as part of learning in a new environment. Learning in a particular situation guides the learn behaviour in another situation.

Relationship between Pupils and the Teacher

Relationship refers to the way in which individuals or group behave toward each other in any organization. In primary education, pupils are taught to develop intellectually, morally and physically, skills that enable them attend to issues at school and in the society. Therefore, pupils are to be obedient, self-disciplined and patient in learning. The teacher becomes their second parent, taking over the role of parenting at school. Pupils-teacher relationship should be cordial; pupils recognizing their teacher as a loco parent who guides, and protects them. The learner should ask question for clarity of information from the teacher. Pupils being honest in relating information to their parents about their teachers with good intention create cordial relationship and love for one another.

Parent Relationship with Teachers

It has been observed recently that teachers, in performing their jobs, smack a child for wrong behaviour, in order to correct the child in the school. So some parents go to the school to abuse the teachers without knowing what the child has done. In some cases parents arrest teachers with police for smacking their children. Remember Proverbs 13-14, which admonishes that parents should with hold not correction from the child; for if thou beatests him with the rod, he shall not die. Thou shall beat him with the rod and shall deliver his soul from hell. Some decade ago, children were spark very well, at school. They were honest, respective, peaceful and are intelligent. Today, they are important citizens. In this generation, teachers should report whatever behaviour of the child to the school authority.

Secondary School Education/Relationships between Students, Academic Staff and Non-academic Staff of the School

Secondary school Education (Post-Basic Education) is the education children receive after successful completion of ten years of Basic Education and passing the Basic Education, Certificate Examination (AJISCE) (National Policy on Education, 2013). Students at the secondary schools are teenagers who are experiencing transition from childhood to adulthood. Many behavioural problems become apparent; they are troubled and may behave in dangerous ways that may harm them and others; they practice what they see and imitate principles that influence them; they seek freedom in talks and social activities.

Hence, it becomes necessary for the school to inculcate in them moral principles, obedient to school rules and regulations. Respect to both academic and non-academic Staff and respecting the worth of other students in the school. Echebe (2019) was of the view that the school also exists for developing other aspect of the individual's personality. The expectation is to contribute towards the training of the adolescents who do not only think of themselves but also other members of the society. The school co-operates with the home to ensure that students' development is achieved. Denga and Denga (2007), opined that the school aims principally at developing the child's intellect, occupational skills and character. It ensures that the educational vocational spiritual aesthetic and physical aspects of the child is developed.

When to Seek Guidance

Guidance is rendered by any person knowledgeable enough to assist individuals in any organization. The school authority stands a better chance to educate students on rules and regulation of the school. The school administrative staff disseminates vital information to students and permit students to ask questions on issues that concern them. Students need to seek guidance after their resumption into the school. The administrative staff, academic staff and the counsellor give guidance to students when the need arises. Guidance is to prevent problem from occurring. Recall that prevention is better than cure. Seek guidance before subject's selection. To develop career of your choice, guidance is very important, to prepare for external examination. Guidance counsellors ensure that students select subjects of their choice without parental or peer influence (Kinanee, 2012). Parents play no small role in influencing the occupational choice of their children. In the first instance, they could talk children into choosing careers which (they the parents) could not fulfil but expect their children to do so. They also influence family occupation by making their children choose careers in that profession.

Peer influence is a very crucial factor on students' career choice. Students like selecting career of their peers and friends to attend the same higher institution Omeje (2002) stated that many adolescents prefer going to their peers for advice on matters of career choice than adults for guidance. A good relationship between students and staff of the school reduces fear, ignorance, violence and failure at school. The school authority, should schedule regular meetings with students and staff at interactive sections (Iwundu, 2019). The idea of constant staff meetings should be encouraged by the executive administrator. It is as well as an avenue to iron out serious administrative and personnel problems. The executive will find himself relieved after the meeting; because it has afforded him the opportunity to unburden his mind and vent his anger. At the end of the day, it reassures the executive that there is no sabotage and all members of staff equally speak their minds where necessary.

Counselling is rendered by a professional known as the counsellor. It is a process by which the counsellor assists a client in a face to face interaction. The counsellor uses his/her counselling skills and knowledge to understand the clients. Clients or counsellees are group of individuals that have similar problems that needff.. the attention of the counsellor or to assist them resolved. Uzoeshi (2003), opined that counselling is the most important function rendered by the counsellor. The counsellor tries to assist individuals who are experiencing problems to be adjusted and effective. Counselling function involves mutual interaction between the counsellor and the client. Henderson and Thompson (2011) stated that behavioural counsellors believed in establishing positive collaborative relationship as clients are expected to get to try new behavours, work between sessions and monitor themselves counsellors support clients by providing positive feedback and reassurance. Counselling is the integral part of guidance. Counselling is rendered in the clinic or office; a conducive environment that makes clients feel secured to narrate problems bothering him. The problem of the client may lean on educational vocational or person social problems.

Relationship between Students and Staff of Tertiary Institution

Tertiary education is the education given to students after Post Basic Education. It is education given at the university and other higher institutions of learning. Uzoeshi (2013), explained that tertiary education is education after secondary education; the education given at the universities, polytechnics, Colleges of Education, Colleges of Technology and Advanced Teacher Training Colleges. Students and staff of the institutions are individuals working together for the common goal of teaching and learning, for successful programme. No part of it can stand alone, as one leads to the other. Teaching and learning cannot be separated. Both take place in an environment. The learner and the teacher, (lecturer) are to work with mutual, and social spirit of co-operation in the university.

The learning environment must be peaceful, safe, clean and conducive for learning to take place, having enough seats and space to accommodate students' easy movement in and out of lecture. In order to promote healthy atmosphere of learning, the lecturer is a model of imitation in character. Denga (2002) viewed the lecturer as a significant figure to all students having verbal fluency for communication, good behaviour and balanced judgement to all students. The lecturer assesses students by giving them complex work that require critical thinking and reasoning through assignments, group presentations, seminars, practical works, project, and many other method of assessment including examinations by the end of a semester. Fair judgement is given to all students; no one is very important than the other (Adeoye, 2016). The lecturers play loco parent roles; act as adviser, mentor, and information dissemination in the class. They contribute to students' knowledge and wellbeing in the institution. Akubuiro (2015) posited that lectures as teachers, should be careful of comments to students regarding their questions, answers and work during lectures in the classroom setting. Encourage them to build confidence by practicing effective study habits and to avoid examination malpractice for successful programme.

Students who realize the difficulties involved in their admission and the goals of tertiary education of which one of it is to contribute to national development through high level manpower learning, will seek guidance after admission into higher institution. Guidance will enable students to adjust better to the new environment and be ready to learn. The problem of young people living home to another social environment may create abnormalities, being more excited to glorify the admission and progress in life, may impede students to absent from classes, involve in dubious character such as drug abuse, drunkenness, indecent dressing, cultism, sex, offences, truancy, premarital sex that causes unwanted pregnancies and other numerous problem not mentioned that affect students at higher institutions. Students are to seek guidance from administrative personnel, academic staff, and the counsellor of the institution. They are knowledge able to direct students to prevent problems. In order to disseminate information to students, the university can promote healthy social climate through regular meetings, to create opportunities for students and staff to share ideas, and ask questions on issues that boarders them.

When to seek Counselling

Counselling is rendered by a professional known as the counsellor. It is the process by which the counsellor assists a client in a face to face interaction. The counsellor uses his/her counselling skills and knowledge to understand the client's problem and assist to solve it. The client is the individual that has problem to solve. He goes to the counsellor for assist in order to solve problems that affect him/her.

At the higher institution, student's career have been chosen and decided for life. Counselling at this level of educaiton provides skills, and knowledge needed for future life. Uzoeshi (2013), this stage is the stage of career specialization. Students have concretized their educational goals. Problem of students at this level includes family problems, financial problems, securing job after school, looking for life partner, becoming independent from parents, making and breaking friendships with the same sex, dating and maintaining steady relationship with opposite sex and passing examination with good grade.

A student seeking personalized dialogue and interaction with the counsellor, implies that the individual is experiencing a problem that needs adequate attention and assistance to resolve. One of the slogan in counselling. A problem shared is a problem solved" when the client meets a competent person, who uses counselling expertise to assist him/her to solve the problem. Denga (2004) explained that counselling service describes as personalized, in the sense that the problem brought by the client is private in nature and require some confidentiality. Such problems include family issues, sexual issues, self-concept problems and many other issues that the student may not like to share with others except the one trusted.

Students should not be afraid or ashamed of seeking the counsellor's advice when problem arises. Seeking the counsellor for information is guidance, preventive measure. Seeking counselling is curative measure. Guidance and counselling are very important to humans for proper adjustment to issues in the society.

The aforementioned problems need the attention of students at the higher institutions to see counselling for proper resolution and adjustment to university programmes. Remember, a stich in time saves nine.

Conclusion

Guidance and counselling assist students to develop the right full mind to study and pass examinations. Students should build friendly relationship with staff of the institution for peaceful atmosphere in the institution of learning. The administrators should create opportunities for staff and students to interact, share ideas and provide solution to problems that affect them from time to time. These will actually inculcate a peaceful environment for learning to take place.

Recommendations

Based on aforementioned issues, the following recommendations are made:

- Students should seek guidance from professionals, knowledgeable to offer assistance in the university after admission into tertiary institution, so that proper adjustment will be made to lectures.
- It is important for students to give respect to those who care for their success. The academic and non-academic staff of the institution.

- Attend lectures, write examinations and participate in other learning activities held in the campus.
- Develop effective study habits in order to pass examinations.
- Avoid examination malpractice; it one of the big crimes in education.
- Students should shun violence, and focus on academic work.
- Seek guidance and counselling from the counsellors to prevent and resolve problems in educational, vocational and personal-social matters.

References

Achuonye, K. A. (2019). The virtuousness of a teacher. An Inaugural lecture Ignatius Ajuru University of Education Port Harcourt Rivers State. Pearl Publishers International Ltd.

Akubuiro, I. M., Denga, I. D. (2015). *Learner Friendly Classroom Environment for Sustained Interest in Science Education. Credible Educational Response to current Challenges Plaguing Nigeria.* Calabar: Rapid Educational Publishers.

Amaele, S. (2019). The Dilemma of Frustrated Nigeria Education System. An inaugural lecture, Ignatius Ajuru University of Education Port Harcourt, Rivers State. Pearl Publishers International Ltd.

Bruce, T. and Megerit, C. (2005). *Child care education.* London: Hodder and Stoughton Education.

Denga, I. A. and Denga, H. M. (2007). *Child parenting in a developing nation, challenges and prospects.* Calabar: Haye Communications.

Denga, I. D. (2002). *Educational and Social Psychology for Schools and other Social Organizations.* Calabar: Clear-Lives Publications.

Echebe, P. (2019). *Adolescence Psychology Basic Principles and Practice.* Port Harcourt: Emhai Books.

Federal Government of Nigeria (2013). *National Policy on Education.* Lagos: NERDC Publishers.

Forture, O. and Osaro, C. A. (2019). Financing education in Nigeria and other issues in education. *Quarterly Journal of Contemporary Research*, 7: 119-129.

Henderson, D. A. and Thompson, C. L. (2011). *Counselling children, International Edition* (3rd Ed). America: Books and Cole Cengage Learning.

Iwundu, C. O. (2019). *Psychology for the Education and Health Professions.* Port Harcourt: Km 7 Shops.

Khana, M. J. (2010). A comparative study of leadership behaviour of principals in relation to job satisfaction of teachers in government and non-government schools. Retrieved 27th July 2010.

Kinanee, J. B. (2012). *The Youth and Career Development.* Port Harcourt: Acheri Books.

Meziobi, K. A. and Opara, J. M. (2007). *Principles of Family living.* Owerri: Acadapeak Publishers.

Nwamadi-Wosu, L. M., Ordu, S. N. Nwamadi-Wosu, L. and Osaro, C. A. (2014) *Educational Psychology theories and Practice.* Port Harcourt: Emhai Books.

Omeje, J. C. (2002). *Educational and Occupational Information in Counselling.* A Foundational approach. Enugu: Chidube Printing Press Company.

The Holy Bible, King James Version (2010). *Reference Edition, giant print concordance. Topical Heading led letter edition.* China: Franchrix Publishers.

Uzoeshi, K. C. (2013). *Guidance and Counselling Foundations and Practice.* Port Harcourt: Harey Publications Coy.

19

Issues in Managing E-Learning in Tertiary Institutions in a Developing Economy

AGI Ugochukwu K. Ph.D

Abstract

Advancement in technologies and the introduction of the internet are twin factors that have revolutionized the ways a number of human endeavours are conducted and achieved. Technology and Internet have caused massive development in commerce, business, medicine, engineering, space travel, and explorations and communication. Similarly, there have been major influences of technology and internet on education. Teaching and learning have benefitted immensely from the availability of these technological facilities as well as the internet in the classrooms, laboratories, workshops, theatres and libraries. Computers, robotics, and other media are evidences that the classrooms have bought into the technological age. This paper focused on the central role of management of E-Learning in tertiary education in maximizing its purposes. Accordingly, the paper considered the issues of rising populations in tertiary institutions, available facilities and structure, capacities of staff, power supply, and capacity for renewal of spent usables, learning environment, availability of internet, and students' attitudes. The challenges of sustaining a viable E-Learning in tertiary institutions are highlighted and suggestions are made.

Key Words: *E-Learning, Managing, Tertiary Institutions, Developing Economy*

Introduction

Internationalization and globalization have pushed international boundaries requiring countries of the world to believe they exist in a global community bridged by internet, fast and efficient communication networks. Education is not an exception (Boholano, 2017). The function of education in the 21st century for every country has a critical role in determining the direction for their national development (FRN, 2014). Nigeria has for decades identified and promoted education for social change, national development and tool for national unity (FRN, 2014; Lauder, Brown, Dillabough and Hasley, 2006). Concerted and deliberate efforts and commitments are made to have an educational system competent to address the aspirations of the nation. To this end plans, policies and programmes are meticulously prepared and rolled out for implementation and matched against estimated expenditure.

Like education in other nations of the world, Nigeria's education and educational system have evolved over the past five decades. There have been changes in policy, administration, curriculum and extension services. Changes in Policy on Education have seen education redirecting its focus from producing docile and dependence-oriented individuals to citizens with creative abilities and critical minds (FRN, 2014) who are able to cope beyond their environments. Thus the contents of curricula have also been drastically modified to respond to these national aspirations. Most recently, the curriculum at the secondary school level has expanded to include skill and trade courses. At the tertiary level, there has also been the introduction of Innovation, Enterprise and Career Education as follow up of skills and trade courses at the secondary level (FRN, 2014; Ugwuadu and Oparah, 2013). Another exciting introduction has been the Information Communication Technology (ICT). The goal of education for Nigeria in introducing changes therefore is to accelerate robust national development capable of causing prosperity and enhance standard of living comparable to the best anywhere. Similarly, administration of education, itself, the epicentre of educational activities, has equally witnessed transformation. Structural and curriculum reforms have further broadened the responsibilities of supervision and funding necessitating the provision for partnerships and decentralization of education provision. Supervision and control are issues of great concern especially as education has been perceived in the private sector as profit driven or oriented. So more than before, the role of administration of education will come to critical focus.

The emphasis on curriculum has not been limited to its contents and appending variables such as its quantity, quality and instructional materials. Current literature on pedagogy is filled with discussions of devising modern teaching and learning strategies germane to the intensive demands of 21st century knowledge, skills and career industry (Arora, 2015). The trend for over a decade now remains using technology in administration and classroom which according to Arora (2015) has numerous learning benefits of promoting intelligence, communication, social interaction and personal skills; as well as efficiency and effectiveness in the discharge of office duties and responsibilities. However, in most tertiary institutions in Nigeria as it stands today, Information Communication Technology Units have been established and are performing several functions. The National Universities Commission (2018) through its Director, of Research, Innovation & Information Communication Technology, argued that since ICT is " driving and shaping activities" in virtually all human endeavour teaching, learning and research in the tertiary institutions be driven by ICT. By implication, tertiary institutions in Nigeria like their contemporaries world over are to be ICT compliant.

A survey conducted by Agyeman (2007) on ICT and Education in Africation covering all tiers of education in Nigeria, revealed that National Universities Commission's guideline for Personal Computer ownership in tertiary institutions in Nigeria should be one computer to four students and two lecturers are to share one. It recommended one personal computer each for lecturers from the rank of senior lecturer (SL). For those at the Professorial cadre, a notebook computer type was recommended as well. The survey also showed that some universities in Nigeria such as Nnamdi Azikwe University, Awka, Obafemi Awolowo University, Ile Ife and University of Jos had made tremendous progress in the adoption and use of ICT. As far back as 2007 when this Report was filled in, OAU, Ile Ife was already having 15 computer laboratories in its campuses. It also noted that University of Jos had equally made progress in developing its e-learning (Agyemen, 2007).

E-Learning

E-learning is teaching and learning through the use of electronic devices and technologies. It is the non-traditional method of teacher-learner verbal exchange in a face to face encounter in the traditional classroom setting. Curriculum and other learning experiences are prepared and conveyed in portable forms that enable learners to learn personally at their paces and deal continuously with issues and tasks arising from learning materials. E-learning has been described as learning done online, virtual, linked to network, web-based learning and distributed learning (wikieduator.org, 18/03/2019). E-learning has also been described as digital learning, computer based learning, and technology based learning (https//www.riemysore.ac.in, 12/03/2019).

E-learning entails utilization of information and communications technology for the delivery of education activities relevant to instructing, teaching, and learning through various electronic media. Characteristically, e-learning is basically electronic driven and diversified learning prepared for individuals or group (Jereb and Smitek, 2006; Koohang and Harman, 2005). E-learning employs technologies as computer, satellite television, audio and video media, intranet, internet, CDROM in the delivery of teaching and teaching learning (https//www.riemysore.ac.in 12/03/2018). This means that learning and teaching can significantly be achieved from any point or distance and with the ease of personal pace and resources. Coincidentally, so much emphasis on learning in tertiary education tends to encourage research, independent and critical thinking as well as the ability to undertake study with very minimal supervision.

Higher Education Institution and e-learning

Tertiary education has enormous responsibility in providing and raising the podium for national development. This task is succinctly captured in the National Policy on Education that spells the goals of tertiary education. Tertiary education is expected to train and develop the high level manpower base, capable of transforming the nation into prosperous and stable country. However, the educational system that is capable of achieving the required standard envisioned to achieve national transformation, while drawing relevance from national needs, must also contemplate the international dynamics of national development. This mix becomes imperative in the light of interconnectivity of world economies. The impact of this for tertiary education is that teaching and learning experiences, teaching methodologies/pedagogy, facilities, technologies, environments, and output are to respond to universal aspirations reflecting global practices. Globalization and internationalization of education certainly require broad approach to both teaching and learning, meaning that online libraries, google, web, and such other teaching and learning resources are part and parcel of the education environment and contribute to the emerging whole.

Recognition, adoption and employment of e-learning in Higher Education Institutions started fairly over one and half decades ago in universities such as Obafemi Awolowo University, Ile Ife; Nnamdi Azikwe University, Awka and University of Jos all in Nigeria. However, most universities and other higher education institutions are vigorously and aggressively pursuing the policy of making the availability of e-learning facilities a priority (Agyeman, 2007). Ahmed (2012) and Iloanusi (2007) both agreed on the relevance of e-learning in tertiary education. This includes reduction of cost construction of classroom facilities, cost of transportation, educational materials. Other importance of e-learning are the ability to cater for the need of a large population of learners at the same time; availability of updated knowledge content, there is also the advantage of fast delivery of learning experiences as well as consistency in learning content which has been programmed and slated (Gupta, 2017). Of a more critical importance in e-learning is the self-pace which the flexibility of facility and methodology permit individual learners to enjoy (Vikoo, 2013). Thus, the relevance of e-learning is such that the National Universities Commission through its Director of Research, Innovation and Information Technology, Babatunde Raymond-Yusuf emphasised that the Commission would leverage the ICT to drive teaching, learning and research in Nigerian universities (PREMIUM Times, Friday April 5, 2019. Npremiumtimesng.com). In the light of its overwhelming relevance, NUC plans to make ICT training compulsory for undergraduates in Nigerian universities. However, much as this plan is laudable and achievable, what is central to its success remains the issue of management. Managing e-learning effectively requires the consideration of a number of vital factors. These factors are discussed below.

Managerial Issues in Providing E-learning

- **Rising population in tertiary learning institutions:** In most universities in Nigeria, there is the tendency to demand for increase in admission quota. The speculations are that it is mainly to satisfy the demand for more places in the university by many candidates who are seeking to enter the university, and again, the political promises made by politicians to provide education as a social good and dividend of democracy. Thus between the year 2003 and 2013, the admission rate had risen from 14.5% to 31.1% (International Organisation for Migration, Abuja, Nigeria, (2014): Needs Assessment of Nigerian Education Sector. https://nigeria.iom.int>files> newsletter. 9/4/2019). Arising from the situation, it is often to have universities that are over populated vis-a-vis its resources, and struggling to provide sufficient facilities to cater for available number of students. However, while universities have managed to cope with squeezing out halls of residence and classroom facilities, the same has not been true of laboratories, workshops, and equipment, library facilities, staff and fund (Fabiyi and Uzorka, (n.d.); Babatope, 2010). Noticeable gaps therefore mean there is the need to strategies to balance resources of institution and people slated to receive their services.

  Managing the population of students admitted into the university against the available resources is engaging and requires strategic plan. The declaration by the National Universities Commission that all students in tertiary institutions should be ICT compliant means Nigerian universities are to provide computers and ICT hubs and laboratories sufficient to match the number of students available, notably because the acquisition of ICT skills is fundamental to e-learning. Achieving that goal by the universities may not be feasible going by the percentage of budget allocated to education both at the federal and the state levels (Ajadi, Salawu & Adeoye, 2008). Universities, while not denying prospective candidates admission, have the responsibility to internally organise its ICT centres to accommodate the students' population. To manage the population and achieve the goal of getting available students to acquire the ICT skills necessary for e-learning, the following managerial strategies are necessary:

  (a) All elective courses, including entrepreneurship courses in the first two years of schooling be ICT courses/computer based courses.
  (b) Use of computer laboratories is on rotational basis with each department taking its turn
  (c) Computer hubs created in the universities are dedicated to use by students after regular classes and arranged according to levels on rotational basis as well.

(d) The first semester of freshmen and women is shared between compulsory courses and ICT programmes.

Planning the use of available ICT facilities to accommodate all students at the various levels, they are to learn, remains the only managerial way to ensure that all students duly registered develop the necessary skill that enable them engage in and benefit from e-learning programmes designed internally and or sourced externally whether in synchronous or asynchronous learning circumstances (hppts://www.slideshare.net/mobile/sspink/e-learning 18/03/2019).

- **Facilities and structures:** E-learning requires that learners possess their electronic gadgets and equipment. Despite this knowledge of what it entails, apparently not all lecturers and learners have financial capacity to acquire these gadgets. This therefore requires that the institutions will provide ICT centres and have them fully equipped. Roadmap for Nigerian Education Sector (2009) identified inadequate funding of ICT development and deployment and lack of implementation of government policy on ICT as some of the obstacles. The implication for universities is for improvisation of structures and facilities to house ICT centres. Managing the situation for e-learning requires that university administrators localise ICT hubs in small rooms at departmental levels. Departments are to create timetable designed to ensure students in these departments have access to ICT to enhance opportunities for e-learning (Mapuva, 2009). Given that most students in Nigeria's tertiary institutions are not able to afford electronic equipment and appliances, and internet connectivity, means that universities will continue to be responsible for the provision of, and access to e-learning through availability of physical structure and other facilities (Oye, Salleh and Iahad, 2011).
- **Managing staff capacity:** Human resource management is critical to the success of e-learning in tertiary education in Nigeria. The introduction of e-learning, being relatively new to most tertiary schools, has all along contended with staff's lack of capacities to deploy the innovation to learning (Oye, Salleh and Iahad, 2011). Lecturers who are not in Computer Science Department have naturally not been concerned with the prospect of e-learning in delivering their courses. The entire blame cannot be put on the unwilling lecturers. Most university administrations do not have any policy regarding acquiring ICT skills (Mapuva, 2009). Thus to develop staff with capacities to deploy ICT for e-learning, university administration would require to:

(a) Put in place a policy regarding ICT skills
(b) Train its existing workforce especially teaching staff and training be conducted periodically

(c) Provide platform for acquisition of computers and needed accessories
(d) Train staff on e-learning
(e) Draw timeline
(f) Implement ICT policies.

Managing staff to develop the needed capacities in leveraging e-learning requires providing all the technical support available in the institution (Islam, Beer & Slack, 2015). Thus Institutions need staff policy not only regarding recruitment but also on development, training and retraining to enhance sustainable capacities (Shahmoradi, Changizi (n.d.) and Hosseini, 2018).

- **Learning environment:** E-learning environment has been defined as collaborative and cooperative interactions for knowledge acquisition based on the online computer facilitated process and system (www.igi.global.com.dictonary. 14/04/2019). The learning environment of the formal classroom setting differs structurally and pedagogically from the e-learning environment and very challenging giving the technologies and individuals involved. Yengin, Karachoca, Karachoca & Yucel, (2010) identified the issues of designing and implementation of e-learning as a critical technical factors. How should e-learning be implemented and what technologies are available and accessible to students? Yengin, Karachoca, Karachoca & Yucel (2010) have emphasised the questions of defining what (a) active learning is in e-learning (b) how students could be motivated to learn actively where physical contact with teacher is not there and (c) how to obtain feedback from learners. In addition, the question of objective assessment of learners who are at various locations using a uniform standard is as important as the previous questions.

  Tied to the pedagogical issues in e-learning is the technologies that are available to school. The available technologies to be used determine quality of delivering of learning experiences, video, computers, tablets, and other mobile devices (Vidyadevi, 2014). How schools are to support their e- learning with limited amount of technologies available to them becomes another contention for efficient management.

- **Managing available internet facility:** In schools where e-learning is adopted, access to internet is taken for granted and assumption can be that users are free to access it at their own paces and as much as they wish. Now, limited funds to purchase data and bandwidth needed for such level of internet usage and consumption would constraint availability. As a measure of control, regulating the use of internet facility would affect teaching and learning as well. To then ensure internet is available for use is to get the school to assign time for accessibility and have staff control their classes to correspond to when internet facility is restored (Eze, Chinedu-Eze and Bello, 2018).

- **Students' attitude to e-learning:** Attitude of an individual is crucial in determining how they perceive and ultimately react to issues, challenges and even solutions before them. Akinbobola (2009) quotes Gagne (1979) as stating that attitude is an "internal state that influences the actions of a person". It is also believed that attitude is linked to belief and behaviour (Rhema & Miliszewska, 2014). What this implies is that the state of the mind of the learner plays a role in learning and then influences the extent to which the learner's preparedness to learn. Learners' attitude to e-learning just like learning other subjects or courses in the tertiary institutions according to Akinbobola (2004), may be cooperative, individualistic or competitive depending on factors such as environment, teaching method and teacher handling the course. Rhema & Miliszewska (2014), additionally, identify other factors which influence students attitude towards e-learning as (a) demographic characteristics which includes gender, age, and student year of study; (b) availability and access to technology in terms of information and communication technology centre sufficiently equipped to sustain student population; (c) student's skills and competence in the use of personal or school provided technology and (d) acceptance of e-learning environment.

  The varying contexts of cooperative, individual and competitive attitude learners bring to e- learning have their relative importance and effects on how learners accomplish learning (Abu & Flowers, 1997; Gul & Sheszad 2015; & Adeyemi & Elphinah, 2016). To maximise the attitude of students towards effective e-learning, there have to be the critical roles of facilities and professional work environment that can engage individually and cooperatively while promoting healthy competition (Ladyshewsky, Barrie and Drake, 1998; Tanner, Chatman and Allen, 2003; Fay, Teh and Kheong, 2008).

Challenges Facing the Management of E-learning in Tertiary Education

The provision and management of e-learning in tertiary education are quite demanding, tedious and present enormous challenges to institutions. Some of these challenges identified are as follows:

(a) **Shortage of skilled and competent information technology compliant teaching staff.** Apparently because the employment of ICT in the classroom is relatively new in most of the developing countries, most countries have not considered the necessity to include it in the curriculum of the Teacher while they are in training.

The effect of this, is that the Lecturer or teacher, in the first instance is not bringing any knowledge of thc use of ICT which should have impacted on the leaner's quest in the use of e-learning (Oroma, Wanga and Ngumbuke, 2012).Two scenarios are possible here. First, the teachers are not able to assist learners adopt e-learning to their studies and secondly, the learners cannot take advantage of e-learning facilities.

(b) **Budgetary allocation to tertiary education and e-learning facilities.** Education receives one of the lowest allocations in Nigeria. Both Federal and State governments do not meet the UNESCO benchmark in funding education. Investigation by Azi (2011) showed that between 2000 and 2010, was observed to have affected development and growth of capital projects in tertiary institutions in Nigeria. In recent years, budgetary allocations to education have been anywhere close to the 26% UNESCO mark. In 2018, it was less than 7.05% (N605.8bn). In 2019, there was a marginal increase which took it to 7.05% being N620.5bn (Ameh and Aluko, 2019). The other years between 2011 and 2018 were neither better in terms of meeting UNESCO's standard. Apparently, this situation has deep implications for capital projects, manpower training and development, staff recruitment, equipment, research and dissemination of information, teaching and students learning. No doubt that e-learning will benefit from availability of funds needed for supply of both equipment and manpower if adequate budgetary allocation is to education (Abada, Okuma &Ugwu, 2016). The tertiary institutions are not likely to promote e-lcarning given that the provision of e- learning facilities are expensive to procure (Olutola& Olatoye, 2015).

(c) **Students' issues.** While the institutions have their numerous challenges in providing e-learning, the students for whom e-learning is designed to assist in facilitating learning also bring their challenges. Most students show lack of background knowledge or skills in computer applications. Olutola and Olatoye (2015) point out that most Nigerian in tertiary institutions exhibit lack of skills in the application of computer skills such as use of 'Microsoft Word, Excel package, Power Point', just as most students equally do not have background in SPSS package. Thus, the result for the students will be shying away from an important source of learning for self-development. The students' readiness with the mentioned skills signifies that they are prepared to be introduced to e-learning. Lack of those skills indicates such students cannot adopt e-learning (Aboderin, 2015). A study by Aboderin (2015) shows that there is positive relation between the availability of e-learning facilities and students interest in its utilization among students of National Open University of Nigeria, Akure study Centre, Nigeria. The study links the situation apparently to students' background in computer application skills they possess as indicated by their responses to the question whether they agree to the use of computer to access their portal, write examinations or login to carry out other assignments.

(d) **Cost of computers and such other devices.** The cost of procuring a piece of computer is almost out of the reach of an average Nigerian student in the tertiary institution. This is not unconnected with the economic realities in the country. Studies carried out by Nwana (2012) on "Challenges in the application of e-learning by secondary school teachers in Anambra State, Nigeria" and Nwana, Egbe and Ugwuda (2017) on "Awareness and Usage of E-Learning among Students of National Open University of Nigeria (NOUN)", clearly indicate that some key hardware facilities such as on-line/internet connected computers, E-mail facilities, Videophone, e-readers and e-books and many others are not within the reach of students. Thus the cost of e-learning facilities poses serious challenge to students' ability to developing skills essential for e-learning.

(e) **The question of connectivity.** Internet connectivity is very critical to e-learning. Most tertiary institutions in Nigeria lack the financial capacity to purchase internet equipment with higher and strong Bandwidth strength enough to reach students outside the Information Technology Centres or classrooms. Thus once they are out of the designated areas, they are no longer hooked to e-learning facilities (Massing, 2017). For students with 4G and 3G capacities handsets, the challenge, where ever they are, around or outside the institution, remains sustained connectivity. Tertiary institutions outside the metropolis or cities, mostly in rural communities are likely to be worst off. With irregular power supply, any idea about internet connectivity becomes really difficult to contemplate. Put together, these factors greatly hinder the essence of e-learning for students in tertiary institutions in Nigeria generally.

(f) **Lack of connection between industry and the tertiary institutions in Nigeria.** The industry sector as well as government which are employers of labour especially graduates from tertiary institutions in Nigeria have continued to employ people without 21st century requisite skills of which E-skills is one. This has continued to encourage a good number of students to think that e-learning skills are not and should not be mandatory. This is perhaps the reason students in Nigerian Universities according to Anene, Imam and Odumuh (2014) in their study, found that "Use of e-learning by students in Nigerian Universities" is very low. They found out that this resulted from low computer literacy and other factors of lack of equipment and policy on e-learning in the universities. Lack of knowledge of the importance in the adoption of e-learning for both learning in school and opportunities by students is quite detrimental to students.

Creating Measures for E- learning Environment in Higher Education Institutions in Nigeria

(a) **Policy on computer literacy:** A policy making computer literacy a requirement for admission into tertiary education be put in place. The policy needs to demand the teaching of computer skills from Basic education level and leading through to senior secondary school. Equipment might pose the basic challenge. However, commencing with theoretical foundation and accompanying with pictorial demonstration can set the tune.

(b) **Ownership of Android 3G & 4G phones and other devices:** Managers or Directors of Information Technology Centres are to guide students make choices of affordable devices that possess strong technologies for receptivity and connectivity especially for institutions in rural settings with internet connectivity. Students are also to be encouraged to purchase and subscribe to affordable internet vendors. ICT Managers are to guide students who to come together to source internet bandwidths as to the best products that could offer the viability and flexibility commensurate with level of economic power and learning space,

(c) **Inclusive fees:** Higher Education Institutions should develop policy to embed charges and fees for devices such as computers, palmtops, tablets and others which should be provided to students and staff on admission or employment. To achieve this without distorting the financial plans of students is to arrange with companies producing such devices and import them in large scale. Then on yearly basis, a proportion of the fees are cut out to pay the manufacturers or their agents. The proprietor of the institutions and the official bankers of the institutions can be brought in to ensure payment compliance by the institutions involved in the scheme. The payment should be in installments and spread over the number of years each student is to spend in the school. This way, students are able to own devices and can now move towards actualizing the move to e-learning.

(d) **The role of the faculty**: The faculty has a crucial role to play in making e-learning accessible to students. The faculties could purchase and install internet facilities that can service their faculties. They can install manageable smaller Bandwidth internet facilities within their enclosures. This can be achieved through subventions and grants received from the management of their institution. Part of the internally generated revenue by the faculties could also be invested in the provision of internet facilities. On most campuses of higher education institutions in Nigeria, there are vendors who provide internet facilities and are highly patronized by students. Faculties and units could follow suit to commercial their ICT units to make them sustainable by charging users marginal fees. This measure is most likely to encourage students' interest in the use of internet facilities for e-learning (OECD, 2005).

(e) **Government needs to increase funding for higher education:** Funding for higher education has been a major challenge in Nigeria. This has been due partly to the disposition of succeeding governments and partly attributed to the dwindling economy. The number of institutions, attendant population and inefficiency in the management of available financial resources, as well as programmes has all contributed immensely to the difficulties associated with adequate provisions for higher education. If the country stands to benefit from the relevance of ICT to learning and opportunities sourcing by its citizenry in a world laden with e-economy, then government should invest in equipping the institutions for e-learning (Afolayan, 2015).

(f) **Partnership/ Private provision:** One way to address the challenge of providing e- learning in higher education is approaching ICT companies for partnership with higher institutions or seeking to cede outright franchise to them to provide and charge for their services. The advantages here will include availability of services, rates based on existing circumstances, proximity to service providers in events of technical issues, employment, transfer of technology, and others (Van-Rooijen, 2013).

Summary and Conclusion

E- learning in higher education is being vigorously pursued by many tertiary education institutions in Nigeria as it the world over. Apparently realizing the numerous advantages associated with e-learning, most tertiary institutions have initiated policies aimed at making their schools completely compliant. The management of tertiary education institutions will have to contend with issues of over population, shortage of facilities, staff capacities, internet facilities, students' attitude and learning environment among others. However, it is pertinent to note that certain challenges likely to confront the management of e-learning may include scanty budgetary allocation to education, students' issues, cost of procurement of e-learning facilities, connectivity, power supply, policy, fees charged per student and vandaliztion.

Something is certain about e-learning in tertiary institutions in Nigeria, as it is in other parts of the world, which is that internalization and globalization which affect all facets of life affects also how education is acquired and how learning is achieved. It therefore stands to reason that institutions of higher learning pursue learning in the ways that enhance quality and meets national and international standards.

References

Abada, D. U., Okuma, C. N. and Ugwu, K. O. (2016). The effects of budgetary allocations on Education Sector Reform Agenda: Evidence from Nigeria Public Sector. *International Journal of Social Sciences and Humanities Review, 6(4)*, 1-9.

Aboderin, O. S. (2015). Challenges and prospect of e-learning at the National Open University of Nigeria. *Journal of Education and Learning, 9(3)*, 207-216. Retrieved from media.neliti.com/media/publication/70837, 26/05/2019.

Abu, R. B., Pendidikan, J. and Flowers, J. (1997). The effects of cooperative learning methods on achievement, retention and attitudes of home economics students in North Carolina. *Journal of Career and Technical Education, 13(2), 54-60.* Retrieved on the 26th May, 2019 from: https://ejournals.lib.vt.edu.

Adedigba, A. (2018). NUC to make ICT training compulsory for Nigerian university undergraduates. *The Premium Times*, Nigeria. Retrieved from: https://www.premiumtimesng.com, 26/05/2019.

Adeyemi, S. R. and Elphunah, N. C. (2016). Effects of cooperative and individualistic learning strategies on students' map reading and interpretation. *GJDS, 13(2),* 154 – 175. Retrieved on the 26th of May, 2019 from: https://www.ajotinfo>article,

Afolayan, F. O. (2015). Funding higher education in Nigeria. *Journal of Research & Method in Education, 5(1),* 63-68. Retrieved from Isorjournals.org/iosr-jrme/vol5.10.20/issue on 16/02/2020.

Agyeman, O. T. (2007). *ICT for education in Nigeria: Survey of ICT and education in Africa.* A Nigeria Country Report. Retrieved from: www.infodev.org, 26/05/2019.

Ahmed, S. A. (2012). *Essentialities for e-learning: the Nigerian tertiary….* SAVAP International. www.savap.org.pk-2012, 26/05/2019.

Ajadi, T. O., Salawu, I. O. & Adeoye, F. A. (2008). E-learning and distance education in Nigeria. *The Turkish Online Journal of Educational Technology, 7(4),* 5-10. Retrieved from: https://files.eric.ed.gov.fulltext, 26/05/2019.

Akinbobola, A. O. (2004). Effects of cooperative and competitive learning strategies on academic performance of students in Physics. *Journal of Research in Education,* 1(1) 71 – 75.

Akinbobola, A. O. (2009). Enhancing students' attitude towards Nigerian senior secondary school physics through the use of cooperative, competitive and individualistic learning strategies". *Australian Journal of Teacher Education*, 34(1), 22-25.

Ameh, J. and Aluko, O. (2019). 2019 budget: Education gets N620.5bn against UNESCO advice. *Punch Newspapers.* Retrieved from punchng.com/2019-budget-educationgets-n620.5bn-against-UNESCO-advice, 26/05/2019.

Aneore, J. N., Iman, H. and Oduma, T. (2014). Problem and prospect of e-learning in Nigeria universities. *International Journal of Technology and Inclusive Education, 3(2),* 325-326.

Arora, A. (2015). *Using e-learning technologies to improve educational quality of language learning.* Retrieved on the 4th of March, 2019 from: https://elearningindustry.com.

Awidi, I. T. (2013). *E-learning implementation strategies for an ICT…….* Edith Cowan University ECU. ro.ecu.au>cgi>viewcontent. Retrieved on 26/05/2019.

Azi, A. S. (2011). An assessment of Nigerian budgeting allocations to the education sector: Implications for the Tertiary education Nigeria. *Journals of Educational Foundations,* 2(1), 12-15. Retrieved from ajol.info/index.php/jet/article/view/ 116445, 26/05/2019.

Babatope B. A. (2010). *Problems of facilities in South-West Nigerian universities and the way forward.* Retrieved on the 9th of April, 2019 from: www.academicjournals.org>app>article.

Benedict, M. (n.d.). *Importance of e-learning in Nigeria.* Retrieved on the 25th of May, 2019 from: https://www.academica.edu.impore.

Boholano, H. B. (2017). Smart social network: 21st century teaching and learning skills. *Research in Pedagogy, 7(1),* 21 – 29.

Fabiyi, A. and Uzorka, N. (n.d.). State *of physics facilities in Nigeria universities: Implication for repositioning tertiary institutions for global competition.* citeseerx.ist.psu.edu>viewdoc>download. Retrieved on 26/05/2019.

Federal Republic of Nigeria (2014). *National Policy in Education.* Lagos: Nigeria Educational Research and Development Council.

Fey, K. L., Teh, P. L., and Kheong, F. H. (2008). The effectiveness of cooperative and individualistic approaches in teaching mathematics and English. *Singapore Journal of Education,* 9(2), 15-20.

Fresh Science News (2015). *Importance and effectiveness of e-learning.* Retrieved on the 3rd of April, 2019 from: https://higheredrevolution.com.

Gagne, R. M. (1979). *The Conditions of Learning* (3rd Edition). New York: Holt Rinehart and Winston.

Gul, F. and Shehzad, S. (2015). Effects of cooperative learning on students achievements. *Journal of Education and Learning,* 9(3), 246 – 255. Retrieved on the 26th May, 2019 from: https://www.researchgate.net

Gupta, S. (2017). *Nine benefits of e-learning Industry.* Retrieved on the 3rd of April, 2019 from: https://elearningindustry.com

Ihanusi, O. N. (2007). The meaning of e-learning and the impact of … African. *Journal Online. Nigerian Journal of Technology, 26(1)*, 12-15. Retrieved on the 25th of May, 2019 from: https://ajol.info>article.

International Organization for Migration, Abuja (2014). *Needs assessment of Nigerian education sector.* Retrieved on the 9th April, 2019 from: https://nigeria.iom.int>files>newsletters

Islam, N., Beer, M. and Slack F. (2018). E-learning challenges faced by academics in higher education: A literature review. *Journal of Education and Training Studies, 3(2)*, 11-14. Retrieved from: http://dx.doi.org/10.11114/jetsvs315.947, 26/05/2019.

Ladyshewsky, R. K., Barrie, S. C., and Drake, V. M. (1998). A comparison of productivity and learning outcome in individual and cooperative physical therapy. *Clinical Education Models, 78(12),* 25-30.

Mapava, J. (2009). Confronting challenges of e-learning in higher education institutions. *International Journal of Education and Development using Information conversation Technology IJEDICT,* 5(3) pp 101–114. Retrieved from: https://www. learntechlib.org>article42, 26/05/2019.

Massing, C. (2017). Success and *challenges in e-learning technology in the higher education system: A case study of the University of Namibia.* An unpublished Bachelor Degree project of the University of SKovDe dira-portal.org/smash/get/diva2.

Nwabufo, B. N., Umoru, T. A. and Olukotun (n.d.). *The challenges of e-learning in tertiary institutions in Nigeria.* Retrieved from: https://conference.pixel-online.net>76E, 26/05/2019.

Nwana, S. E (2012). Challenges in the application of e-learning by secondary school teachers in Anambra State, Nigeria. *African Journal of Teacher Education (AJoTE), 2(1),* 14-22.

Nwana, S. E., Egbe, C. I. and Ugwuda, S. O. (2017). Awareness and Usage of E-learning among Students of National Open University of Nigeria (NOUN). *World Journal of Education, 7(6),* 75-79.

Olutola, A. T. and Olatoye, O. O. (2015). Challenges of e-learning technologies in Nigerian university education. *Journal of Educational Social Sciences. 5(1),* 301-305.

Organisation for Economic Co-operation and Development (2005). *E-learning in tertiary education*. Where do we stand? Paris: Center for Educational Research and Innovation. Retrieved from Oecd.library.org/docserver, 16/02/2020.

Oye, N. D., Salleh, M. and Lahad, N. A. (2011). Challenges of e-learning in Nigerian University Education Based on the Experience of Developed Countries. *International Journal of Managing Information Technology*, 3(2), 39 – 48.

Patil, V. (2014). Technologies used in e-learning. *Scholarly Research Journal for Humanity Science and English Language, 1(11),* 12-15.

Rhema, A. and Miliszewska, I. (2014). Analysis of students' attitude towards e-learning: The case of Engineering Students in Libya. *Issues in Informing Science and Information Technology,* 11: 170 – 188.

Tamara, K., Chatman, L. and Allen, D. (2003). *Approaches to cell biology teaching: cooperative learning in science classroom – beyond students working in groups.*

Ugwuadi, E. L. and Oparah, Z. C. (2013). A catalogue of existing reforms and Innovation in Nigeria Education. In E. Kpangbam, P. E. Eya & P. C. Igbojinwaekwu (Eds.). *Reforms and Innovations in Nigeria Education.* Onitsha: West and Solomon.

Van-Rooijen, M. (2013). *E-learning through public partnerships.* University World News (Global Edition). Universityworldnews.com/post.php?Story retrieved 16/02/2020.

Vikoo, B. (2013). Exploring the use of some information and communication technology-based materials and methods in Nigerian education. In E. Kpangbam, P. E. Eya and P. C. Igbojinwaekwu. *Reforms and Innovations in Nigeria Education.* Lagos: West and Solomon Publishing Ltd.

Yengin, I., Karachoca, D., Karachoca, A. and Yucel, A. (2010). Roles of teachers in e-learning: How to engage students and how to get free-learning and the future. *Procedia Social and Behavioural,* 2, 5775 – 5787.

20

Investigation of Friction Condition between Human Skins at Lower Limb Stump with Different Textiles

EMAD Kamil H., KUSSAY Ahmed S. & ANDREI Tudor

Abstract

Human skin is considered as an important organ in the human body since it works as a barrier between outside environment and the internal components, also it covers approximately two squared meter in total area and around 18% of human weight in adult. In case of lower limb amputation, the stump will be in direct and continuous touch with textile material in between the polymeric socket and stump itself, so to avoid skin injuries or ulcers which are causes if bad contact conditions occur for long time duration. In the present work, coefficient of friction of different textiles with in-vivo human skin for both male and female at the stump region are investigated, this specific contact area is influenced by many factors such as skin humidity, nature of the employed textile itself, temperature, and other factors. This paper will clarify how coefficient of friction varies together with different textile to provide comfortable ambience at this sensitive region.

Key Words: *Skin Friction, Biotribology, Lower Limb; Viscoelastic Materials*

Introduction

Biotribology is defined as the science that deals with tribiological aspect of biological systems like human skin, bone, etc. This field is still relatively recent and need more investigations due to the various cases of medical problems like limps amputation [1]. More complicated cases are friction between human skins in vivo with other artificial textile materials; this is because of the complex nature of the human skin topography. Furthermore, the contact conditions such as humidity, temperature, the nature of the other surface in touch. Human skin consists of multilayers and treated as a viscoelastic material and its thickness varies from less than one millimetre in the eyelid up to few centimetres at the abdomen. In this paper, the employed skin is at the above knee region with thickness of approximately 1centimetre.

Figure 1 below shows in details the main layers of the skin; they are Epidermis, Dermis, and Hypodermis, for two cases, thick (hairless) and thin skin (hairy).

Human skin is considered as a viscoelastic material as a result of its behavior when loaded and shows similarity to viscoelastic mechanical system due to its specific structure. 978-1-5386-3540-7/18/31.00$©2018 IEEE with fibers and others [2] it is well known that elastic materials obey the general laws of friction where friction

Force is always proportional directly to the normal force *Ffriction* µ *Normal Force* and independent of the generated contact area between the two mated surfaces, but the situation in viscoelastic materials is completely different where two important components of friction where raised: adhesion and deformation: adhesion component (major contribution) of friction sometimes is called the pull-off force i.e. negative force required to break down the adhesive links between the surfaces, mean while the other component is named deformation (minor contribution) refers as to the deformation contacted bodies [3]. Other parameters have taking into account: volunteer sex, age, anatomical region. Many other recent papers investigated other parameters but in other places in human body i.e. interaction between hands and daily handled objects [4], interaction between human skin for two regions started with index finger then lower edge of the human hand and rough and smooth glass plate was investigated by S. Derler et al [5] with two conditions dry and wet. Another study of skin friction with smooth steel ball tip probe at the forearm dry skin with humidity ratio of 50% was done by M. Kwiatkowska et al [6] Comparison to values of the effective indentation stiffness of the skin presented variances in the effects of the applied load and ball tip diameter that may be attributable to differences in the extent of the deformation field within the skin and the complex structure and anisotropic mechanical properties of the diverse skin layers. W. Li et al [7] have examined three types of human skin at the lower limb stump; natural, prosthetic, and scar skin as a tribological behavior and comfort sensation.

Experimental Preparations

Due to the high increase in lower limps amputation population, Iraq reached the highest value all over the world [8] as a results of land mines, bombing, wars, gangrene, diabetes, etc. (see Figure 2 below).

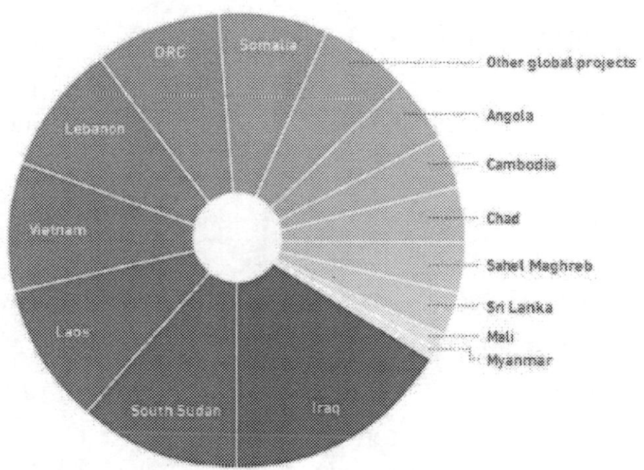

Fig. 2: Annual International Statistics of Amputees [8]

The need for prosthesis is rising, including a special kind of socks covered by hard polymeric sockets for below or above knee amputation, so that leads to examine five types of commercially available socks fabrics plus natural leather fabricated socks to simulate real contact conditions. Figure (3) below shows microscopic images for the above mentioned materials. Also, many volunteers are adopted in this research with different ages varies between 18 up to 52 years old, with two types of amputations below and above knee, all of them are free of diabetes and normal blood pressure, they have weights ranging within the normal standard according to the ISPO matrix of weight and job of the amputee person, this standard noted as 22 for moderate weight and job duty.

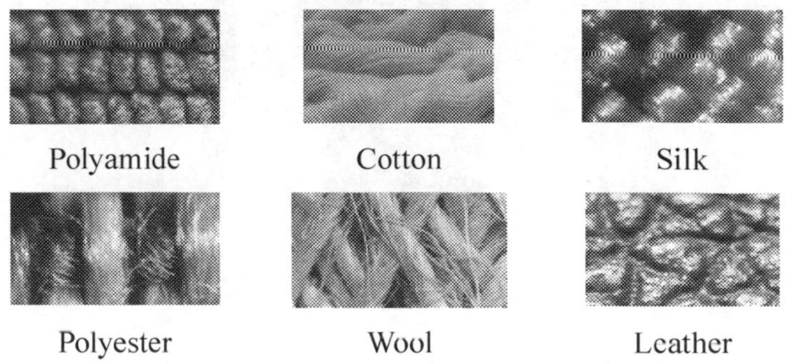

Fig. 3: The selected Fabrics and Leather

Experimental Considerations

According to the common nature of atmospheric weather in the region of Babil governorate where all tests are done, some boundary conditions were considered. Table I clarifies these conditions.

Table I: Experimental considerations

Temp.	Humidity	Skin moisture	Skin type	Skin region	sex	Age years
25°C±2	50%±10	Wet skin	Natural not scar	AK stump	F&M	18-52

Furthermore, all friction tests were done by using the well-known Tribometer rig of type Universal Micro Materials Tester of model UMT-II multi-specimen Biomedical Micro-Tribometer manufactured by the CETR corporation, Campbell, CA, USA [9]. The most important facility of this tribometer is a computer-controlled bench top instrument employed to measure tribological parameters on the human skin as shown in figure (4). As revealed at the end tip of this device, there is a semi spherical stylus attached to electric force sensing system working by strain gauges. This tip allowed to be moved in a three dimensional coordinates to ease touching process with the selected residual limp under a computerized controlled perpendicular force of course with so suitable value in order not to hurt the amputee person through moving linearly with constant speed and keeping in touch along experiments time durations. Table II below summarized all working conditions of this tribometer to conduct this paper.

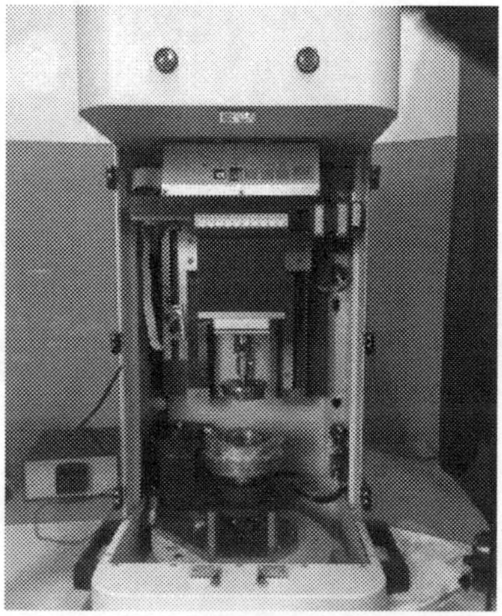

Fig. 4: Tribometer UTM-II, [9]

Table II: General Features of the used Tribometer [9]

Name	Contact ball dia.	Total load Normal force	Contact pressure	Resolution	Measurement Principle
UTM- II	Φ8 mm	2 N	≈40 KPa	1 μm	Measure ment of COF

Table (III) below demonstrates the two collaborated amputee persons, each of them are Iraqi people, they are injured in two cases of land mine explosions which caused AK amputation or the so called transfemoral amputation. Also, they have no medical problems such blood pressure, diabetes, or ulcer at the residual stump, in addition their weight fall in the accepted rates region and all soft tissues at the stump were completely healed.

Table III: Amputees Outlines CVS

Age (years)	Sex	Average weight Kg(N)	Type of amputation	Time after amputation (years)	Ethnicity	No.
≈18	F	≈45(441)	AK	≈3	Asian, Iraqi	1
≈52	M	≈60(588)	AK	≈11	Asian, Iraqi	1

The applied contact pressure in this work was approximately 40 KPa, and the associated maximum contact pressures for the two cases were 24.25 and 32.34 KPa respectively. According to the above mentioned data, the applied contact pressure was greater than the actual values both for the female and male amputee, this will locate the obtained results at the safe side with good margin of the expected error. Many prior papers stated that the maximum contact pressure between stump skin and the used prosthetic socket, Jumaa S. [10], measured it of around ≈30 KPa related to amputee weight of ≈600N, by using a developed sensing matrix distributed all over around the internal area of a above knee amputation socket as shown in figure (5) below, and by comparing this measured result with the above suggested values, it is seen that all these values lie in safe region, and by respected help of the expert technician at the laboratory, all other important experimental parameters are well adjusted and calibrated of course in cooperation with the two amputee persons. K. A. Subhi et al [11], and K. A. Subhi et al [12] studied frictional mechanical properties including adhesion and hysteresis of human skin as a biomaterial based on three well-known theories: Johnson-Kendall-Roberts (JKR), Derjaguin-Muller-Toporov (DMT), and Maugis-Dugdale (MD).

Final results showed that the mechanical adhesion component of the friction is representing many times of the other component, hysteresis component with the same boundary conditions like the total applied load, direct contact velocity, and the skin-artificial material interface characteristics. K. A. Subhi et al [12], investigated an alternative biomaterial, cow skin, instead of human skin to study relationship between coefficient of friction as a function of the employed indenter angular velocity and a wide range of the applied pressure on this substitute skin, followed by calculating the indenter trace or contact area plus its depth. Gained result indicates that coefficient of friction is proportional inversely with the applied pressure and directly with the angular velocity.

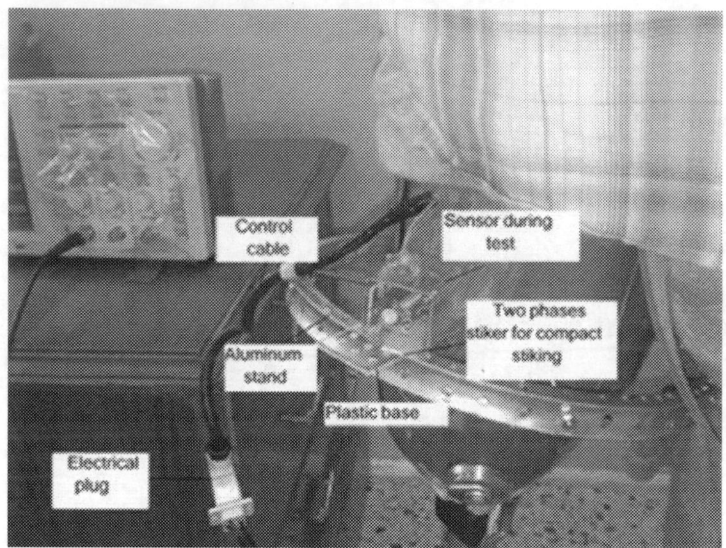

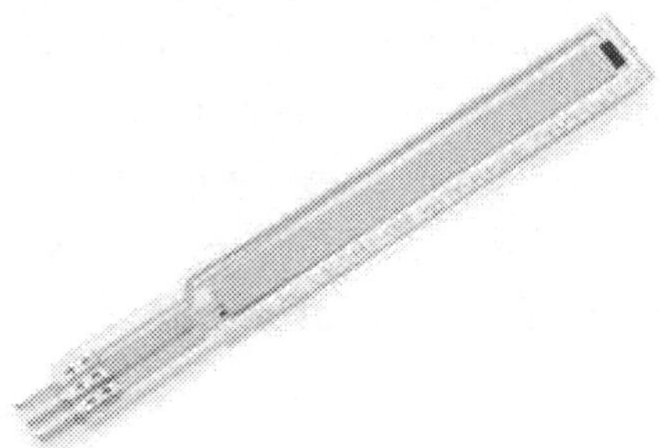

Fig. 5: The Developed Pressure Sensing System [10]

Experimental Investigation

One of the main experiments done in this paper is measuring coefficient of fraction as a function of different selected fabrics that is in continuous contact with in-vivo human skin in the ordinary day life especially for amputee persons, and by using sliding method to measure coefficient of friction, the gained results are showed in detail in Figure 6 below. According to these results, cotton exhibits a lowest value of CoF followed by silk, polyester, wool, polyamide, then leather for both male and female, also all results indicated that male skin has higher values of CoF than that for female, in spite of using the same boundary conditions for the two cases.

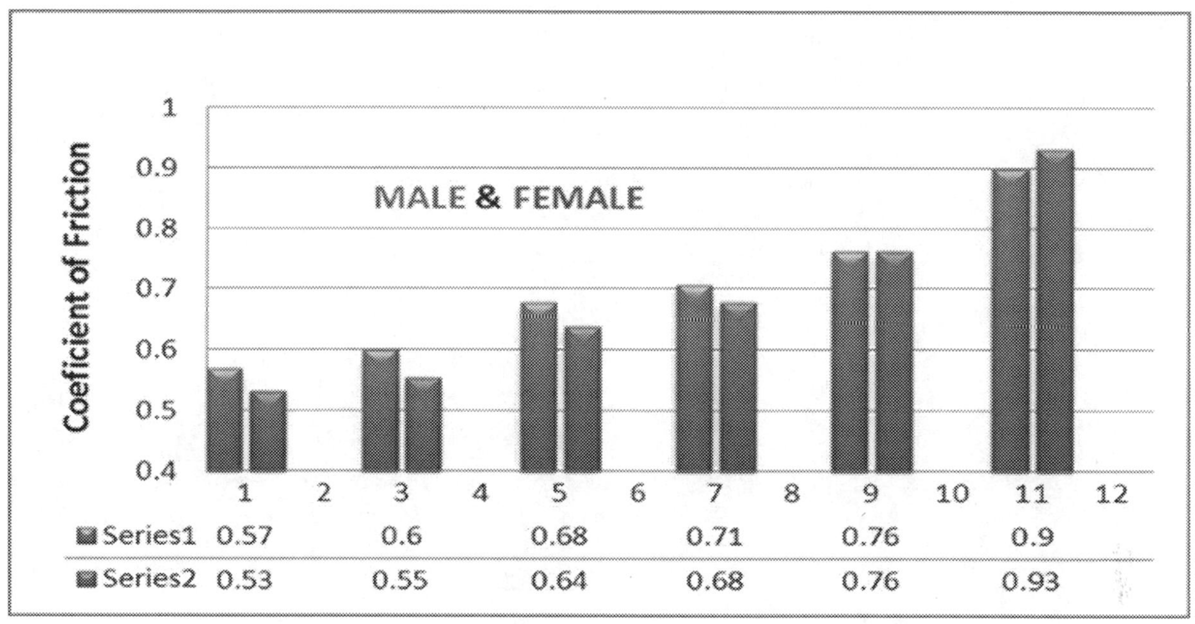

Cotton Silk Polyester Wool Polyamide Leather

Fig. 6: Coefficient of Friction as a Function of Different Fabrics

1. Pain Sensation Test

Another test done by means of interaction between the two amputees and the technician, it may be named as pain sensation test, in this test, a suitable value of contacting pressure was selected according to the above mentioned criteria, also the designated time interval for each test was 10 minutes, this ten minutes represent full contacting pressure between stylus tip and stump, besides that a suggested scale of pain sensation has been adopted, where this scale on the vertical axis as seen in figure (7a, b) below consists of six stages along 10 steps starting from zero with no pain up to ten with worst pain possible, and the intermediate grades are mild, moderate, severe, and very severe pain, each grade colored with an meaningful explanation, i.e. for no pain it is green up to worst pain possible is red, so for example by attaching cotton fabric at the stylus tip and adjusting time duration for only ten minutes with the correlated contact pressure for both male and female and asking the amputee about his pain sensation and recording his feeling on the proposed pain scale every one minute for allover broad ten minutes.

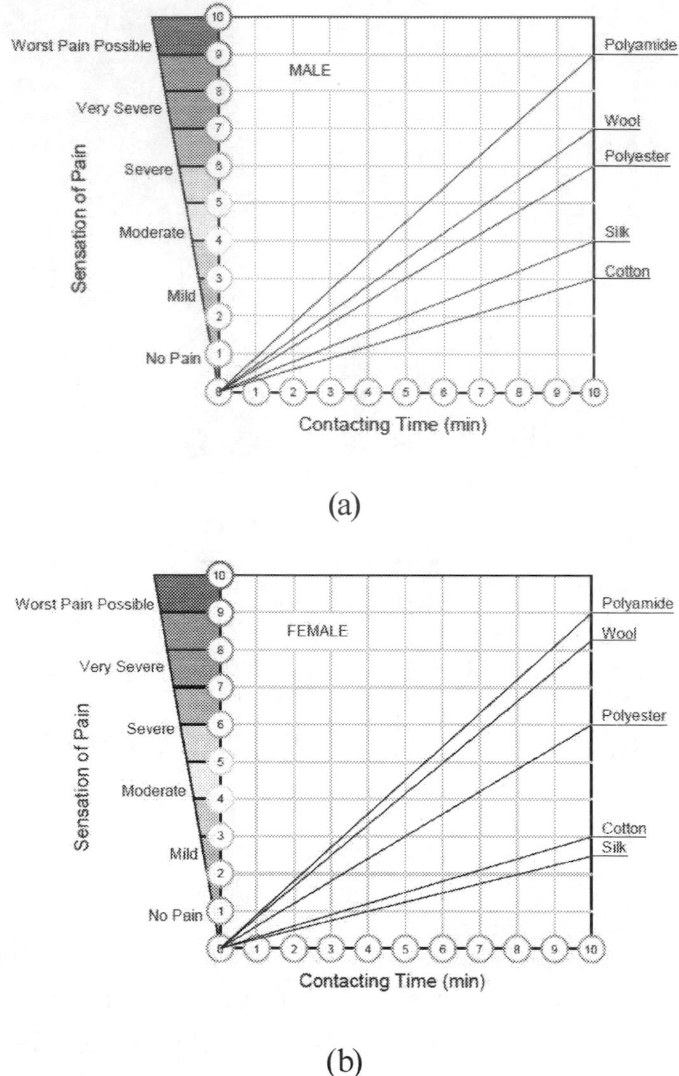

Fig. 7: Pain Sensation Tests a and b.

The two amputees were aware not to use any cosmetic powders, body lotions, skin softeners before at least 24 hours and wash the stump skin with sterilized water and keep it dry as possible as could. In addition, no physical activities are allowed at that time. Final indications of pain sensation tests displayed, for male, the most comfortable fabric with no pain along the ten minutes' test was cotton followed by silk, after that, polyester and wool start pain in friction area causes severe pain meanwhile polyamide fabric caused a high level of pain reaches to worst pain possible level at the tenth minute of test. At the other part of this investigation, female reveals no pain sensation for both silk and then cotton respectively, and matched sense with male regards to polyester, severe pain. Wool and polyamide showed the highest level of pain. This slight difference in pain sensation tests are due to topography of male skin is to some extent different from female skin, also thickness of skin plays an important role in transferring sensation of friction to the nerve system, so in many hard cases, it is found that male can sustain more than female.

2. Fluctuation of CoF Test

To complete investigation of interaction between in-vivo human skin with many selected fabrics, another important test has to be done. It is analysis for fluctuation in coefficient of friction as a function of number of cycles in the tribometer, also the six materials (five fabrics and natural leather) were fixed at the stylus end for ten minutes, also the amputee were instructed to be kept at full static situation without any movement to ensure get accurate value of contacting pressure and then precise series of coefficient of friction values, in Figure 8 below, number of cycles lies on x-axis with initial value of zero up to final value of 300 cycles, on the y-axis coefficient of friction take a range of 0.4 approximately.

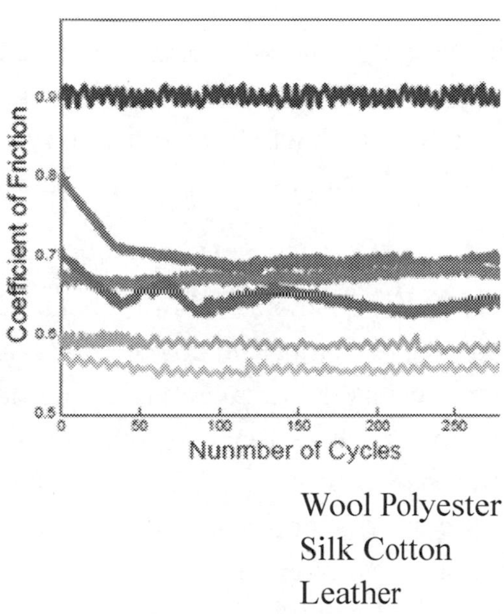

Fig. 8: Fluctuation of CoF

As expected, cotton fabrics have the lowest value of CoF comparing with the other used fabrics and natural leather has the highest values, and the other four fabrics occupied the intermediate region starting by silk, polyester, wool, and polyamide. Due to the softness of cotton fabrics, it showed semi linear value of CoF along total time period of the test and no high varies in CoF, the situation in the silk case is similar to that of cotton but with few higher in the mean value of the CoF. The attitude in wood, polyester, and polyamide is entirely different in both the high value a clear fluctuation of CoF, it is attributed to many collaborated factors such as their rough texture surfaces and tough protruding material yarns. In addition, any slight movement in stump will cause considerable deviation and fluctuation in the measured values of the CoF, so it is hard to resist friction force by the amputee when using such fabrics.

Conclusion

The conclusions that can be drawn from this work are largely dependent on two important factors: first, in-vivo human skin tribology is a complex issue due to its mechanical behavior where other frictional components will rise and affecting coefficient of friction such components is adhesive component of friction, it will lead to the so called friction hysteresis, meantime dependent coefficient of friction, exactly similar to mechanical behavior of polymers when loaded for a specified period of time, forming the two well-known phenomena stress relaxation and creep, so this is to some extent just happening in human skin under search, moreover, there is alteration between male and female human skin.

Second factor is the inclusive properties of fabrics, for example, size of weaves either coarse or small, where the coarse weave gives relatively higher values of CoF, bulging textile fibers works as a scratcher which will be as a difficulty to ensure smooth contacting condition and then increasing CoF leading to un comfortable sense in case of using suck fabrics.

In addition to the above mentioned factors, environmental surroundings have a strong effect on the CoF, so, it is thought that the obtained results may be accepted within the proposed ambient conditions, but as the temperature or humidity or both vary, this sure will lead to dramatic changes in the expected results, so these gained results may be considered as a limited reference for values of CoF depending on the suggested working conditions! Since this work concerns stump skin friction, it is thought that other values of CoF at other regions in human body will give completely different results, taking into account the historical and medical conditions of the amputee persons. All above friction test is done on natural human skin and not prosthetic or scar skin. Finally, the researchers used natural leather as a separation layer to check friction interaction, so it gives an extreme value of CoF, this may be considered as a putative test only, just to compare results with other fully different material.

Acknowledgment

The present work was undertaken under the support of the State Company for Fabrics Industries (SCFI), for the preparing and providing of all fabrics, and funded by Al- Furat Al-Awsat Technical University (ATU), Iraq. Also many thanks for the all amputee persons. The author acknowledges the constant support encouragement of Professor Dr. Eng.

Andrei Tudor, Politehnica Univ. of Bucharest, Romania, and Prof. Dr. Eng. Muhsin J. J. Head of P & O Eng. Dept. at College of Engineering, Nahrain University, Baghdad, Iraq.

References

[1] Z. R. Zhao, Z. M. Jin, "Biotribology: Recent progress and future perspectives", Sciencedirect, Biosurface and Biotribology, 1 (2015) 3- 24.

[2] Silver et al "Viscoelastic properties of human skin and processed dermis" skin research and technology 2001; 7:18-23.

[3] C. Pailler et al "Analysis of Adhesive Behavior of Human Skin in vivo by an Indentation Test" Tribology International 39 (2006) 12-21.

[4] W. Li et al "Effect of Prosthetic socks on the frictional properties of residual limb skin" Wear 271 (2011) 2804-2811.

[5] S. Derler "Friction of human skin against smooth and rough glass as a function of the contact pressure" Tribology international 42 (2009) 1565-1574.

[6] M. Kwiatkowska et al "Friction and deformation behavior of human skin" Wear 267 (2009) 1264–1273.

[7] https://www.scribd.com/doc/296310884/MAG-s-Annual- Summary- 2015.

[8] http://www.courage-khazaka.de/index.php/en/products/scientific/268- frictiometer-e#st1

[9] CETR, INC. 1715 DELL AVE, CAMPBELL, CA 95008 PHONE 408.376.4040 FAX 408.376.4050 INFO@CETR.COM

[10] Jumaa S. Chiad, "ANALYSIS AND OPTIMUM DESGIN OF THE ABOVE KNEE PROSTHETIC SOCKET", Ph.D. Thesis, Dept. of Mechanical Engineering, University of Technology, 2009, Baghdad, Iraq.

[11] K. A. Subhi et al, "The Adhesion and Hysteresis Effect in Friction Skin with Artificial Materials", 13th. International Conference on Tribology, ROTBRIB'16, IOP Publishing. IOP Conf. Series: Materials Science and Engineering 174 (2017) 012918, DOI: 10.1088/1757- 899X/174/1/012018.

[12] A SUBHI, Kussay; TUDOR, Andrei; K HUSSEIN, Emad. Ex-Vivo Tribological Behavior of Cow Skin. American Scientific Research Journal for Engineering,

Technology, and Sciences (ASRJETS), [S.l.], v. 34, n. 1, p. 54-61, July, 2017. ISSN 2313-4402. Available at: http://www.asrjetsjournal.org/index.php/American_Scientific_Journal/article/view/3229. Date accessed: 02 Nov. 2017.

NOMENCLATURE

ATU	Al-Furat Al-Awsat Technical University
CoF	Coefficient of friction
P&O	Prosthetics & Orthotics
SCFI	State Company for Fabrics Industries

21

Emotional Intelligence and Self-Efficacy as Determinants of Bullying Behaviour of Adolescents in Police Barracks in Rivers State

ORDUA Victor N. Ph.D

Abstract

The study investigated Emotional Intelligence and Self-Efficacy as determinants of Bullying Behaviour of Adolescents in Police Barracks in Rivers State, Nigeria. A correlational design was used in this study. The study was guided by five research questions and five hypotheses. The population of this study comprised all adolescents living in Police Barracks in Rivers State. The sample was 200 respondents sampled from three Police Area Commands in Rivers State namely; Port Harcourt Area Command, Ahoada Area Command and Bori Area Command. The study used three instruments adopted from various authors, namely Bullying Behaviour Scale, Emotional Intelligence Scale and General Self-Efficacy scale to collect data. The content and face validation of the Instruments was determined by five specialists two from measurement and evaluation and three from educational psychology. A 36 item questionnaire on emotional intelligence and self-efficacy was administered to respondents. The data collected were analyzed using mean and standard deviation to answer research questions while Pearson Product Moment Correlation Coefficient and Multiple Regression analysis were used to test the hypotheses at 0.5 level of significant. The result obtained showed that a weak and negative relationship existed among emotional intelligence, self-efficacy and bullying behaviour of adolescents living in Police Barrack in Rivers State. It was recommended that emotional intelligence and self-efficacy training should be included in the orientation programme of adolescents living in Police Barracks. This is to enable them develop the necessary life skills for optimal functioning not only in Police Barracks but also in other future purposes.

Key Words: *Intimidation, Abuse, Provocation, Victim, Bully*

Introduction

There is need for awareness of the complex nature of bullying behaviour and the extent to which it affects Nigerian adolescents especially those living in police barracks. Themes in classic literature and memories of adolescent students all over the world attest to the common presence of intimidation, threat, abuse and bullying of students by other peers. Thus, a single adolescent who bullied in the school and immediate environment creates a climate of fear and intimidation to victims and fellow peers as well as in the society. Adolescents exposed to bullying are much more likely to experience deteriorated self-esteem, suffer from isolation and become fearful and avoidant after being victimized. It is actually a behavioural pattern that deviates from certain rules or laws enacted by constituted authorities and also contrary to the societal norms and moral standards. It is a form of aggressive behaviour that is characterized by deliberate, repeated show of power (Tsang, Hui & Law, 2011). Kokkimos and Kiprits (2012) see bulling as unprovoked, intentional and repetitive act which displays an imbalance of power that aims at causing physical or psychological harm. Bullying includes a range of behvaiour that results in an imbalance of power between the aggressor and the victim. Such behaviours include not only physical aggression but also verbal harassment and public humiliation (e.g name calling and spreading rumors) (Thompson & Sharp 2013).

Bullying can lead to negative outcomes for both the bully and the victim because adolescent who participate in bullying are at risk of lacking compassion and concern for others by becoming desensitized to bullying which becomes part of their normal daily life. They are at an increased risk for dropping out of school and failing academically which can lead to involvement in gangs and participating in delinquent and anti-social behvaiour. In later life they might have difficulty sustaining healthy intimate relationship and can become abusive spouses and parents. This can lead to a higher risk of depression and suicide (Tsang, Hui & Law, 2011). Agulanna (2014) opined that long term exposure to bullying may also have consequences for the victim's livelihood through absenteeism and even ruin a career. Bullied children may experience headaches, sleeplessness, anxiety, depression and psychosomatic complaints (Sourander, Klomek, Ikonen, Lindroos, Huntamo, Koskelainen and Helenius in Agulanna, 2014). This circumstances if not checked could affect educational and social development of the young persons.

Numerous programmes have been created for bullying prevention and safety of adolescents. Research suggests that in order for intervention programmes to be effective, they must be long term. (Schutte, Malouff, Hall, Haggerty, Cooper, Golden & Dornheim 1998) and part of a comprehensive school counselling programmes (Limber, 2002). However, many of these prevention strategies which include focus on the social environment of the school, assess bullying at schools, Garner staff and parent support for bullying prevention, form a group to coordinate the schools bullying prevention activities, increase adult supervision in hot spots where bullying occurs, intervene consistently and appropriately bullying situation, train your staff in bullying prevention and establish and enforce school rules and policies related to bullying etc (Health Resources and Services Administration, 2014) Although many of these strategies to prevent school violence could be utilized, the effectiveness of a violence prevention program depends on the quality of implementation of the intervention as much as the type of intervention selected (Hermann & Finn, 2002). To this end, it is noted that an effective intervention should take into consideration major correlates and determinants of the problem. Despite the numerous interventions bullying still persist in police barracks. The extent to which bulling is influenced by factors as emotional intelligence and self-efficacy have not been given much priority in research. For instance, emotions are primary sources of human energy, aspiration and drive activating their inner most feelings and purpose in life, and transforming them from things we think about to values we live. The key factor is the way that we interpret our circumstances, based on our prior experiences and belief system, to either respond reactively like a stimulus response machine with an emotion that is outside our control may be inappropriate and self defeating or to respond proactively with self determined responsibility and freedom of choice (George, 2000).

Hence, emotional intelligence plays an integral role in defining character and determining both their individual and group destinies. It involves the ability to monitor among them and to use the information to guide one's thinking and actions (Goleman, 1998). Ayodele and Sotonade (2014) define emotional intelligence as the capacity of creating positive outcomes in relationship with others and oneself, as well as adequate relationship with the immediate environment which will promote peaceful co-existence among significant others. Mayer and Salovey citied in Ayodele and Sotonade (2014) see emotional intelligence as the ability to monitor one's own and other feelings and emotions, to discriminate among them, and use this information to guide ones thinking and actions. Therefore, emotional intelligence training is one of the major skills needed by individual, especially adolescents for self-control, self-awareness, cooperation and empathy that are necessary for sound decision-making. Smith (2007) asserts that such a skill is critical to making the right choices and in molding the adolescents' brain for making strong emotional responses to meet daily life challenges. According to Stein (2009), emotional intelligence creates self-awareness among adolescents, which is the ability to understand ones emotions and feelings. It enables an individual to tune into and evaluate his or her true feelings. An understanding of one's true feelings, grants the individual the power to manage his or her emotions. Emotional intelligence has been seen as the capacity of creating positive outcomes in relationship with others and oneself, as well as adequate relationship with immediate environment which will promote peaceful coexistence among significant others. It is the thinking of the researcher that there may be a relationship between the emotional intelligence and bullying behaviour of adolescents.

Furthermore, self-efficacy is defined as the belief in one's ability to execute successfully a certain course of behaviour. Bandura (1997) and Carver (2005) opined that self-efficacy influences choice of actions and the amount of energy invested in a task and the length of time during which we persevere before achieving the desired result. Tsung, Hui, and Law (2011) defined self-efficacy as a person's belief in his capabilities to organize and execute a plan of action to obtain certain goals or activities. It is a person's belief in his capabilities to successfully organize and execute a particular action required to produce the desired result. Self-efficacy can be seen to play a critical role in whether students get involved in bulling behaviour or remain passive (Tsung, Hai & Law 2011). The self-efficacy of an individual refers to that person's judgment about how well they can, "organize and execute a course of action required to deal with prospective situations that contain many ambiguous, unpredictable and often stressful elements" (Bandura, 1981). Bandura, as cited in Ukozor (2010) states that self-efficacy represents an individual's belief about his/her ability to successfully execute a course of action in a difficult or challenging situation. Self efficacy is an execute predictor of performance. People with low self-efficacy about an activity will tend to a void that activity, whereas people with high self-efficacy will make vigorous and persistent effort and will therefore be more likely to complete the test successfully (Bandura, 1981).

Gender is the range of physical, biological, mental and behavioural characteristics pertaining to and differentiating between masculinity and femininity (Haig, in Onuigbo 2012). Depending on the context, the term may refer to biological sex (i.e the state of being male, female or intersex), sex based social structure (including gender roles and other social roles) or gender identity. To Okeke (2013), gender refers to the socially and culturally constructed characteristics and roles which are ascribed to males and females in any society. Gender is a major factor that determines the level of bullying behaviour of adolescents in the society. Okeke (2013) described the male's attribute as bold, aggressive, tactful and economical on the use of words, while the females are fearful, timid, gentle, dull, submissive and talkative. May be that is the reason Salmivalli, (2010), Salmivali and Voeten (2004) stated that boys are the more actively involved in bullying process and are more likely to acquire the participant roles of the reinforcers and the assistants in bullying situations whereas girls are more likely to participate in the roles of the defender and the passive bystanders in bullying situations. Girls are nominated as defenders more often than boys both by their classmates and victims. Thus, in today's society boys are brought up to be aggressive and involved in tough and tumble play while girls are brought up to be sensitive and caring and to behave in more pro-social and helping ways (Salmivalli, Lagerspratz, Bjorkqvist, Osterman and Kukiaine, 1996).

Despite the effort of schools, parents, psychologists, government and non-governmental organizations to prevent or stop bullying, it still occurs worldwide and is common in Police

Barracks. The most prevalence of bullying in the Police Barracks include name calling, put-downs, insults, harassment, assault, threats, coercion and extortion etc. Barhight, Hubbahg and Hyde (2013) states that victims of frequent bullying have been reported to experience a range of psychological, psychosomatic and behavioural symptoms including anxiety and insecurity, low self esteem and low self-efficacy, low self-worth, considerable mental health problem, sleeping difficulties, bed wetting, feeling of sadness and frequent headaches and pains. Bullying thus is likely to evoke a range of ideas and situation in different people's minds. Some of these common behaviours are hitting, kicking, extortion of money etc. Others are likely to be less common, for instance, children and adolescents who bully thrive on controlling or dominating others. They have often been the victims of physical abuse or bullying themselves. Bullies may also be depressed, angry or upset about events at school or at home. In essence, bullying behaviour is a compulsive need to displace aggression which is achieved by the expression of inadequacy (social, personal, interpersonal, behavioural, professional) by projection of that inadequacy onto others through control and subjugation (criticism, exclusion, isolation etc.) (Albiero, Benetle and Altoe, 2007). This is sustained by abdication of responsibility (denial, counter accusation, pretences of victimhood) and perpetuated by a climate of fear, ignorance, indifference, silence, denial, disbelief, deception, evasion of accountability, tolerance and reward (e.g promotion) for the bully and victim (Thomberg and Jungert, 2013). Though a number of studies by Abbitt in Agulanna (2014), and Rigby (2014) and Wang, Iannotti, Nansel (2009) on school bullying among adolescents, seminars, symposia as well as rallies have been done before now, a lot still needs to be done to create awareness and check the menace of bullying behaviour in their society and also educate adolescents on the causes, effects, predictors and consequences of bullying, both in relation to being a bully and being a victim of bullying behaviour on mental health and academic performance. Hence, this study is to examine emotional intelligence and self-efficacy as determinants of bullying behaviour of adolescents in police barracks in Rivers State.

Statement of the Problem

Bullying is a social phenomenon that is a major problem in today's society, and studies have shown that children exposed to bullying are much more likely to experience long-term, as well as immediate negative psychological impacts. Persistent bullying may lower victims' self-confidence, induce serious health problems and ruin careers. More bulled children may suffer headache, sleeplessness, anxiety, depression and psychosomatic complaint. Some of the bullied children equally develop post-traumatic stress disorder, unheard victims may turn to inward violence, suicide or outward violence. Bullies are described as anxious, academically uneducated, and insecure and tend to be aggressive and coercive. They display negative attitude towards their peers and tend to solve their problems with violence. Youth violence in the barracks is also seen as more likely to involve weapons and gangs, to be more destructive and to involve adolescents than ever before. While there is a lack of hard evidence to support an actual increase in the prevalence and severity of adolescents bullying behaviour, there is, nonetheless a growing sense of complex social issue. Clearly, bullying behaviour among adolescents is an issue that needs to be examined, understood and ameliorated through effective, concerted and sustained efforts. The understanding of the functioning of emotional intelligence and self-efficacy in the occurrence of bullying behaviour could provide for better development of a lasting and effective intervention. It is towards this end that this study is designed to examine emotional intelligence and self-efficacy as determinants of bullying behaviour of adolescents in police barracks in Rivers State.

Purpose of the Study

The main purpose of this study is to investigate the emotional intelligence and self-efficacy as determinants of bullying behaviour of adolescents. Specifically, the researcher sought to:

(i) determine the relationship between emotional intelligence and bullying behaviour of adolescents living in police barracks.
(ii) determine the relationship between self-efficacy and bullying behaviour of adolescents living in police barracks.
(iii) determine the relationship among emotional intelligence, self-efficacy and bullying behaviour of adolescents living in police barracks.
(iv) ascertain if gender is a factor in the relationship between emotional intelligence and bullying behaviour of adolescents living in police barracks.
(v) determine if gender is a factor in the relationship between self-efficacy and bullying behaviour of adolescents living in police barracks and

Research Questions

The study was guided by the following research questions:

(i) What is the relationship between emotional intelligence, and bullying behaviour of adolescents living in police barracks?
(ii) What is the relationship between self-efficacy and bullying behaviour of adolescents living in police barracks?
(iii) What is the relationship among emotional intelligence, self-efficacy and bullying behaviour of adolescents living in police barracks?
(iv) To what extent is gender a factor in the relationship between emotional intelligence and bullying Behaviour of adolescents living in police barracks?
(v) To what extent is gender a factor in the relationship between self-efficacy and bullying Behaviour of adolescents living in police barracks?

Hypotheses

The researcher formulated the following hypotheses to guide the study and was be tested at 0.05 level of significance.

(i) There is no significant relationship between emotional intelligence and bullying behaviour of adolescents living in police barracks.
(ii) There is no significant relationship between self-efficacy and bullying behaviour of adolescents living in police barracks.
(iii) There is no significant relationship among emotional intelligence, self-efficacy and bullying behaviour of adolescents living in police barracks.
(iv) Gender is not a significant factor in the relationship between emotional intelligence and bullying behaviour of adolescents living in police barracks.
(v) Gender is not a significant factor in the relationship between self-efficacy and bullying behaviour of adolescents living in police barrack.

Methodology

The research design adopted for the study is correlational design, the area of the study was Rivers State, the population of this study was 2573 adolescents from the various Police barracks in the three Area Command in Rivers State. The study adopted a cluster sampling technique, in which three Area Command in Rivers State namely; Port Harcourt Area Command, Bori Area Command and Ahoada Area Command. A sample size of 200 adolescents from the population of the study was selected for the study.

Instrumentation

The researcher used three instruments for the study. They are Bullying Behaviour Scale (BBS), Emotional Intelligence Scale (EIS) and General Self Efficacy Scale (GSES). The first instrument Bullying Bahaviour Scale (BBS) was adopted from Williams (2003) to elicit information of bullying behaviour which has 14 items. A modified four point likert scale of Exactly true = 4, Moderately true = 3, Barely true = 2, and Not of all true = 1 was used.

The Second Instrument Emotional Intelligence Scale (EIS) was adopted from low and Drawn (2000) to elicit information on Emotional Intelligence with 12 items. A modified likert four (4) point scale of Exactly true = 4, moderately true = 3, Barely true = 2 and Not of all true = 1 was used.

While the third instrument General Self Efficacy Scale was adopted from Jerusalem and Schwarzer (1993) with 10 items were used to elicit information on Self – Efficacy. A modified four point likert scale of Exactly true = 4, Moderately true = 3, Barely true = 2 and Not of all true = 1. These are positively keyed items in both three instruments. The researcher employed direct delivery technique in the administration of the instruments to the research subject. This implies that the researcher administered the instruments personally to the respondents with the help of two (2) trained research assistants from the Police barracks, one for each cluster and the two were found to have been correctly filled and fit for use in further analysis. That data were collated to obtain mean and standard deviation and Pearson Product Moment Correlation Coefficients.

Results

Research Question One: What is the Relationship between Emotional Intelligence and bullying behaviour of adolescents living in police barrack.

Table 1: Pearson Product Moment Correlation on Emotional intelligence and bullying behaviour of adolescents living in Police Barracks

Variables	n	x	SD	r
Emotional Intelligence (EI)	200	33.082	2.702	-0.106
Bullying Behaviour (BB)	200	32.160	2.800	

n= number of Subjects, x = Mean. SD = standard deviation, r = Reliability coefficient.

Table 1 shows the r-value calculated as -0.106 indicating that the relationship between Emotional intelligence and bullying behaviour is negatively weak. Also the mean and standard deviation of the two variables, emotional intelligence and bullying behaviour of adolescents living in police barracks, Emotional intelligence (EI) has the highest mean(x=33.082) followed by bullying behaviour (BB) the lowest mean(x=32.160).

Hypothesis One: There is no significant relationship between emotional intelligence and bullying behaviour of adolescents living in Police Barrack.

Table 2: Correlations matrix showing relationship between emotional intelligence and bullying behaviour of adolescents living in police barrack.

Variables	E. I.	B. B
Emotional Intelligence (EI)	1.000	
Bullying Behaviour (BB)	-0.106	1.000

Table 2 shows the correlations between Emotional Intelligence and bullying behaviour is -0106 indicates a very weak negative relationship.

Research Question Two: What is the Relationship between Self-efficacy and bullying behaviour of adolescents living in police barrack.

Table 3: Pearson Product Moment Correlation on self-efficacy and bullying behaviour of adolescents living in police barracks.

Variables	n	Mean (x)	SD	r
Self-Efficacy (SE)	200	31.704	2.062	-0.041
Bullying Behaviour (BB)	200	32.160	2.800	

n=Number of subjects, x=Mean, SD =Standard deviation, r= reliability coefficient.

Table 3 presents the r-value calculated as-0.041indicating that the relationship between self-efficacy and bullying behaviour is negatively weak. Also the mean and standard deviation of the two variables, self-efficacy and bullying behaviour of adolescents living in police barracks. Bullying behaviour has the highest mean (x=32.160) while self-efficacy lowest mean (x= 31.704).

Hypothesis Two: There is no significant relationship between self-efficacy and bullying behaviour of adolescents living in Police Barrack.

Table 4: Correlations matrix showing relationship between self-efficacy and bullying behaviour of adolescents living in police barracks

Variables	S. E.	B. B
Self-efficacy (SE)	1.000	
Bullying Behaviour (BB)	-0.041	1.000

Table 4 shows the correlations between self-efficacy and bullying behaviour is -0.041 indicates a very weak negative relationship.

Research Question Three: What is the relationship among emotional intelligence, self-efficacy and bullying behaviour of adolescents living in police barracks?

Table 5: Pearson Product Moment Correlation on emotional intelligence, self-efficacy and bullying behaviour of adolescents living in police barracks

Variables	n	Mean (x)	SD	r
Emotional Intelligence (EI)	200	33.082	2.702	-0.106
Self-Efficacy (SE)	200	31.704	2.062	-0.041
Bullying Behaviour (BB)	200	32.160	2.800	

n=Number of subjects, x=Mean, SD= standard deviation, r= reliability coefficient.

Results from Table 5 reveal that there is a significant negative relationship between emotional intelligence, self-efficacy and bullying behaviour of adolescents (r= -0.106 and -0.041 respectively). The mean, standard deviation of emotional intelligence has the highest mean and standard (x=33.082 and SD=2.702), followed by bullying behaviour mean and standard (x=32.160 and SD= 2.800) and Self-Efficacy (SE) the lowest mean and standard deviation (x= 31.704 and SD= 2.062).

Hypothesis Three: There is no significant relationship among emotional intelligence, self-efficacy and bullying behaviour of adolescents living in police barracks.

Table 6: Correlations matrix showing interrelationship among emotional intelligence, self-efficacy and bullying behaviour of adolescents living in police barracks

Variables	E. I.	S. E.	B. B
Emotional Intelligence (EI)	1.000		
Self-efficacy (SE)	-0.033	1.000	
Bullying Behaviour (BB)	-0.106	-0.041	1.000

From Table 6 above shows the correlations between emotional intelligence and self-efficacy is -0.033 which indicates a very weak negative correlation, also emotional intelligence and bullying behaviour -0.106, indicates a very weak negative correlation and also self-efficacy versus bullying behaviour is -0.041 which indicates a very weak negative relationship.

Table 7: Summary of multiple regression showing prediction of bullying behaviour on the combination of emotional intelligence and self-efficacy

Model	R	R-square (R^2)	Adjusted R^2	Std. Error of the Estimate
1	0.112[a]	0.012	0.001	2.780

Table 7 shows that for the mode 1 used the multiple regression (R) of 0.112[a], regression squared (R^2) is 0.012, adjusted R^2 of 0.001, standard error of estimate is 2,780, change of statistics of R^2 change is 0.012. This means that all the predictors (actually those that contributed significantly to the prediction) account for 12% of the variance in bullying behaviour of adolescents living in police barracks and this is statistically significant ($P>0.05$).

Table 8: Analysis of Variance table based on prediction of bullying behaviour of adolescent by emotional intelligence and self-efficacy

ANOVA

Model	Sum of Square	Df	Mean Square	F.	Sig
Regression	17.315	2	8.658	1.120	.329[b]
Residual	1368.346	197	6.946		
Total	1385.661	199			

a. *Dependent variable: Var. 0001*

b. *Predictors (constant) Var. 0003, Var. 0002*

The result in Table 8 above revealed that F-ratio value of 1.120 not statistically significant at 0.05 alpha level because the P-value of 0.329 is greater than the chosen alpha level of significance at df (2,197). Therefore the null hypothesis is accepted as F (2,197) = 1.120 P>0.05.

This means that taken together the variables emotional intelligence and self-efficacy do not jointly determine bullying behaviour of adolescents living in police barracks.

Table 9: Coefficient of unstandardized multiple regression

Model	Unstandardized Coefficients		Std. Coefficient	t	Sig
	B	Std. Error	Beta		
Var. 0002	-.045	.092	-0.037	-.493	.622
Var. 0003	-.103	.072	-0.107	-1.432	.154

Note: *A negative value indicates that as the predictor increases the criterion decrease.*
Variable 0002 (Emotional intelligence)
Variable 0003 (Self-efficacy)
Their Beta (B) actually tested for significance.
B for Emotional intelligence is – 0.037 which is not significant P>0.05, t = -.0493.
B for self-efficacy is -.107, which is not significant, P>0.05, t = -.107

Contributions

Emotional intelligence does not significantly contribute to the determination of bullying behaviour of adolescents living in police barrack. Self-efficacy does not significantly contribute to the determination of bullying behaviour of adolescents living in police barracks.

Therefore emotional intelligence and self-efficacy do not independently determine significantly bullying behaviour of adolescents living in police barracks.

Research Question Four: To what extent is gender a factor in the relationship between emotional intelligence and bullying behaviour of adolescents living in police barracks?

Table 10: Pearson Product Moment Coefficient on gender as a factor in the emotional intelligence and bullying behaviour of adolescents living in police barracks

Variables	n	Mean (x)	SD	r
Emotional intelligence of Males	**100**	**33.311**	**2.835**	**-.023**

Emotional intelligence of Females	**100**	**33.033**	**2.737**	

n= Number of subjects, x= Mean, SD= standard deviation, r= reliability coefficient.

The result from Table 10 revealed that there is significant weak negative relationship between gender as a factor in emotional intelligence and bullying behaviour of adolescents. (r= -.023). Emotional intelligence of male adolescent group mean (x) is 33.311 with standard deviation of 2.835 while that of emotional intelligence of female adolescents group is 33.033 with standard deviation of 2.737. The mean scores are almost equal.

Hypothesis Four: Gender is not a significant factor in the relationship between emotional intelligence and bullying behaviour of adolescents living in police barracks.

Table 11: Correlations between gender as a factor in the emotional intelligence and bullying behaviour of adolescents living in police barracks

Variables	Emotional Intelligence of Males	Emotional Intelligence of Females
Emotional Intelligence of Males	1	-.023
Emotional Intelligence of Females	-.023	1

Correlation is not significant at 0.05 (2-tailed), n = 90.

Pearson Product Moment Correlations Coefficient were calculated in Table 11 for a relationship between Emotional intelligence of males and females adolescent living in Police barracks. A negative weak correlation was found r (88) = -.023, P>0.05) indicating no significant linear relationship between the two variables.

Research Question Five: To what extent is gender a factor in the relationship between self-efficacy and bullying behaviour of adolescents living in police barracks.

Table 12: Pearson Product Moment Correlation on gender as a factor in the self Efficacy and bullying behaviour of adolescents living in Police barracks

Variables	n	Mean (x)	SD	r
Self-efficacy of Males	**100**	**30.611**	**2.311**	**.351*** **
Self-efficacy of Females	**100**	**29.078**	**2.505**	

n= Number of subjects, x= Mean, SD= standard deviation, r= reliability coefficient.

Data from Table 12 demonstrate that there is a positive significant relationship between gender as a factor in the self-efficacy and bullying behaviour of adolescents living in Police barracks (r= .351). The self-efficacy of male adolescents group mean (x) of 30.611 with standard deviation of 2.311 while that of females adolescents group mean (x) is 29.078 with standard deviation of 2.505. The mean score are almost equal.

Hypothesis Five: Gender is not a significant factor in the relationship between self - efficacy and bullying behaviour of adolescents living in police barracks

Table 13: Correlations between gender as a factor in the self-efficacy and bullying behaviour of adolescents living in police barracks

Variables	Self-Efficacy of Males	Self-Efficacy of Females
Self-efficacy of Males	1	.351***
Self-efficacy of Females	.351***	1

**** Correlations is significant at 0.05 (2-tailed) n = 100*

Pearson Product Moment Correlation Coefficient was calculated in Table 13 for relationship between self-efficacy of males and females adolescents living police barracks. A weak positive correlation was found r (98) = 0.351, P<0.05 indicating that there is a significant linear relationship between the two variables.

Summary of Findings

1) There is a very weak negative relationship between emotional-intelligence and bullying behaviour of adolescents living in police barracks.
2) There is a very weak negative relationship between self-efficacy and bullying behaviour of adolescents living in police barracks.
3) The variables Emotional Intelligence, Self-Efficacy do not jointly determine bullying behaviour of adolescents living in police barracks.
4) There is a weak negative relationship between gender as a factor in the Emotional intelligence and bullying behaviour of adolescents living in police barracks.
5) There is a weak positive relationship between gender as a factor in the self-efficacy and bullying behaviour of adolescents living in police barracks.

Recommendations

Based on the findings of the study, the following recommendations were made:

1) It becomes imperative that stakeholders in police barracks should mount serious enlightenment campaigns in the form of rallies, workshops and Seminars geared towards teaching parents the best way to live a healthy life in Police barracks
2) Psychologists and guidance counseling should enlighten parents and adolescents the best ways to live a healthy life which is devoid of violence on police barracks in order to promote good mental health.
3) Non-governmental organizations should organize rallies, symposia programmes of letting them to know that negative effects of bullying behaviour on adolescents themselves ie parents, family, peers, etc.

4) Consequently, professional helpers such as counselors, health workers etc who are serving in the police and living in the barracks should be saddled with responsibilities of providing guidance and counseling services and disseminating information that will help reduce the incidence of bullying behaviour among adolescents in police barracks.
5) In addition, parents, religious bodies and schools should guide adolescents through moral lessons that would discourage bullying and aggressive behaviour by building the child's emotional state (i.e teaching adolescents to be emotionally intelligent).
6) In summary, parents, government health workers, counseling psychologists and other stakeholder of adolescents as a matter of urgency encourage emotional development training, this will help the child to be more successful in handling any bullying episode.

Conclusion

The study investigated the emotional intelligence and self-efficacy as determinants of bullying behaviour of adolescents in police barracks in Rivers State. Bullying is a social phenomenon that is a major problem in today's society, and studies have shown that children exposed to bullying are much more likely to experience long-term as well as immediate negative psychological impacts. The main purpose of this study is to investigate the emotional intelligence and self-efficacy as determinants of bullying behaviour of adolescents.

References

Agulanna, G. G. (2014). Issues in adolescence: Gender issues, deviant behaviour and moral values. *The Educational Psychologist.* 8 (1) pp. 9-22

Albiero, P., Benelli, B. and Altoe, G. (2007). Does empathy predict adolescent's bullying and defending behaviour? *Journal of Aggressive Behaviour.* 33, 1-10. http://DOI: 10.1002/ab.20204.

Ayodale, K. O. and Sotonade, O. A. T. (2014). Comparative effectiveness of self-management, emotional intelligence and assertiveness training progress in reducing the potential for terrorism and violence among Nigerian adolescents. *International Journal of Applied Psychology* 4(6): 214-222. http://Dol. 10.5923/j.ijap-2014040602.

Bandura, A. (1981). Self-referent thought. A development analysis of self-efficacy in J.H. Flarell & L. Ross (eds.). *Social cognitive development frontiers and possible features (pp. 205-239).* New York. Cambridge University Press.

Bandura, A. (1997). *Self-efficacy: The exercise of control.* New York: Freeman

Barhight, L. R., Hubbard, J. A. and Hyde, C. T. (2013). Children's physiological and emotional reactions to witnessing bullying predict bystander intervention *Journal of Child Development.* 84(1), 375-390. http://DOI; 10.1111/j.1467-8624.2012.01839.x.

Carver, C. S. (2005). Impulse and constraint perspectives from personality psychology, convergence with theory in other areas and potential for integration. *Personality and Social Psychology Review,* 9:312-333.

George, J. (2000). Emotions and leadership. The roles of emotional intelligence. *Human Relations,* 53 (8): 1027 – 55.

Goleman, D. (1998). *Working with emotional intelligence.* New York: Bantam Book.

Health Resources & Services Administration. 2014 Press Releases.

Hermann, M. and Finn, A. (2002). School violence prevention: Legal and ethical issues and crisis response. *Professional School Counselor.* 6(1): 46-54.

Jerusalem, M. and Schwarzer, R. (1993). Generalized self-efficacy scale. In J. Weinman, S. W. and Johnson, N. (Eds.). *Measures in Health Psychology. A user's portifolio. Causal and control beliefs Windsor,* V/C: NFER-Nelson, 35-37.

Kokkinos, C. K., and Kipritsi, E. (2012). The relationship between bullying victimization, trait emotional intelligence, self-efficacy and empathy among preadolescents. *Journal of Social Psychology Education.* 15, 41-58. http://DOI; 10.1007/s11218-011-9168-9.

Limber, S. (2002). Youth bullying: Addressing youth bullying behaviours. American Medical Association. *Educational Forum on Adolescent Health.* Retreived June 8, 2005. Available: http://www.ama-assn.org/ama//pub/upload/mm/39/youthbullying paf.

Low, R. and Darwin, E. (2000). *Exploring and developing emotional intelligence skills.* Cambridge England, Cambridge University Press.

Okeke, P. E. (2013). *Effect of simulation on students' achievement in senior secondary school chemistry in Enugu East L.G.A.* Unpublished research work of Department of Science Education, University of Nigeria, Nsukka.

Onuigbo, C. N. (2012). Gender issue and deviant behaviour of adolescent. *The Educational Psychologist.* 8(1): 9-22.

Rigby, K. (2014). Self-efficacy differences between perpetrators and victims (M.Sc Thesis), The Faculty of Humboldt State University.

Saimivalli, C., Lagerspetz, K., Bjokqvist, K., Oysterman, K. and Kaukiainen, A. (1996). Bullying as a group process: Participant roles and their relations to social status within the group. *Aggressive Behaviour*, 22, 1-15.

Salmivalli, C. (2010). Bullying and the peer group. A review. *Journal of Aggression and Violent Behaviour,* 15, 112-120. http://DOI; 10.1016/j.avb.2009.08.007.

Salmivalli, C., and Voeten, M. (2004). Connections between attitudes, group norms and behaviour in bullying situations. *International Journal of Behaviour Development,* 28, 246. http://DOI; 10.1080/01650344000488.

Schuttle, N. S., Malouff, J. M., Hall, L. E., Haggerty, D. J., Copper, J. T., Golden, C. J. and Dobnheim, L. (1998). Development and validation of a measure of emotional intelligence personality and individual differences, 25. 167-177.

Scutte, N., Malouff, J. J., Coston, C., and Tracie, D. (2001). Emotional intelligence and interpersonal relations. *Journal of Social psychology,* 4, 523-526.

Smith, P. K. (2007). The silent Nightmare: Bullying and victimization in school peer groups. *The Psychologist,* 4, 243-248.

Stein, S. (2009). *Emotional intelligence for dummies.* New York. NY: John Wiley & Sons.

Thomberg, R. and Jungert, T. (2013). Bystander behaviour in bullying situation, basis moral sensitivity, moral disengagement and defender self-efficacy. *Journal of Adolescence,* 36(3): 475-483. http://Dol.org/10.1016/3.adolescence.

Thompson, D., and Sharp, S. (2013). The dynamics of victimization and rejection in school. In D.Thompson & S. Sharp (Eds.), *Improving schools: Establishing and integrating whole school behaviour policies* (pp. 11-25). London: David Fultons.

Tsung, S. K. M., Hui, E. K. P., and Law, B. C. M. (2011). Bystander position taking in school bullying. The role of position identity, self-efficacy and self-determination. *Journal of the Scientific World.* 11, 2278 – 2286. http://Dol; 10.1100/2011/531474.

Ukazor F. I. (2008). Effect of constructurist approach teaching strategy on the senior secondary school student achievement and self-efficacy in Physics. Unpublished Ph.D Dissertation, Enugu State University of Science and Technology (ESUT), Enugu.

Wang, J., Iannotti, R. J. and Nansel, T. R. (2009). School bullying among adolescents in the United States. Physical, verbal, relational and cyber. *Journal of Adolescence Health,* 45(4), 368-375.

Williams, K. (2003). Bullying behavior and attachment styles. Electronic Thesis and Dissertations. Paper 444.

22

Causes, Types and Consequences of Mental Disorder among Women in Nigeria: Implications for Guidance and Counseling

UDECHUKWU Joachim A. Ph.D & ANAZODO C. E. Ph.D

Abstract

Mental disorder is a psycho-social and psychiatric problem that manifests in behavioral display that falls short of societal standards. Mental disorder is the opposite of mental health. Mental disorder generally refers to psychological syndrome associated with illogical thinking, depression, mood swing, immature frantic approach to stress, delusion of perfection, hallucination, self-talk and self-exaltation, feeling of persecution, withdrawal syndrome, distorted perception, faulty and unfounded mind-reading, unwarranted quarreling with self and others etc. These conditions recently appear to be more prevalent among women in Nigeria. The focus of this paper therefore is to identify some of the causes and effect of these phenomena as they affect Nigerian women. Considerable efforts were also made by the researchers to bring to the forefront the strategic positive difference guidance and counseling can make to ameliorate these ugly health situations.

Key Words: *Mental Health, Mental Disorder, Guidance and Counseling*

Introduction

Mental disorder is a psychological condition that is said to have set in when an individual gradually manifests behaviors that are not only considered as deviant but are judged unwanted and therefore not acceptable to the immediate society to which the victim belongs. Mental disorder is a health challenge which is not readily accepted or noticed by the victim. It is therefore a psych-social or psychiatric concept that refers to a psychological syndrome associated with legion of maladaptive behaviors. It is said to be a syndrome because it manifests at anytime, in diverse ways and has many labels attached to it. These labels include attack from mammy-water spirit, madness, seasonal health condition associated with the appearance of the moon, unprovoked aggression, excessive cleanliness and/or dirtiness and mood-swing, among others. According to Nnachi (2007), a mentally disordered person has serious intellectual and reasoning problems. Such a person has certain mental dysfunctions that affect thinking, coordination or reasoning, producing behaviour that is inappropriate within the context of the person's culture and in relation to the person's social standing, age or sex. The same author posits that "Mental disorder seriously and negatively affects thinking, coordination or reasoning, the phenomenon has a serious impact on learning. It brings about learning impairment, emotional instability, psychological distress and intellectual disorganization".

Definition of Concepts

Mental health: This is an effective and enjoyable living. It is living a purposeful life of accepted accomplishment which gives consuming satisfaction and enjoyment with a minimum of friction and conflict either within the individual or between the individual and others around him. Also, the current concept of positive mental health describes three ideas that characterise the mentally healthy person, viz:

a. That the human person understands himself including his own motivation, drives, wishes and desires.
b. That the person accomplishes self actualization and self realization and,
c. That the human person lives an integrated balances life.

Mental health is a pathological concept and condition that is akin to the psychological state of the human person. The psychological state of a person determines how that person relates, reasons, interacts, socializes, performs, reacts and behaves and even does things within his/her environment (Okafor, 2000 and Nnachi, 2007).

Following from the above, one can see that the concept of mental health is neither here nor there and does not lend itself to easy definition and understanding. Hence, as a scholar from the South-East Nigeria where such concepts as ala- ikirika, ala-ogbanje, ala-uka, ala-iba, ala-otu are all grouped under the heading onye ala (ara). That is to say, that all kinds of mild mental ill-health are labeled as mental disorder. Hence anybody who is not in a positive condition of his environment and appears not to be joyful, happy, free from worries, loving, acceptable, appreciative and kind, shows affection, peace and is well protected can be categorized as mentally unhealthy and in simple language, suffering from mental disorder. The rest of the analyses in this research will be done using the concept of mental disorder for all categories of persons suffering from levels of mental illness. Consequently mental disorder is a psychological concept that refers to syndrome associated with stress, distress, illogicality, dysfunction in a crucial area of performance, or major deviant behavior as a result of old age, diseases of the brain, acute and generalized deprivation/poverty etc. Though it can be argued that mental health is positive while mental disorder is negative, the layman has come to see any reference to mental state as a signal of inability to coordinate affairs of life as a result of mental dysfunction. Hence the term mental disorder will be used to refer to all kinds of mental disequllibruim.

The concept of women on the other hand, is the plural form of woman which means a female human being, a girl, lady. Women are members of the feminine sex. Women have softer muscles, soften voices, longer hair than men. Women also have bigger breasts, wider hips and more beautiful skin than men. Women are created and packaged to perform so many tasks at a time and are readily given to "falling in love" than men. The love atmosphere and environment should be threat-free. They also operate better in an economically secure environment. Their traditional roles as assigned by the society include house-care, cooking for the family and looking after their husbands and children. However, more recently women perform all the roles that the society affords including leadership roles, in politics, the role of the clergy in religious organisations and chief executive officers' role in institutions and industries.

Causes of Mental Disorder

Ordinarily, it appears that women are playing the traditional roles of motherhood, child-bearing and child-rearing, and being good wives to their husbands and recently combining these roles with their careers. It is also suspected that these additional roles have combined to make the average Nigerian woman vulnerable to mental disorders. The following therefore are some of the causes of mental disorder among Nigerian women:

1. Hereditary-related causes
2. Environmental-related causes
3. Drug-related causes
4. Stress-related causes
5. Age/Disease related causes
6. Religion related causes
7. Evil Local technology-related causes
8. Accident-related causes
9. Poverty-related causes

We shall now go ahead to explain all but briefly.

1. Hereditary-related Causes

Hereditary is the transfer of behavioural and intellectual traits from parents to their children. According to Ngwoke and Eze (2010), the fact that some children of pure African origin have a dark skin while the Caucasian child has a pink skin is manifestation of heredity. The tendencies to behave in certain peculiar ways may be explained by inheritance or the actions of genes. It follows therefore that negative traits such as mental disorders can be transferred from parents to their children, including their female children. As if to confirm the above statements, Egbule (2009) observes that "through the phenomenon of genotype, certain pathological behaviours are inherited by offspring from their progenitors. This is essentially a function of genes from either of the parents".

2. Environmental-related causes

Closely following endowment as transferred from parents to their children is the impact of the environment also known as nurture in activating what is dormant in a person's gene. If environment does not cooperating (with genetic endowments), there will be distortions and aberrations in the individual's development (Ngwoke and Eze, 2010). Hence, generalized poverty, deprivation, marital conflict, disappoints and frustrations can combine to stir up mental disorder especially among women because of their susceptibility to emotional imbalance.

3. Drug-related causes

It is now known that the use of certain drugs such as alcohol, marijuana, tobacco, caffeine, amphetamines etc. can be deleterious to health. Women, even from peer learning, are influenced to smoke cigarette, sniff cocaine, heroin and morphines while the local women do take overdose of tobacco, kolanut which some of them take as elixir for teeth and gum infections. These stimulants are drugs that tend to increase the activities of the organs and/or system, especially the central nervous system. Nnachi (2007) observes that "stimulants are generally dangerous to mental health. This is because they alter the individual's natural feelings. They can cause brain damage and may lead to mental sickness".

4. Stress-related causes

Akinboye and Adeyemo (2002) describe stress as the body's response to any undesirable mental, physical, emotional social or environmental demand. They argue that stress causes physical trauma, strenuous organic exercise, metabolic disturbances of anxiety or homeostasis (well-being). Chronic and accumulated stress can be detrimental to health and well-being and can result in, higher levels of stress which can lead to worsening of a wide variety of physical conditions, including cardiovascular disease, octopuses, arthritis, type–2 diabetes, certain cancers, among other conditions (such as mental disorders) (Keitcolt-Glasser, MCGuire, Roblesand Glaiser, (2004), in Obikeze, (2008). In fact there is an established relationship between pressure and mental illness (Weitan, 1988).

5. Age/Diseases-related causes

Diseases such as cerebral malaria, stroke, syphilis, dementia, stress etc can alone and/or in combination, cause mental disorder. According to Taylor (1999), approximately 500,000 individuals experience stroke every year, and more than 4 million of these neurologically-impaired individuals live with significant cognitive and emotional problems. Since most stroke cause damage to the left-brain, cognitive disturbances, intellectual decline and motor-coordination are usually affected. This is mostly because patients with left-brain respond to their plight with anxiety, depression, memory dysfunction and mood alteration.

6. Over-religiosity

Over-religiosity is an active dependence on religious activities, relics, sacrifices and observation of religious days, festivals and symbols of faith (symbolo fidei) with doing the will of God. Over-religiosity is an aberration which occurs when a person become over-religious and over-dependent on prophets, prophecies, sacrifices, relics, incantations and invocation, religious prostitution, during strange things such as wearing over-sized cross (symbol of Christian religion), white garment with signs of cross round the garment, speaking esoteric language, withdrawal from day-to-day activities, Commenting in this regard, Nmah (2004) refers to this condition as "Psychological disequilibrium, which according to him is a "state of mental imbalance leading to unsound and distorted mentality in religious and spiritual matters... as he is largely guided not by sound reason, but by the mere force of emotions and religious sentiments...as a hidden mental case, generally tends to perceive and interpret the right thing the wrong way".

7. Evil Local Technology:

Evil Local technology as used in this context refers to the use of local and native medicinal process, through invocation and incantation to derail the mental equilibrium of a perceived enemy to the extent that the victims degenerate to a state of insanity and mental disorder. Witches and wizards, sorcerers and powerful native medicine-men can be hired to inflict mental disorder on a normal person.

8. Accident-related causes:

Accident-related cause of mental disorder can be traced back even from conception. Accident can, and does manifest in birth is implicated and when the baby is too big for natural birth, the use of instruments such as forceps can be used to assist the baby out. However, because the head of the child is very soft like the egg-shell accidents can occur. It is because both human error and the instrument can cause brain damage to the baby. Also in adult situation, accidents can also lead to brain damage which can also lead to mental disorder.

Types of Mental Disorder

Mental disorder is not a one-shot affair, for it is now known that in some cases it takes some time for both the victim and those around him/her to realize that things have fallen apart and that the centre cannot hold. In other words, mental disorder manifest in different ways. While some are aggressive, others are withdrawn, sedate and extremely slow and quiet. It is upon this background that we want to X-ray types of mental disorders.

They include the following:

1. Psychosis
2. Neurosis
3. Psychosomatic disorders
4. Personality disorders
5. Affective disorders

We shall now go ahead to explain them one after the other.

1. Psychosis

Psychosis (singular from of psychoses) is characterized by a distortion and impairment in mental activities that extremely interfere with the human person's ability to meet the demands of day-to-day life activities. There is great distortion of reality. It is so massive that the human person may no longer separate illusion from reality. These may take the form of, or manifest in, delusions and/or hallucinations. According to Hilgard, Alkinson and Atkinson (1979), a delusion is a false belief maintained despite contradictory evidence or experience. Psychotic delusions often centre around ideas of grandeur(I am the King of the Universe or I am Jesus Christ). Other forms of Psychoses include, persecution, external control, and depersonalization. "The psychotic individual may also show profound changes of mood (from hilarious excitement to depressive stupor) as well as defects in language and memory".

2. Neurosis

Neurosis (singular form of neuroses) is usually a lesser form of abnormal behaviour, those suffering from neurosis are however troublesome and quarrelsome to the extent that they require expert help and intervention. From time to time they may need hospitalization. However, they still with effort, maintain responsible touch with reality. Okafor (2000), observes that "they (neurotics) suffer from unreasonable fears, obsessions, compulsions, depressed feelings and unwarranted exhaustion".

3. Personality Disorder

Personality disorders are usually enduring patterns of socially maladaptive behaviour. Extreme dependency, antisocial or sexually deviant behaviour, alcoholism and drug addiction are some of the disorders included in this category. Back-boning the above assertion Okafor (2000) posits that included in the category are "the alcoholics, drug addicts, delinquents, criminals, sexual deviants and individuals with difficult personalities". Persons in this group show signs of immaturity, weak ego and manifest anti-social behaviour. The victim's personality disorders affect both their families and the society, (Fieldmen, 2009 & Nnachi 2007). Personality disorders are separated from neuroses and psychoses in the sense that personality disorders are longstanding patterns of maladaptive behaviour, rather than reactions to conflict or stress. This distinction is essentially a matter of degree.

4. Affective Disorders

Affective disorders are disturbances of affect, or mood. The person may be severely depressed, manic (wildly elated), or may alternate between periods of depression and elation (happiness). These mood swings are often so serious that the human person may require hospitalization (Hilgard, Atkinson and Atkinson, 1979).

5. Psychosomatic Disorders

This type of disorder refers to a cluster of psychological syndromes that affects bodily activities. Such psychological disorders usually cause damage to the tissues or organs of the body or they may prevent or distort the effective use of physiological processes of the body. This type of psychological diseases can easily lead to physical disability. According to Nnachi (2007) "they include such diseases as stroke, high blood pressure, skin disorder and acute headache. Sometimes, psychosomatic disorders may involve crawling sensation all over the body. This type of disorder also affects the nervous system and the entire body. There is no gainsaying that it leads to impairment in learning and negatively affects intellectual process.

It is obvious that the mental disorders identified and discussed above are not peculiar to women. It is however, a truism that women are more emotional than men; hence they usually "stress" themselves into most of these typologies more often than their male counterparts.

Effects of Mental Disorders (Women)

1. Personal hygiene is neglected

A mental disordered woman may fail to take her bath for several days, forget to wash her mouth, keep her hair or even dress in clean clothes.

2. Irrational and Illogical Reasoning

The mentally unhealthy woman finds it difficult to discuss issues rationally and logically. This is because she can slip from logicality to illogicality, including the use of esoteric language that appears unreasonable to a normal and healthy person.

3. They are prone to Accidents

Mental disorders usually decrease every sense of security from their victims, especially women. They cross the tarred-roads at will not minding, the speed of vehicles and/or motorcycles. They drink bad water and eat from dust-bins.

4. Sexual Exploitation

The mental unhealthy women are usually sexually exploited by unscrupulous men. These men it is speculated include watch-nights, ritualists and mentally derailed persons. It is common to see women with mental disorders carrying pregnancy without ante-natal and/or post-natal care.

5. Self-centered

Women with mental disorders are not only self-centered but also not in touch with the world around them. Hence they can become threats to themselves, their children and husbands. As far as they are concerned, the world rotates around them.

6. No respect for self and others

Women with mental disorders can go to the market place completely naked. Such persons have no respect for self, members of her family and others. Hence, through their actions they bring shame, disgrace and ridicule to their immediate family members.

7. Information

Women ordinarily talk more than men. In support of the above assertion, Matlin (2000) said "an individual man can be less talkative than most women, similarly, an individual woman may be more talkative than most men". It is said that an average woman speaks about 25,000 words per day. If this is true, one can then imagine the number of words a mentally derailed woman can speak.

8. Suicide

Suicide tendency is common among women. They always, out of frustration and anxiety, try to take their lives. In their houses, they may drink such poisonous chemicals as poison of rat, kerosene, or any harmful substance around, including over-dose of both expired and unprescribed drugs in their house.

9. Effect on Children

This situation can adversely affect the female children of the women with mental disorders. This is because it renders them unmarketable to eligible suitors who may want to select them as marriage partners. The young men and the family will be afraid that the mental disorder can be transferred to the female children and may manifest when they have married them.

Characteristics of Mentally Healthy Women

It is indeed expected that even before discussing the management of mental disorders among women, the reader is expected to be able to differentiate between the characteristics or mentally healthy and unhealthy women. To guide one's competence in the regards, the following description by Okafor regarding the basic characteristics of a mentally healthy woman will now be mentioned.

According to Okafor (2000),

1. Healthy and happy people are those who live well balanced lives in which some time and energy are devoted to work, recreation and companionship.
2. Develop some impelling interest or interests, in which you can lose or forget yourself. These may be your job or profession, your family, your home, nature, sports, music, literature, etc.
3. Set goals for yourself that are reasonably attainable. A long step towards good mental health is accepting one's self and one's limitations. On the other hand, it is dangerous to use one's handicaps as an excuse for not attempting some useful

and satisfactory work. Everyone has her capacities as well as her limitations. One should take stock of these assets so as to direct their efforts along lives in which they may expect the greatest degree of continuing accomplishments and lasting personal satisfaction.

4. Find someone professional or matured friend-with whom your problems can be talked out in a confidential relationship. Confused attitudes and feelings are often clarified by putting them into words spoken to someone who will not tell you what to do and will be a good listener.
5. Healthy individuals are people with a keen sense of integrity. The continuing development of one's conscience is an important part of attaining mental health.
6. A sense of right and wrong and a feeling of moral responsibility for one's behavior are very important. It is also important that the individual try to free herself from the feelings of unnecessary guilt and the inevitable sense of failure.
7. Appreciate that mental health is not something you practice at specific intervals but is a way of living and meeting the normal adjustments of life. It constantly seeks to develop the ability to face frustrations realistically rather than to run away from them. (cf. Okafor, 2000;155).

Implication for Guidance and Counselling

Counselling by way of definition is that process which takes in a one-to-one relationship between an individual troubled by problems with which he cannot cope alone, and a professional worker whose training and experience have qualified him to help others reach solutions to various types of personal difficulties (Hahn and Maclean in Udechukwu, 2014). This definition clearly shows that counseling is not limited to what happens within the inner perimeters of the school setting. Hence, counselling, especially marriage counselling, can be organized of Nigerian Women as a preventive measure for mental disorder.

It is therefore, within the scope of counseling to make her services available for the Nigerian women in a warm and threat-free atmosphere. The counsellors can organise awareness seminars, workshops and/or conferences where they would interact with the women to discuss their challenges, stressful conditions and anxiety-provoking incidents and striking events in their lives. These types of interactive sessions will be free from the usual support given by kindred meetings that are usually backed with rules and regulation with corresponding sanctions, which is also different from the kind of support given by the church where, after singing, dancing and prayers, the women are asked to give/pay offering, tithe, seed faith and/or first fruits. These payments usually act as stressors to the already stressed women. The counselling interaction must be cordial, free, warm, friendly, threat-free and devoid of any kind of payment and/or sanctions. This interactive session can be organized in synergy with the church. This is because women usually find it easier to assemble in church environments or setting such as town halls, civic centres and village squares.

It is upon this background that these researchers suggest that the training of guidance counsellors in Nigeria must be upgraded to include proffiency and needed competencies in the crucial areas of the use of biofeedback's machines, indepth training in the use and application of diagnostic equipment, training in hypnosis, aerobic exercise, adequate relaxation techniques. This will act as prerequisite for their relevance in counselling mentally derailed person (s).

These interactive sessions will help the women to air their views on any matter that worries them, share their views, issues like pregnancy, child-spacing, child rearing, patterns that work, coping strategies for adolescent children and young persons, coping with irresponsible husbands and way-ward spouses. This intermittent interactive sessions give the women a sense of "we are in the same boat". Such meetings are in themselves refreshing, preventive and curative. Specifically, counselling and counsellors can be of great help in preventing mental derailment on its own or together with health personnel in the following ways.

1. Treatment of the Mental disorders

Ab-initio mental disorders were seen as possession of evil-spirit, attack from witchcraft coven and the master-mind of household enemies. It is however, now known that mental disorders has its origin in genetic endowment and environmental conditions of the victims. Today the medical treatment option is in vogue, this is where victims are taken to psychiatric hospital for medical treatment.

2. Psychotherapy

This is the treatment and/or management of mental disorders by psychological methods. One of the psychological methods is through techniques in behavior modification such as self-management, which is an attempt to expand the coast of counseling. It involves self-study and analysis, self- monitoring, self-reinforcement and self-punishment, though stopping technique.

3. Biofeed Back

Biofeed-back is a procedure of monitoring the functioning of a particular response system of the body and presenting the information to the individual. Bio-feed-back consists of the use of modern gadgets to create awareness and control the body process. The result can be used to change the functions of the body voluntarily. It can be used in clinical conditions to modify a number of instinctive functions such as acceleration and deceleration of heart rhythms, lowering of high blood pressure and the control of brain waves. Hypertension, angina, asthma, heart attack are ailments that experts can use bio-feedback technique to manage and/or control (Essuman, Nwaogu, Nwachukwu, 1990).

4. Hypnosis and Free-Association

Hypnosis is one of the oldest techniques for managing mental disorder. This was first made popular by the Psychiatrist Sigmund Freud. This technique relies on several pain and anxiety reduction methods. It is used to elicit from the client information regarding his fears, anxieties, most deep-seated aspirations, feelings, shocks, interests, wishes, hostilities and concerns; and more especially the nature of his past life, such as the experiences of his childhood (Nwoye, 1988 and Taylor, 1999).

5. Clinical/Counseling Method

The modern trend in the management of mental disorder is the use of both psychiatrists and clinical psychologists whose methods involve the application of "a variety of research and diagnostic techniques such as interviews, life histories, testing projective techniques and case observation. It is more known that more emphasis is now on positive environment, air-conditioned room, soft music and a threat-free atmosphere as well as warm acceptance by the clinical psychologists yield positive result. Also where the patient is destructive and aggressive, drugs such as tranquilizers; major tranquilizing drugs include Miltown or Equanil to alleviate anxiety and tension (Coleman, 1969 and Okoye, 2001).

6. Social Support

Social ties, friendship, acquaintances and other healthy family friends relationship are forms of antidote to anxiety, stress and mental disorders. This is in line with the popular saying that: "man is a social animal".

Since it is uncommon for women in black Africa to go to beer parlours and recreation centres for the release of accumulated tension. It's only natural that they make and maintain friendship. However, where for one reason or the other they keep to themselves they are likely to experience mental disequilibrium.

Hence, Myer (2001) reported that it is likely that those who bore their grief alone have more health problems than those who express their painful feelings openly. This will become clearer when sympathizers rally-round the bereaved for the period of mourning; women even go to sleep with their fellow women to give social support, comfort and this proximity act as source of strength and restoration to the bereaved.

7. Relaxation Methods

Relaxation is achieved when the senses and the muscles are tensed and released. It will eventually lead to relaxation of the entire body system. The process of relaxation alone and/or in combination with other behavior modification strategies such as systematic desensitization procedures can be used to reduce stress, anxiety and panic that could lead to mental disorder over a period of time. Research has found out that relaxation methods can be successfully used to treat/manage problems of insomnia, indigestion, severe headache, menstrual clamps and mild forms of depression (Essuman, Nwaogu and Nwachukwu, 1990).

African women need relaxation from several activities of cooking, farming, child-bearing, child rearing, service to her husband both in kind and other motoric services rendered to both her husband children and extended family members as well as friends and acquaintance.

Conclusion

It is the humble position of these writers to state that mental disorders are caused by almost the same factors both for the male and female folks. However, it is important to note that men's ability not to degenerate into mental disorder easily is as a result of their mental strength, mental activity, out-going nature, shock-absorbing strategies and a strong belief in a better tomorrow. On the other hand, women manage their stress and challenges poorly. It is therefore being made available for the women through creation of awareness, education and subtle urging to visit guidance counsellors and share their burdens with them instead of dying in silence.

Recommendations

- **Love**: Men should love their wives and practically demonstrate this love by hugging their wives in public. This practical demonstration of love makes women happy, excited and joyful; it of course reduces tension, anxiety and stress among women and puts them in a state of mental and well-being.
- **Support:** Men (husbands) should also support their wives in everything they do at home, including cooking, washing clothes and utensils, making school-runs, dropping them off at work places etc. This type of support adds spice to their (women) lives.
- **Avoid idleness through alternative education**: Women, especially the rural women, should be encouraged to enroll into alternation education instead of staying at home and wasting away, Alternative education are any type of education outside

the four walls of formal education and schools, learning a trade and all kinds of motoric and/or skill acquisition.

- **Infrastructure**
  Government at all levels should provide social amenities such as electricity, pipe-borne water, good roads, good transportation system to make life easier for the rural women and in turn reduce their stress.
- **Creation of Employment Opportunity**: Government at all levels should also create employment opportunities for the teaming graduates and school leavers. This will be a big relief to the women whose children continue to waste away after school before their very eyes, their husbands, some of whom have lost their jobs and are all relying on the women for succour. This will lift up heavy stressful burden from the women.

References

Akinboye and Adeyemo in Obikezie N. J. (2008). *Development Psychology: Educational Perspectives.* Onitsha: Fabag Prints Ltd.

Coleman, J. C. (1969). *Psychology and Effective Behaviour.* London: Scott, Foresman and Company.

Feldman, R. S. (2005). *Understanding Psychology* (Seventh Edition). New York: McGraw-Hill Companies Inc.

Egbule, J. F. (2009). *Methodology of Guidance and Counselling: Professional Manual for Counselling Psychologists.* Benin City: Goodnews Express Communication.

Hahn and Maclean in Udechukwu J. A. (2014) *Social Horizon: Journal of Social Science.* Edited by Mezieobi .K. Dept. of Social Studies. Ignatuis Atturah University of Education, Port Harcourt.

Hilgrad, E. R., Alkinson, R. L. and Alkinson, R. C. (1979). *Introduction to Psychology* (7th ed). New York: Harcourt Brace Jovanovich, Inc.

Essuman, J. K., Nwaogu, O. and Nwachukwu, V. C. (1990). *Principles and Techniques of Behaviour Modification.* Owerri: International Universities Press.

Keicolt-Glasser, McGuire, Robles and Gluiser in Obikezie (2008). *Developmental Psychology* Onitsha: Fabag prints Ltd.

Myers, D. (2001). *Psychology* (6th ed.). New York: Worth Publishers.

Ngwoke, D. U. and Eze, U. N. (2010). *Developmental Psychology and Education: Theories, Issues & Trends*. Enugu; Timex Enterprises.

Nmah, P. E. (2004). *Basic & Applied Christian Ethics: An African Perspective*. Onitsha: Gucks Systems Int'l.

Nnachi, R.O. (2007). *Advanced Psychology of Learning and Scientific Enquires.* Enugu: John Jacob's Classic Publishers Ltd.

Nwoye, A. (1990). *Counselling Psychology for Africa*. Jos: Fab Anieh (Nigeria) Ltd.

Okafor, J.O. (2000). *Functional Approach to School, Health Education* (2nd ed.). Onitsha: Erudite Publishers.

Okoye, N. N. (2001). *Some Basic Issues in Psychology.* Awka: Erudition Publishers.

Taylor, S. E. (1999). *Health Psychology* (4th ed.). New York: McGraw-Hill Companies, Inc.

23

Constructivist Approach in the Teaching of Christian Religious Education – HIV and AIDS Education Integrated content in Senior Secondary Schools in Nasarawa State, Nigeria

YARO, Joseph Bawa

Abstract

Constructivist approach in teaching and learning represents a big idea in the learning process. The implications of using constructivist approach in teaching and learning Christian Religious Education are enormous. If our efforts to help the Nasarawa state secondary school students to stay safe from HIV and AIDS can only be understood better if the students are given analyses from the global and national contexts of HIV and AIDS related issues. It could also help in reforming education for all students and the Nigerian society. In view of this, the focus must be on students. With the constructivist approach, the focus on student-centered learning may well be the most important contribution of the essential approach of the constructivism. The paper, therefore, explains how constructivist approach in the teaching and learning of Christian religious education integrated content in Senior Secondary Schools in Nasarawa State can be achieved. Philosophers emphasised the need to actively involve the students in the teaching and learning process. In constructivist approach, students internalise and utilise better the knowledge in which they have actively participated to generate knowledge. Constructivism is learning theory found in Psychology which explains how people might acquire knowledge and learn. It therefore has direct application to education. The theory suggests that humans construct knowledge and meaning from their experiences. Conceptual understanding of the theory was discussed as well as basic characteristics of constructivists learning environment. The article outlined the benefits of constructivism, basic characteristics of constructivist approach, important differences between the traditional classroom and the constructivist classroom, principles of constructivism and several implications of constructivism for teaching and learning. The study, therefore, recommended that teachers need to reflect on their practice in order to apply these ideas and method to their teaching in order to encourage students to constantly assess how the activity is helping them gain understanding and knowledge of HIV and AIDs education. It will help the students to stay safe from HIV and AIDs and other related diseases.

Keywords: *Constructivist, Knowledge, Learning, Teaching and Theory*

Introduction

Constructivism is a concept that informs and influences practice (Aggarwal, 2002). Therefore if a teacher understands "teaching" as giving, imparting or inculcating knowledge, he/she will choose and implement methods that help him/her to "give" students knowledge. In most cases, such methods are teacher-centred. Teacher-centred methods make learners passive recipients of knowledge (Aggarwal 2001). Such methods promote rote learning. Much of the knowledge acquired through the rote methods is never internalised, owned or applied to new situations by students (Okaka, 2009). This rhymes well with the puzzling question as to why people do not put into practice the knowledge they have about HIV and AIDS (Bruyn & France, 2001; Okaka, 2009). A more acceptable definition of teaching emphasises dialogue and interaction between a teacher and a student (Aggarwal, 2002). This definition requires the teacher to use methods that encourage and allow students to contribute actively to their learning (Twoli et al, 2007). The teacher, more so the Christian Religious Studies (CRS) teacher, ought to know that students have a lot of experiences, knowledge, feelings, views and interests that need to be shared and utilised to understand better what the teacher has prepared for them. Previous experience helps learners to understand new experiences (Aggarwal, 2002). The approach to teaching using people's own experiences is actually not new. Socrates (470 BC-399 BC), (Rusk & Scotland, 1979) and Jesus (United Bible Societies, 1994) guided their inquirers to answer their own questions.

An important restriction of education is that teachers cannot simply transmit knowledge to students, but students need to actively construct knowledge in their own minds (Poonam, 2017). That is, they discover and transform information, check new information against old, and revise rules when they do not longer apply. These constructivist views of learning consider the learner as an active agent in the process of knowledge acquisition. Constructivist conceptions of learning have their historical roots in the works of Philosophers of Education such as Rousseau (1717 – 1778) and Dewey (1856-1950) who emphasised the need to actively involve the students in the teaching/learning process (Callahan & Clark, 1983). Therefore CRS, or any other subject, will not adequately help students on HIV related issues if correct methods, based on the correct concept of teaching, are not used. Efforts to help the Nasarawa state secondary school students to stay safe from HIV and AIDS can only be understood better if students are given analyses from the global and national contexts of HIV and AIDS related issues. By the end of 2011, there were 34 million people living with HIV (UNAIDS, 2012 Report). Although the rate of new HIV infections has decreased, the total number of people living with HIV continues to rise in Sub-Saharan Africa. Sub-Saharan Africa alone has 22.5 million people living with HIV. This amounts to 68% of the global total number of people living with HIV.

The countries with the highest number of HIV infected people in Africa are Ethiopia, Nigeria, South Africa, Zambia and Zimbabwe. Out of 1.7 million deaths attributed to the epidemic in 2011, 1.3 million (72%), were from Africa. Although the UNAIDS Executive Director, Mr. Sidibe, claims that "we have halted and begun to reverse the epidemic" (UNAIDS 2012 Report: 5). He also concedes that it is too early to say "The mission is accomplished". UNAIDS Vision of "Zero new infections" is far from being realized. Similarly, despite the progress made, many countries will fail to achieve Millennium Development Goal (MDG) number Six by 2015 that is, "halting and reversing the spread of HIV" (UNAIDS Report, 2012).

Benefits Constructivism

1. Students learn faster, and learning becomes interesting and they enjoy the learning because they are actively involved, rather than passive listeners.
2. Education works best when it concentrates on thinking and understanding, rather than on rote memorization. This is because constructivism concentrates on learning how to think and understand.
3. Constructivist learning is transferable. In constructivist classrooms, students create organizing principles that they can take with them to other learning settings.
4. Constructivism gives students ownership of what they learn, since learning is based on student's questions and explorations, and often the students have a hand in designing the assessments as well. Constructivist assessment engages the student's initiatives and personal investments in their journals, research reports, physical models, and artistic representations. Engaging the creative instincts develops students' abilities to express knowledge through a variety of ways. The students are also more likely to retain and transfer the new knowledge to real life.
5. By grounding learning activities in an authentic, real - world context, constructivism stimulates and engages students. Students in constructivist classrooms learn to question things and to apply their natural curiosity to the world.
6. Constructivism promotes social and communication skills by creating a classroom environment that emphasizes collaboration and exchanges of ideas. Students must learn how to articulate their ideas clearly as well as to collaborate on tasks effectively by sharing in groups projects. Students must therefore exchange ideas

and so must learn to "negotiate" with others and to evaluate their contributions in a socially acceptable manner. This is essential to success.

Basic Characteristics of Constructivist Learning Environment

Poonam (2017) lists the following four basic characteristics of constructivist learning environments, which must be considered when implementing constructivist instructional strategies:

1. Knowledge will be shared between teachers and students in the classroom.
2. Teachers and students will share authority during teaching and learning.
3. The teacher's role in the class is one of a facilitator or guide.
4. Learning groups will consist of small numbers of heterogeneous students.

Differences between Traditional Classroom and Constructivist Classroom

In the constructivist classroom, the students activities segment of the lesson plan become strictly in use. The focus tends to shift from the teacher to the students during the lesson presentation. The teaching in the classroom is no longer teacher's activity alone where the expert pours knowledge into passive students, who wait like empty vessels to be filled. In the constructivist model, the students are urged to be actively involved in their own process of learning. The teacher functions more as a facilitator who coaches, mediates, prompts and helps students develop and assess their understanding and thereby their learning. And, in the constructivist classroom, both teacher and students think of knowledge not as inert factoids to be memorized, but as a dynamic, ever-changing view of the world we live in and the ability to successfully stretch and explore that view.

The chart below compares the traditional classroom to the constructivist classroom. According to Poonam (2017), there is a significant difference in basic assumptions about knowledge, students learn shown on the table 1 below.

Table 1

Traditional Classroom	Constructivist Classroom
Curriculum begins with the parts of the whole. Emphasizes basic skills.	Curriculum emphasizes big concepts, beginning with the whole and expanding to include the parts.
Strict adherence to fixed curriculum is highly valued.	Pursuit of student's questions and interests is valued.
Materials are primarily textbooks and workbooks.	Materials include primary sources of material and manipulative materials.
Learning is based on repetition.	Learning is interactive, building on what the students already knows.

Teachers disseminate information to students; students are recipients of knowledge.	Teachers have a dialogue with students, helping students construct their own knowledge.
Teacher's role is directive, rooted in authority.	Teacher's role is interactive, rooted in negotiation.
Assessment is through testing, correct answers.	Assessment includes student works, observation and a point of view, as well as tests. Process is as important as product.
Knowledge is seen as inert.	Knowledge is seen as dynamic, ever changing with our experiences.
Students work primarily alone.	Students work primarily in groups.

Principles of Constructivism

Constructivist teaching is based on recent research about the human brain and what is known about how learning occurs. Caine and Caine (1991), suggest that brain-compatible teaching is based on 12 principles:

1. The brain is a parallel processor. It simultaneously processes many different types of information, including thoughts, emotions and cultural knowledge. Effective teaching employs a variety of learning strategies.
2. Learning engages the entire physiology. Teachers can not address just the intellect.
3. The search for meaning is innate. Effective teaching recognizes that meaning is personal and unique, and that students' understandings are based on their own unique experiences.
4. The search for meaning occurs through 'patterning'. Effective teaching connects isolated ideas and information with global concepts and themes.
5. Emotions are critical to patterning. Learning is influenced by emotions, feelings, and attitudes.
6. The brain processes parts and whole simultaneously. People have difficulty learning when either parts or whole are overlooked.
7. Learning involves both focused attention and peripheral perception. Learning is influenced by the environment, culture and climate.
8. Learning always involves conscious and unconscious processes; Students need time to process 'how' as well as 'what' they have learned.
9. We have at least two different types of memory: a spatial memory system and a set of systems for rote learning. Teaching that heavily emphasizes rote learning does not promote spatial, experienced learning and can inhibit understanding.
10. We understand and remember best when facts and skills are embedded in natural, spatial memory. Experiential learning is most effective.
11. Learning is enhanced by challenge and inhibited by threat. The classroom climate should be challenging but not threatening to students.

12. Each brain is unique. Teaching must be multifaceted to allow students to express preferences.

Implications of Constructivist Approach

Christian Religious Education (CRE) was simply referred to as one of the secondary school subjects, through which HIV and AIDS Education messages could be passed on to students (Kamuli & Ruhweza, 2005). The study established that the full potential of using CRE to teach HIV and AIDS Education had not been realized because most teachers were not using good methods to teach it. The study realised that if teachers used the constructivist approach regularly and put their positive attitudes towards the constructivist approach into practice, they would have helped students not only to gain knowledge but also to acquire skills necessary to protect themselves against HIV and AIDS. What is more urgent is the rational and good decision making skills than mere acquisition of knowledge on HIV and AIDS. Given the influence of teachers' methods of teaching, development of skills among secondary school adolescents cannot be realized unless they improve on the methods they choose to use.

The study explains how students have interest in HIV and AIDS Education as long as it is taught well. The students will develop positive attitudes towards the constructivist approach, if it is regularly used in the classroom. Although some other students may still value teachers' advice. All this implies that there are many opportunities for the secondary school HIV and AIDS Education interventions to succeed because students are receptive to any intervention. Secondary school students are still in their formative years of character formation, without prefixed and rigid attitudes and life styles "As they learn, they change" (Callahan & Clark, 1983). The study established that students responded and reacted differently to different aspects of teaching, learning, sexuality and HIV and AIDS. Given these characteristics of secondary school students, it therefore follows that good HIV and AIDS interventions must be flexible and responsive to all learning styles of students. Many educators have advocated the constructivist approach because it takes care of all differences among students. In a nutshell, whoever wants to help adolescents must be ready to avoid ideas and strategies which are not flexible.

Central to the tenet of constructivism is that learning is an active process that involves the two parties. Information may be imposed, but with the help of constructivist approach, understanding cannot be applied, for it must come from within. Constructivism requires a teacher to act as a facilitator whose main function is to help students become active participants in their learning and make meaningful connections between prior knowledge, new knowledge and the processes involved in learning. Brooks and Brooks (1991), summarize a large segment of the literature on descriptions of 'constructivist teachers'. They conceive of a constructive teacher as someone who will:

1. Encourage and accept students' autonomy and initiative in the teaching and learning process;
2. Use a variety of materials, such as raw materials, data, primary sources and interactive materials and encourage students to use them;
3. Seek to know students' understandings of concepts before sharing his/her own understanding of those concepts;
4. Encourage group study so as students will engage in dialogue with the teacher and with one another;
5. Encourage his/her students to be involved in enquiry by asking thoughtful, open-ended questions and encourage them to ask questions to each other and seek elaboration of students' initial response;
6. Encourage students' initiative experiences that will show no contradictions to initial understanding and then encourage discussion during and after teaching and learning procedure;
7. Provide time for students to construct relationships and create metaphors;
8. Assess students' understanding through application and performance of open-structured tasks.
9. Encourage students to construct knowledge how to provide solutions to the existing problems.

Conclusion

This study established that most teachers avoided using constructivist approaches in teaching HIV and AIDS Education using CRE syllabus. Many CRE teachers rely on dictation and elaboration of notes as a method of teaching HIV and AIDS Education. They relied on this method because they were more pre-occupied with final WAEC, NECO and JAMB CRE results than with the moral development of the students. The affective domain, though emphasised in the CRE syllabus was being given little attention by teachers. It can, therefore, be concluded that unless good methods are used to teach CRE it's potential to help secondary school adolescents avoid HIV and AIDS will not be fully realised. The teachers' positive attitude to the constructivist approach should be regarded as an opportunity to help them teach HIV and AIDS Education well.

Recommendation

1. Continuous Professional Development (CPD) workshops should be organised for CRE Teachers. The need to organise Continuous Professional Development (CPDs) workshops for them as a strategy of revitalising to improve their knowledge and skills of teaching content related to HIV and AIDS.

2. The National Policy on Education should review the secondary school syllabus and recommend the accompanying text books related to HIV and AIDs education so as to incorporate HIV and AIDS as an explicit and a critical area of study.
3. Improvement on Examination and Assessment Techniques should be encouraged. The Examination bodies need to improve on the quality of questions so that emphasis ceases to be on the regurgitation of crammed facts. But the emphasis should also cut across board.
4. Questions should spread across such as; applications, analysis, synthesis and evaluation are to be included in the examinations papers.
5. There is a need for initiating and managing school -based strategies. It will help to supplement CRE Teachers' efforts. Schools need to improve or re-activate. strategies that can help students on sex-related challenges.
6. There is a need for the empowerment of Parents on Adolescent issues. This is to say that schools, Churches and Community-Based Organizations should organize seminars for parents.
7. There is a need for the improvement on the role of the school patrons or Chaplains. They have an important role to play in the education of the secondary school students.

References

Aggarwal, J. C. (2001). *Principles, Methods and Techniques of Teaching.* New Deihi: Vikas Publishing House Ltd.

Aggarwal, J. C. (2002). *Theory and Practice of Education.* New Delhi: Vikas Publishing House Ltd.

Brooks, J. G. and Brooks, M. G. (1991). *In Search of Understanding: the case for Constructivist Classroom.* Alexandria, VA: American Society for Curriculum Development.

Bruyn, M. and France, N. (2001). *Gender or Sex: Who cares?* New York: Ipas.

Caine, R. N. and Caine, G. (1991). *Making Connections: Teaching and the Human Brain.* Alexandria, VA: Association for Supervision and Curriculum Development.

Callahan, J. F. and Clark, L. H. (1983). *Foundations of Education.* New York: Macmillan Publishing Co. Inc.

Okaka, W. (2009). Assessing Uganda's public communications campaigns strategy for effective national health policy awareness. *Journal of Media and Communication Studies,* 1 (4): 073-078.

Poonam, S. (2017). Constructivism: A New Paradigm in Teaching and Learning. *International Journal of Academic Research and Development,* 2 (4).

Rusk, R. R. and Scotland J. (1979). *Doctrines of Great Educators.* London: Macmillan.

Twoli, N. (2007). *Instructional Methods in Education.* Nairobi: Kenya Institute of Education.

UNAIDS (2012). World AIDS Day Report. Joint United Nations Programme on HIV/ AIDS (UNAIDS).

United Bible Societies (1994). *The Good News Bible.* (Mark 10:1 – 16; and Luke 20: 20 – 26).

24

Instructional leadership: Its role in sustaining school improvement in South African Schools context

George N. Shava & Lwazi Sibanda

Abstract

Recent studies conducted the world over have indicated a direct relationship between the instructional role of principal leadership and the effectiveness of a school. Instructional leadership, which seeks to promote a culture of teaching and learning, was seen to be the ingredient for effective teaching and sustaining school improvement in the South African context of education. Initiatives introduced by the South African Government to reform education include the increase in site-based management responsibilities, which are based on instructional leadership perspectives. Principals of schools in South Africa are accountable for the academic improvement in schools. The goal of this qualitative study was to explore the role of principals in sustaining school improvement in the North West Province of South Africa. Premised in the qualitative research approach, a purposive sampling technique was used to select 6 schools which had sustained school improvement for some years. Our findings revealed that principals play a pivotal role in sustaining school improvement. The study findings reinforce recent literature that identifies instructional leadership as a cornerstone for school improvement.

Keywords: *Instructional Leadership, Principals, School Improvement, School Leadership, Teaching and Learning*

Introduction

Instructional Leadership a Historical Perspective

Instructional leadership (IL) has a long-rooted history which emerged out of the effective school literature in the 1960s (Leithwood, Harris and Hopkins 2008; Robinson, Lloyd and

Rowe 2008).IL by its nature is unique to the field of education and it differs from other types of leadership because it is related to students, teachers, curriculum and learning processes (Hoy and Hoy 2003). On the other hand, Hallinger (2011) argue that in the new millennium IL helps principals identify a school vision, empower and inspire teachers, and innovate school classroom- based strategies in order to improve teaching and learning for teachers and students. IL focuses on the organization as much as individuals in the school environment by promoting positive learning conditions for all students, helping teachers and learners in meeting curriculum standards and supporting teacher development, all the while being mindful of the culture and context of schools in order to match improvement strategies with changing context over time (Hoy 2012). Successful school improvement and the enhancement of learning through focusing on the teaching- learning process and the conditions that support it is changing, learning environments are also changing and the crop of learners in schools is changing such that school principals today must possess and demonstrate an increasingly complex and diverse set of technical and adaptive leadership skills. Hoy (2012) show that effective principals today recognize the complicated dynamics of school organizations and work deliberately in ways that promote innovative and healthy learning environments that positively impact school performance. The essence of IL suggests that the more focused a principal's work is on the processes of teaching and learning, the more positive the influence on students learning outcomes will be (Robinson et al 2008; Supovitz and Buckley 2008). According to the Policy on Standards for Principals (South African 2016) principals as instructional leaders should lead the learners to ensure that the school is a professional learning community and promoting a culture of achievement for all learners by communicating and implementing a common vision and mission that is shared by all stakeholders.

Historically, in South Africa and other developing countries, principals traditionally have been responsible for managing a well-run school including the management of teaching which include managing teaching and learning. Managing staff members, developing rules, procedures, and attending to the general operations of the school have been always been part of the job (Bush and Glover 2009). The conception of school management began to shift in the late 1970s, where effective schools were characterized by a climate or culture oriented towards learning, as expressed in high achievement standards and expectations of learners, an emphasis on basic skills, a high level of involvement in decision making and professionalism among teaches (Robinson et al 2008).

A further shift in the principal's role, beginning in the mid-1990s, involved the expectations that principals should provide IL (Marks and Printy 2003). This implied that the principal's role had changed from management to IL. Bush and Glover (2009) also referring to the

South African context claim that principals as instructional leaders focus strongly on the following activities but not limited to:

- Oversee the curriculum across the school.
- Ensure the availability of appropriate learning and teaching support materials.
- Arrange a programme for class visits followed by feedback to educators.
- Promote school wide professional development.
- Define and communicate shared goals.

In short, the principal working with teachers create the conditions and structures to support effective learning and teaching for all.

It is therefore the purpose of our study to explore the IL practices of six principals in the North West Province in South Africa. The paper begins by providing a conceptualization of IL as expounded in the literature. We then go on to give a brief account of the research methodology adopted in the study. This was followed by the presentation of our study findings. Thereafter we present a discussion on the salient issues pertaining to IL in the context of the South African education system. We conclude by providing conclusions derived from the findings of the study.

Rationale

The theoretical foundations for this study conducted in the North West Province of South Africa is based on the belief that school principals who exhibit effective IL behaviors are essential for improving underperforming schools towards sustainable improvement. The South African standards for school principals (2016) for example, in setting the core purpose of principalship underscores the need for principals to enable and create conditions under which every staff member in South African schools should understand that every learner must be supported by creating conditions that will prepare learners for the future. With reference to IL in South Africa what remains unclear and not elaborated through empirical research is the function IL play in the principal's organisational management of the school, the everyday lives of principals in schools, how the principal practices IL and towards which instructional outcome they focus. Making reference to issues about IL shifts towards teaching and learning yet there are other outcomes that are desirable from an educational context. The school principal according to the mandated role expectations as prescribed by the SASA (1996) and its amendment (SA2007). The personnel Administration Measures (PAM) (2003) indicates the duties and responsibilities of the principal which include administrative, personnel, teaching, extra- curricular and co-curricular, interaction with stakeholders and communication. From the South African perspective, the principal leads the Senior Management Team (SMT) and is held accountable for all activities concerned with the academic achievement of learners in both internal and external examinations.

Instructional Leadership: An Overview

Born out of the effective school movement of the late 1970s, the strategy of IL gained significant prominence during the standards based reform movement of the early 1990s(Terosky 2014). Evidence from other recent reviewers of the literature on principal leadership (eg., Hallinger 2011; Southworth 2002; Terosky 2014) suggest that twenty years later, the IL construct is still alive in the domains of policy, research, and practice in school leadership and management. Indeed, since the turn of the twentieth-first century, the increasing global emphasis on accountability seems to have reignited interest in IL (Hallinger 2005), Klasik and LoebMarzano and McNulty).

Despite the plethora of studies on IL, as well as the attention it receives the world over, questions remain around the definition, implementation, and usefulness of the concept. Some scholars argue that the concept of IL remains poorly defined and the behaviors associated with its enactment rather too broad. Critics also assert that the concept tends to focus on transactional leadership practices and surface-level slogan (Leithwood et al. 2008 and Hallinger & Heck 1996). Moreover, educational studies continue to find that despite an emphasis on IL as of late, the vast majority of principal's day is comprised of managerial tasks such as the management of school facilities, school safety, compliance paperwork, and non-instructionally based services, thereby calling into question the effective implementation of IL (Horng et al 2009; Jenkins 2009; Kafka 2009).

In spite of the critique on instructional leadership, it is therefore the purpose of the article to explore the practices of six principals in the North West province in South Africa and to determine how this practice enhances school improvement.

Conceptual Dimensions of Instructional Leadership

Several notable models of IL have been proposed (Hallinger&Murphy 1985; Hallinger 2003, 2011, Leithwood &Montgomery 1982). We will focus on the model proposed by Hallinger and Murphy (1985), since it is the model that has been used most frequently in empirical investigations. Hallinger &Murphy (1985) developed a specific conceptualization of IL consisting of three dimensions for the IL role of the principals consisting of: (1) Defining the school's mission (2) Managing the instructional program and (3) Promoting a positive school climate. These three dimensions are further delineated into ten instructional leadership functions (see figure 1). Two main functions, framing the school's goals and communicating the school's goals, comprise the first dimension, defining the school's mission. Defining the school's mission includes working with the staff to ensure that the school has clear and measurable goals that are clearly communicated throughout the school community. The dimension focuses on the principal's role in working with staff to ensure that the school has clear, measurable, time based goals focused on the academic process of students. The focus of goal development is considered less critical than the outcome. The goals are primarily concerned with the academic progress of students. The second dimension, managing the instructional program, focuses on the coordination and control of instruction and curriculum. This dimension incorporates three leadership functions of supervising and evaluating instruction, coordinating the curriculum and monitoring learner progress. This dimension requires the principal to be deeply engaged in stimulating, supervising, and monitoring teaching and learning. Obviously, these functions demand that the principal has expertise in teaching and learning, as well as commitment to school improvement. The third dimension, promoting a positive school learning climate, which includes several functions: protecting instructional time, promoting professional development, maintaining high visibility, providing incentives and rewards for teachers and learners. This dimension is broader in scope and purpose. It confirms to the notion that effective schools create an academic press through the development of high standards and expectations for students and teachers. The principal also leads improvement of the school's climate by ensuring that there is a high standard of excellence. The principal must model values and practices that create a climate and support the continuous improvement of teaching and learning (Dwyer 1986; Hallinger &Heck 1996; Hallinger and Murphy 1985). Figure 1 shows the instructional management framework by Hallinger and Murphy 1985.

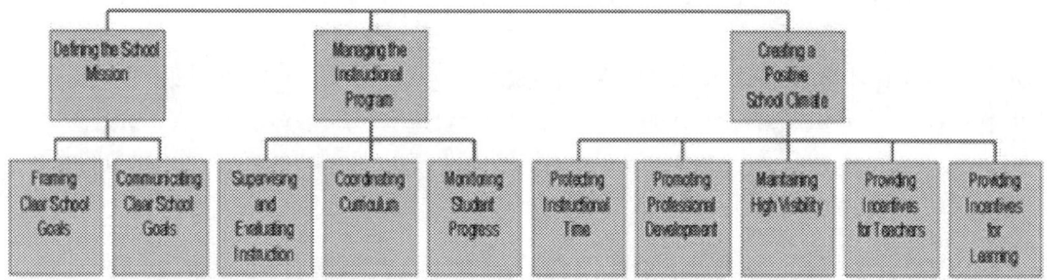

Adapted from Hallinger & Murphy, (1985)

Instructional Leadership: A Core Strategy for influencing Learner Achievement

Proponents of IL argued that if the main business of schools was instruction and student learning, then the main job of school leadership should be likewise (Firestone and Riehl, 2005). Education leadership is synonymous with instructional leadership in that principals are expected to direct their attention to creating conditions for enhanced teaching that ultimately improves students' achievement (Hallinger 2011; Terosky 2014). Previous research has demonstrated that the leadership style of the principal can strongly influence various elements of school environment, including teacher and staff attitudes, student learning, and academic achievement (Bush 2013). Of the several theories in the literature,

IL has received the most attention (Robinson et al 2008). IL focuses predominantly on the role of the school principal in coordinating, controlling, supervising, and developing curriculum and instruction in the school (Hallinger 2010; Supvitz et al 2009)

IL is a deliberate process of behaviors and practices adopted by principals to promote teacher instructional improvement and these activities are tightly aligned to student achievement (Robinson et al 2008; Supovitz and Buckley 2008). In their review of school leadership and student learning outcomcs, Leithwood et al (2004) concluded that, “leadership is second only to classroom instruction among all school related factors that contribute to what students learn at school” (p.5). This idea was supported by Robinson at al 2008; Hoy and Miskel 2013) who show that school leadership and specifically instructional leadership positively impact student achievement. This is an indication that principals by virtue of their instructional role clearly play an essential role in improving student learning. The impacts of leadership are underestimated and the combination of direct and indirect effects account for approximately 25% of school effectiveness (Leithwood et al 2004).

Principals who operate as instructional leaders aim to increase instructional effectiveness in their schools through quality interactions with teachers and in an informative process of supervision. As instructional leaders, principals primarily direct teaching for effective learning and support teachers and student in their work towards educational excellence (DeMatthews 2014). According to DeMetthews (2014) IL is the leadership function associated with teaching and learning specifically with reference to duties and responsibilities principals need to perform on daily basis to support teachers and learners towards educational excellence. The principal’s major role in IL is considered to be communicating high expectations for teachers and students, supervising instruction, monitoring assessment and student progress, coordinating the school’s curriculum, promoting a climate for effective learning and creating a supportive work environment (Marks and Printy 2003). From these conceptual issues, we propose the following working definition of IL: a school principal who develops a clear vision, team, culture and structure that prioritizes and enhances the instructional environment of a school. Our definition could be in line with Jita and Mokhele (2013) who are of the view that IL incorporates the process of creating and sustaining an environment in which the highly complex, socially textured tasks of effective schooling can take place.

Instructional Leadership and Learner Achievement

Several studies have been conducted examining IL. Hallinger (2011) conducted a review of the IL and he noted that several studies have concluded that principals who employ an IL style have some influence over student outcomes, usually through teacher or organizational means. Marks and Printy (2003) found that a principal’s IL had an indirect effect on student reading achievement and direct effects on school climate variables in schools. The relationship between instructional leadership and student achievement is often mediated by school- level factors such as school climate or classroom-level factors such as teacher efficacy, motivation and job satisfaction. DiPaola and Hoy (2015) also supported the argument by indicating that several comprehensive meta-analyses have linked IL to student learning achievement. They concluded that several empirical studies have established that the principal's IL behaviors indirectly and positively impacted on school climate, culture, and organization. School mission, goals and high academic expectations were IL behaviors that manifested themselves in classroom instruction to positively impact student outcomes (May & Supovitz 2011). Studies published between 1978 and 2006, the authors found that practices associated with establishing school goals, supervision of instruction, and professional learning were highly impactful and concluded, "the more leaders focus their relationships, their work, and their learning on core business of teaching and learning, the greater their influence on student outcomes" (Robinson et al 2008, p.636).

Instructional Leadership and Its Impact on Teaching Practices

Multiple educational studies in the last 15 years have demonstrated the significance of high-quality, focused principal- teacher interactions about specific instructional strategies that impact on teaching practices (May &Supovitz 2011; Robinson et al 2008). On the other hand, Supovitz & Buckley (2008), Supovitz et al (2009) in their studies concluded that there is a positive relationship between the IL behaviors of the principal and teachers' innovation, creativity, professionalism, and commitment to school and colleagues. More recent research has broadened the focus of IL, such as collaboration among teachers, creating opportunities for professional growth, and the development of professional learning communities (Marks and Printy 2003). Blasé and Blasé (1999) uncovered two significant themes from the teachers' perspectives that impacted their motivation, creativity, efficacy, and their varied use of instructional strategies. When principals engage in discussions with teachers about instruction, the dialogue promotes teacher reflection. Where principals supported collaboration among teachers to study teaching and learning, as well as opportunities for teachers to plan and facilitate quality professional learning aligned with learning principles, the reflective attitudes and behaviors of classroom teachers improved significantly (Blasé & Blasé 1999). Supovitz and Buckley (2008) refer to these themes as, "high- leverage IL: evidence-based feedback given by principals that induces teachers to examine their instruction in order to improve the effectiveness of their practice" (p.5). Targeted IL activities, such as providing specific feedback about an observed lesson, are more likely to change an individual teacher's practices. In conclusion, the time a principal specifically allocates to IL activities is a predictor of positive classroom instructional change and sustained school improvement. The international research on school improvement shows that the two main factors influencing the quality of education are classroom practice and leadership (Bush 2013).

Methods

Juxtaposing the ongoing emphasis on IL for principals with scholarly critiques of the ongoing conceptualization and implementation of IL, we designed a qualitative study exploring the experiences of eight principals from South African school context in hopes of better understanding their perceptions and experiences in enacting the concept of IL and sustaining school improvement especially in light of the managerial imperatives they face.

In order to explore participants' perspectives and actions through the conceptual lens of IL, we followed the tradition of interpretive research (Bogdan &Biklen 1998; Creswell 2012). In this qualitative research, we examined the experiences of six public school principals who are noted by the area manager as instructional leaders through their ability to change underperforming schools to sustainable school improvement. A qualitative approach emphasizes the qualities of entities, processes and meanings that are not experimentally examined or measured in terms of quantity, amount or frequency (Denzin & Licolin 2000). Through semi-structured interviews we worked to understand the world from the participants' points of view, to unfold the meaning of peoples' experiences. Researchers suggest the need for qualitative studies of educational leadership (Firestone &Riehl 2005) in order to capture the thinking and actions of principals within their context. Ultimately, we were interested in the general issue of IL and how individuals enact their roles as instructional leaders to change underperforming schools towards sustainable improvement. In order to bound our cases by recognizable features of IL we applied purposeful sampling method (Creswell 2012; Denzin and Lincolin 200). We requested referrals for participants from the education area manager from which the schools were selected. The area manager position was credibly suited to determine principals who have managed to change underperforming schools through the emphasis of IL. We provided the area manager with the following working definition for IL: a principal who develops a vision, team, and structure that prioritizes and enhances instructional environment to change underperforming schools to sustainable improvement. We chose this definition because it succinctly synthesizes the extent literature on IL as well as establishing a broad yet bounded base for nominations. The six schools nominated were three secondary schools, two primary schools and one combined farm school. Two participants were men and four were women, years of experience as principal ranged from five to more than ten years (see table 1).

To gather a breath of contextual information about each case, we took about one hour or longer with each principal. This was the intended length of our interviews, but some interviews took longer depending on the participants' schedules. We took descriptive field notes detailing information on activities, people, and settings that we directly got from the participants. To ensure trustworthiness of the study we used Lincolin and Guba (2011)'s norms of trustworthiness, namely, credibility, transferability, dependability and conformity. Prolonged engagement, member checks and peer debriefing were used to promote confidence that the researchers had accurately recoded the phenomena under investigation. Schools were coded as school A to F to protect their identity. We made contacts with each participant telephonically to establish a good working relationship. Consent was obtained from the Ethics committee of the North West University, Potchefstroom Campus, North West Department of Education and the participants. Participants were made aware that they may withdraw from the study at any time, and that confidentiality and anonymity would be observed during and after the study was completed.

Research questions

We set out on a profound investigation of the principals' instructional leadership to sustain school improvement in South Africa guided by three research questions:

1. How do principals as instructional leaders influence effective teaching and learning?
2. What is done by principals as instructional leaders to change underperforming schools?
3. How do principals perceive instructional leadership in schools as an approach to enhancing the quality of teaching and learning?

Findings

The purpose of our study was to better understand how principals of six selected schools as instructional leaders influence effective teaching and learning in their schools to change underperforming schools to sustainable improvement. With the study's purpose in mind, data analysis of the six principals noted for their instructional leadership yielded several key themes of which we will discuss in this article. The study participants were made up of two men and four women. The schools location breakdown was one combined school from the farms, two primary schools and three secondary schools. Years of experience for principals ranged from five to ten years (see table 1) The five schools are from a black and coloured township. We collected numerous types of data to locate the cases within their contextual nuances (Creswell 2012).The interpretation of data commenced soon after the interviews were completed.

Table 1: Participating principals and the schools' demographics

School	Location	Number of learners	Number of Trs	Years as Principal	Qualification of Principal
A	Township	1452	44	20 yrs+	B.Ed hons Mgt
B	Township	1475	40	14yrs+	Masters in Public Admin
C	Township	1037	30	5yrs	Masters Edu. Mgt
D	Township	526	19	10yrs+	BA Hons Lit
E	Farm School	618 Gr R to 12	20	7yrs	Bed Hons Mgt
F	Township	1023	30	10yrs+	Bed Hons Mgt

From our interviews with the principals we established that the communities served by the six schools exhibited a range of problems which include; poverty especial at the farm school, teenage pregnancy including learners especially in the townships, unemployment, lack of parental support to schools especially secondary schools, child headed families, school break ins especially in the townships and premature deaths due to the prevalent of HIV and AIDS in both the townships and the farming communities. While these mostly external school conditions have a significant impact on school improvement, all the six principals indicated that these challenges affected their school leadership but they try as much as possible to do the best under such conditions in the interest of learner improvement. All the six schools have enough classrooms for the learners. The buildings are in good shape although in two primary schools the structures looked old but they are well looked after which creates a conducive learning environment.

Perceptions of Principals of their Core Instructional Functions

The analysis of data gathered from principals indicated that principals as instructional leaders play a key role to improve teaching and learning in the schools. All the six principals emphasised the important role they played in ensuring school improvement. The six principals interviewed all had a clear understanding of their core instructional functions.

Principal A commented in this regard:

> *This school was a trap school, this means it was underperforming; the school had a lot of problems. I did not wait for the department to came and solve these problems but to solve the problems by ensuring that effective*

> *teaching and learning takes place. I instructed every teacher to focus on the core business of the school ie teaching and learning and that is it.*

Principal B:

> *I do a lot to ensure effective teaching and learning takes place. Every day i move from class to class to ensure that its business all the time while the academic deputy head is in charge of the academic side, i also ensure that all teachers are doing their work every day. I make sure that teaching and learning takes place in every class by closely monitoring the teaching process.*

Principal F:

> *I do not teach, but every day i am here, i go around the classrooms assisting teachers, i also go around asking teachers how they expect me to help them improve their classroom teaching. I also relay more on my HODs but i monitor a lot.*

Participants C, D and F spoke extensively of their key roles as instructional leadership which in summary includes:

- Monitoring the teaching and learning process closely on a daily basis.
- Direct supervision of teachers by both principal and SMT.
- Providing the necessary resources and support for teaching and learning.
- Allocating a larger budget to teaching and learning (school D)
- Managing the instructional program in the schools.
- Creating conditions for effective teaching and learning by motivating both teachers and learners.
- Communicating with learners, teachers and parents.
- Coordinating and evaluating curriculum activities.
- Monitoring students' progress and attendance
- Designing systems for effective teaching and learning
- Management by walking around the school.

These views from principals coincide with Blase and Blase(1999) who found in their research on instructional leadership that even "walking through" visits without dialogue or feedback by the principal has a positive impact on the teachers and encourage motivation, better planning, focus and innovation(p. 361). All the six principals indicated that they visit classes regularly and provide support in an informal rather than in a formal way. The principal for school (C) noted that:

> *Just in an informal way—usually its more of an informal visit, i just walk into a class or walk past a class or decide to go in the class and greet both the learners and their teacher. During such a visit i talk to learners as well as their teacher on their leaning progress. I have discovered that such visits motivate both the learners and their teacher. I avoid faultfinding visits to classrooms as this demotivates teachers. I visit to reward.*

While the direct class visits for classroom observation is delegated to SMT in some cases principals also do direct classroom teaching observations and according to the interviewed principals this helps them to have a comprehensive understanding of what takes place in the classrooms. This also helps the principal to have a comprehensive record of the class and their teacher.

Promoting a Culture of Teaching and Learning in the Schools

As explained earlier, principals of schools adopt several strategies to change underperforming schools using their instructional function. In carrying out most important roles as instructional leaders, principals confirmed the existence and the nature of a high-level dependence on their HODs and SMTs. A common comment:

> *—minus our HODs and SMT I really doubt whether we can change underperforming schools.*

Such comments were raised by almost all the six principals though they were stated differently. The following comment from one of the principals (school B) is similar to many we heard in the six schools:

> *It is important that with our teachers we set our targets, that we tackle problems in the school together, we work as a team, we connect our efforts, we seek for effective communication, we provide space for teachers to talk, we remove the fear element among our teachers and that way we are assured of changing our schools towards improved performance.*

All the principals interviewed considered their duties to include promoting a culture of teaching and learning by:

- Creating an environment where teachers and learners may reach their full potential.
- Managing learner discipline.
- Promoting teaching and learning by securing resources.
- Monitoring and evaluating teaching and learning.
- Ensuring a climate conducive to teaching and learning.

- Communicating with parents on issues affecting to teaching and learning.
- Coordinating curriculum activities in the school.
- Proactive in and involved in continuous professional development.

In all their comments principals indicated that they were overwhelmed by the work of their teachers and they were professionally obliged to coordinate and implement the state curriculum. There was also consensus among the interviewed participants that they conducted class observations on regular basis to ensure effective teaching and teachers are happy about these visits since they are meant to develop them. Principal (A) described his efforts to work collaboratively with a mining company which has since financial assistance to build computer science labs in the school, an accomplishment that is indirectly related to the improvement of teaching and learning. The main subject in the schools was teaching and learning and everyone was focused on issues related to teaching and learning.

Managing Instructional Programme

During our interviews with principals we established that principals as managers of instructional programmes in schools ensured an environment where teachers felt safe to extend their capacity so that others could similarly thrive and grow. This was done through professional development programmes facilitated by teachers or HODs to improve teaching skills of their colleagues. In all the secondary schools there are positions of subject heads who are also responsible for the management of all aspects of the particular subject including work load allocation, time tabling and supervision. Despite subject heads assuming the responsibility of curriculum supervision, principals also supervise both the subject head and teachers. It emerged that while the subject head is responsible for subject policy, planning for the subject in the school and the implementation of any new techniques or approaches are co-ordinated and approved by the principal who is overall in charge of planning, organising, leading and controlling instructional programmes in the school.

Academic excellence is one of the cornerstones of the success of all schools the world over. In this area of instructional leadership the principal plays a major role to ensure the achievement of academic excellence by creating a culture that is focused on teaching and learning. Academic excellence can only be achieved if all stakeholders in the school set up are directly focused on teaching and learning and this can be achieved through initiatives by the principal. At school (D) the principal explained as follows:

> *With regards to examination results my intervention is very strong. I make sure all teachers produce good results. I also closely monitor the performance of learners through a comprehensive analysis of the examination results both internal and external examinations.*

Similarly, at school (B) the principal remarked that:

> *I keep a record of the analysis of results for all teachers through a spreadsheet showing learner averages and subject averages. This record is discussed with the teachers and we seek ways to improve where learners are not performing well. Where there is always high performance we reward both the teacher and learners. We always seek to motivate and encourage hard working among our teachers and learners. My leadership is not only limited to teachers but i also consider communicating with parents and learners especially where performance is poor.*

In all the six schools the instructional time is protected and managed properly. Principals and HODs are involved in the allocation of work and the design of personal time table for teachers and they ensure that these time tables are followed. Teachers however have an input into the academic allocation of work and usually they feel comfortable with the subject and work load allocation. The involvement of teachers in subject allocation and decision making about the allocation of work stimulates their professional growth and influences the organisational culture of teaching and learning.

Discussion and Implications

The study contributes to the existing evidence base on the role of instructional leaders in enhancing school improvement by identifying insights into roles of instructional leadership in South African schools contexts. Our findings expand the current knowledge base and add several nuances to instructional leadership. Regarding our research questions, we found that in all the six schools the impact of leadership in securing school improvement was great. The school principal is considered as the key ingredient for success especially in academic performance of learners in the schools. Principals as instructional leaders play a major role by effectively managing external and internal environments to create a culture of teaching and learning, which is a condition for school academic success. The six principals take priority on continuous professional development and motivating teachers as the hallmarks of a successful leader. Lithwood et al (2008) agree that a successful school leader is effective in setting direction, and managing communities, as well as managing the teaching and learning programmes of the school. Our study in the six schools in the North West Province of South Africa established that the six schools have high quality leadership, which is dedicated to ensure school improvement. We established that principals achieve school improvement by setting direction of the schools and charting a clear course of action that everyone understands including the community, and establishing high expectations for their schools. Principals prioritized teaching and learning activities together with staff development and giving the necessary support and training to succeed. They ensure that the entire range of conditions and incentives in the schools fully support rather than inhibit teaching and learning.

Conclusion

The school principal is the key ingredient for effective teaching and school improvement, setting the tone for the school and assuming responsibility for instructional programmes in the school. No doubt then an instructional leader is the cornerstone of school improvement due to his or her key role of promoting a culture of teaching and learning in the school. Our research also confirms that the school principal together with the SMT is the thick foundations for school improvement while the principal remain the central source of leadership influence. In all cases we realised that principals distribute tasks to other members and this deliberate effort to share leadership responsibilities had an influence on learner achievement. Within the framework of exercising distributed leadership teachers would contribute in sharing their expertise with colleagues. The traditional perspective on instructional leadership focuses on the role of principals as leaders of hierarchical structures that isolated teachers from making decisions or taking leadership roles. The thrust of reform in the education practice in South Africa today have influenced the nature of leadership in such a way that they have to devise new and innovative practices of instructional leadership with elements of shared participative and democratic leadership. In this study the following summary provide some of our important findings with regards to instructional leadership in the six schools we interviewed:

- In all schools there is an emphasis on academic success by all stake holders.
- Principals adopt current leadership style of distributing leadership among teacher.
- Ensuring a culture of teaching and learning among all stakeholders.
- Principals with their SMTs ensuring that learners and teachers are motivated to build a productive school culture.
- Establishing a culture of winning by focusing on teaching and learning.
- Empowering of teachers by offering both management and pedagogical responsibilities.
- Setting a vision of continuous improvement for teachers.
- Setting school goals and ensuring their accomplishment.

All in all the findings illustrate a move away from the traditional authoritarian type of instructional leadership towards a more collaborative and democratic approach which proved successful in school improvement. The approach to establish and maintain a sound culture of teaching and learning through sharing of the instructional leadership responsibilities was found to be effective, applicable to all the six school, and hence resulting in school improvement. Findings from our interviews resonate with the findings from our literature review, which established that principals through their instructional leadership are the cornerstones of school improvement and ingredients for success in schools.

References

Blasé, J. and Blasé, J. (1999). Principal's instructional leadership and teacher development: Teachers' perspectives. *Educational Administration Quarterly*, 35, 349-378.

Bogdan, R. C. and Biklen, S. K. (1998). *Qualitative research for education: An introduction to theory and methods.* (3rd ed.) Boston: Allyn Bacon.

Bush, T. (2013). Instructional leadership and leadership for learning: global and South African perspectives. Education as Change, Vol 17. No SI, 2013, pp. S8-S20

Bush, T. and Glover, D. (2009). *Managing Teaching and learning: A concept paper.* MGSLG. Johannesburg.

Creswell, J. W. (2012). *Education research: Planning, conducting, and evaluating quantitative and qualitative research.* (4th ed.) Boston: Pearson.

DeMatthews, D. E. (2014). How to improve curriculum leadership: Integrating Leadership Theory and Management Strategies: *The clearing House: A Journal of Education Strategies. Issues and ideas*, 87(5), 192-196.

Denzin, N. K. and Lincolin, Y. S. (2000). *Hand book of Qualitative Research*. Thousand Oaks: Sage Publications Inc.

DiPaola, M. F. and Hoy W. K. (2015). *Leadership and School Quality. A Volume in Research and Theory in Education Administration*. New York: IAP Information age Publishing, INC.

DuFour, R. (2002). Learning centered principals. *Educational Leadership*, 59 (8), 12-15.

Dwyer, D. (1986). Understanding the principal's contribution to instruction. *Peabody Journal of Education,* 63(1): 3-18.

Elmore, R. F. (2000). *Rebuilding a new structure for school leadership.* Washington, Dc: The Albert Shanker Institute.

Firestone, W. A. and Riehl, C. (2005). *A new agenda for research in educational leadership.* New York: Teachers College Press.

Hallinger, P. and Heck, R. H. (1996). Reassessing the principal's role in school effectiveness: A review of empirical research. *Education Administration Quarterlly,* 32(1), 5.

Hallinger, P. and Murphy, J. (1985). Assessing the instructional leadership behavior of principals. *Elementary School Journal.* 86(2): 217-248.

Hallinger, P. (2003). *School leadership development: Global challenges and opportunities.* Lisse, Netherlands: Swets &Zeitlinger Publications.

Hallinger, P. (2005). Instructional Leadership and the School Principal: A Passing Fancy that Refuses to Fade Away. *Leadership and Policy in Schools.* 4: 221-239.

Hallinger, P. (2010). Leading Educational Change: reflections on the practice of instructional and transformational leadership. *Cambridge Journal of Education,* 33 (3): 330-351.

Hallinger, P. and Murphy, J. (2013). *Running on empty? Finding the time and capacity to lead learning.* NASSP Bulletin, 97(5)

Hallinger, P. (2011). Leadership for learning: Lessons from 40 years of empirical research. *Journal of Educational Administration,* 49: 125-142.

Horng, E. L., Klasik, D. and Loeb, S. (2009). Principal *time-use and school effectiveness.* (CALDER), Washington, DC: The Urban Institute.

Hoy, A. W., and Hoy, W. K. (2003). *Instructional leadership: A learning- centered guide.* Boston: Allyn Bacon.

Hoy, W. K. (2012). School characteristics that make a difference for the achievement of all students. A 40 year academic odyssey. *Journal of Educational Administration,* 50, 76-97.

Hoy, W. K. and Miskel, C. G. (2013). *Educational administration: Theory, research, and Practice* (9th ed.). New York, NY: McGraw- Hill.

Jenkins, B. (2009). What it takes to be an instructional leader. *Principal.* Washington, DC: National Association of Elementary School Principals.

Jita, L. C. and Mokhele, M. L. (2013). The role of leading teachers in instructional leadership: A case study of environmental learning in South Africa: Education as change 17(1), 123-135.

Kafka, J. (2009). *The principalship in historical perspective*. Peabody Journal Education, 84, 318-320.

Kanapp, M. S., Copland, M. A., Honig, M. I., Pleck, M. L. and Portin, B. S. (2010). *Learning-focused leadership and leadership support: Meaning and practice in urban systems*. Seattle: University of Washington, Center for the Study of Teaching and Policy.

Leithwood, K. and Montgomery, D. (1982). The role of the elementary principal in program improvement. *Review of Educational Research*, 52(3): 309-339.

Leithwood, K., Harris, A. and Hopkins, D. (2008). Seven strong claims about successful school leadership. *School leadership and management* 28:27-42.

Leithwood, K., Louis, K., Anderson, S. and Wahlstrom, K. (2004). *How leadership influences student learning*. New York: The Wallace Foundation.

Lincolin, Y. and Guba, E. (2011). *Naturalistic enqiry*. Beverly Hills, CA: SAGE.

Marks, M. H, and Printy, M. S. (2003). Principal leadership and school performance: An integration of transformational and instructional leadership. *Educational administration Quarterly,* 39 (3):370-397.

May, H. and Supovitz, J. A. (2011). The scop of principal efforts to improve instruction. *Education Administration Quarterly*, 47(2): 332-352.

Republic of South Africa (RSA). (2016). National Education Act (27/1996) Policy on the South African Standards for Principals. No 39827 of 2016. *Government Gazette,* vol 609, no 39827.Pretoria Government Printers. Available on line at www.gpwonline.coza.

Robinson, V., Lloyd, C. and Rowe, K. (2008). The impact of leadership on student outcomes: An analysis of the different effects of leadership types. Educational Administration Quarterly 44:635-674.

Shelton, S. (2011). *Strong leadership strong schools: 2010 school leadership laws*. Washington, DC: National Conference of State Legislatures.

Southworth, G. (2002). Instructional leadership in schools: Reflections and empirical evidence. *School Leadership &Management*, 22(1):73-92.

Supovitz, J. and Buckley, P. (2008). How principals enact Instructional leadership. Paper presented at the meeting of American Educational Researchers Association, New York. NK.

Supovitz, J., Sirimides, P. and May, H. (2009). How principals and peers influence teaching and learning. *Educational Administration Quarterly*, 46(1): 31-56.

Terosky, A. L. (2014). From a Managerial Imperative to a Learning Imperative: Experiences of Urban, Public School Principals. *Educational Administration Quartely,* 50(1): 3-33.

Waters, T., Marzano, R. J. and McNulty, B. (2003). *Balancing leadership: What 30 years of research tells us about the effects of leadership on student achievement.* Aurora, CO: Mid- Continent Research for Education and Learning.

Printed in the United States
By Bookmasters